Shojo Beat

O.T.OMEN

Story & Art by
Aya Kanno

Volume
THREE

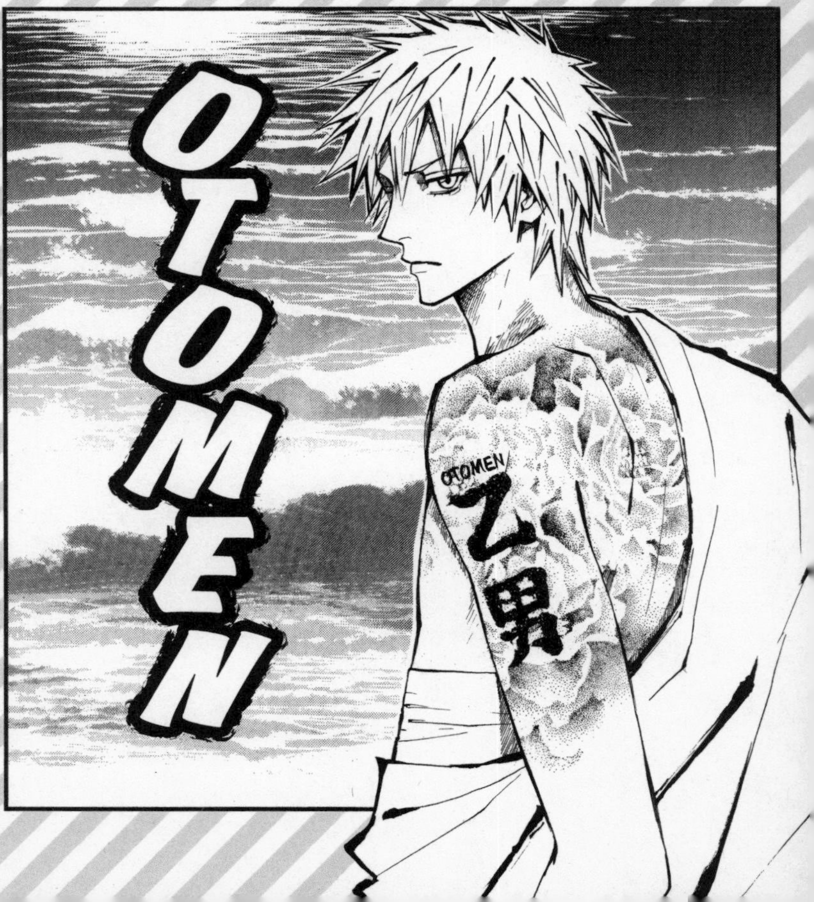
OTOMEN
OTOMEN
乙男

OTOMEN CHARACTERS & STORY

What is an OTOMEN?

O•to•men *[OH-toe-men]*

1) A young man with girlish interests and thoughts.
2) A young man who has talent for cooking, needlework and general housework.
3) A manly young man with a girlish heart.

Asuka Masamune

The captain of Ginyuri Academy High School's kendo team. He is handsome, studious and (to the casual observer) the perfect high school student. But he is actually an *otomen*, a man with a girlish heart. He loves cute things ♥, and he has a natural talent for cooking, needlework and general housekeeping. He's even a big fan of the girls' comic *Love Chick*.

STORY

Asuka Masamune, the kendo captain, is actually an *otomen* (a girlish guy)— a man who likes cute things, housework, and girls' comics. When he was young, his father left home to become a woman. His mother was traumatized, and ever since then, he has kept his girlish interests a secret. However, things change when he meets Juta, a guy who is using Asuka as the basis for the female character in the shojo comic he is writing (←top secret). Asuka also starts having feelings for a tomboy girl who is good at martial arts. Because of this, he's slowly reverting to his true *otomen* self!

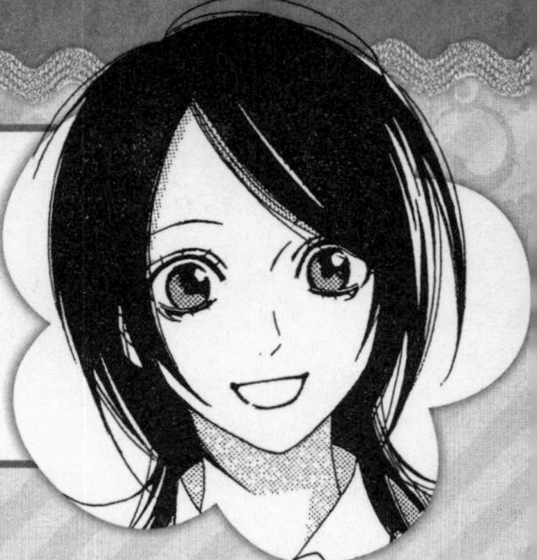

Ryo Miyakozuka

Asuka's classmate for whom he has feelings. She has studied martial arts under her father ever since she was little, and she is very good at it. On the other hand, her housekeeping skills are disastrous. She's a very eccentric beauty.

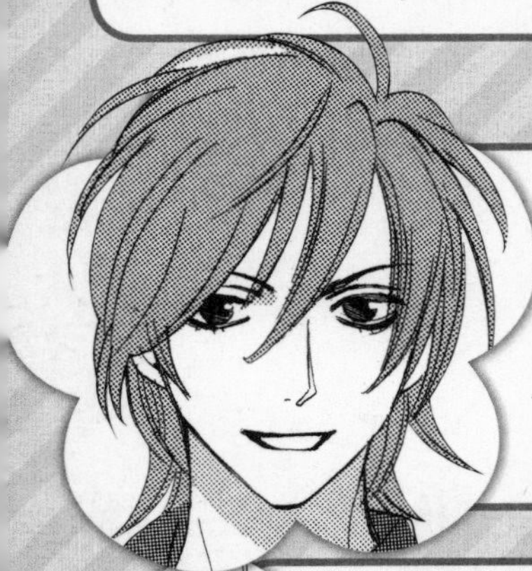

Juta Tachibana

Asuka's classmate. He's flirtatious, but he's actually the popular shojo manga artist Jewel Sachihana. He is using Asuka and Ryo as character concepts in his manga *Love Chick*, which is being published in the shojo magazine *Hana to Mame*. His personal life is a mystery!

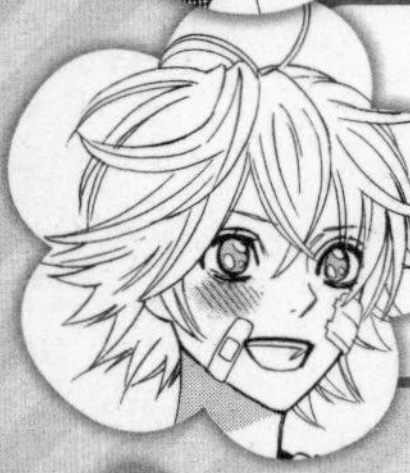

Yamato Ariake

Underclassman in Asuka's school. He looks like a girl, but in reality, he admires manliness and has long, delusional fantasies about being manly. He fondly calls Asuka "sensei." He doesn't realize that Asuka is an *otomen*.

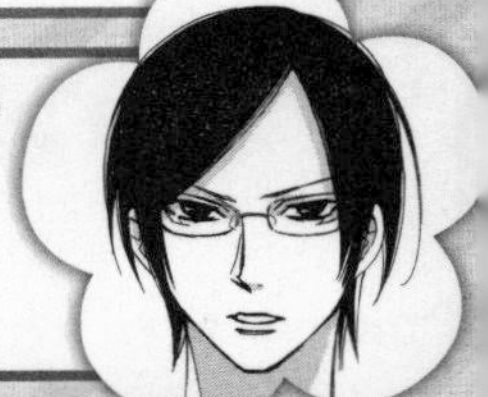

Hajime Tonomine

His first appearance. He sees Asuka as his lifelong rival. He is the captain of Kinbara High School's kendo team.

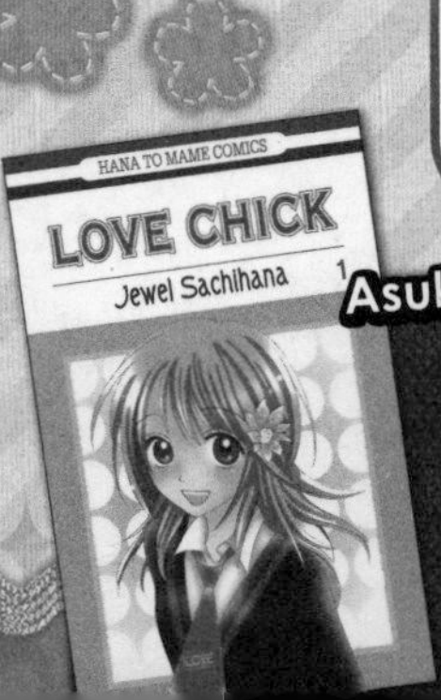
HANA TO MAME COMICS
LOVE CHICK
Jewel Sachihana
1

Asuka is also a BIG FAN!

Hana to Mame Comics

LOVE CHICK by Jewel Sachihana

(Now serialized in *Hana to Mame*)

The very popular shojo comic that Juta writes (under the pen name Jewel Sachihana). It is a pure-love story about Asuka, a tomboy girl who falls head-over-heels in love with a boy named Ryo!

OTOMEN *volume 3* CONTENTS

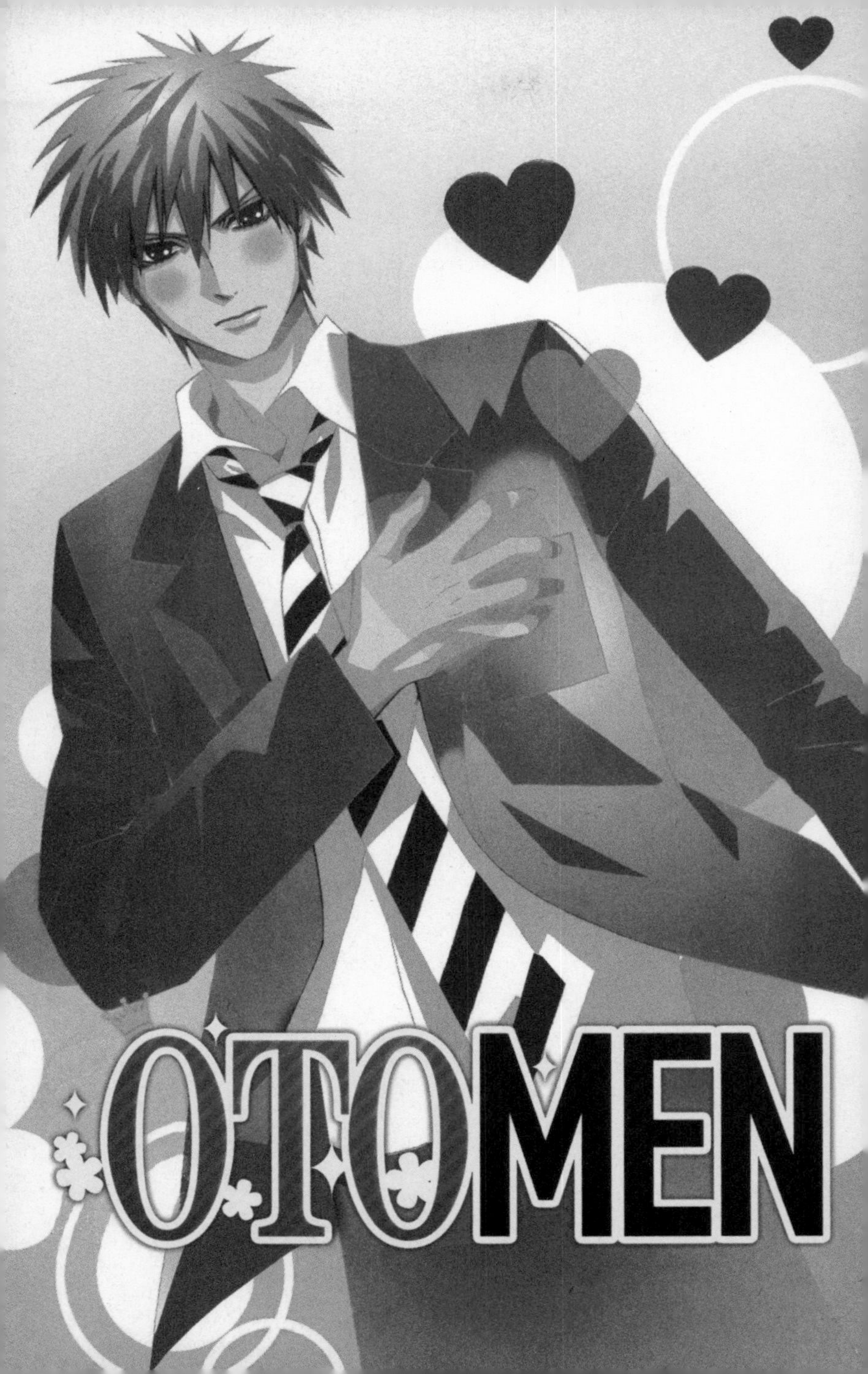
OTOMEN

OTOMEN

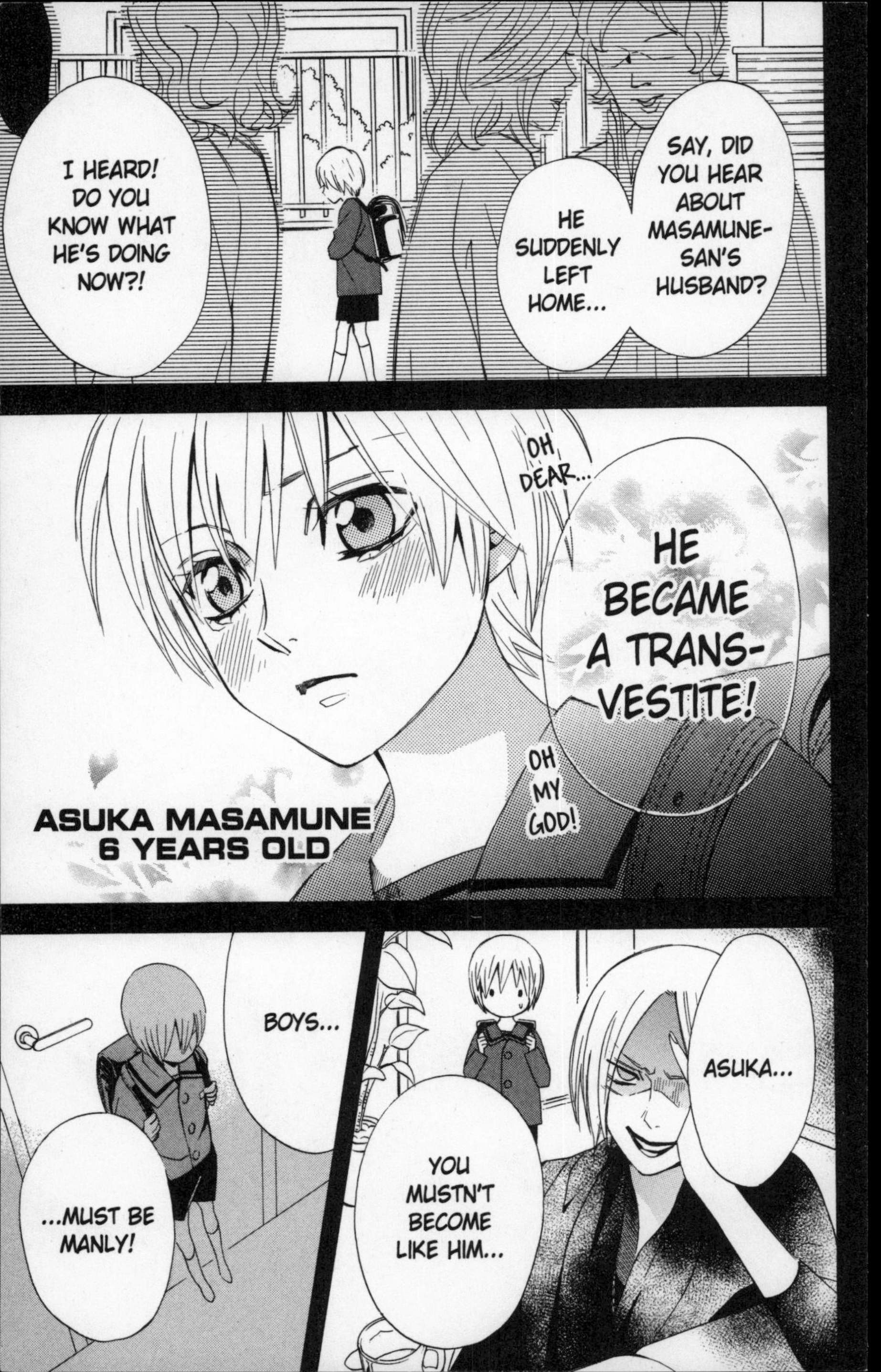
SAY, DID YOU HEAR ABOUT MASAMUNE-SAN'S HUSBAND?
HE SUDDENLY LEFT HOME...
I HEARD! DO YOU KNOW WHAT HE'S DOING NOW?!
OH DEAR...
HE BECAME A TRANS-VESTITE!
OH MY GOD!
ASUKA MASAMUNE 6 YEARS OLD
ASUKA...
YOU MUSTN'T BECOME LIKE HIM...
BOYS...
...MUST BE MANLY!

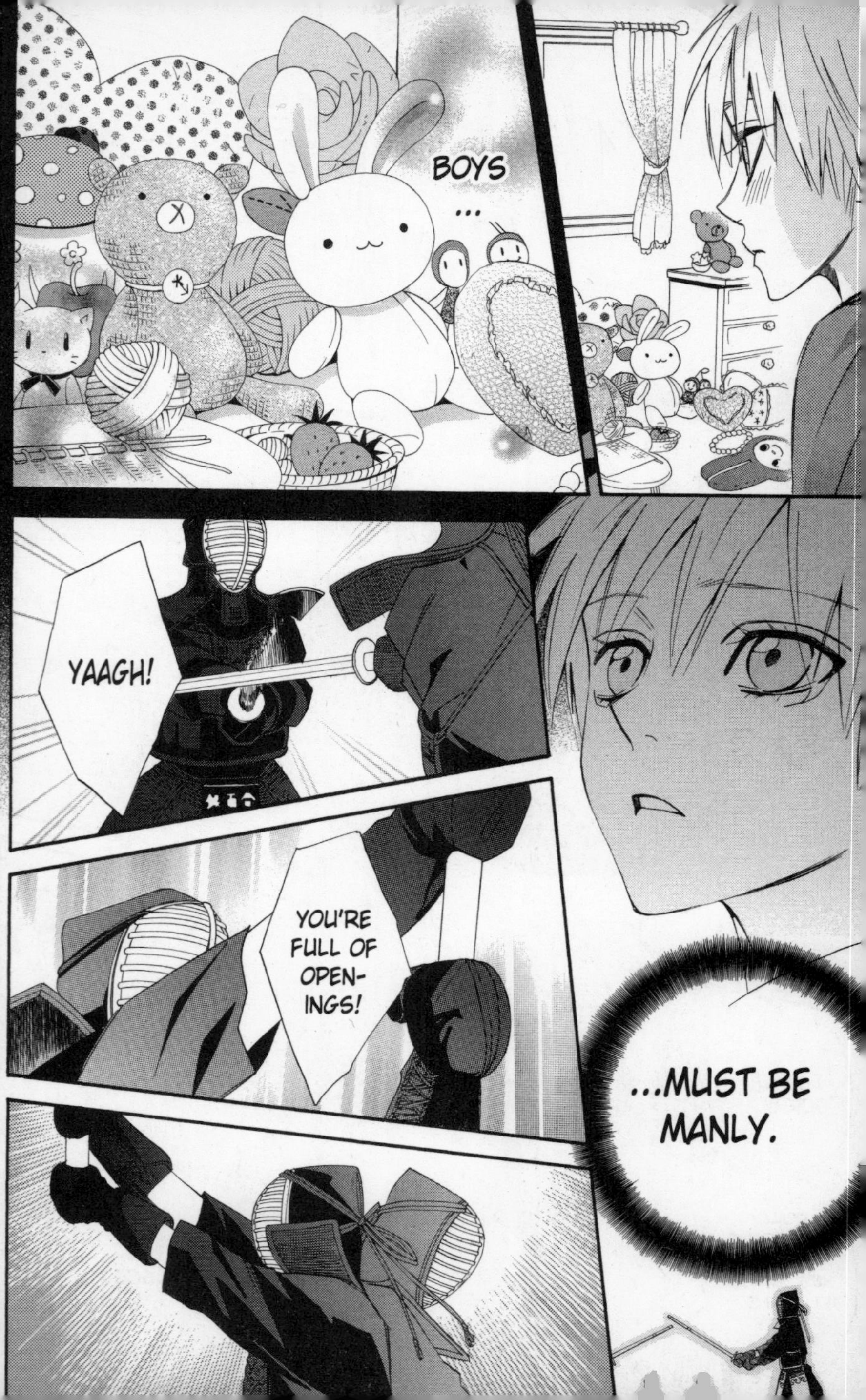
BOYS
...
...MUST BE MANLY.
YAAGH!
YOU'RE FULL OF OPENINGS!

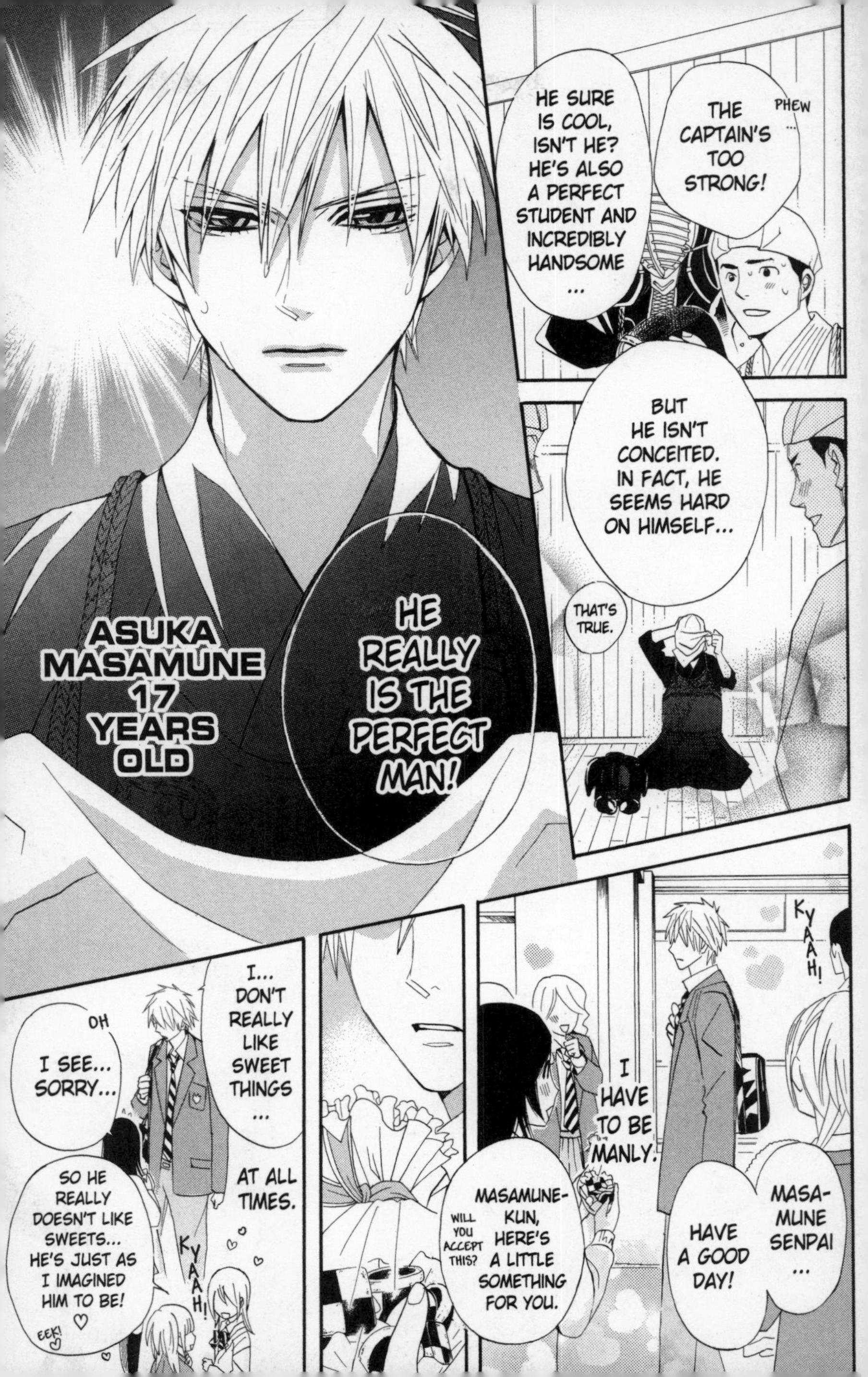
PHEW ...
THE CAPTAIN'S TOO STRONG!
HE SURE IS COOL, ISN'T HE? HE'S ALSO A PERFECT STUDENT AND INCREDIBLY HANDSOME ...
BUT HE ISN'T CONCEITED. IN FACT, HE SEEMS HARD ON HIMSELF...
THAT'S TRUE.
HE REALLY IS THE PERFECT MAN!
ASUKA MASAMUNE 17 YEARS OLD
KYAAAH!
MASAMUNE SENPAI ...
HAVE A GOOD DAY!
MASAMUNE-KUN, HERE'S A LITTLE SOMETHING FOR YOU.
WILL YOU ACCEPT THIS?
I HAVE TO BE MANLY.
AT ALL TIMES.
I... DON'T REALLY LIKE SWEET THINGS ...
OH
I SEE... SORRY...
SO HE REALLY DOESN'T LIKE SWEETS... HE'S JUST AS I IMAGINED HIM TO BE!
KYAAAH!
EEK!

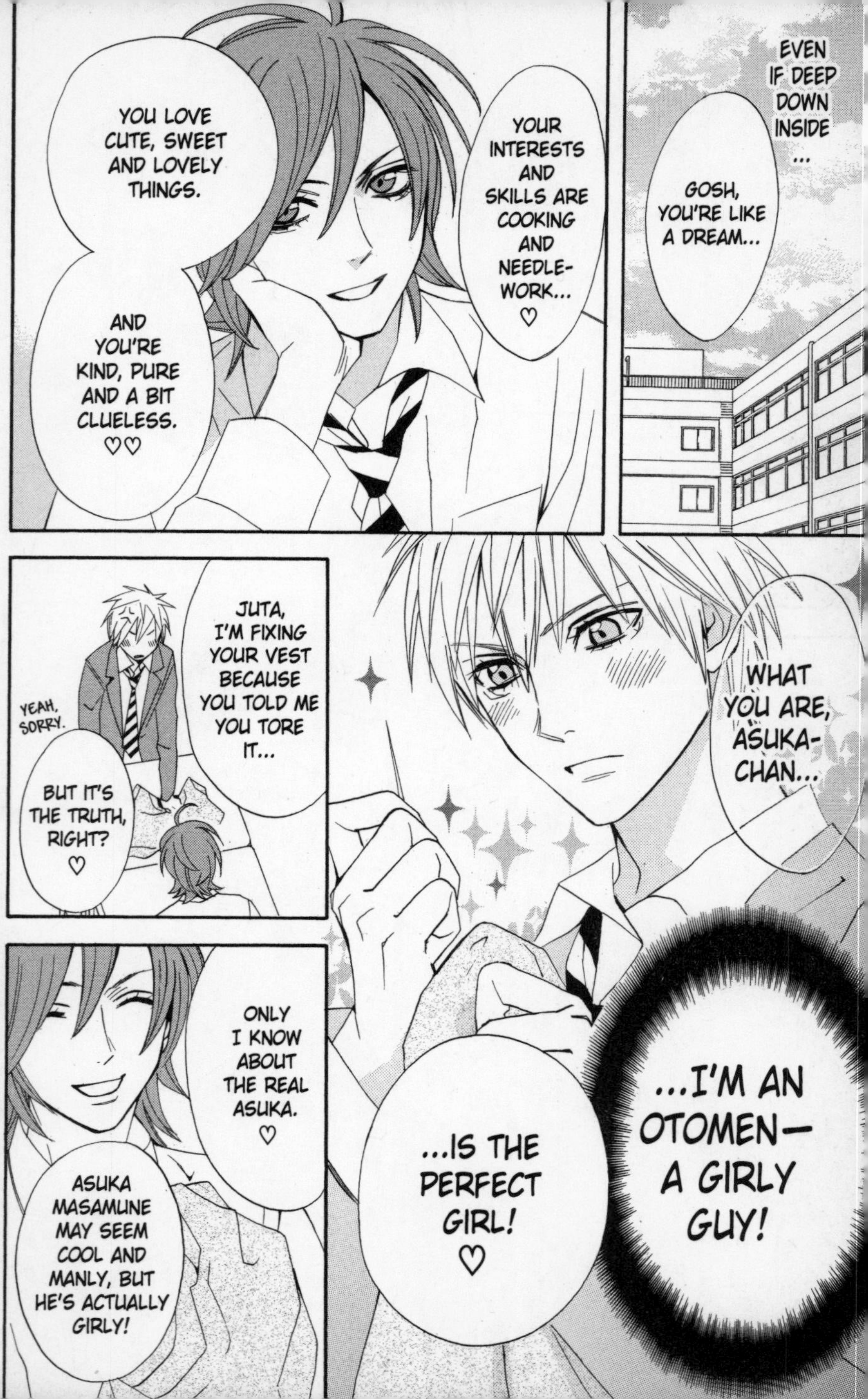
EVEN IF DEEP DOWN INSIDE ...
GOSH, YOU'RE LIKE A DREAM...
YOUR INTERESTS AND SKILLS ARE COOKING AND NEEDLE-WORK... ♡
YOU LOVE CUTE, SWEET AND LOVELY THINGS.
AND YOU'RE KIND, PURE AND A BIT CLUELESS. ♡♡
WHAT YOU ARE, ASUKA-CHAN...
...IS THE PERFECT GIRL! ♡
...I'M AN OTOMEN— A GIRLY GUY!
JUTA, I'M FIXING YOUR VEST BECAUSE YOU TOLD ME YOU TORE IT...
YEAH, SORRY.
BUT IT'S THE TRUTH, RIGHT? ♡
ONLY I KNOW ABOUT THE REAL ASUKA. ♡
ASUKA MASAMUNE MAY SEEM COOL AND MANLY, BUT HE'S ACTUALLY GIRLY!

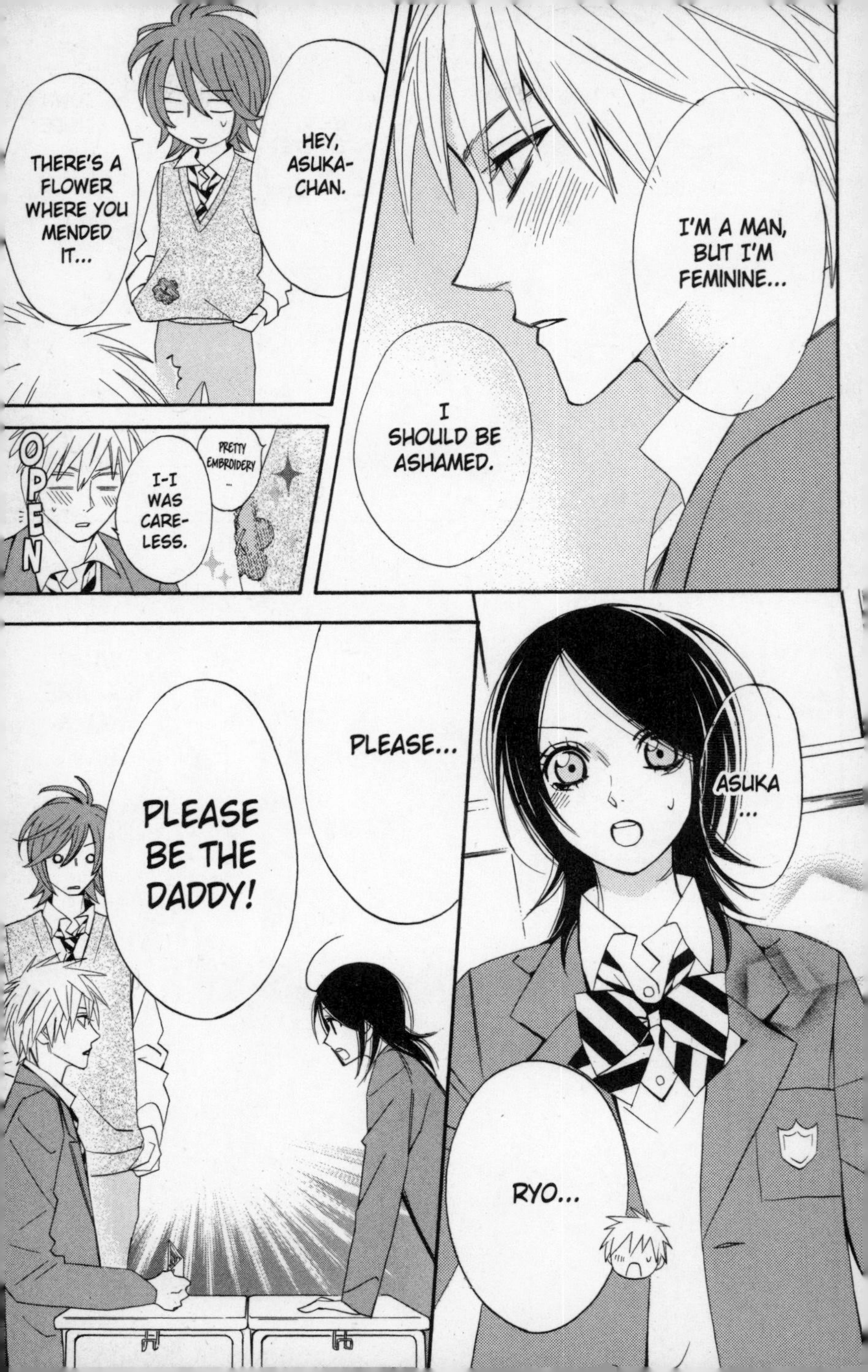
I'M A MAN, BUT I'M FEMININE...
I SHOULD BE ASHAMED.
HEY, ASUKA-CHAN.
THERE'S A FLOWER WHERE YOU MENDED IT...
PRETTY EMBROIDERY ...
I-I WAS CARELESS.
OPEN
ASUKA ...
RYO...
PLEASE...
PLEASE BE THE DADDY!

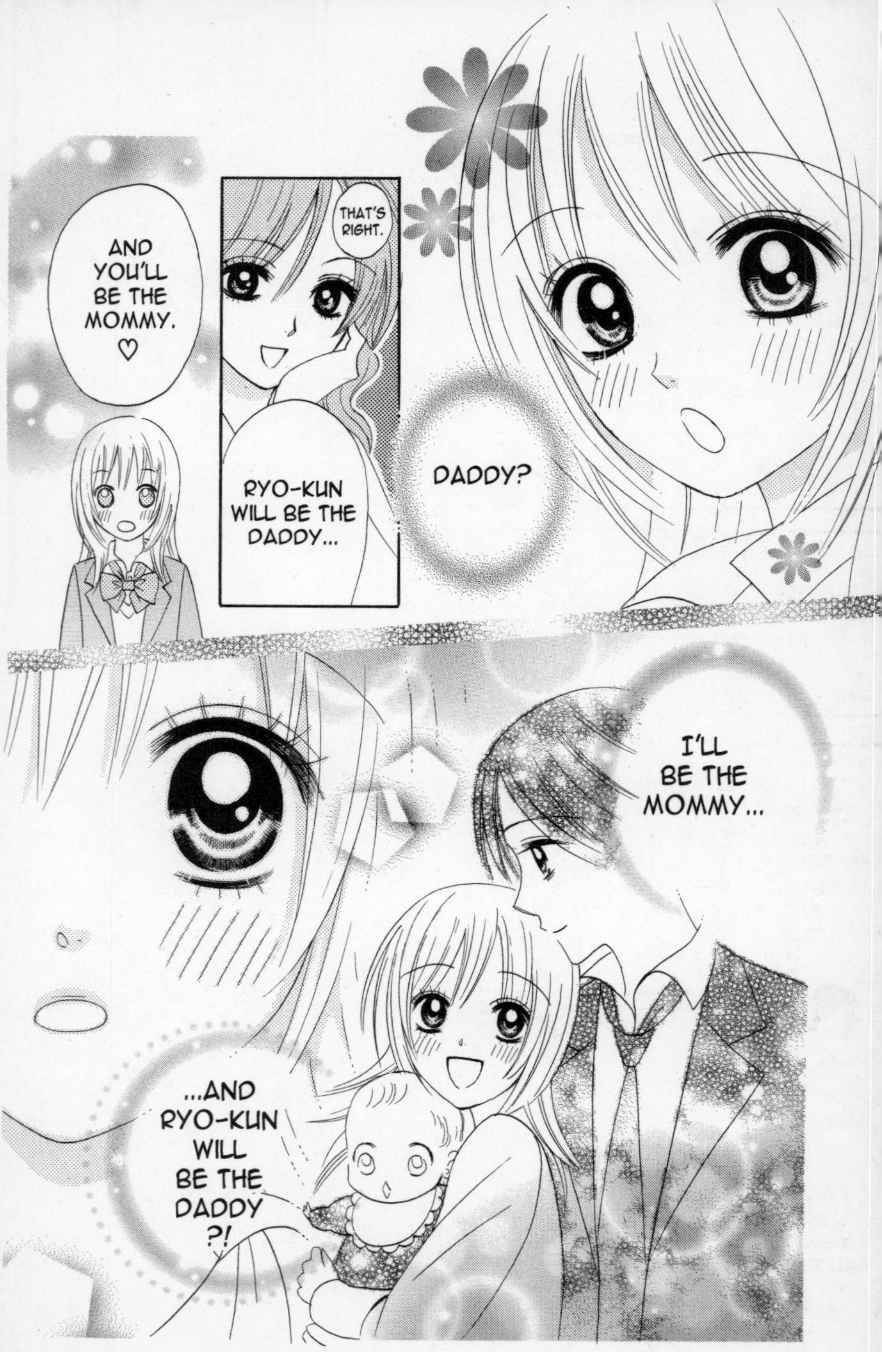
DADDY?
THAT'S RIGHT.
RYO-KUN WILL BE THE DADDY...
AND YOU'LL BE THE MOMMY. ♡
I'LL BE THE MOMMY...
...AND RYO-KUN WILL BE THE DADDY ?!

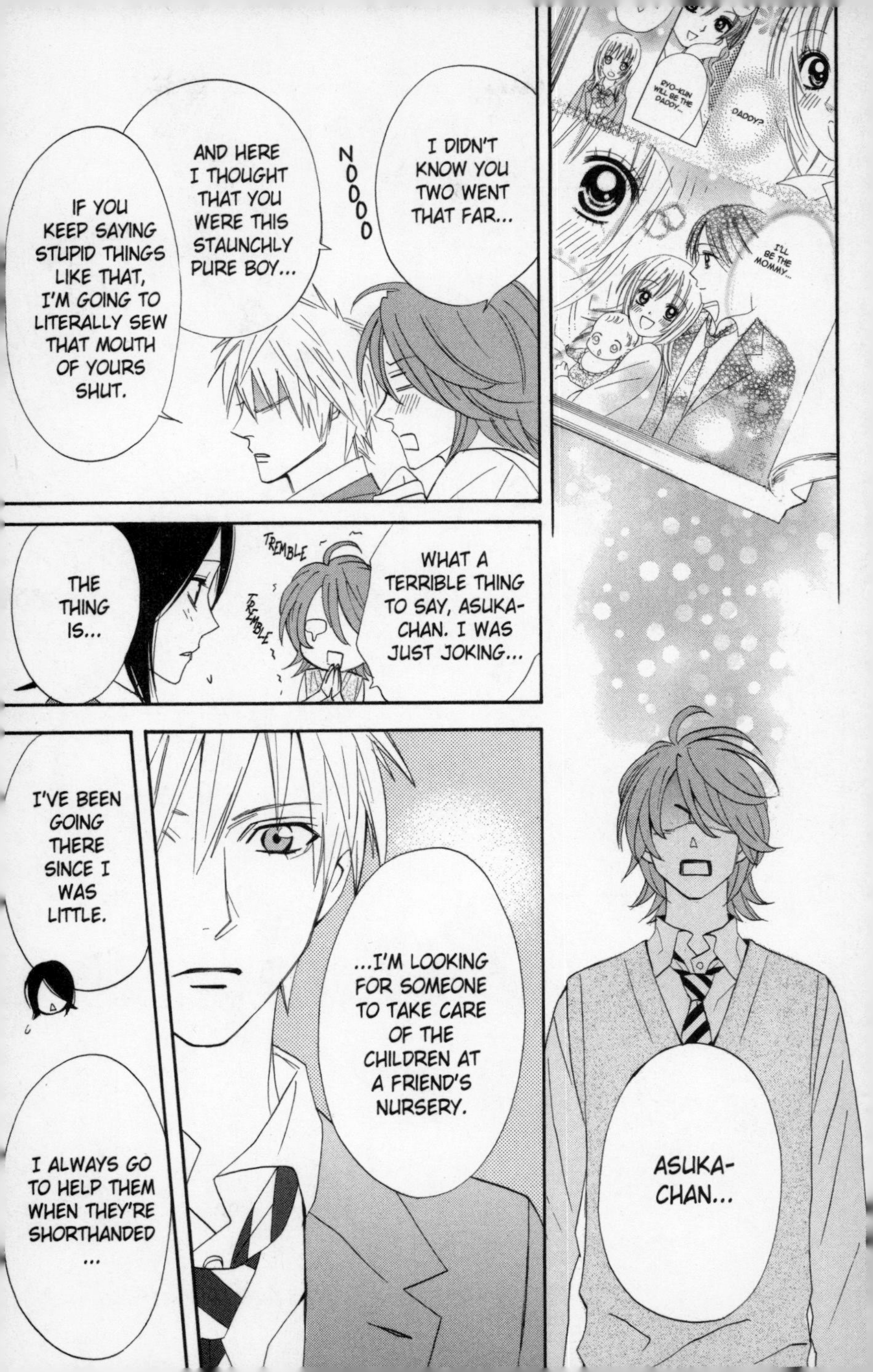
RYO-KUN WILL BE THE DADDY...
DADDY?
I'LL BE THE MOMMY...
ASUKA-CHAN...
I DIDN'T KNOW YOU TWO WENT THAT FAR...
NOOOO
AND HERE I THOUGHT THAT YOU WERE THIS STAUNCHLY PURE BOY...
IF YOU KEEP SAYING STUPID THINGS LIKE THAT, I'M GOING TO LITERALLY SEW THAT MOUTH OF YOURS SHUT.
WHAT A TERRIBLE THING TO SAY, ASUKA-CHAN. I WAS JUST JOKING...
TREMBLE
TREMBLE
THE THING IS...
...I'M LOOKING FOR SOMEONE TO TAKE CARE OF THE CHILDREN AT A FRIEND'S NURSERY.
I'VE BEEN GOING THERE SINCE I WAS LITTLE.
I ALWAYS GO TO HELP THEM WHEN THEY'RE SHORTHANDED...

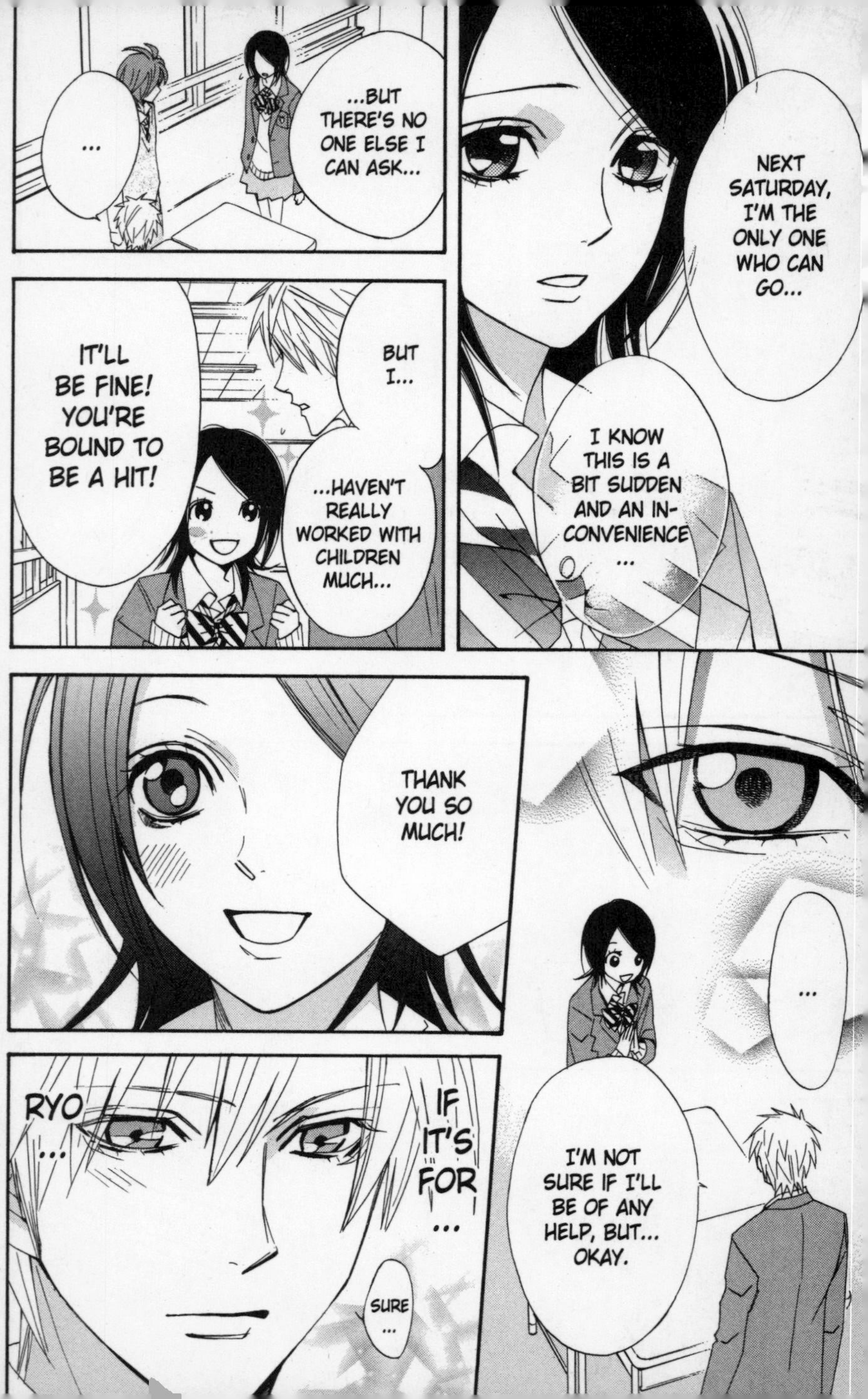
NEXT SATURDAY, I'M THE ONLY ONE WHO CAN GO...
I KNOW THIS IS A BIT SUDDEN AND AN IN-CONVENIENCE ...
...BUT THERE'S NO ONE ELSE I CAN ASK...
...
BUT I...
...HAVEN'T REALLY WORKED WITH CHILDREN MUCH...
IT'LL BE FINE! YOU'RE BOUND TO BE A HIT!
...
I'M NOT SURE IF I'LL BE OF ANY HELP, BUT... OKAY.
THANK YOU SO MUCH!
IF IT'S FOR ...
RYO ...
SURE ...

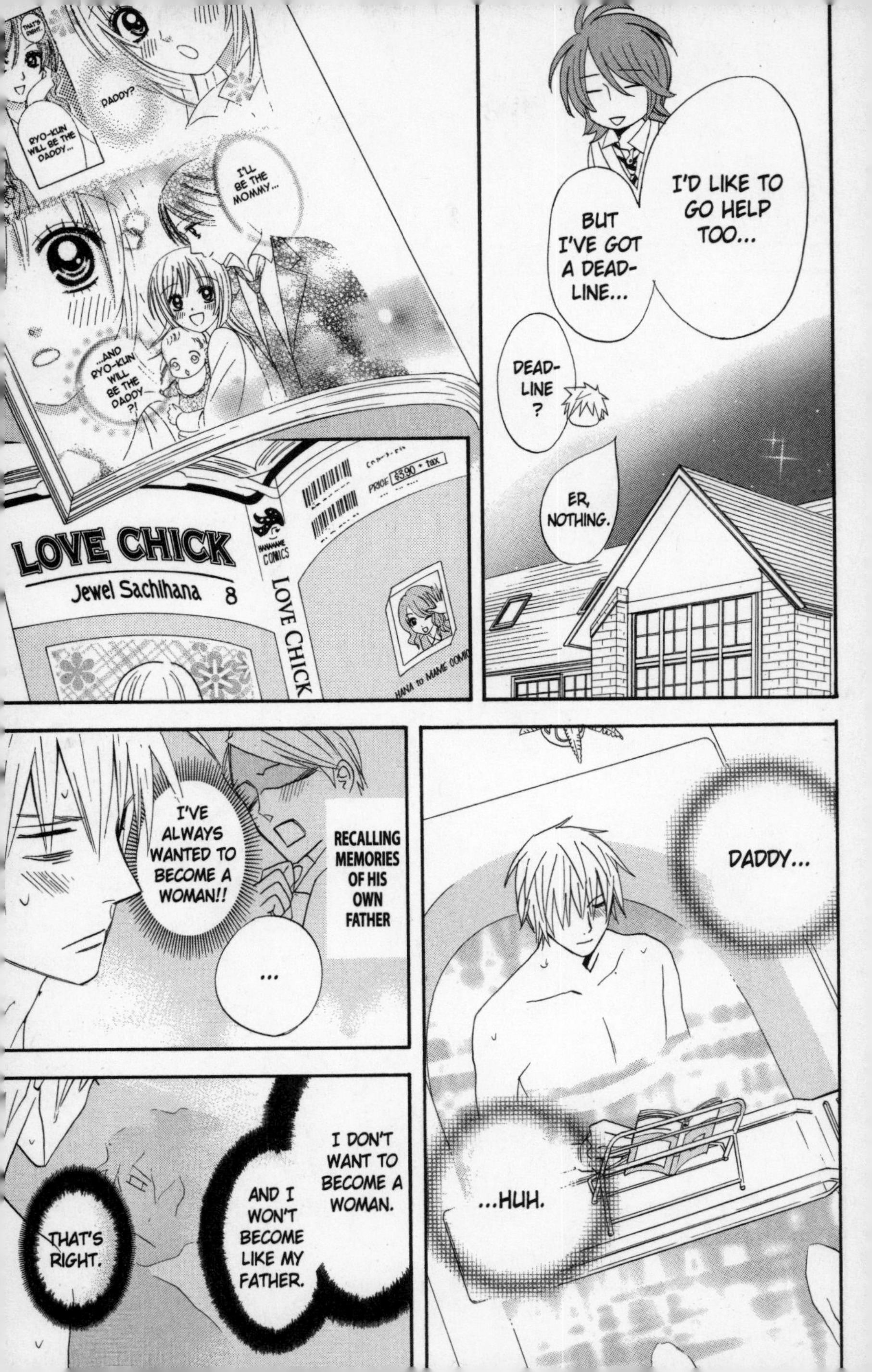
I'D LIKE TO GO HELP TOO...
BUT I'VE GOT A DEAD-LINE...
DEAD-LINE?
ER, NOTHING.
THAT'S RIGHT.
DADDY?
RYO-KUN WILL BE THE DADDY...
I'LL BE THE MOMMY...
...AND RYO-KUN WILL BE THE DADDY—?!
LOVE CHICK
Jewel Sachihana 8
HANAMAME COMICS
LOVE CHICK
HANA to MAME COMIC
DADDY...
...HUH.
RECALLING MEMORIES OF HIS OWN FATHER
I'VE ALWAYS WANTED TO BECOME A WOMAN!!
...
I DON'T WANT TO BECOME A WOMAN.
AND I WON'T BECOME LIKE MY FATHER.
THAT'S RIGHT.

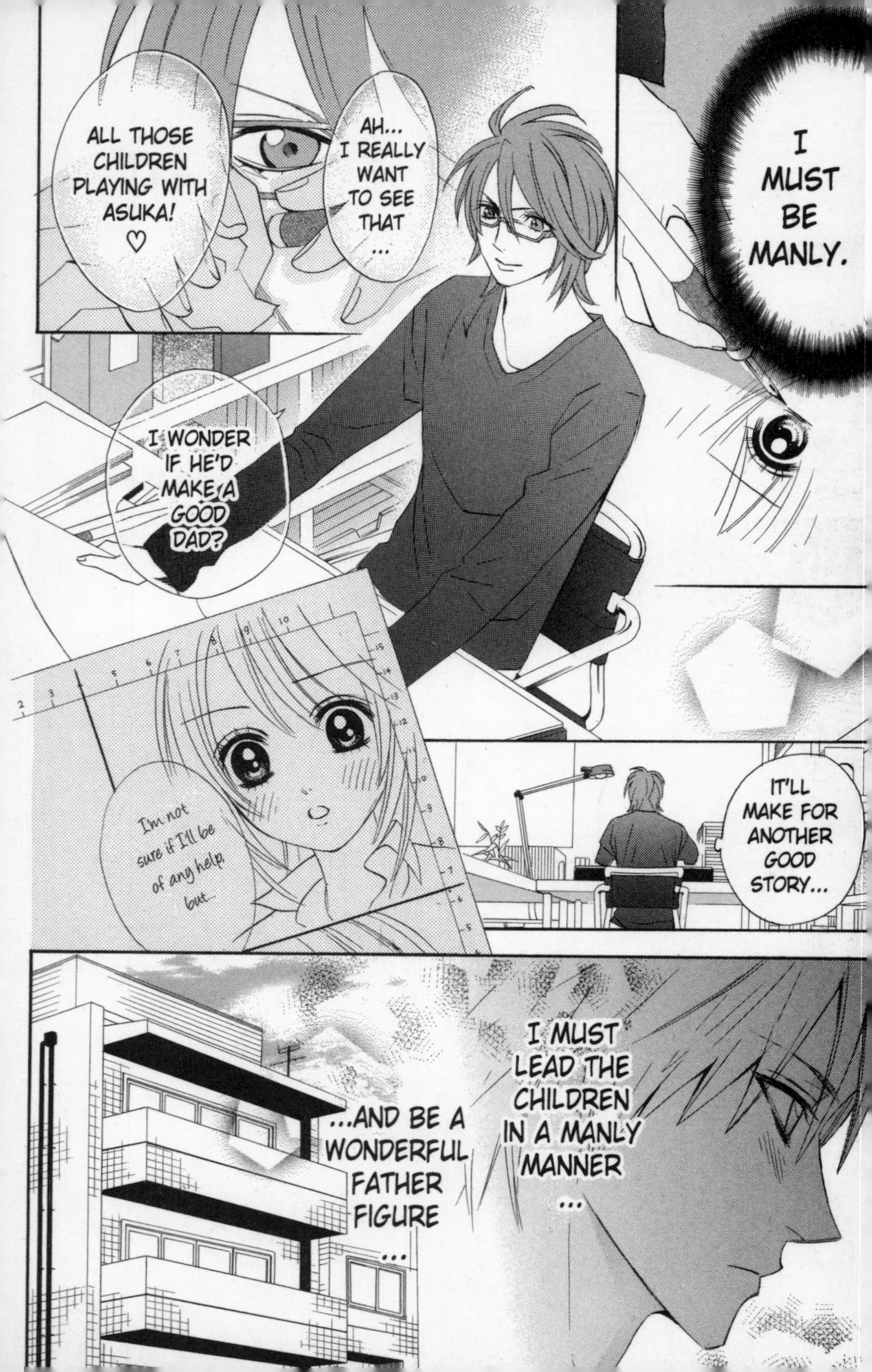
I MUST BE MANLY.
AH... I REALLY WANT TO SEE THAT...
ALL THOSE CHILDREN PLAYING WITH ASUKA! ♡
I WONDER IF HE'D MAKE A GOOD DAD?
I'm not sure if I'll be of any help, but...
IT'LL MAKE FOR ANOTHER GOOD STORY...
I MUST LEAD THE CHILDREN IN A MANLY MANNER...
...AND BE A WONDERFUL FATHER FIGURE...

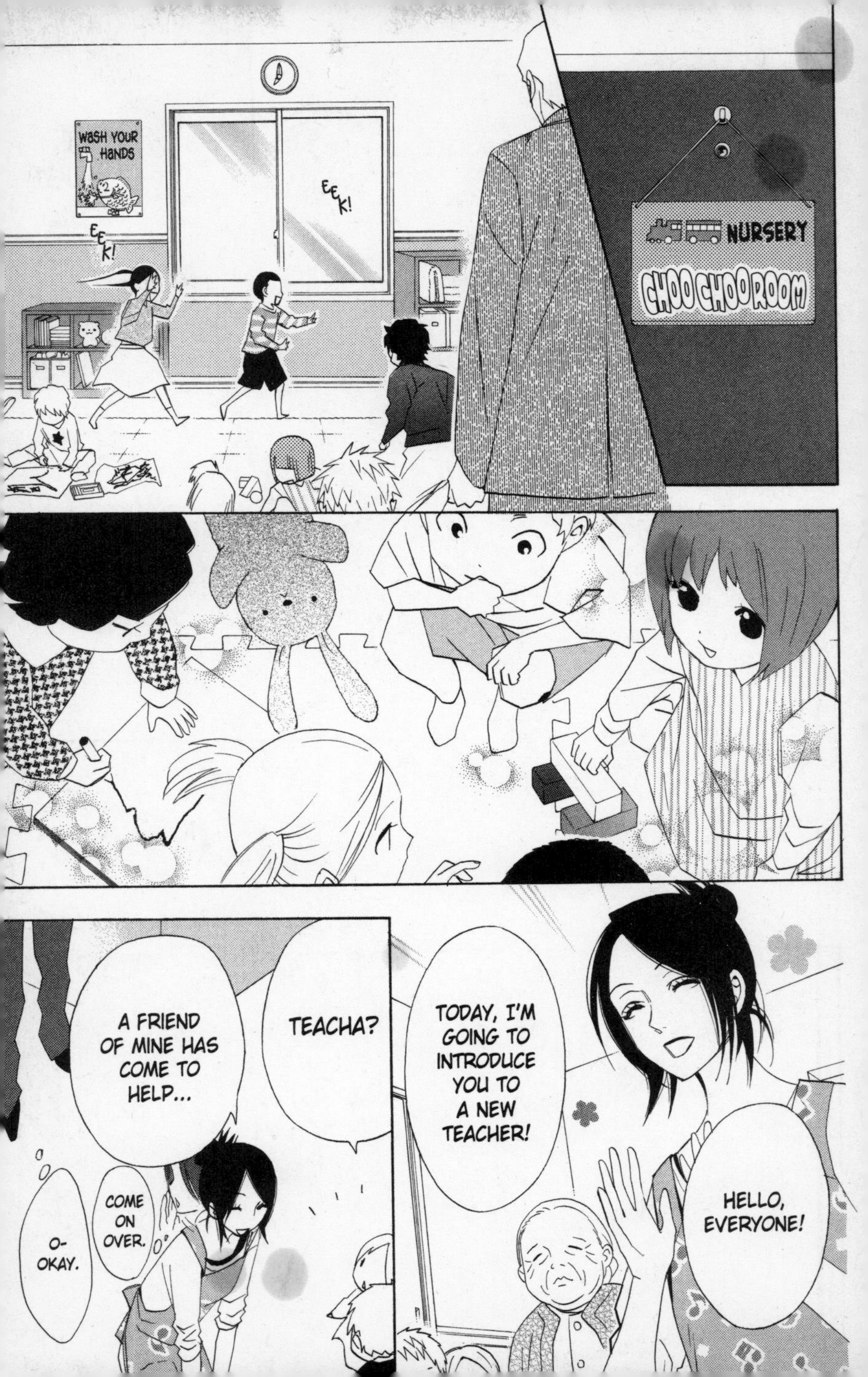
NURSERY
CHOO CHOO ROOM
EEK!
WASH YOUR HANDS
EEK!
HELLO, EVERYONE!
TODAY, I'M GOING TO INTRODUCE YOU TO A NEW TEACHER!
TEACHA?
A FRIEND OF MINE HAS COME TO HELP...
COME ON OVER.
O-OKAY.

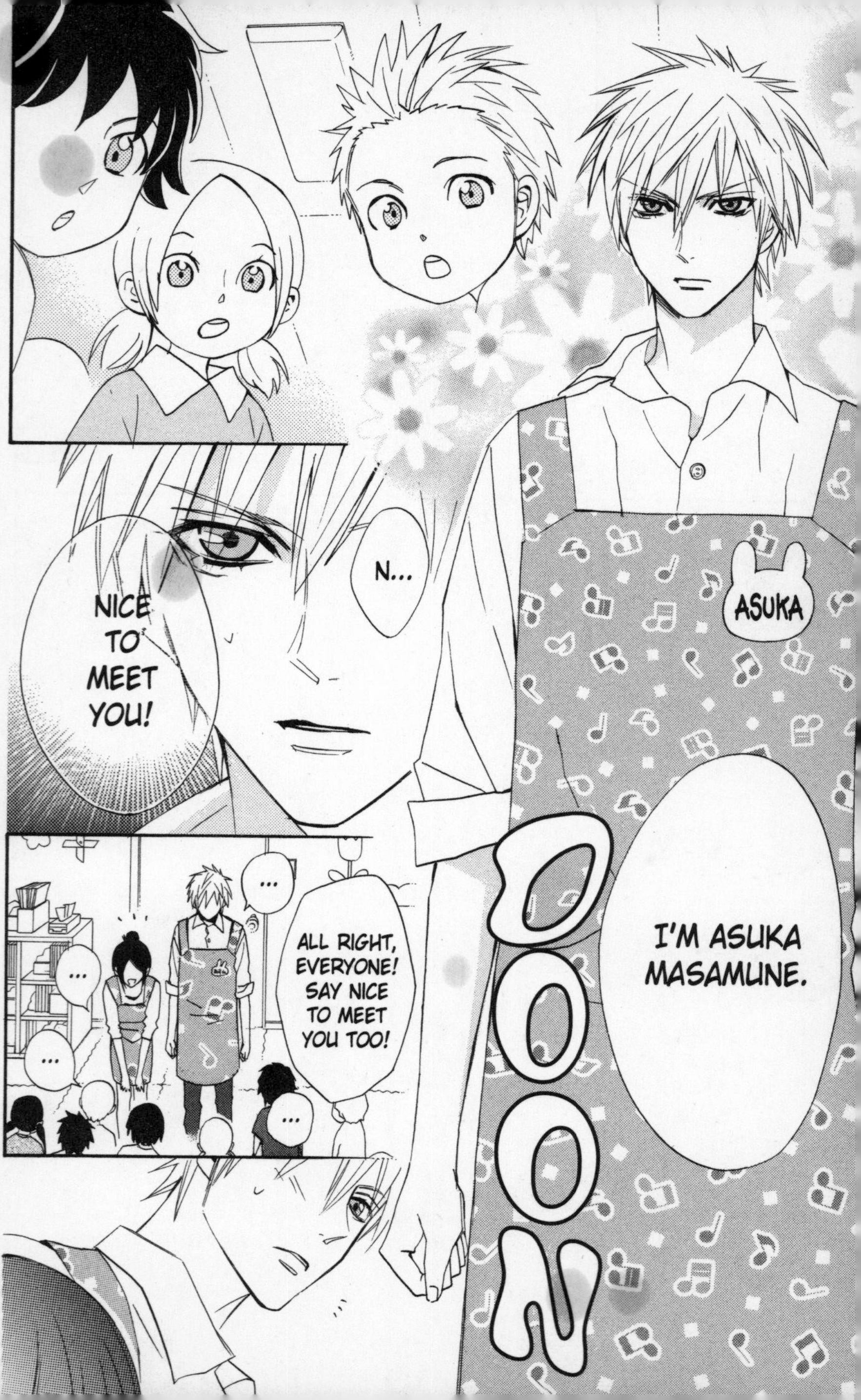
ASUKA
I'M ASUKA MASAMUNE.
DOON
N...
NICE TO MEET YOU!
...
ALL RIGHT, EVERYONE! SAY NICE TO MEET YOU TOO!
...
...
...
...

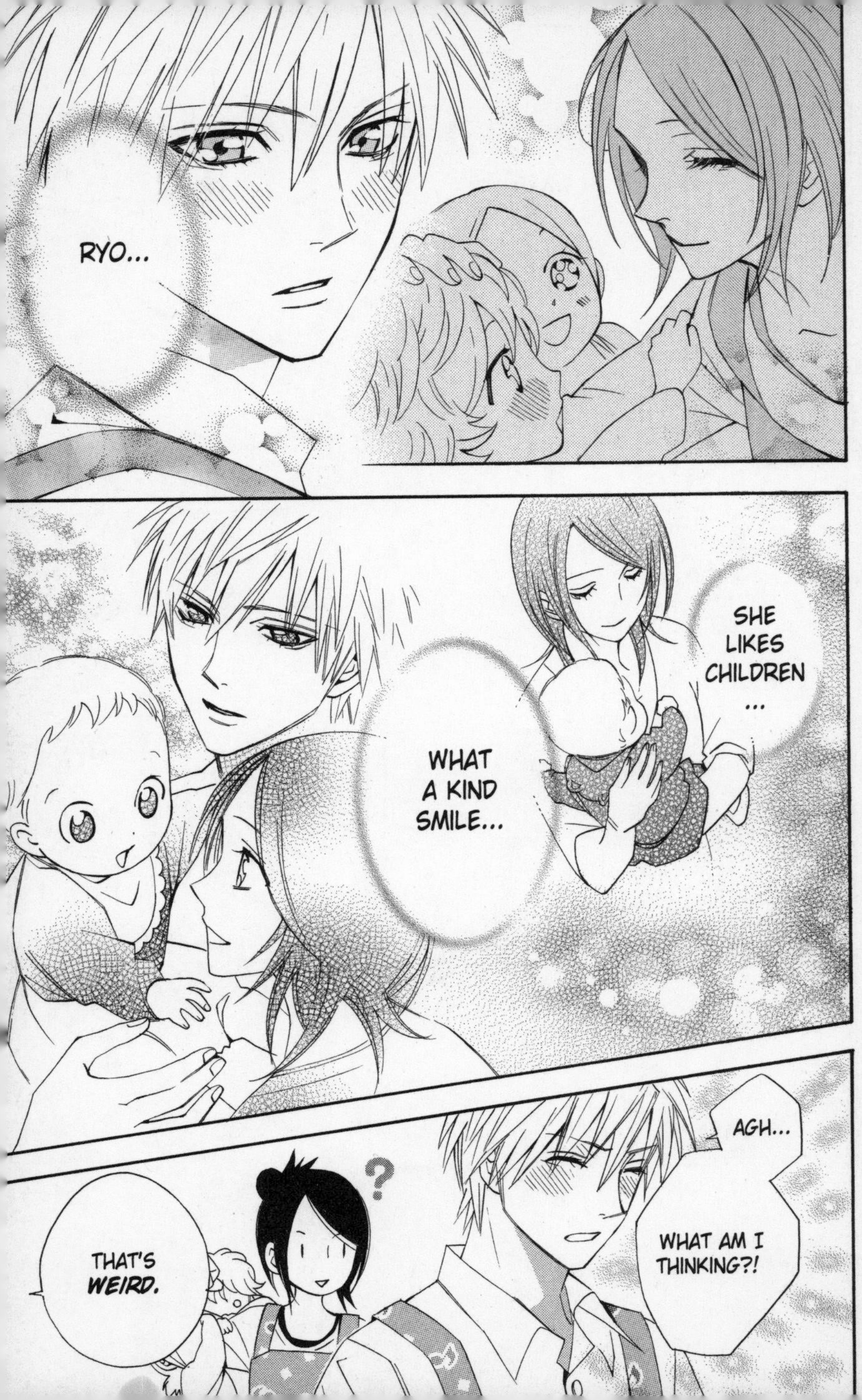
RYO...
SHE LIKES CHILDREN ...
WHAT A KIND SMILE...
AGH...
WHAT AM I THINKING?!
THAT'S *WEIRD.*

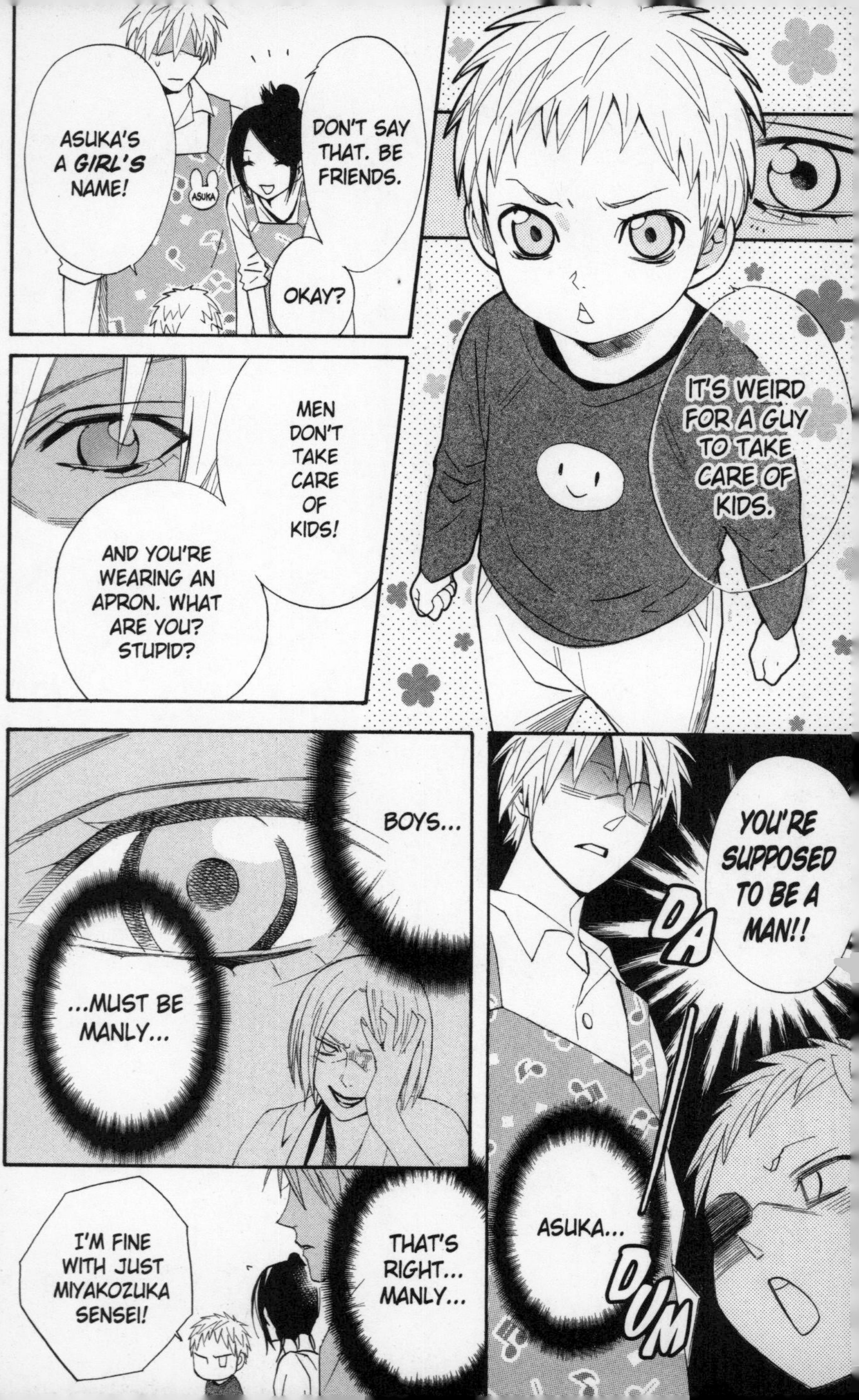
IT'S WEIRD FOR A GUY TO TAKE CARE OF KIDS.
DON'T SAY THAT. BE FRIENDS.
OKAY?
ASUKA'S A GIRL'S NAME!
ASUKA
MEN DON'T TAKE CARE OF KIDS!
AND YOU'RE WEARING AN APRON. WHAT ARE YOU? STUPID?
YOU'RE SUPPOSED TO BE A MAN!!
DA
ASUKA...
DUM
BOYS...
...MUST BE MANLY...
THAT'S RIGHT... MANLY...
I'M FINE WITH JUST MIYAKOZUKA SENSEI!

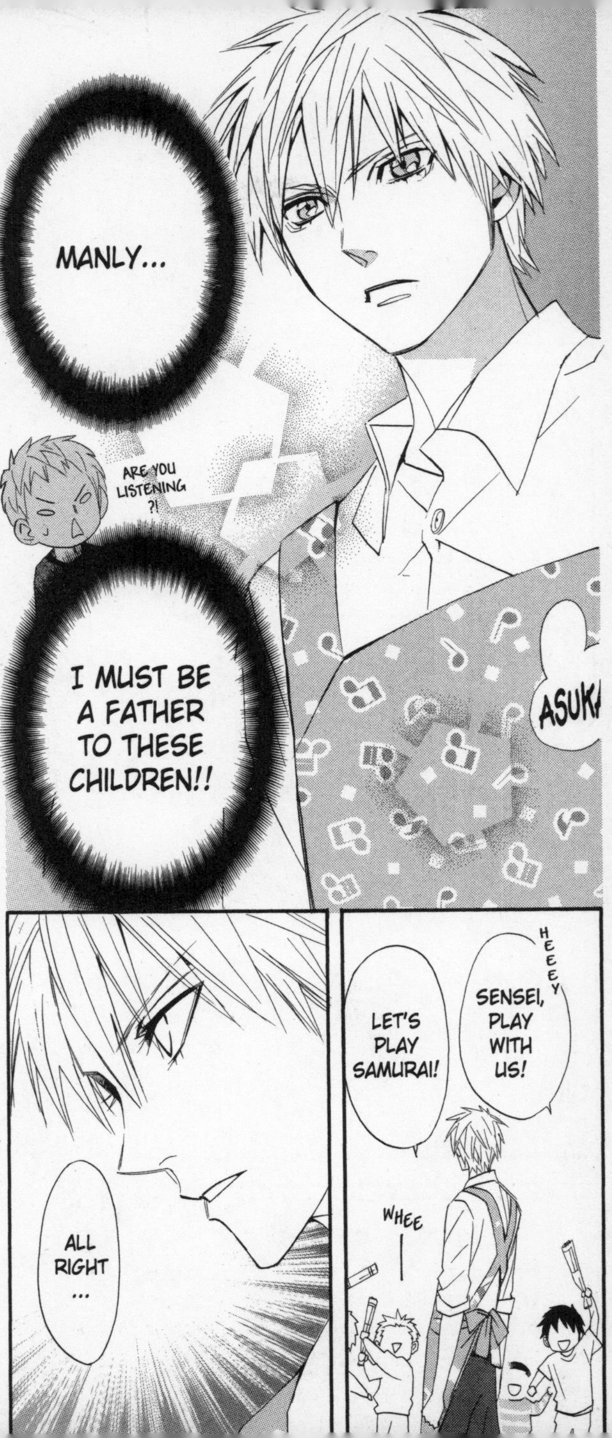
MANLY...
ARE YOU LISTENING ?!
ASUKA
I MUST BE A FATHER TO THESE CHILDREN!!
HEEEY
SENSEI, PLAY WITH US!
LET'S PLAY SAMURAI!
WHEE
ALL RIGHT ...

Hello, it's Aya Kanno.

Thankfully, *Otomen* has reached volume 3! I've done six series so far, but this is the first time I've reached three volumes. I'm grateful to my readers and everyone involved with *Otomen*. I was a two-volume series writer for a while, but I've finally broken away from that...

The first story in volume 3 takes place in a nursery. This story is obviously fiction. I don't think that such an irresponsible nursery exists. It's fiction, so please overlook some parts of it. This chapter ran in the main *Hana to Yume* magazine, so the beginning sounds like an overview, doesn't it?

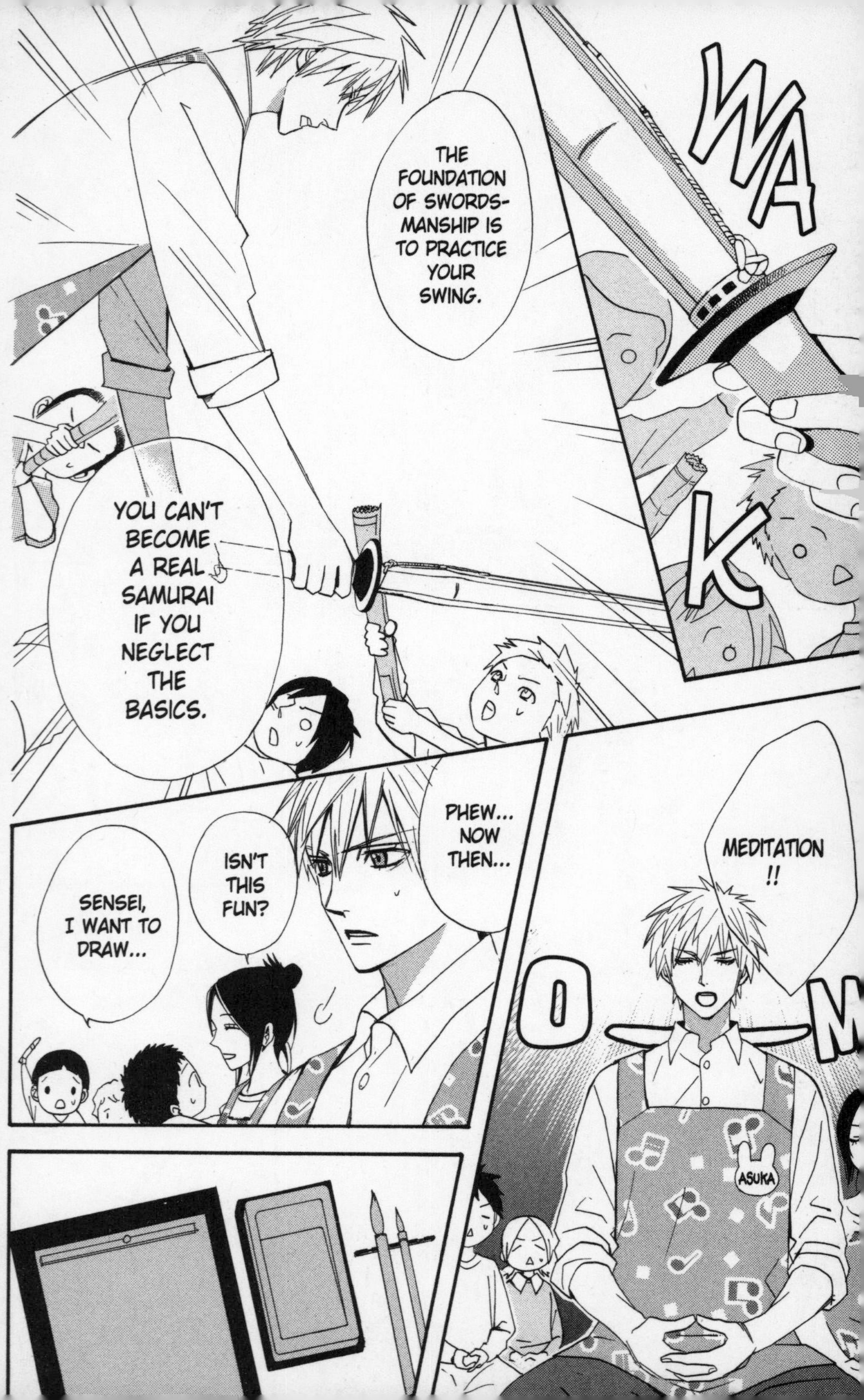
WAK
THE FOUNDATION OF SWORDS-MANSHIP IS TO PRACTICE YOUR SWING.
YOU CAN'T BECOME A REAL SAMURAI IF YOU NEGLECT THE BASICS.
MEDITATION !!
O—M
PHEW... NOW THEN...
ISN'T THIS FUN?
SENSEI, I WANT TO DRAW...
ASUKA

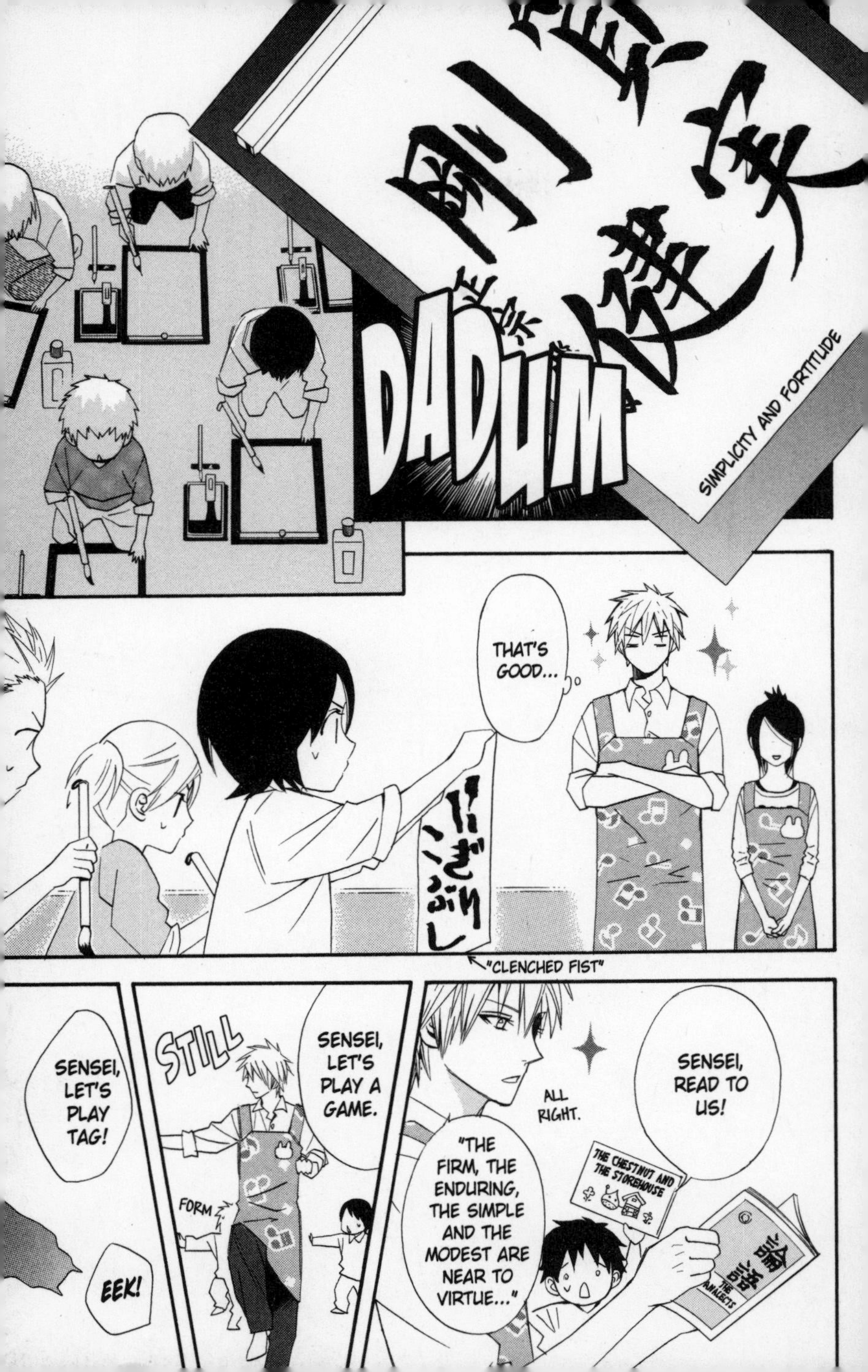
DADUM
SIMPLICITY AND FORTITUDE
THAT'S GOOD...
にぎりこぶし
"CLENCHED FIST"
SENSEI, READ TO US!
ALL RIGHT.
THE CHESTNUT AND THE STOREHOUSE
"THE FIRM, THE ENDURING, THE SIMPLE AND THE MODEST ARE NEAR TO VIRTUE..."
論語
THE ANALECTS
SENSEI, LET'S PLAY A GAME.
STILL
FORM
SENSEI, LET'S PLAY TAG!
EEK!

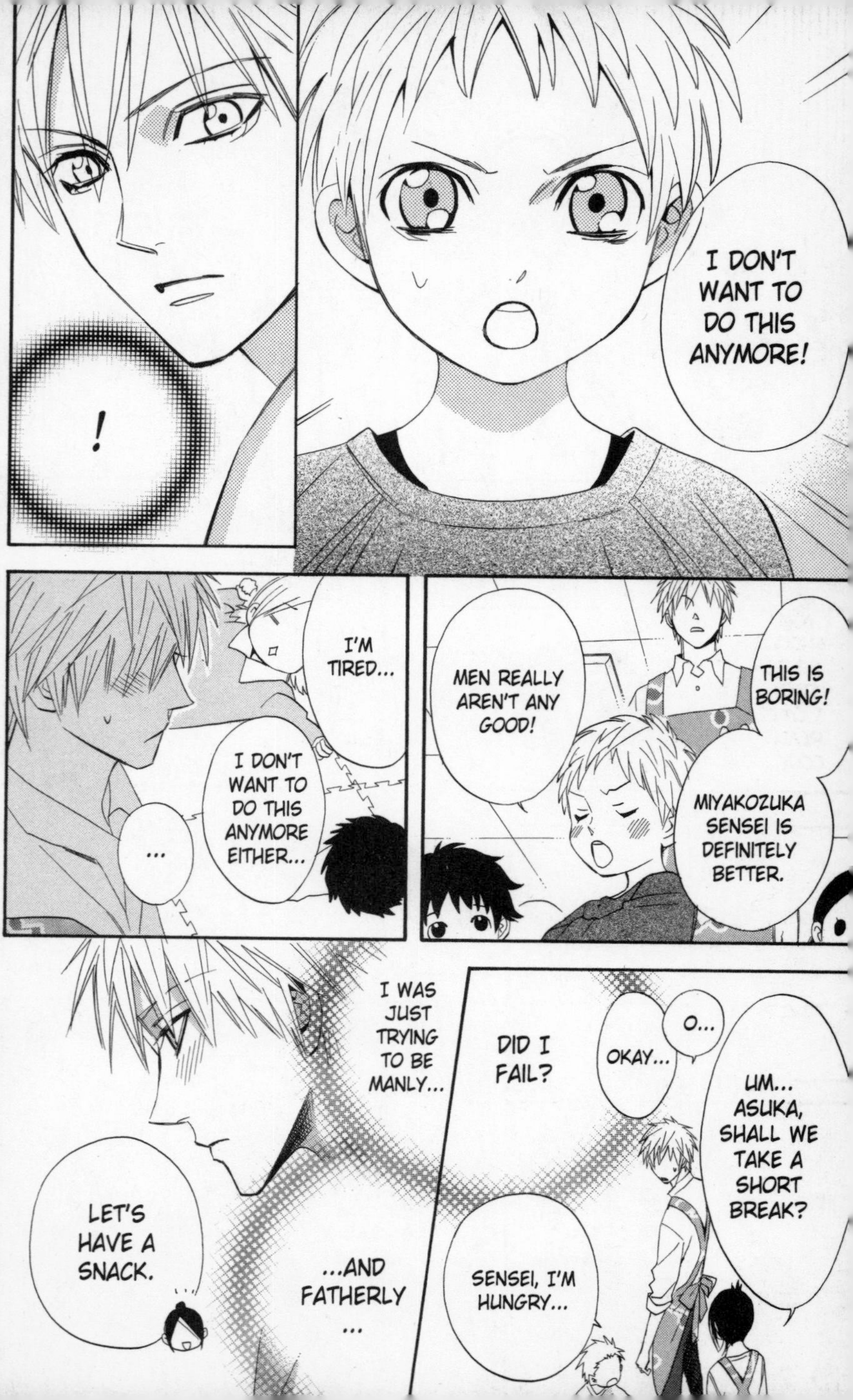
I DON'T WANT TO DO THIS ANYMORE!
!
THIS IS BORING!
MEN REALLY AREN'T ANY GOOD!
MIYAKOZUKA SENSEI IS DEFINITELY BETTER.
I'M TIRED...
I DON'T WANT TO DO THIS ANYMORE EITHER...
...
O...
OKAY...
UM... ASUKA, SHALL WE TAKE A SHORT BREAK?
DID I FAIL?
SENSEI, I'M HUNGRY...
I WAS JUST TRYING TO BE MANLY...
...AND FATHERLY...
LET'S HAVE A SNACK.

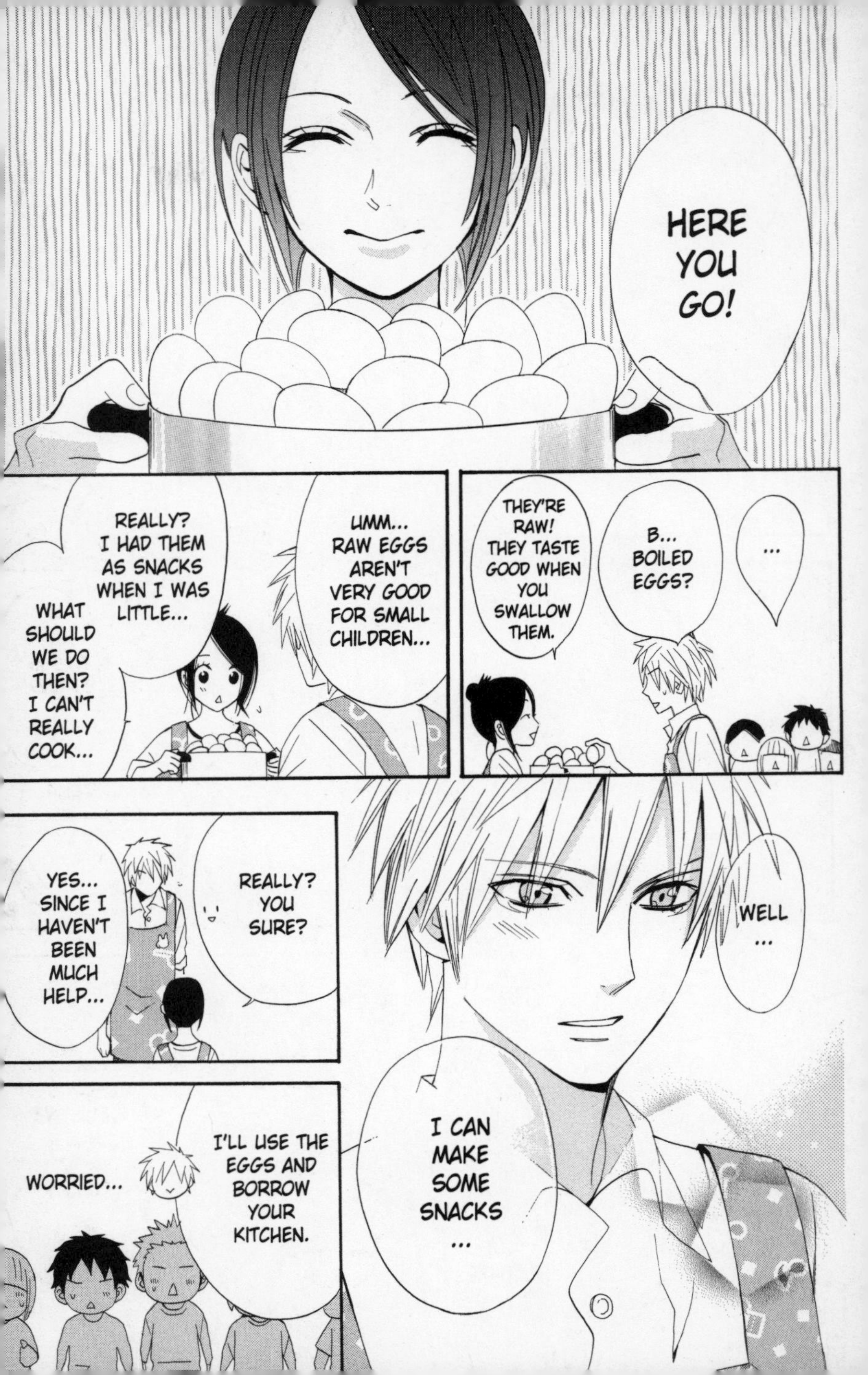
HERE YOU GO!
...
B... BOILED EGGS?
THEY'RE RAW! THEY TASTE GOOD WHEN YOU SWALLOW THEM.
UMM... RAW EGGS AREN'T VERY GOOD FOR SMALL CHILDREN...
REALLY? I HAD THEM AS SNACKS WHEN I WAS LITTLE...
WHAT SHOULD WE DO THEN? I CAN'T REALLY COOK...
WELL ...
I CAN MAKE SOME SNACKS ...
REALLY? YOU SURE?
YES... SINCE I HAVEN'T BEEN MUCH HELP...
I'LL USE THE EGGS AND BORROW YOUR KITCHEN.
WORRIED...

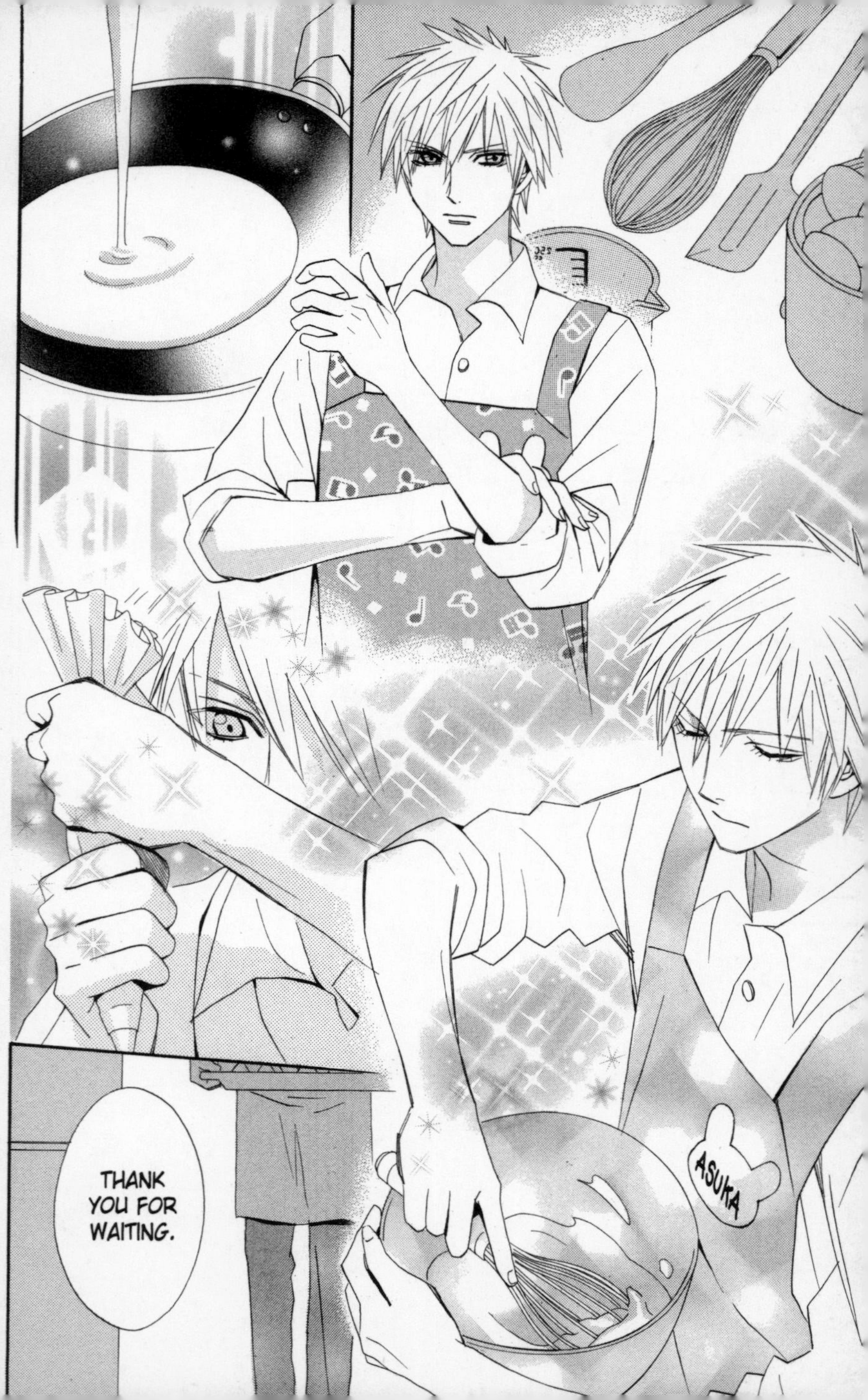
ASUKA
THANK YOU FOR WAITING.

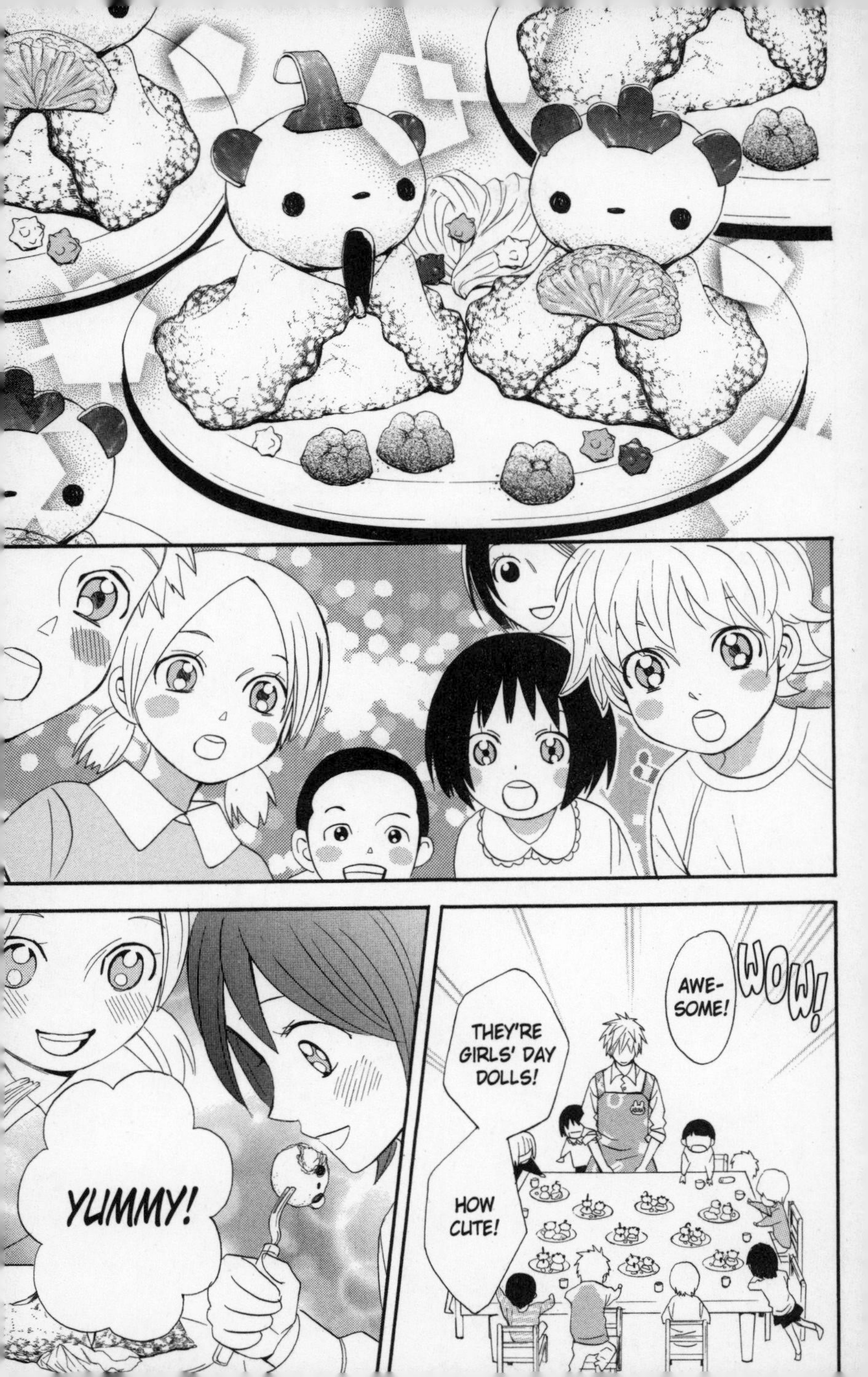
WOW!
AWE-SOME!
THEY'RE GIRLS' DAY DOLLS!
HOW CUTE!
YUMMY!

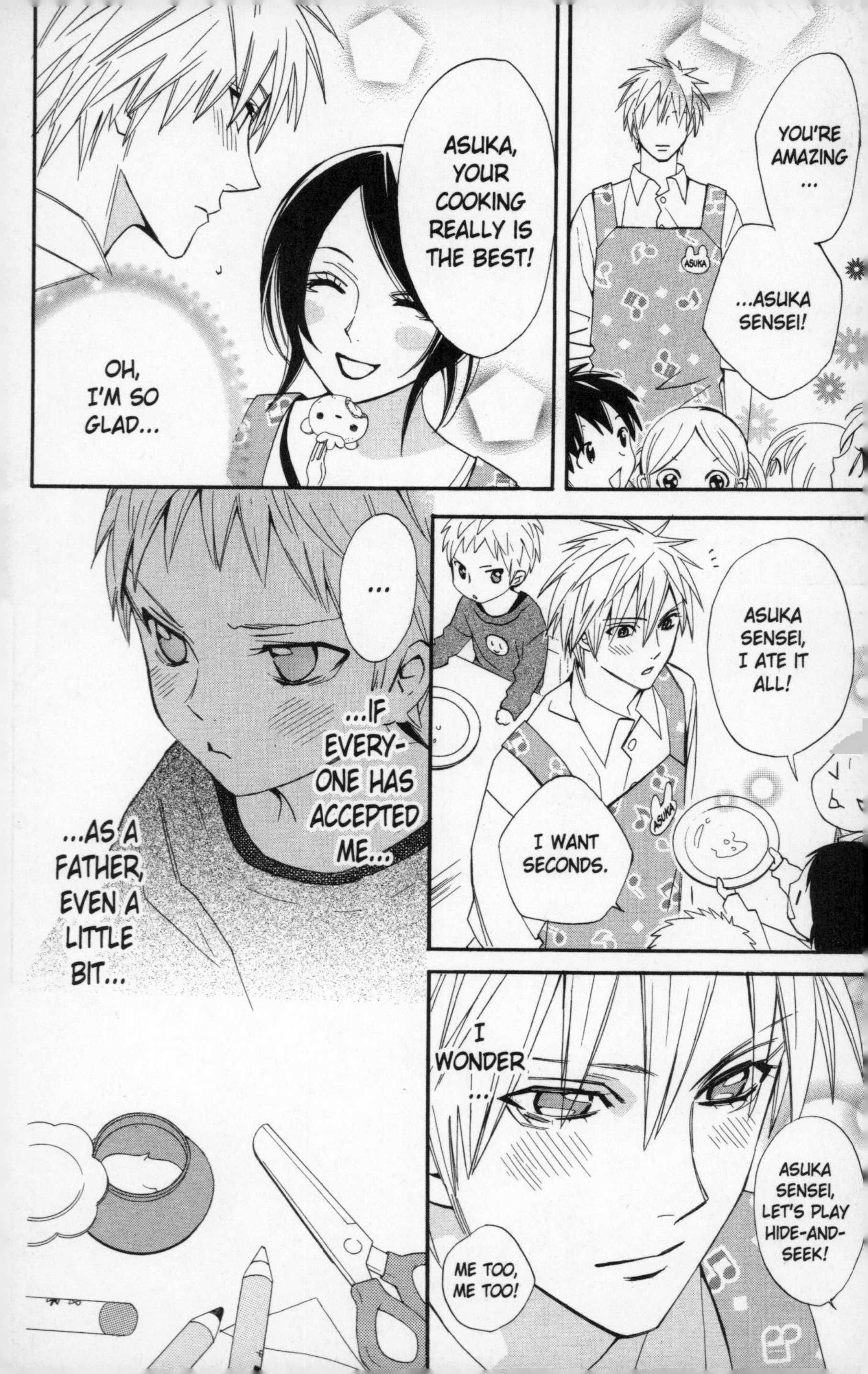
YOU'RE AMAZING ...
...ASUKA SENSEI!
ASUKA, YOUR COOKING REALLY IS THE BEST!
OH, I'M SO GLAD...
ASUKA SENSEI, I ATE IT ALL!
I WANT SECONDS.
...
...IF EVERY-ONE HAS ACCEPTED ME...
...AS A FATHER, EVEN A LITTLE BIT...
I WONDER ...
ASUKA SENSEI, LET'S PLAY HIDE-AND-SEEK!
ME TOO, ME TOO!

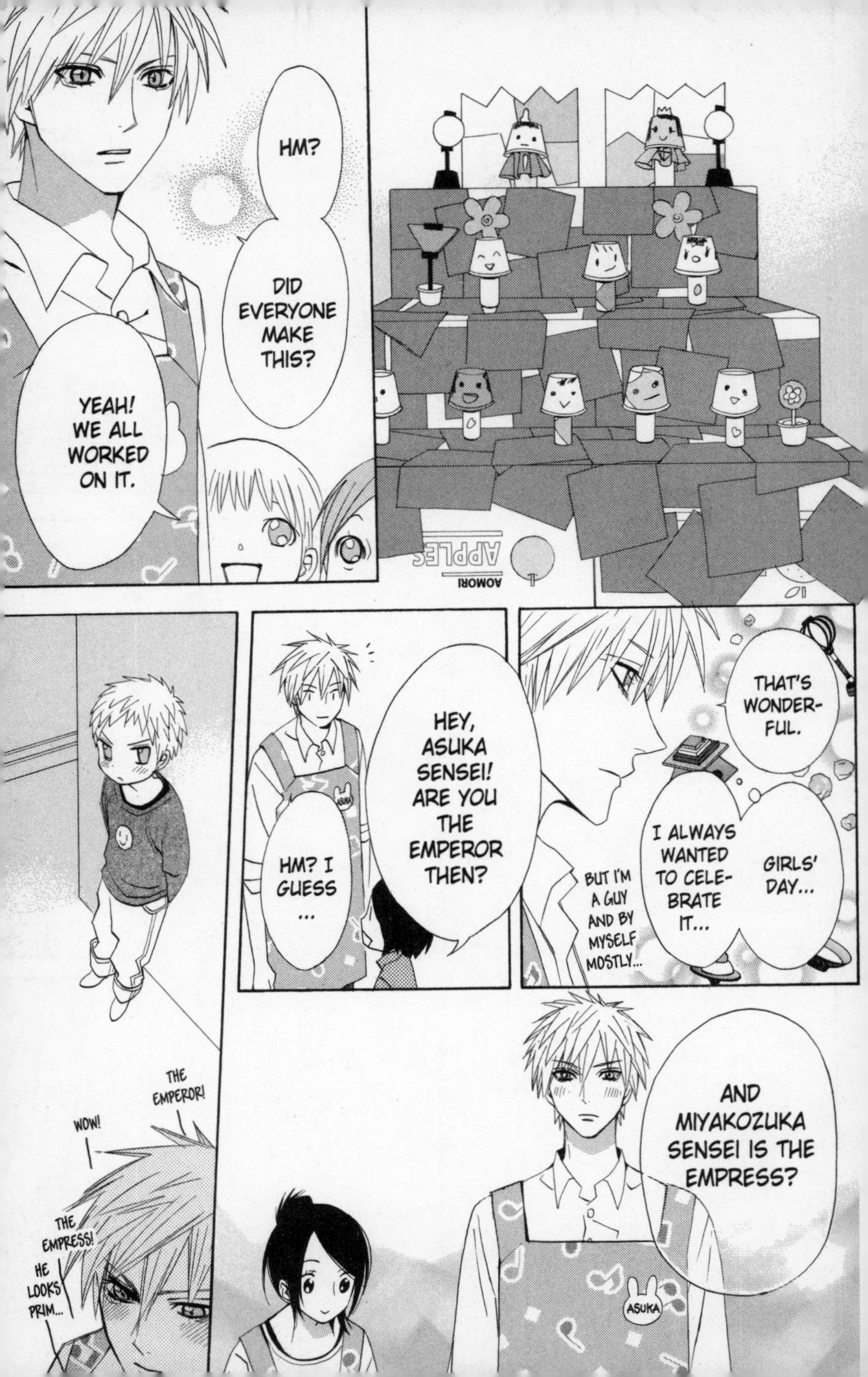
HM?
DID EVERYONE MAKE THIS?
YEAH! WE ALL WORKED ON IT.
THAT'S WONDERFUL.
GIRLS' DAY...
I ALWAYS WANTED TO CELEBRATE IT...
BUT I'M A GUY AND BY MYSELF MOSTLY...
HEY, ASUKA SENSEI! ARE YOU THE EMPEROR THEN?
HM? I GUESS...
AND MIYAKOZUKA SENSEI IS THE EMPRESS?
ASUKA
THE EMPEROR!
WOW!
THE EMPRESS!
HE LOOKS PRIM...

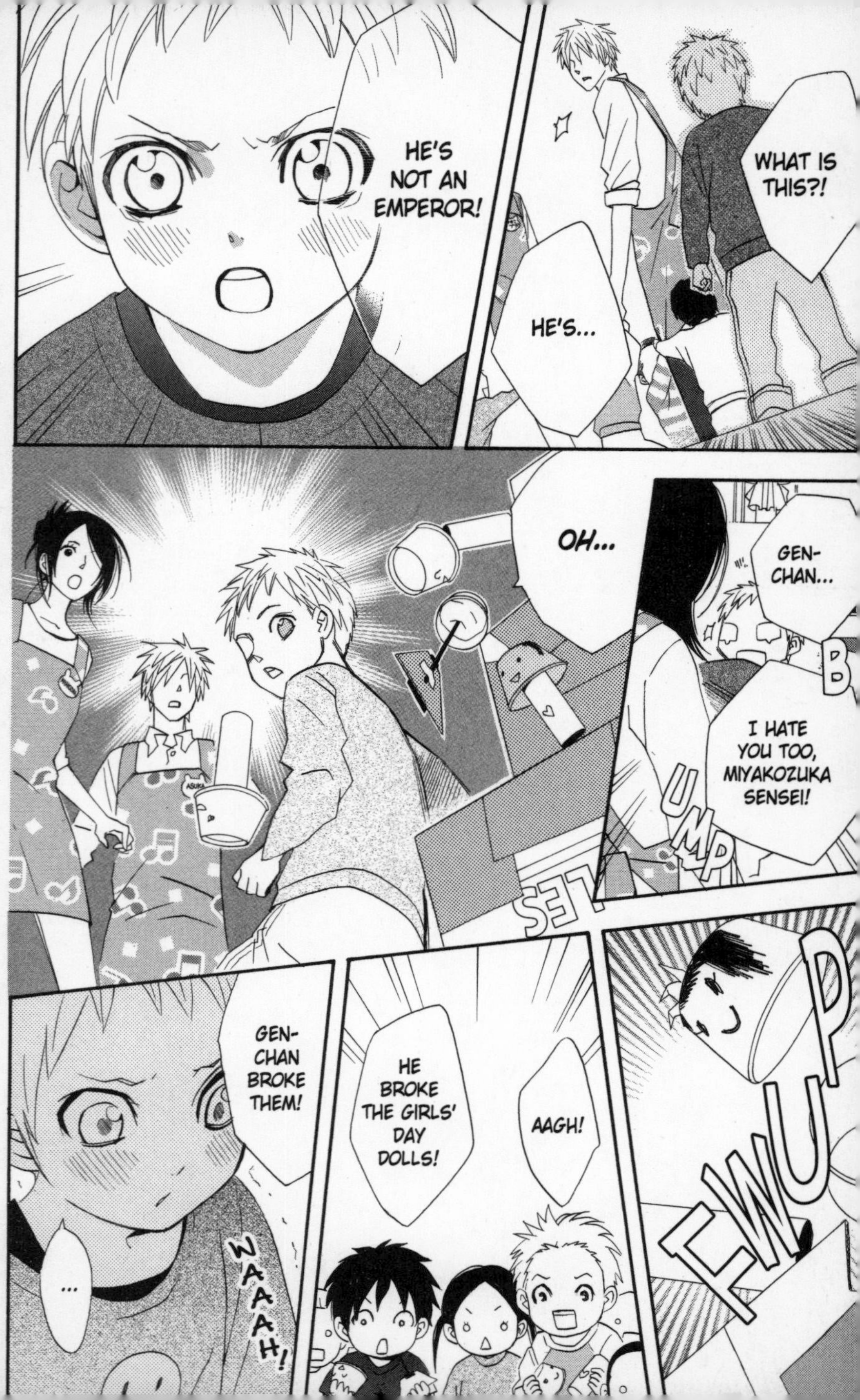
WHAT IS THIS?!
HE'S...
HE'S NOT AN EMPEROR!
GEN-CHAN...
BUMP
I HATE YOU TOO, MIYAKOZUKA SENSEI!
OH...
FWUP
AAGH!
HE BROKE THE GIRLS' DAY DOLLS!
GEN-CHAN BROKE THEM!
WAAAH!
...

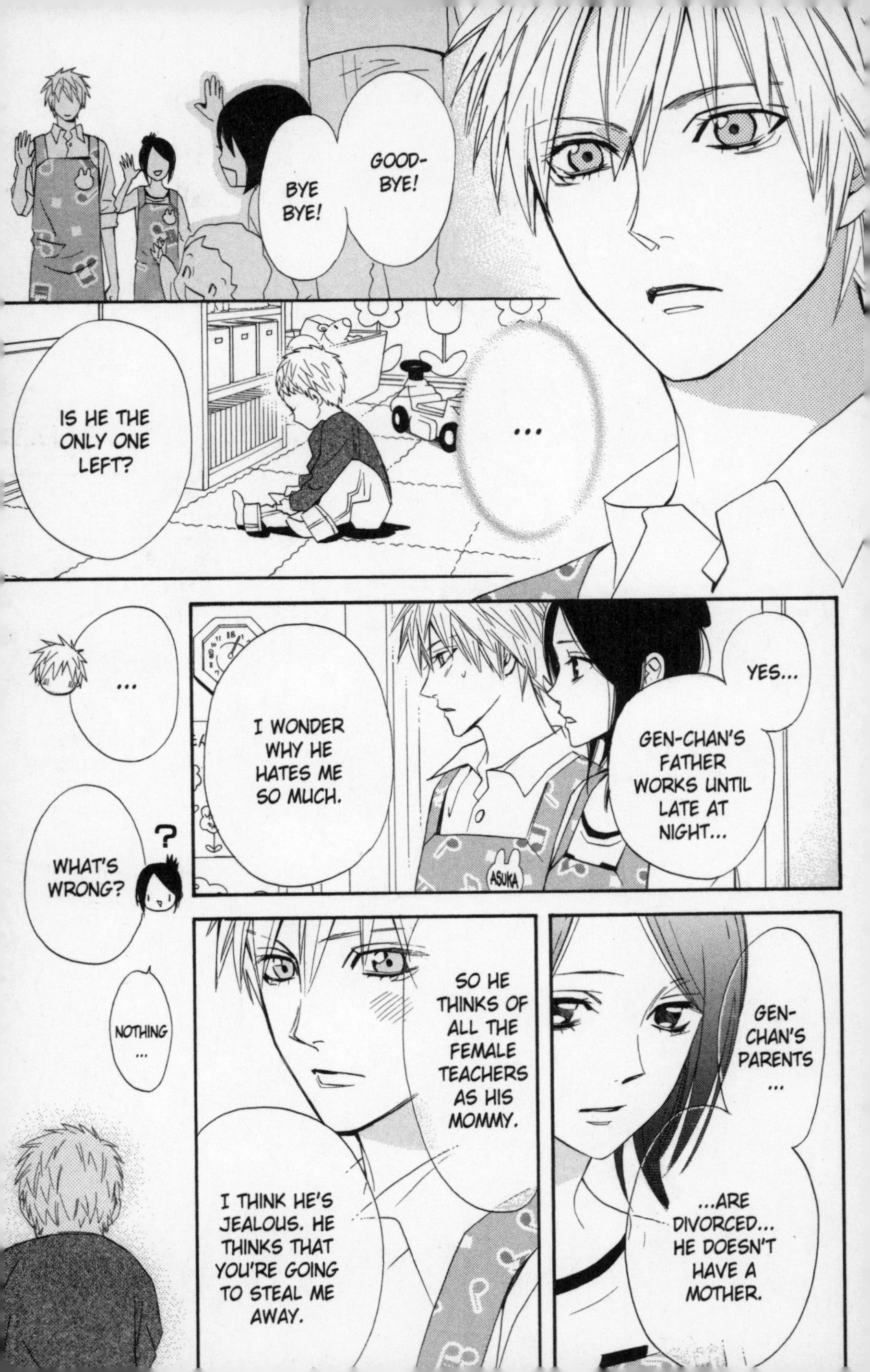
GOOD-BYE!
BYE BYE!
...
IS HE THE ONLY ONE LEFT?
YES...
GEN-CHAN'S FATHER WORKS UNTIL LATE AT NIGHT...
I WONDER WHY HE HATES ME SO MUCH.
...
WHAT'S WRONG?
NOTHING...
GEN-CHAN'S PARENTS...
...ARE DIVORCED... HE DOESN'T HAVE A MOTHER.
SO HE THINKS OF ALL THE FEMALE TEACHERS AS HIS MOMMY.
I THINK HE'S JEALOUS. HE THINKS THAT YOU'RE GOING TO STEAL ME AWAY.
ASUKA

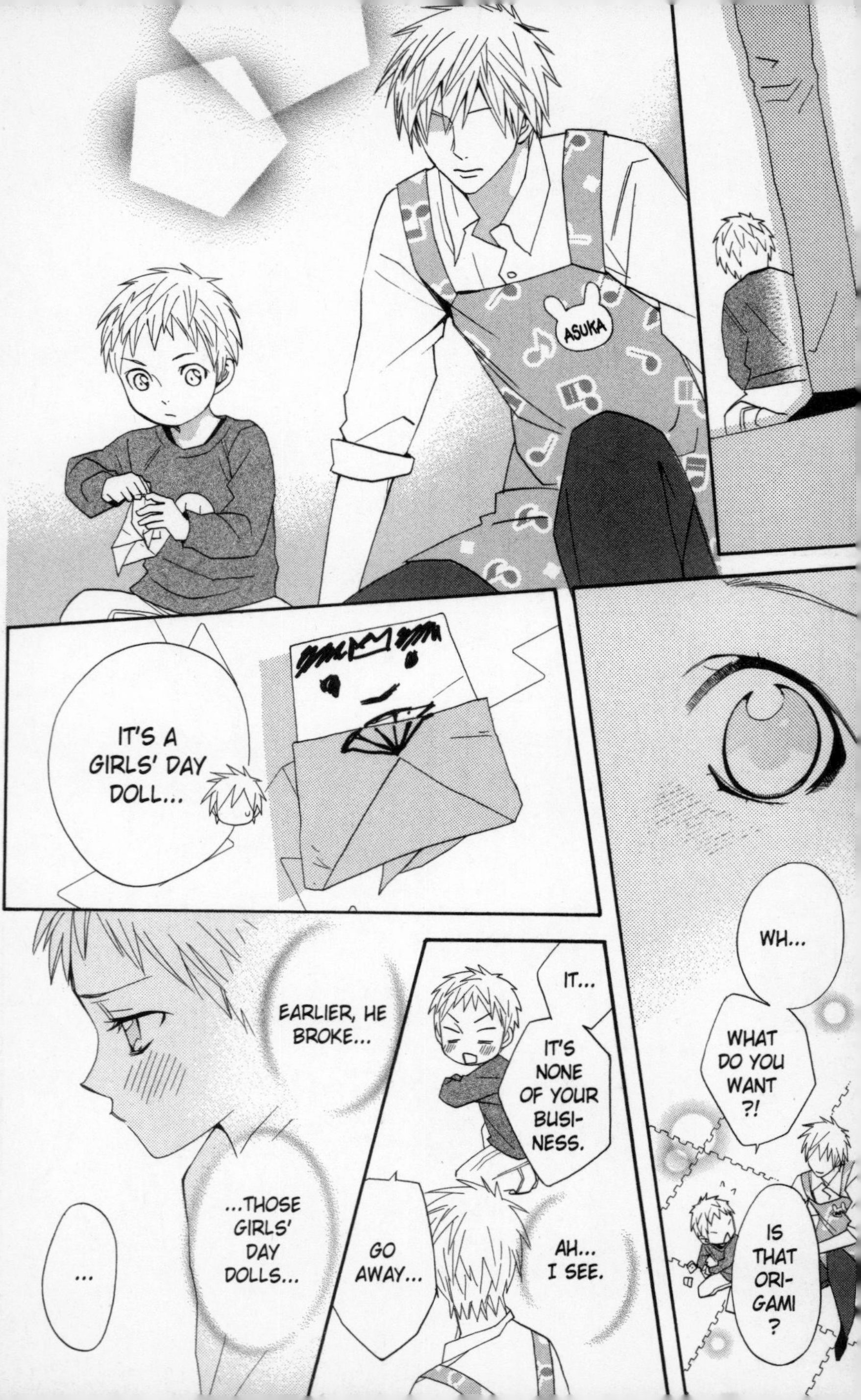
ASUKA
WH...
WHAT DO YOU WANT?!
IS THAT ORIGAMI?
IT'S A GIRLS' DAY DOLL...
IT...
IT'S NONE OF YOUR BUSINESS.
AH... I SEE.
GO AWAY...
EARLIER, HE BROKE...
...THOSE GIRLS' DAY DOLLS...
...

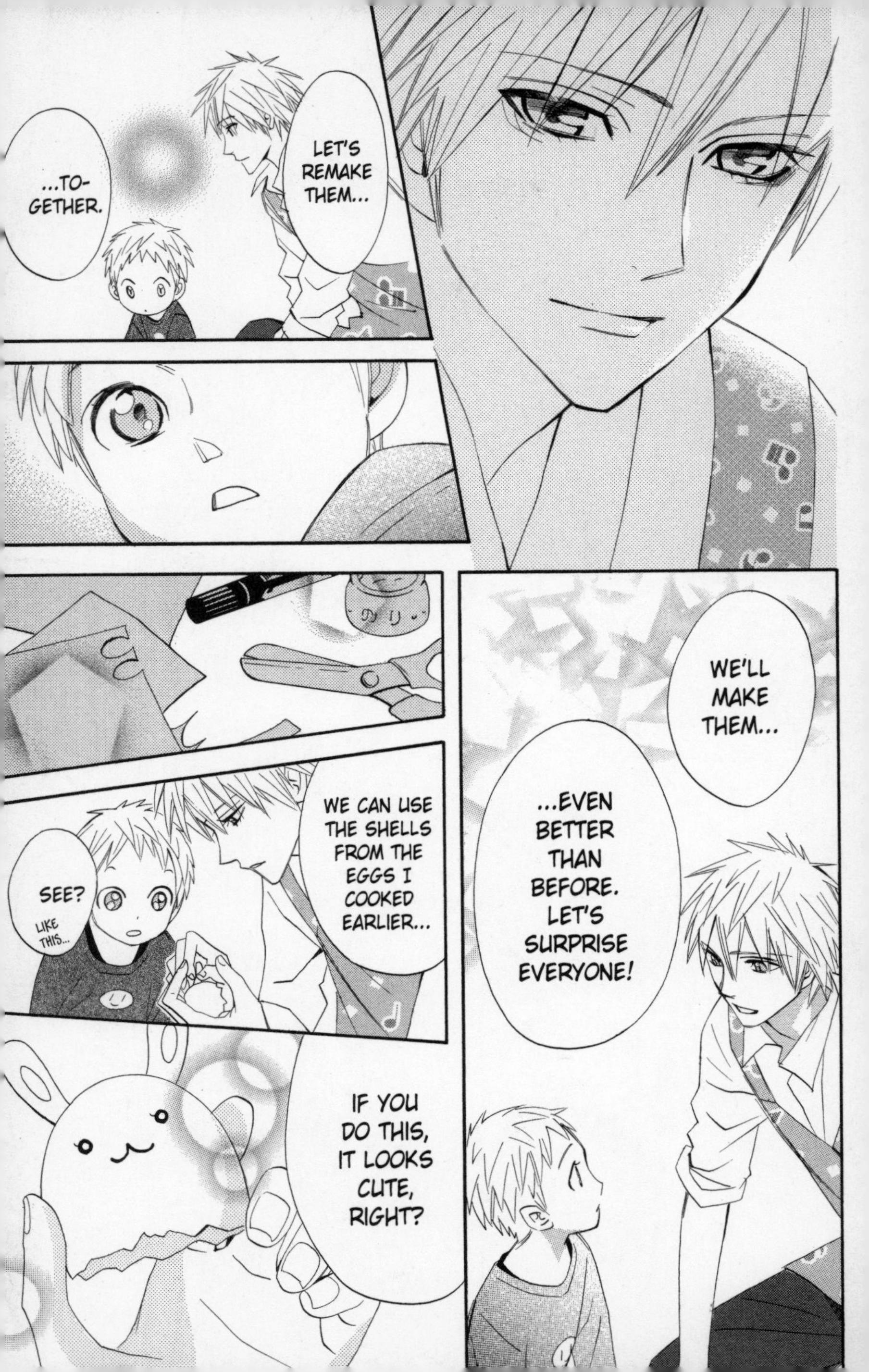
LET'S REMAKE THEM...
...TO-GETHER.
WE'LL MAKE THEM...
...EVEN BETTER THAN BEFORE. LET'S SURPRISE EVERYONE!
WE CAN USE THE SHELLS FROM THE EGGS I COOKED EARLIER...
SEE?
LIKE THIS...
IF YOU DO THIS, IT LOOKS CUTE, RIGHT?

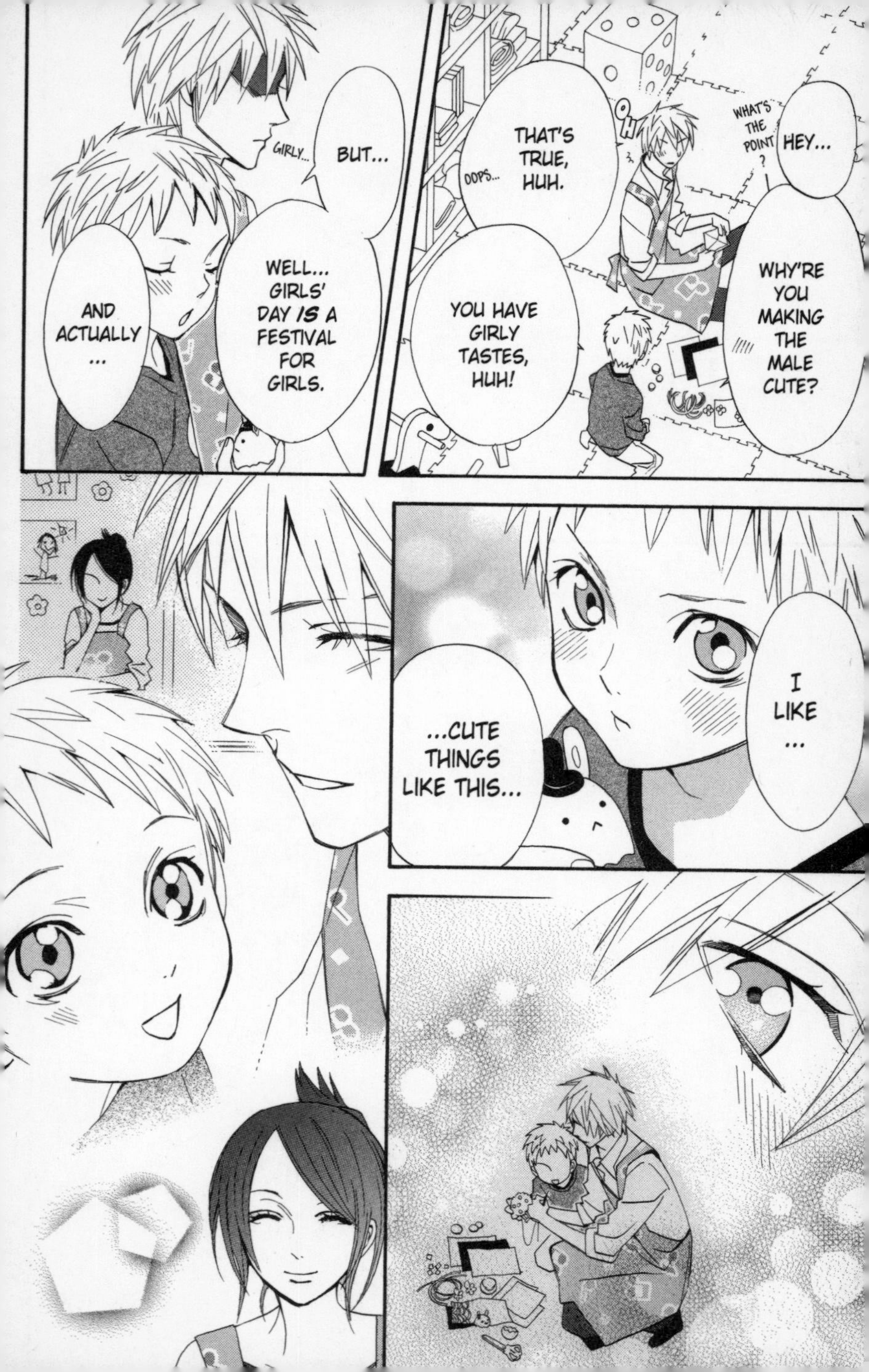
HEY...
WHAT'S THE POINT?
WHY'RE YOU MAKING THE MALE CUTE?
THAT'S TRUE, HUH.
OOPS...
YOU HAVE GIRLY TASTES, HUH!
BUT...
GIRLY...
WELL... GIRLS' DAY *IS* A FESTIVAL FOR GIRLS.
AND ACTUALLY...
I LIKE...
...CUTE THINGS LIKE THIS...

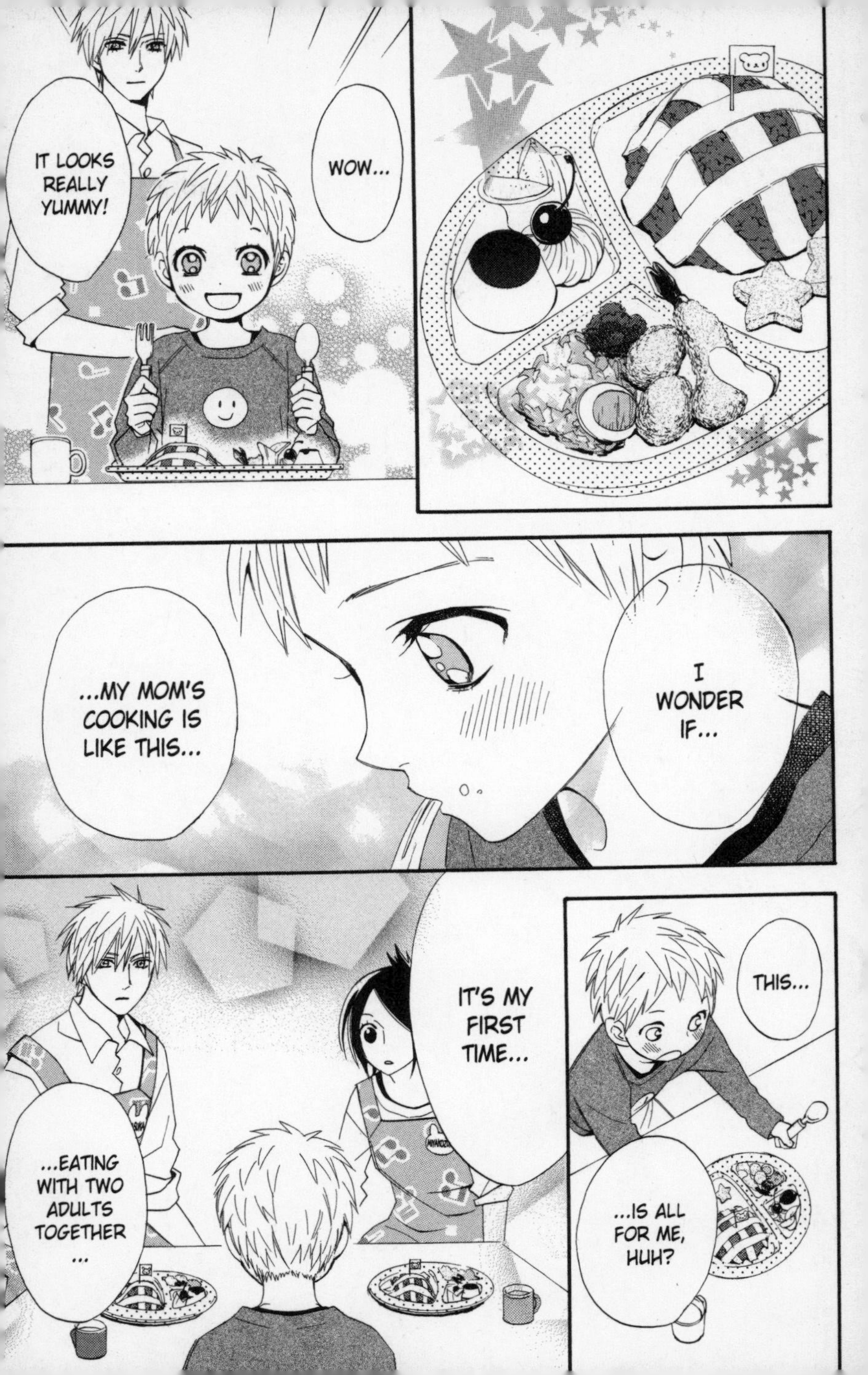
WOW...
IT LOOKS REALLY YUMMY!
I WONDER IF...
...MY MOM'S COOKING IS LIKE THIS...
THIS...
...IS ALL FOR ME, HUH?
IT'S MY FIRST TIME...
...EATING WITH TWO ADULTS TOGETHER ...

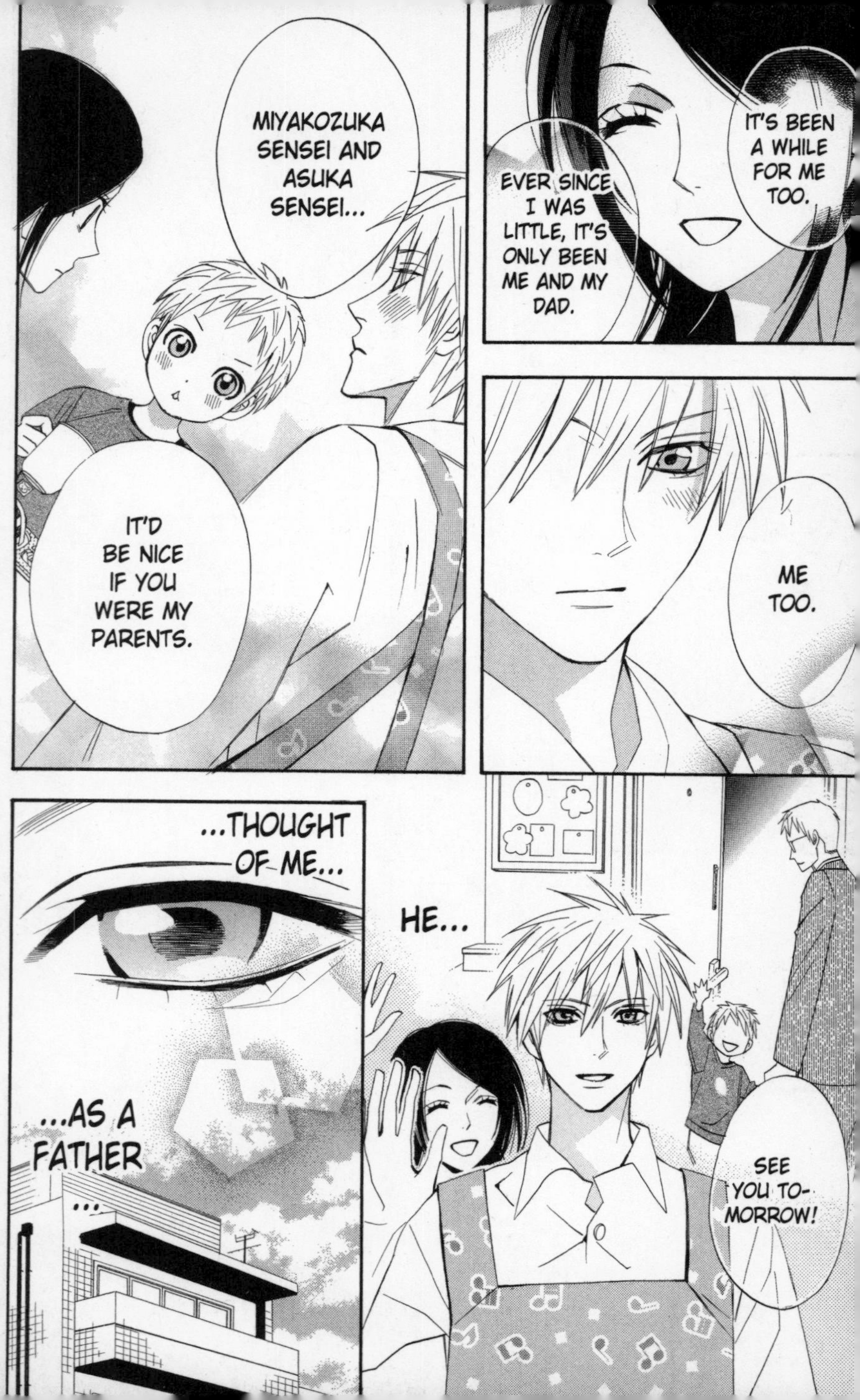
IT'S BEEN A WHILE FOR ME TOO.
EVER SINCE I WAS LITTLE, IT'S ONLY BEEN ME AND MY DAD.
ME TOO.
MIYAKOZUKA SENSEI AND ASUKA SENSEI...
IT'D BE NICE IF YOU WERE MY PARENTS.
SEE YOU TO-MORROW!
HE...
...THOUGHT OF ME...
...AS A FATHER
...

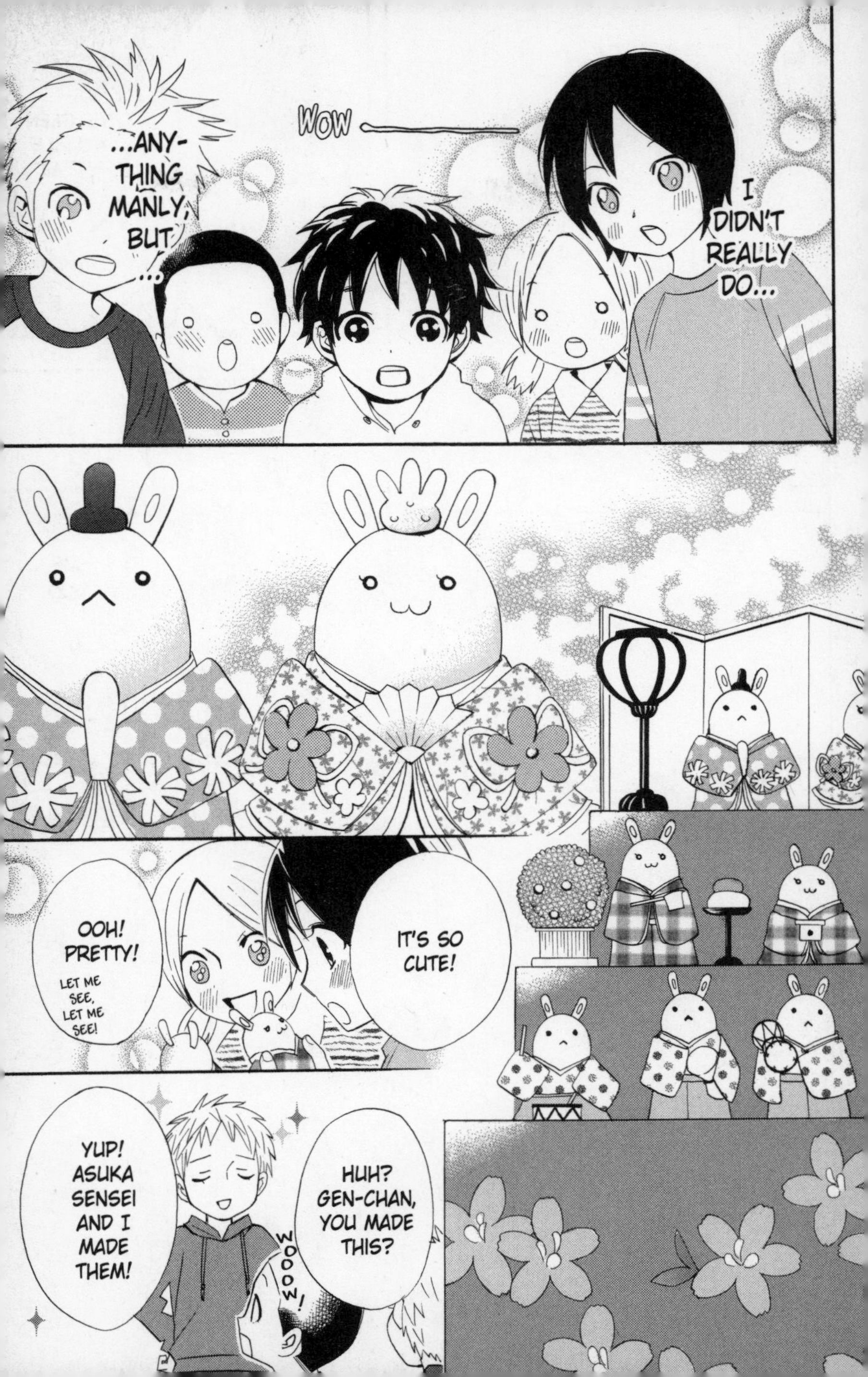
I DIDN'T REALLY DO...
WOW
...ANYTHING MANLY, BUT...
IT'S SO CUTE!
OOH! PRETTY!
LET ME SEE, LET ME SEE!
HUH? GEN-CHAN, YOU MADE THIS?
WOOOOW!
YUP! ASUKA SENSEI AND I MADE THEM!

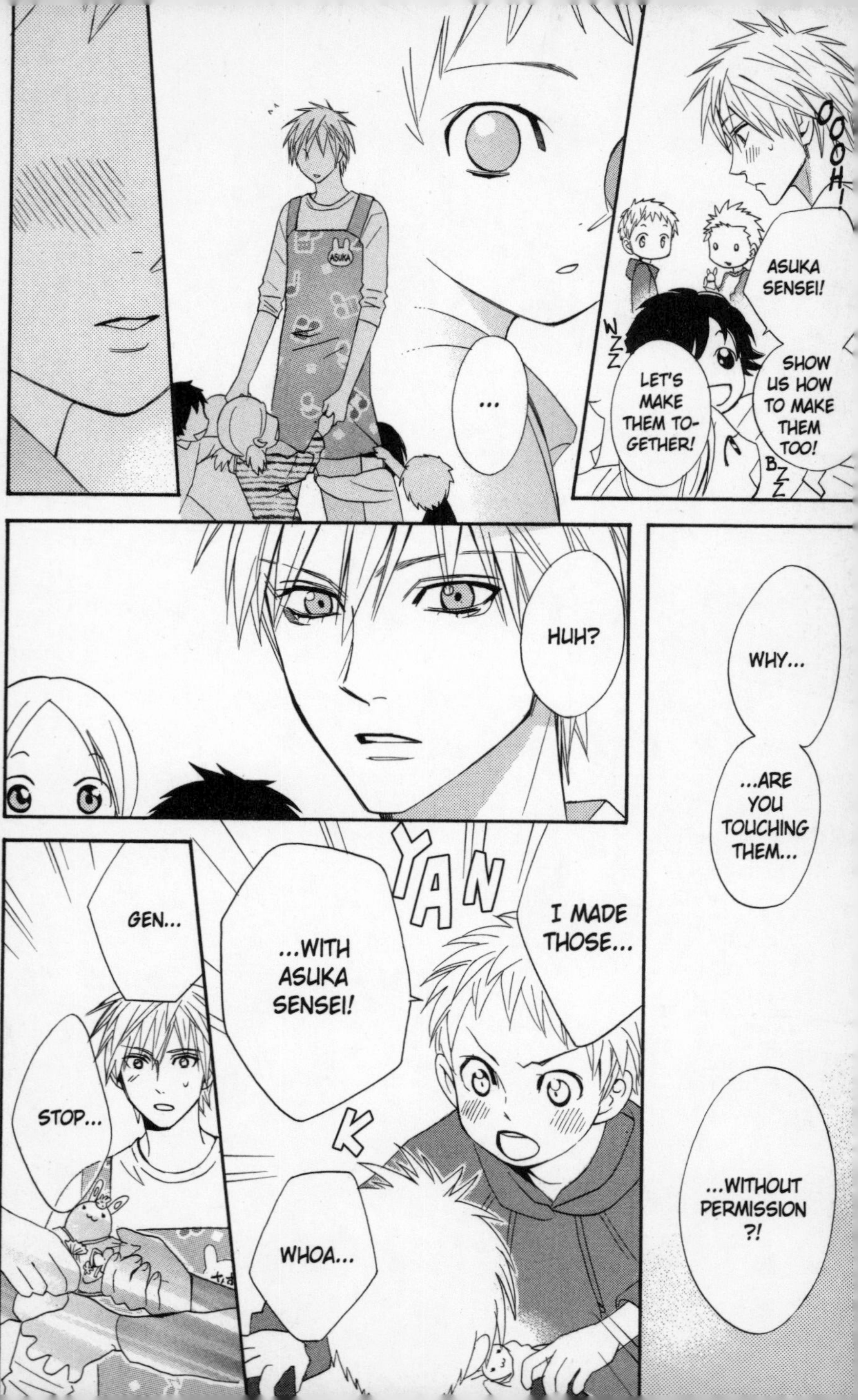
OOOH!
ASUKA SENSEI!
SHOW US HOW TO MAKE THEM TOO!
BZZ
LET'S MAKE THEM TO-GETHER!
WZZ
...
WHY...
...ARE YOU TOUCHING THEM...
...WITHOUT PERMISSION ?!
HUH?
I MADE THOSE...
YAN
...WITH ASUKA SENSEI!
K
GEN...
WHOA...
STOP...

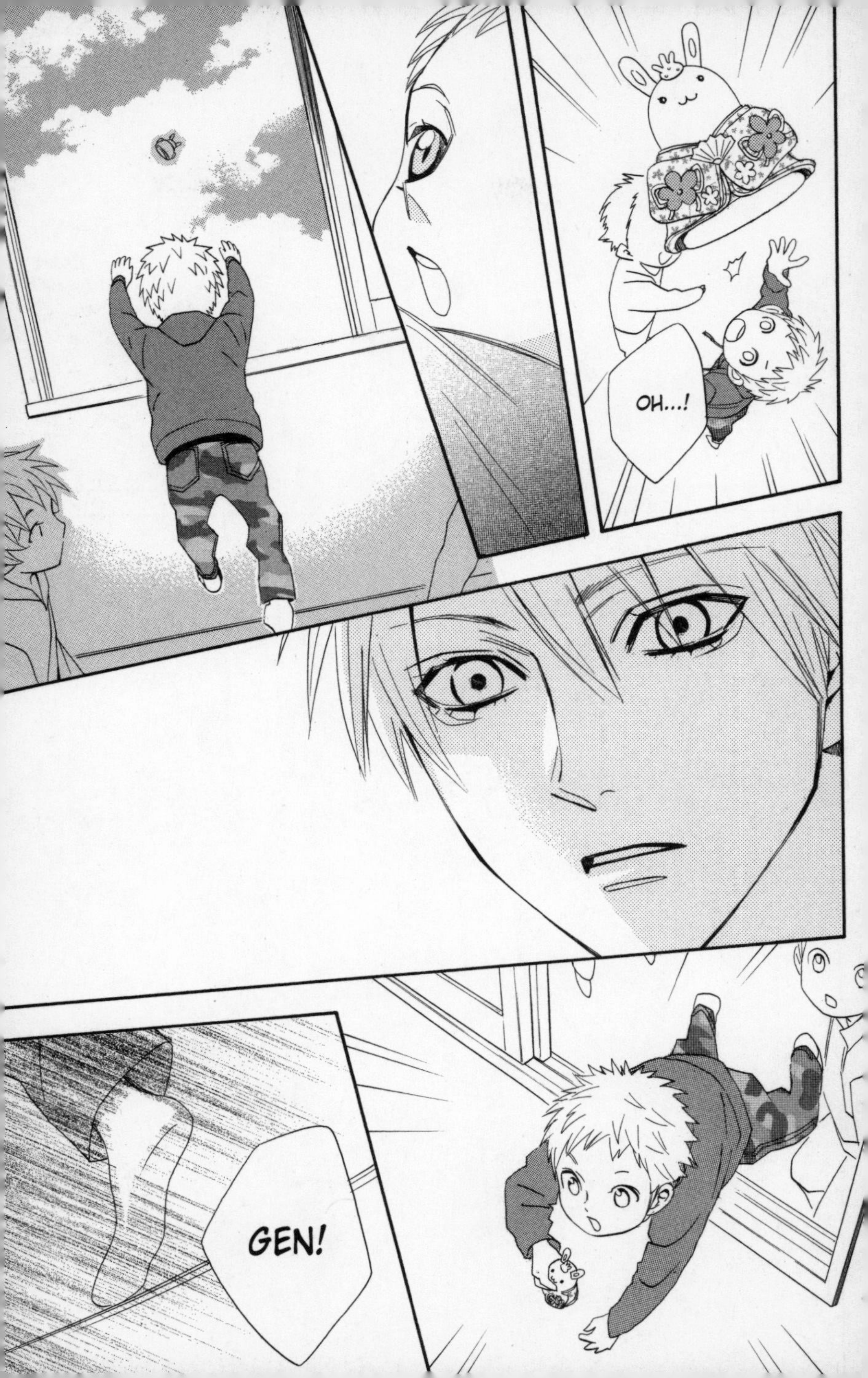
OH...!
GEN!

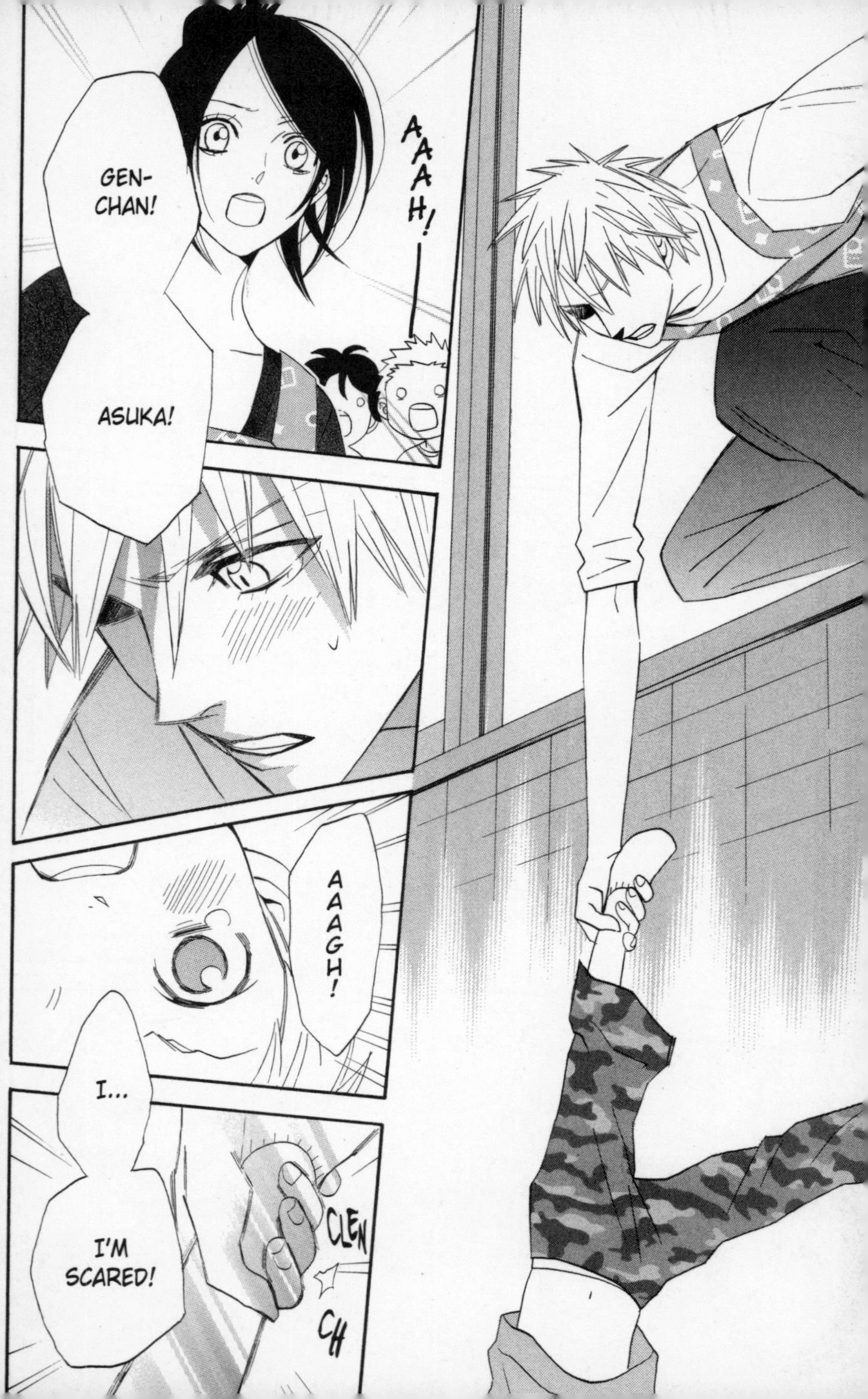
AAAAH!
GEN-CHAN!
ASUKA!
AAAGH!
I...
I'M SCARED!
CLENCH

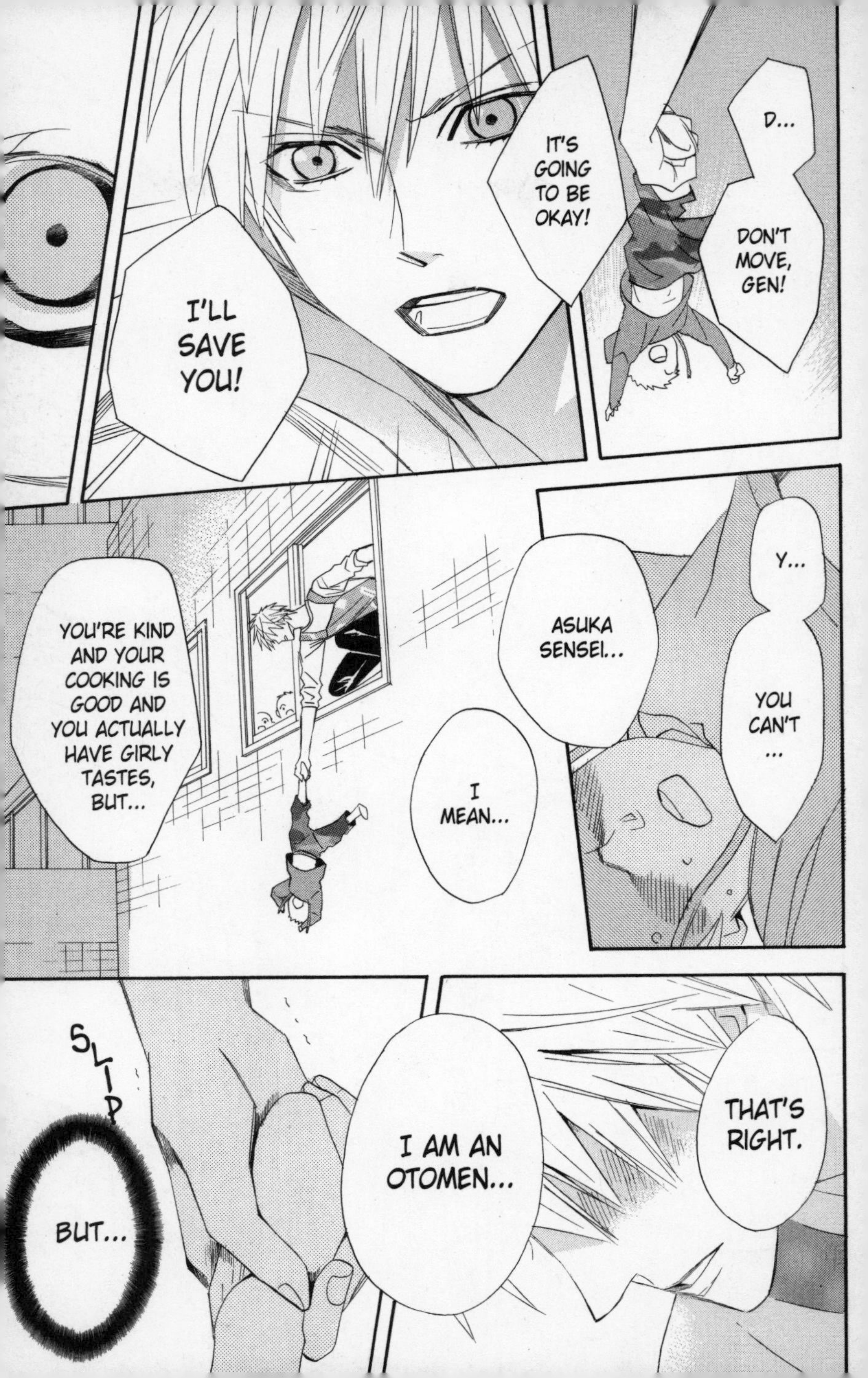
D...
DON'T MOVE, GEN!
IT'S GOING TO BE OKAY!
I'LL SAVE YOU!
Y...
YOU CAN'T ...
ASUKA SENSEI...
I MEAN...
YOU'RE KIND AND YOUR COOKING IS GOOD AND YOU ACTUALLY HAVE GIRLY TASTES, BUT...
THAT'S RIGHT.
I AM AN OTOMEN...
SLIP
BUT...

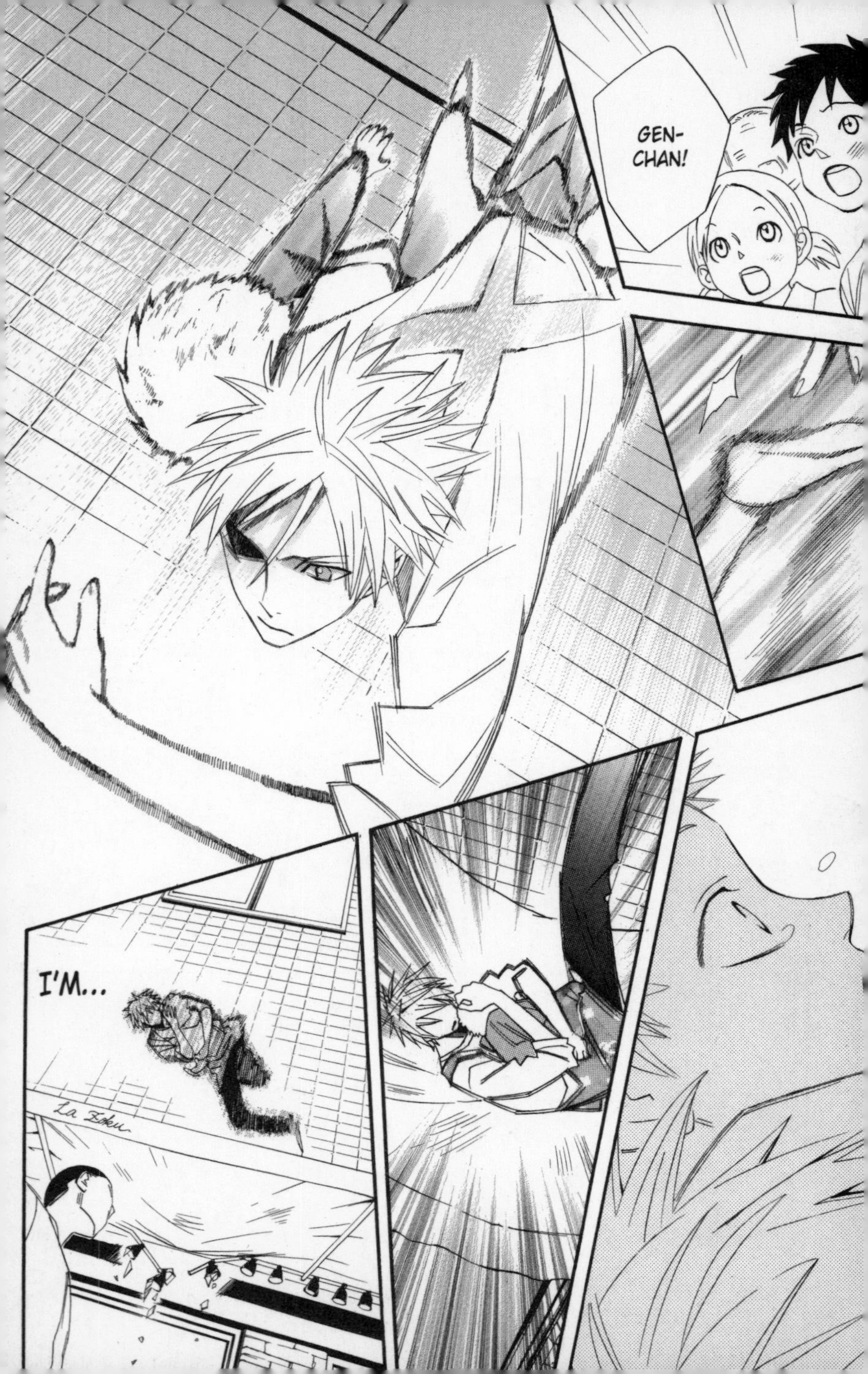
GEN-CHAN!
I'M...

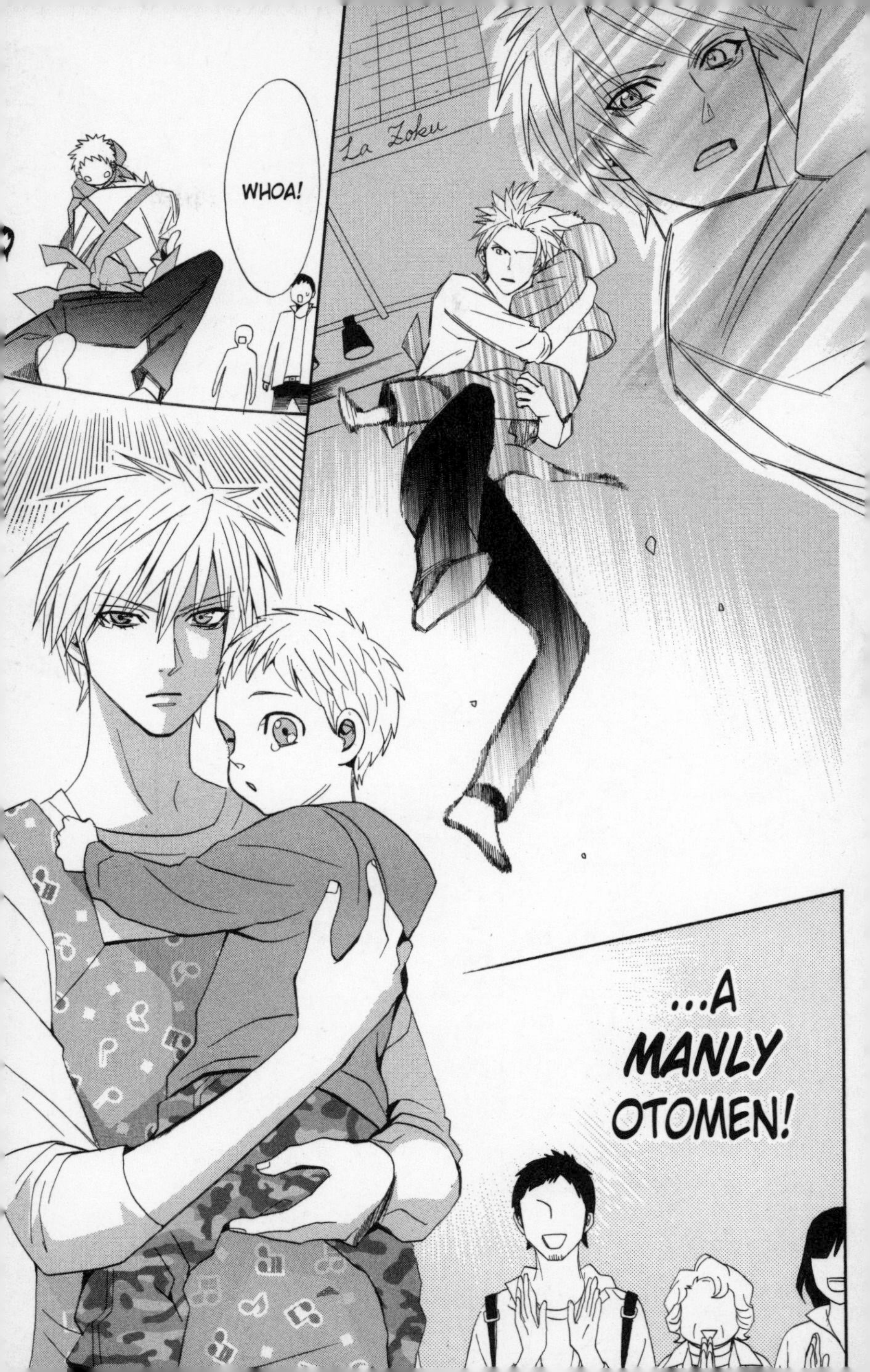
La Zoku
WHOA!
...A MANLY OTOMEN!

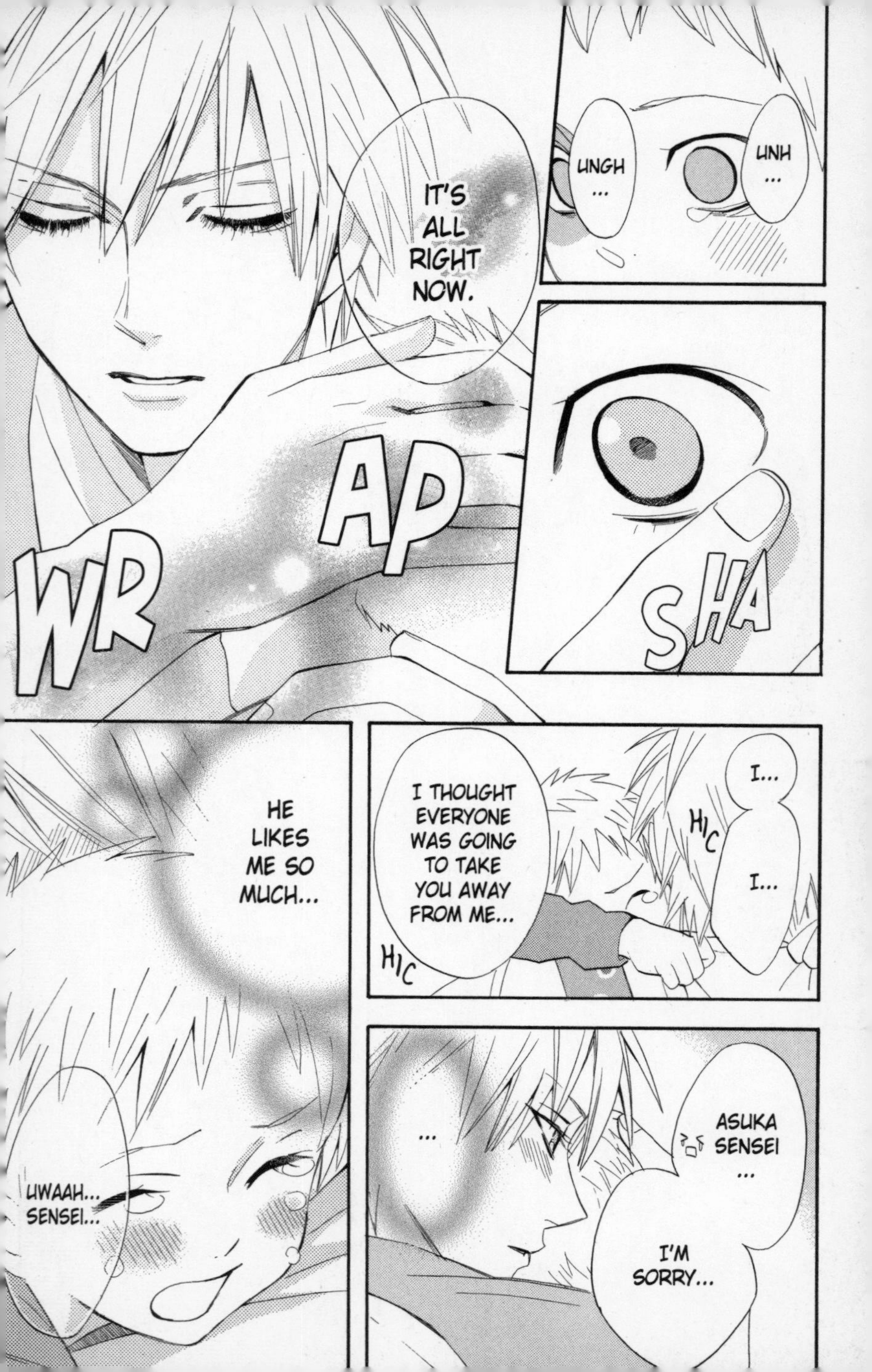
UNH...
UNGH...
SHA
IT'S ALL RIGHT NOW.
WRAP
I...
HIC
I...
I THOUGHT EVERYONE WAS GOING TO TAKE YOU AWAY FROM ME...
HIC
ASUKA SENSEI ...
I'M SORRY...
...
HE LIKES ME SO MUCH...
UWAAH... SENSEI...

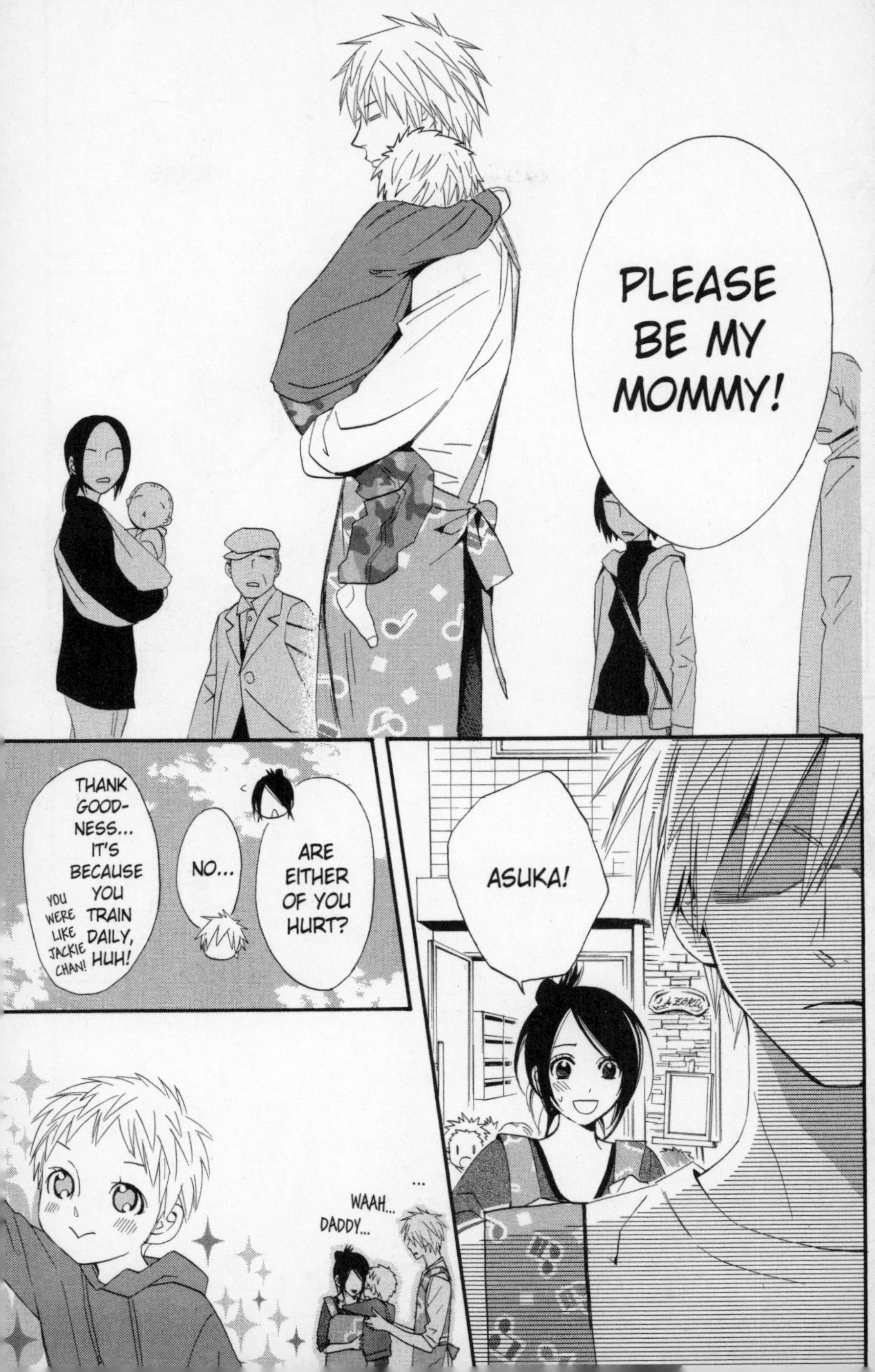
PLEASE BE MY MOMMY!
ASUKA!
ARE EITHER OF YOU HURT?
NO...
THANK GOODNESS... IT'S BECAUSE YOU TRAIN DAILY, HUH!
YOU WERE LIKE JACKIE CHAN!
...
WAAH... DADDY...

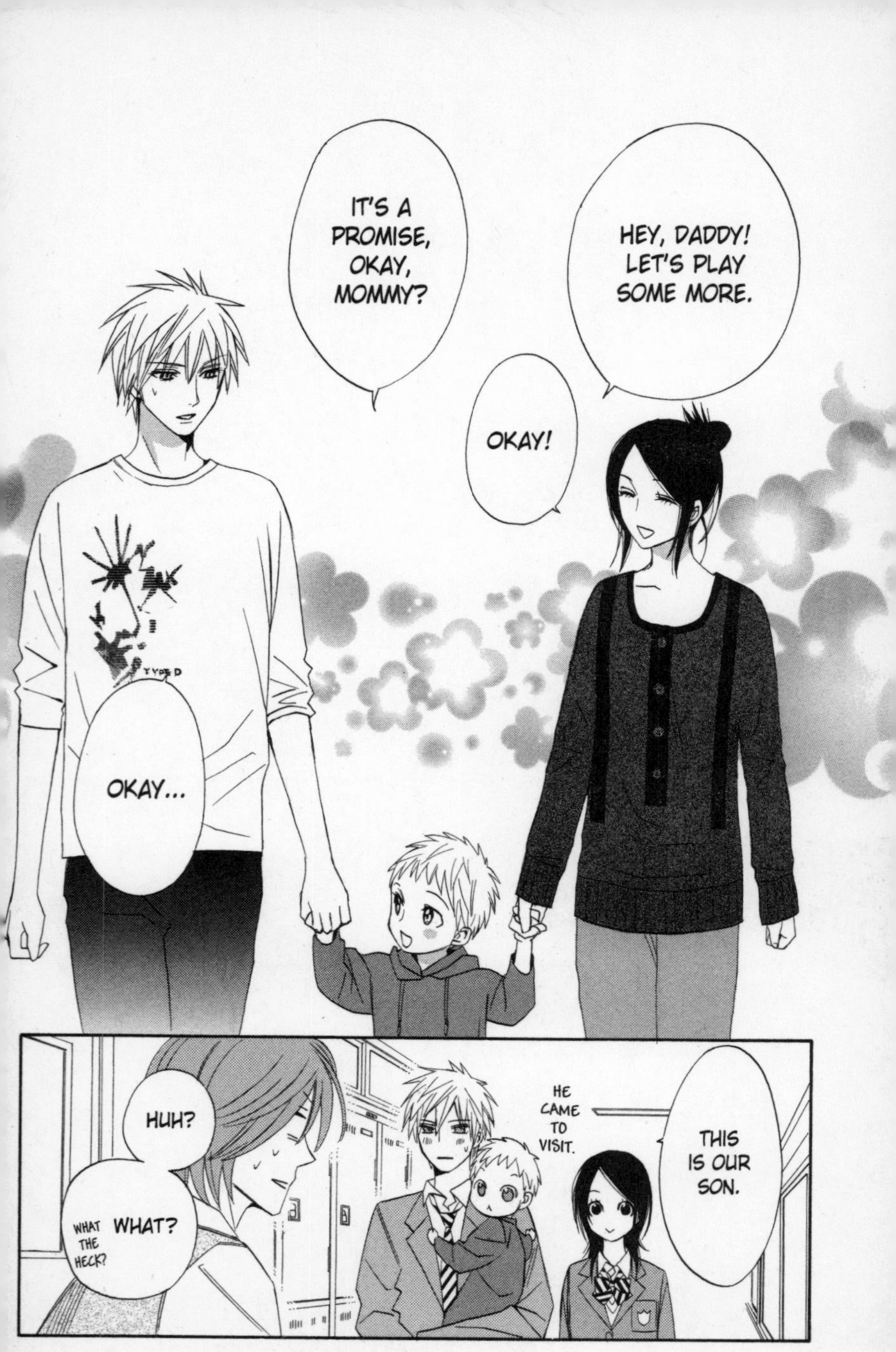
HEY, DADDY! LET'S PLAY SOME MORE.
IT'S A PROMISE, OKAY, MOMMY?
OKAY!
OKAY...
THIS IS OUR SON.
HE CAME TO VISIT.
HUH?
WHAT?
WHAT THE HECK?

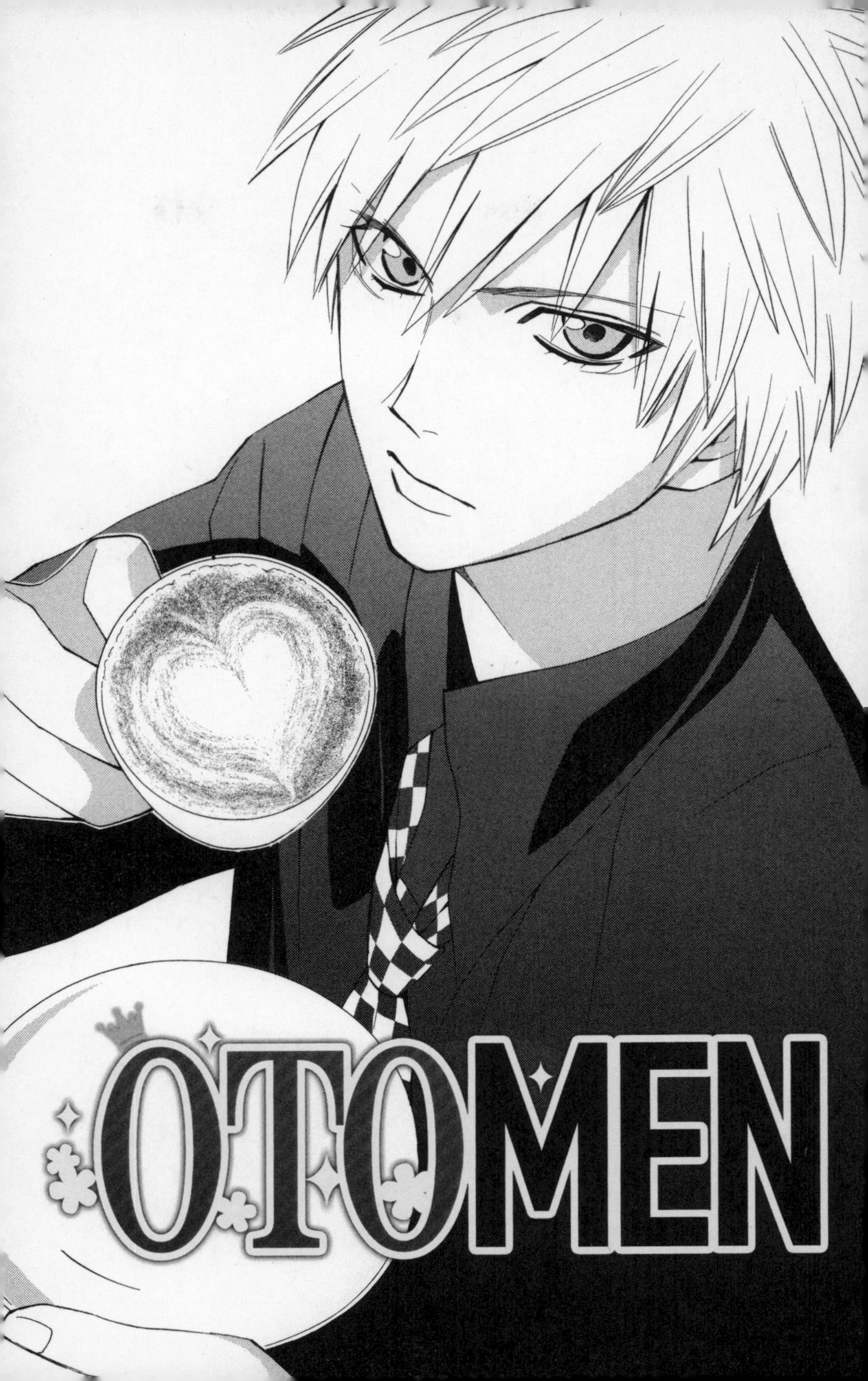
OTOMEN

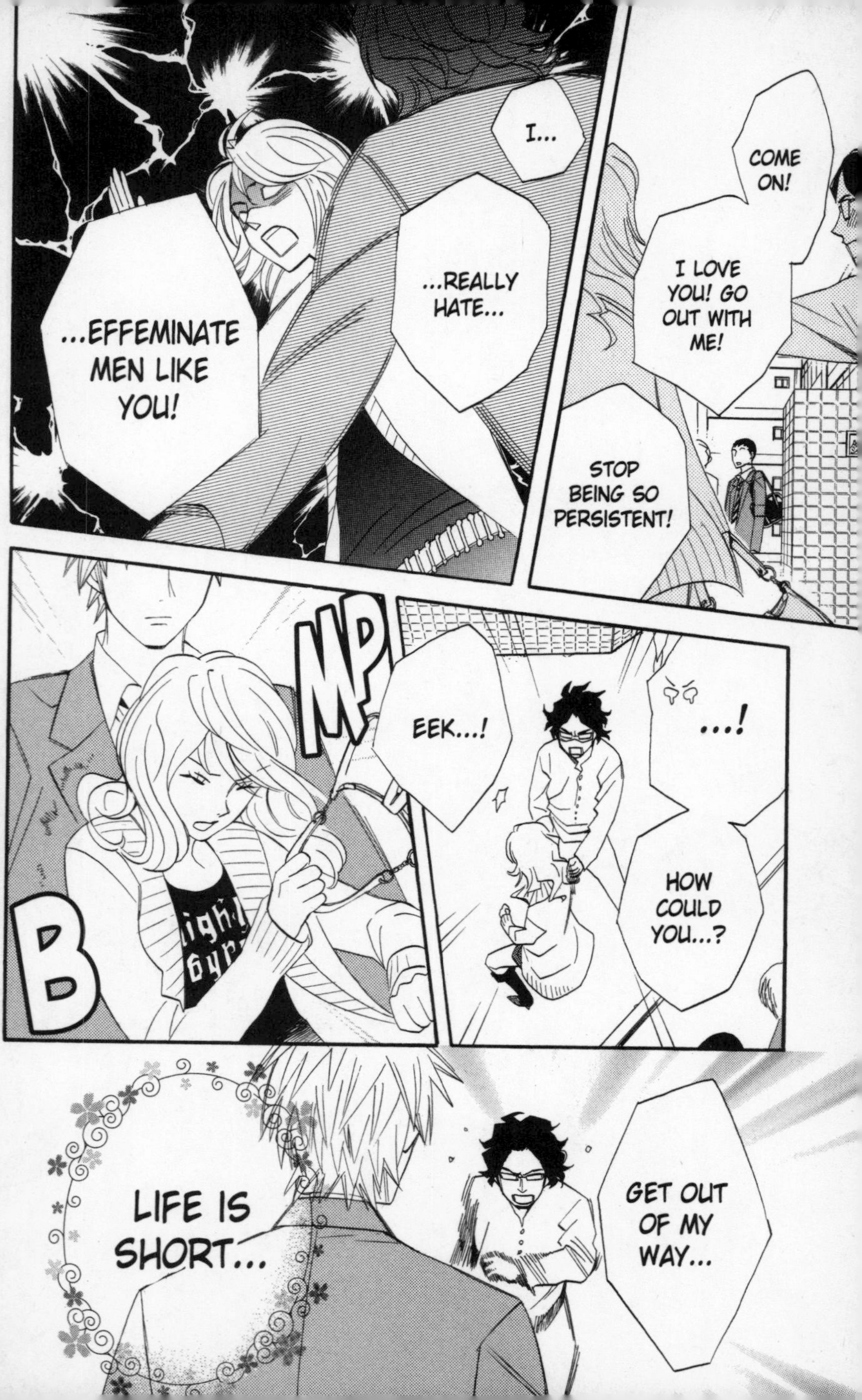
COME ON!
I LOVE YOU! GO OUT WITH ME!
STOP BEING SO PERSISTENT!
I...
...REALLY HATE...
...EFFEMINATE MEN LIKE YOU!
...!
HOW COULD YOU...?
EEK...!
MP
B
GET OUT OF MY WAY...
LIFE IS SHORT...

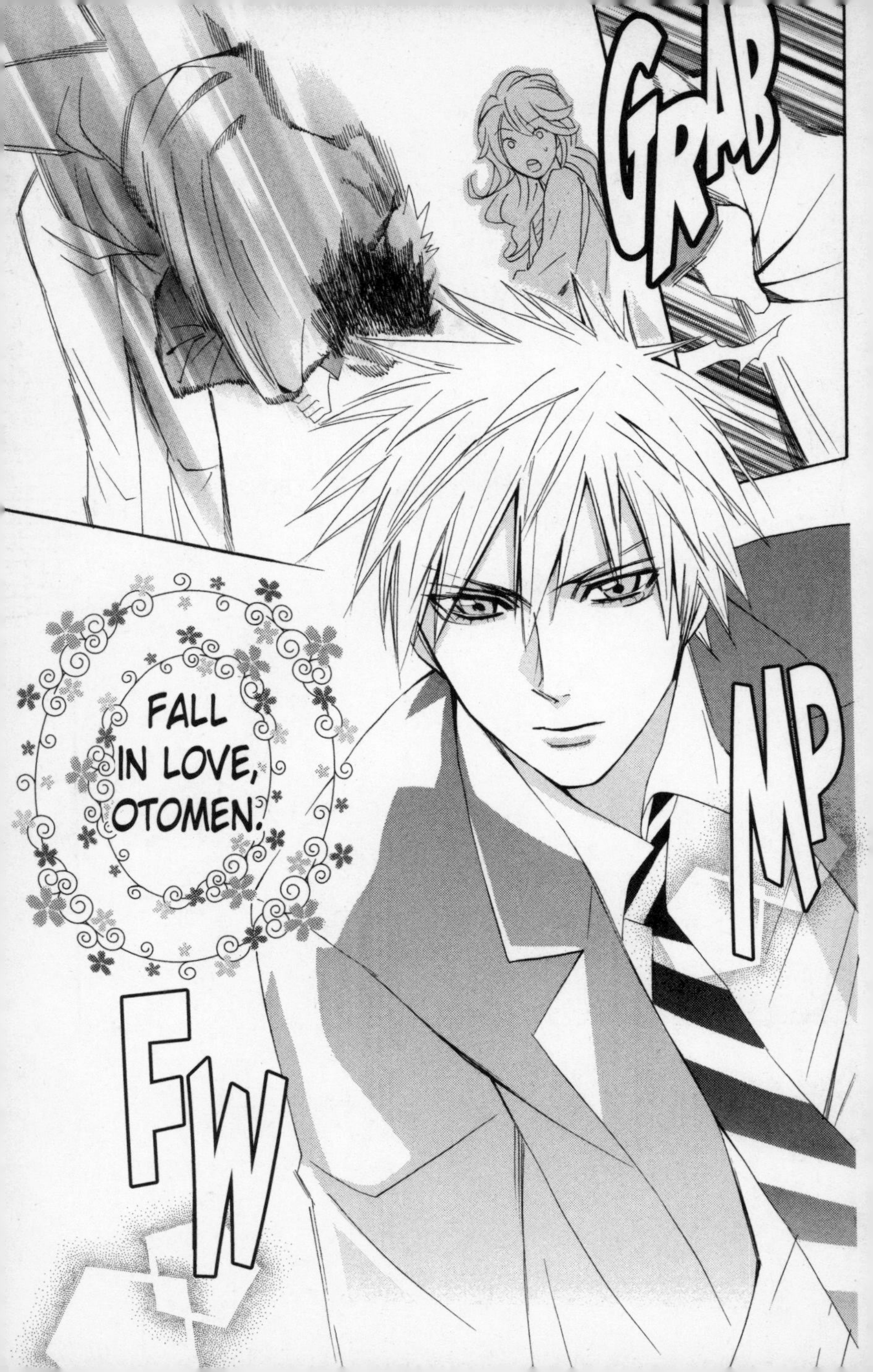
GRAB
MP
FALL IN LOVE, OTOMEN.
FW

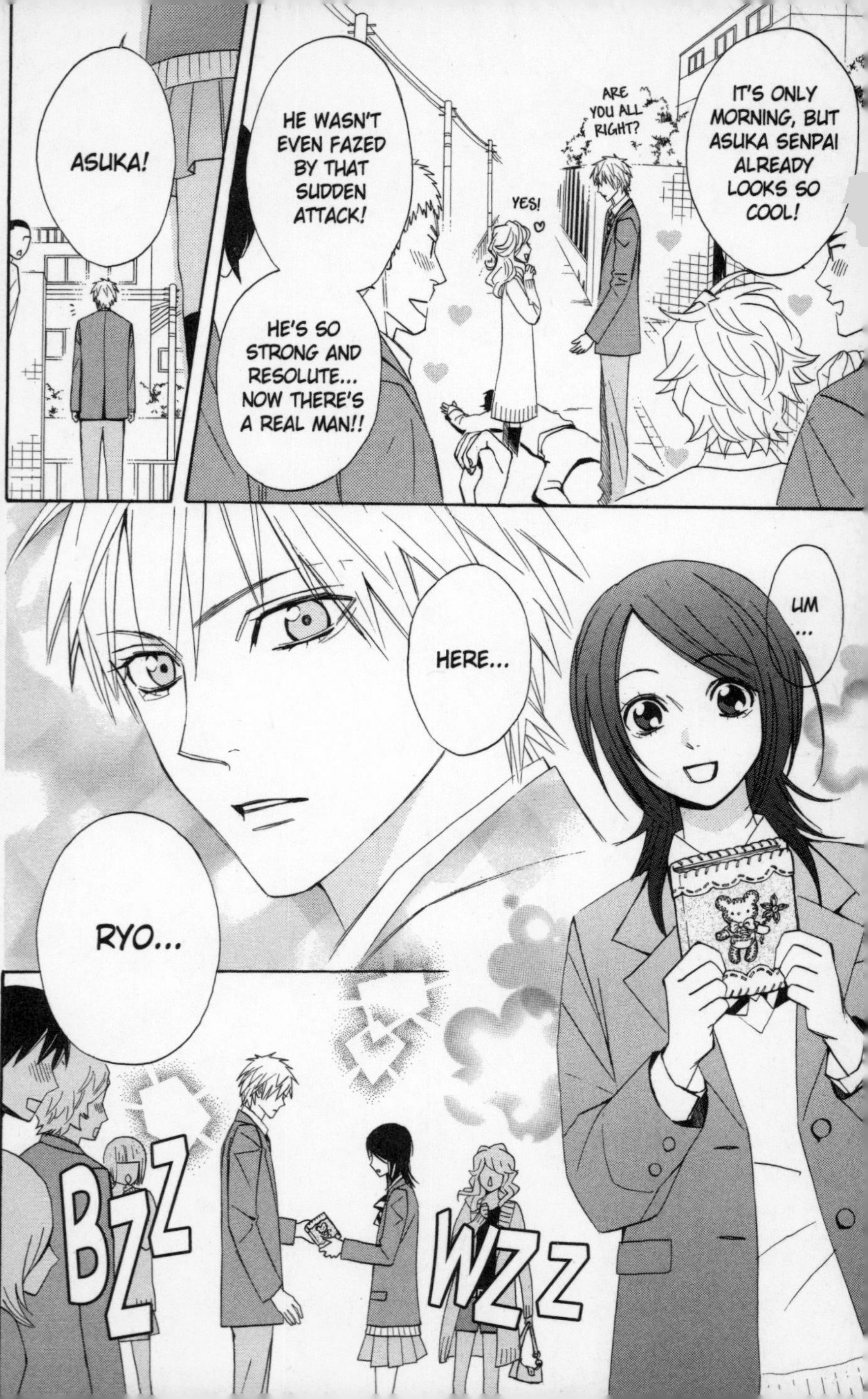
IT'S ONLY MORNING, BUT ASUKA SENPAI ALREADY LOOKS SO COOL!
ARE YOU ALL RIGHT?
YES!
HE WASN'T EVEN FAZED BY THAT SUDDEN ATTACK!
HE'S SO STRONG AND RESOLUTE... NOW THERE'S A REAL MAN!!
ASUKA!
UM ...
HERE...
RYO...
WZZ
BZZ

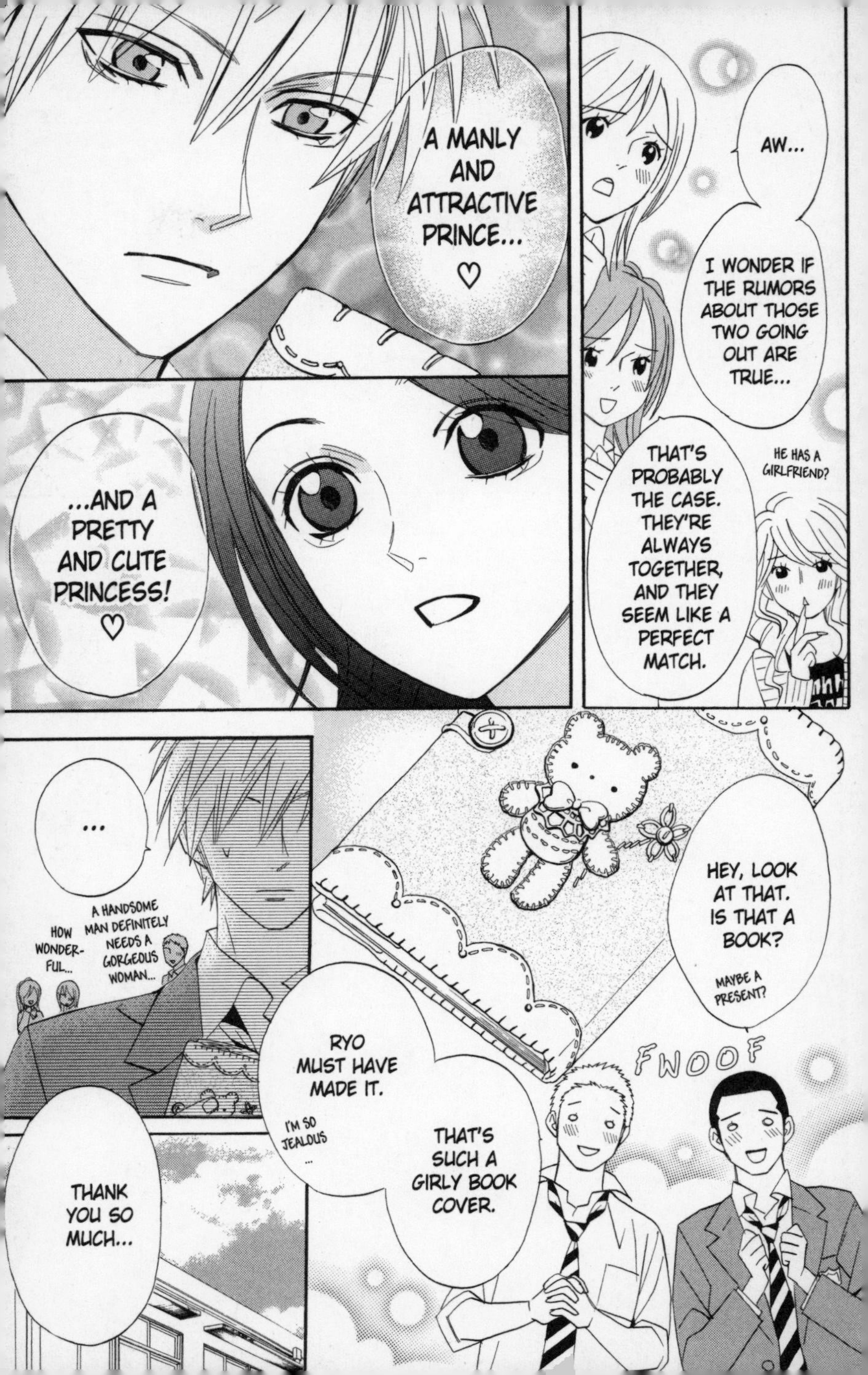
AW...
I WONDER IF THE RUMORS ABOUT THOSE TWO GOING OUT ARE TRUE...
HE HAS A GIRLFRIEND?
THAT'S PROBABLY THE CASE. THEY'RE ALWAYS TOGETHER, AND THEY SEEM LIKE A PERFECT MATCH.
A MANLY AND ATTRACTIVE PRINCE... ♡
...AND A PRETTY AND CUTE PRINCESS! ♡
HEY, LOOK AT THAT. IS THAT A BOOK?
MAYBE A PRESENT?
FWOOF
RYO MUST HAVE MADE IT.
I'M SO JEALOUS...
THAT'S SUCH A GIRLY BOOK COVER.
...
A HANDSOME MAN DEFINITELY NEEDS A GORGEOUS WOMAN...
HOW WONDERFUL...
THANK YOU SO MUCH...

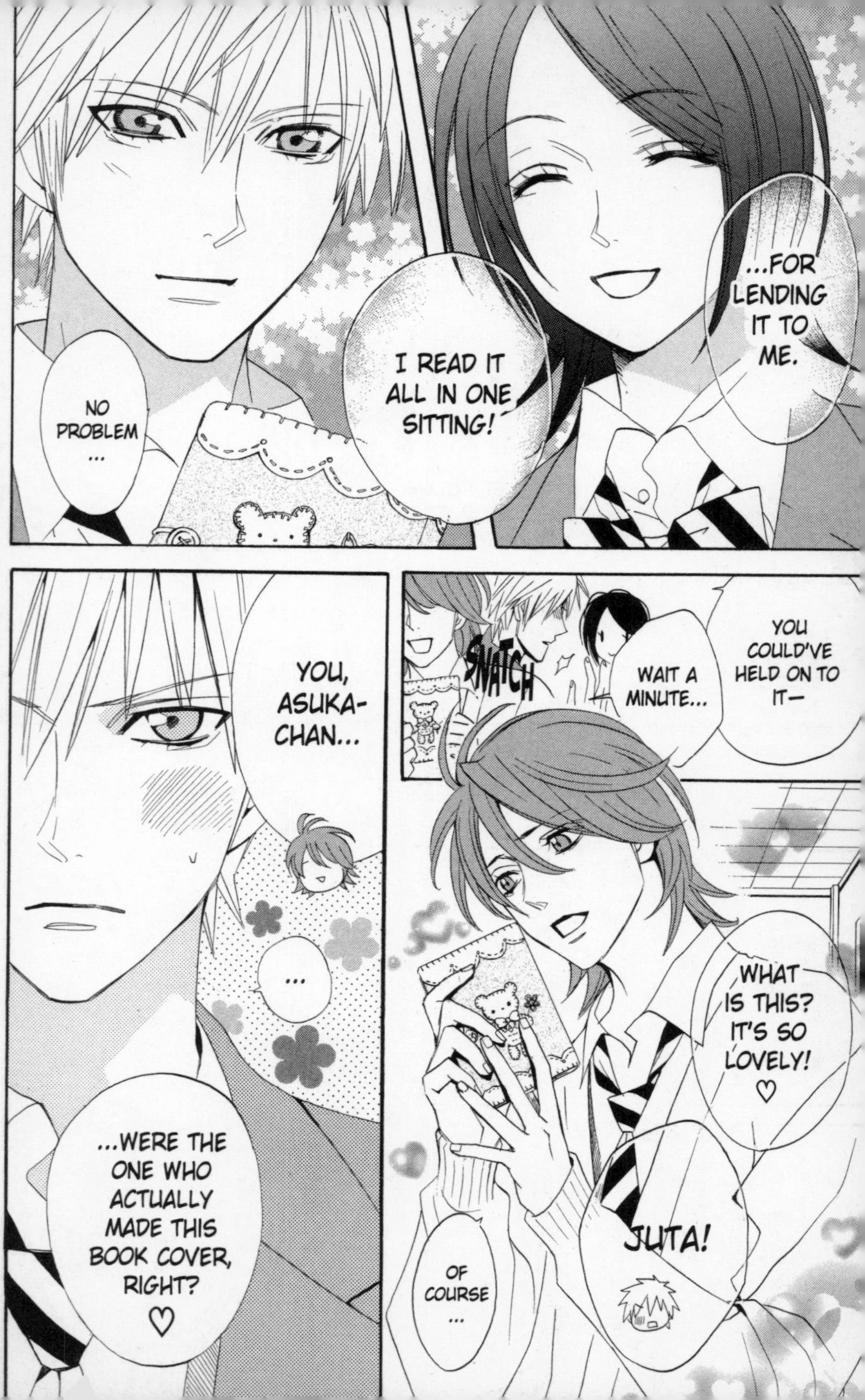
...FOR LENDING IT TO ME.
I READ IT ALL IN ONE SITTING!
NO PROBLEM...
YOU COULD'VE HELD ON TO IT—
WAIT A MINUTE...
SNATCH
WHAT IS THIS? IT'S SO LOVELY! ♡
JUTA!
OF COURSE...
YOU, ASUKA-CHAN...
...
...WERE THE ONE WHO ACTUALLY MADE THIS BOOK COVER, RIGHT? ♡

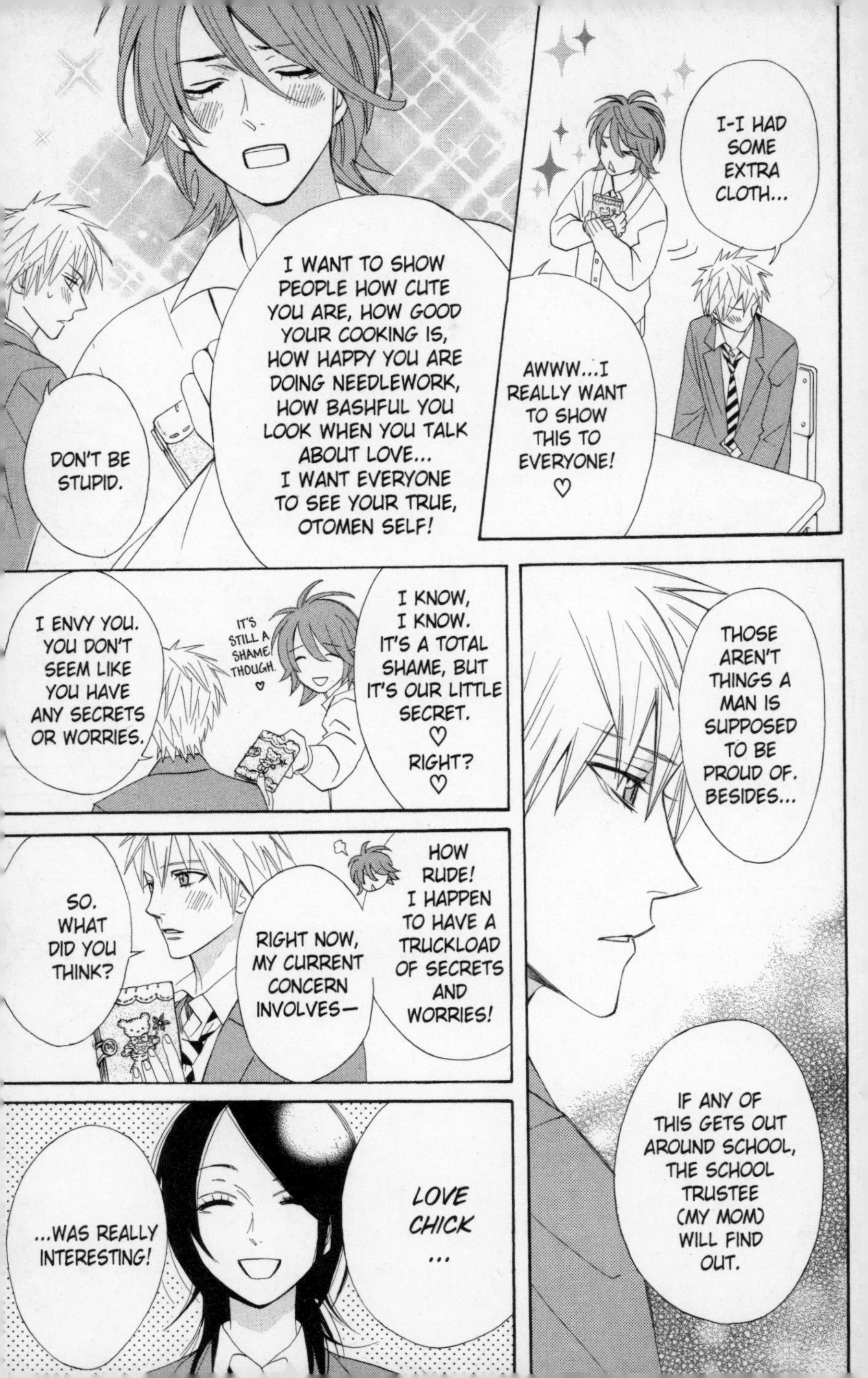
I-I HAD SOME EXTRA CLOTH...
AWWW...I REALLY WANT TO SHOW THIS TO EVERYONE! ♡
I WANT TO SHOW PEOPLE HOW CUTE YOU ARE, HOW GOOD YOUR COOKING IS, HOW HAPPY YOU ARE DOING NEEDLEWORK, HOW BASHFUL YOU LOOK WHEN YOU TALK ABOUT LOVE... I WANT EVERYONE TO SEE YOUR TRUE, OTOMEN SELF!
DON'T BE STUPID.
THOSE AREN'T THINGS A MAN IS SUPPOSED TO BE PROUD OF. BESIDES...
IF ANY OF THIS GETS OUT AROUND SCHOOL, THE SCHOOL TRUSTEE (MY MOM) WILL FIND OUT.
I KNOW, I KNOW. IT'S A TOTAL SHAME, BUT IT'S OUR LITTLE SECRET. ♡ RIGHT? ♡
IT'S STILL A SHAME THOUGH. ♡
I ENVY YOU. YOU DON'T SEEM LIKE YOU HAVE ANY SECRETS OR WORRIES.
HOW RUDE! I HAPPEN TO HAVE A TRUCKLOAD OF SECRETS AND WORRIES!
RIGHT NOW, MY CURRENT CONCERN INVOLVES—
SO. WHAT DID YOU THINK?
LOVE CHICK ...
...WAS REALLY INTERESTING!

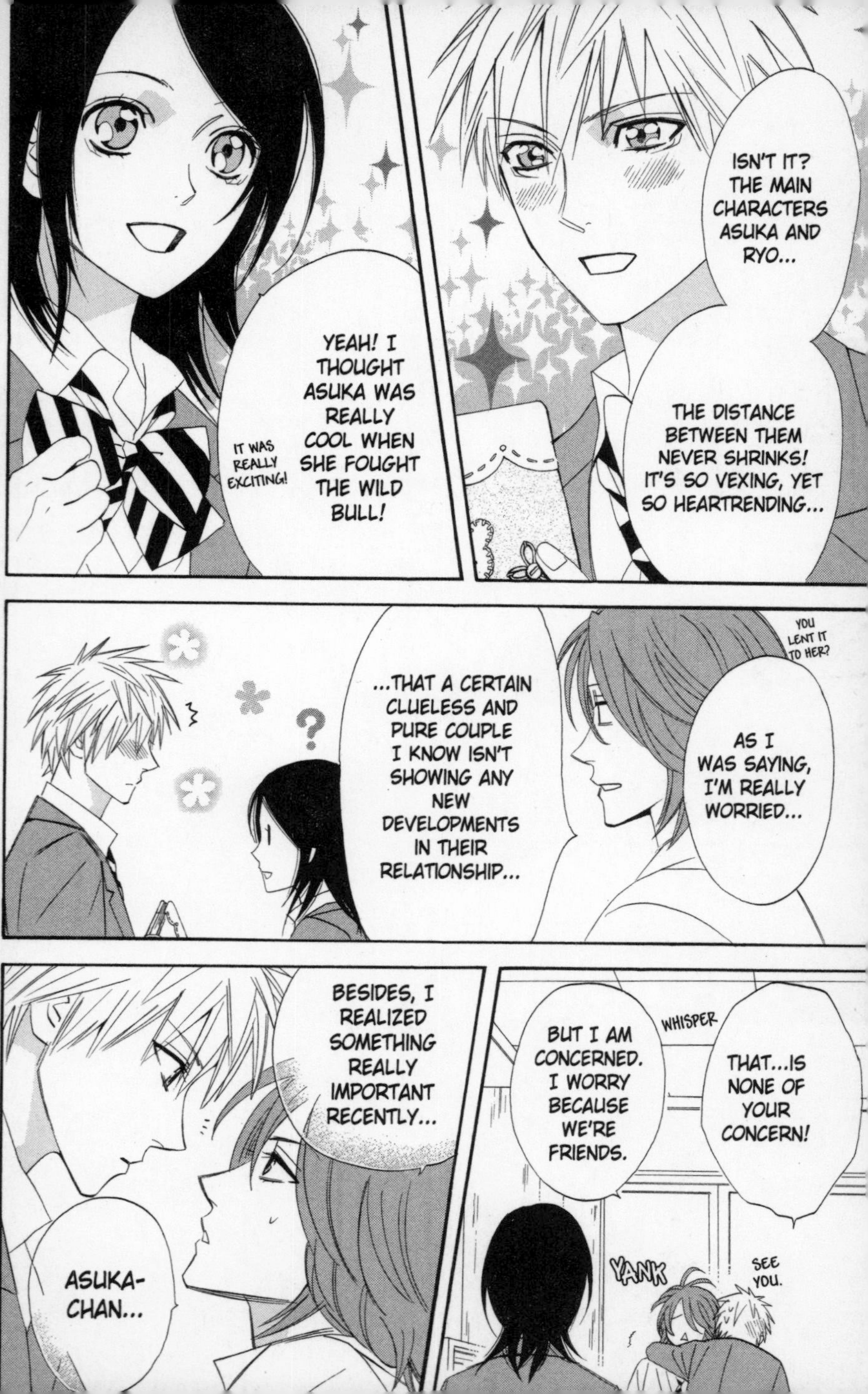

ISN'T IT? THE MAIN CHARACTERS ASUKA AND RYO...
THE DISTANCE BETWEEN THEM NEVER SHRINKS! IT'S SO VEXING, YET SO HEARTRENDING...
YEAH! I THOUGHT ASUKA WAS REALLY COOL WHEN SHE FOUGHT THE WILD BULL!
IT WAS REALLY EXCITING!
YOU LENT IT TO HER?
AS I WAS SAYING, I'M REALLY WORRIED...
...THAT A CERTAIN CLUELESS AND PURE COUPLE I KNOW ISN'T SHOWING ANY NEW DEVELOPMENTS IN THEIR RELATIONSHIP...
THAT...IS NONE OF YOUR CONCERN!
WHISPER
BUT I AM CONCERNED. I WORRY BECAUSE WE'RE FRIENDS.
SEE YOU.
YANK
BESIDES, I REALIZED SOMETHING REALLY IMPORTANT RECENTLY...
ASUKA-CHAN...

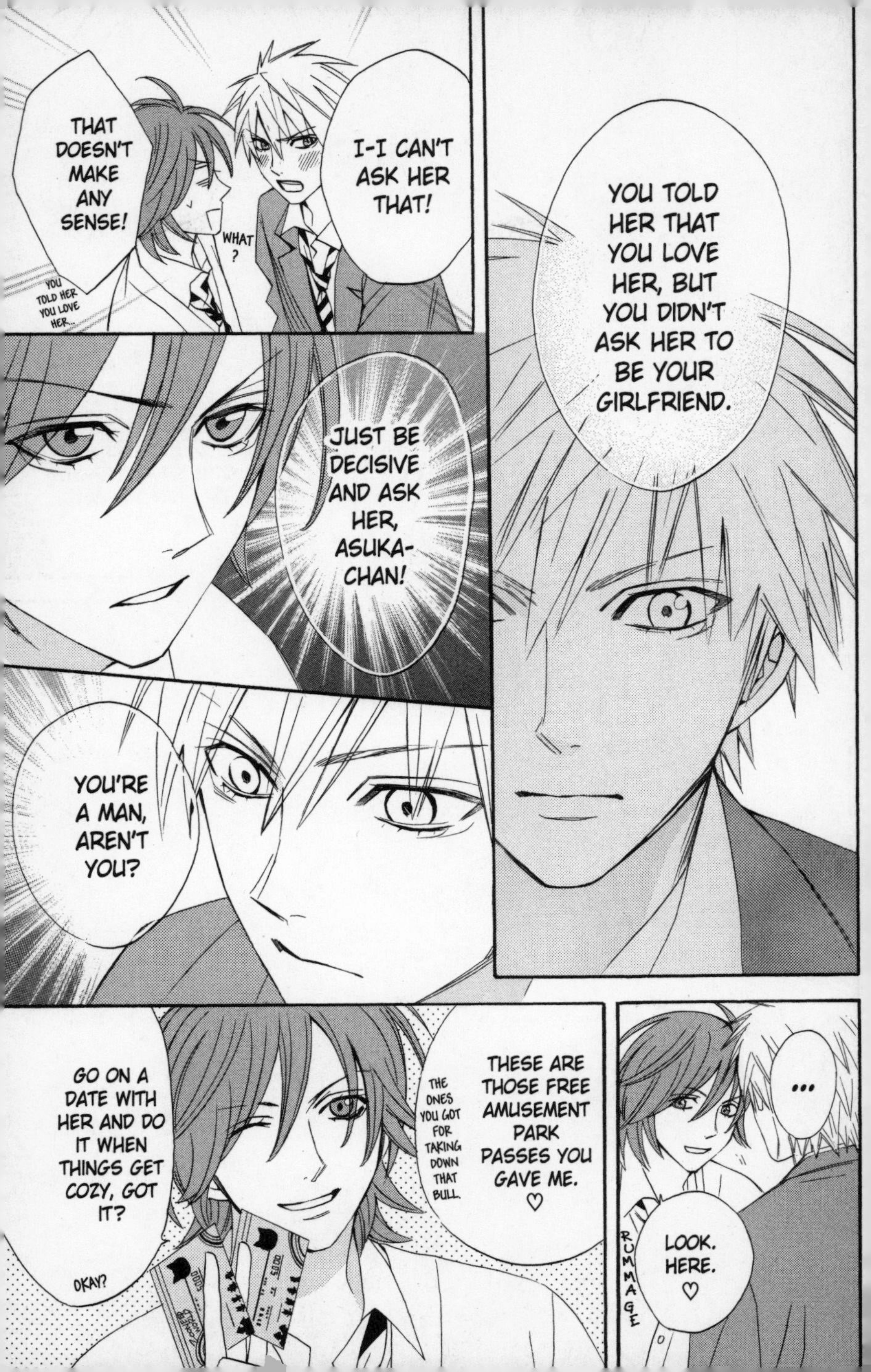
YOU TOLD HER THAT YOU LOVE HER, BUT YOU DIDN'T ASK HER TO BE YOUR GIRLFRIEND.
I-I CAN'T ASK HER THAT!
WHAT?
THAT DOESN'T MAKE ANY SENSE!
YOU TOLD HER YOU LOVE HER...
JUST BE DECISIVE AND ASK HER, ASUKA-CHAN!
YOU'RE A MAN, AREN'T YOU?
...
LOOK. HERE. ♡
RUMMAGE
THESE ARE THOSE FREE AMUSEMENT PARK PASSES YOU GAVE ME. ♡
THE ONES YOU GOT FOR TAKING DOWN THAT BULL.
GO ON A DATE WITH HER AND DO IT WHEN THINGS GET COZY, GOT IT?
OKAY?

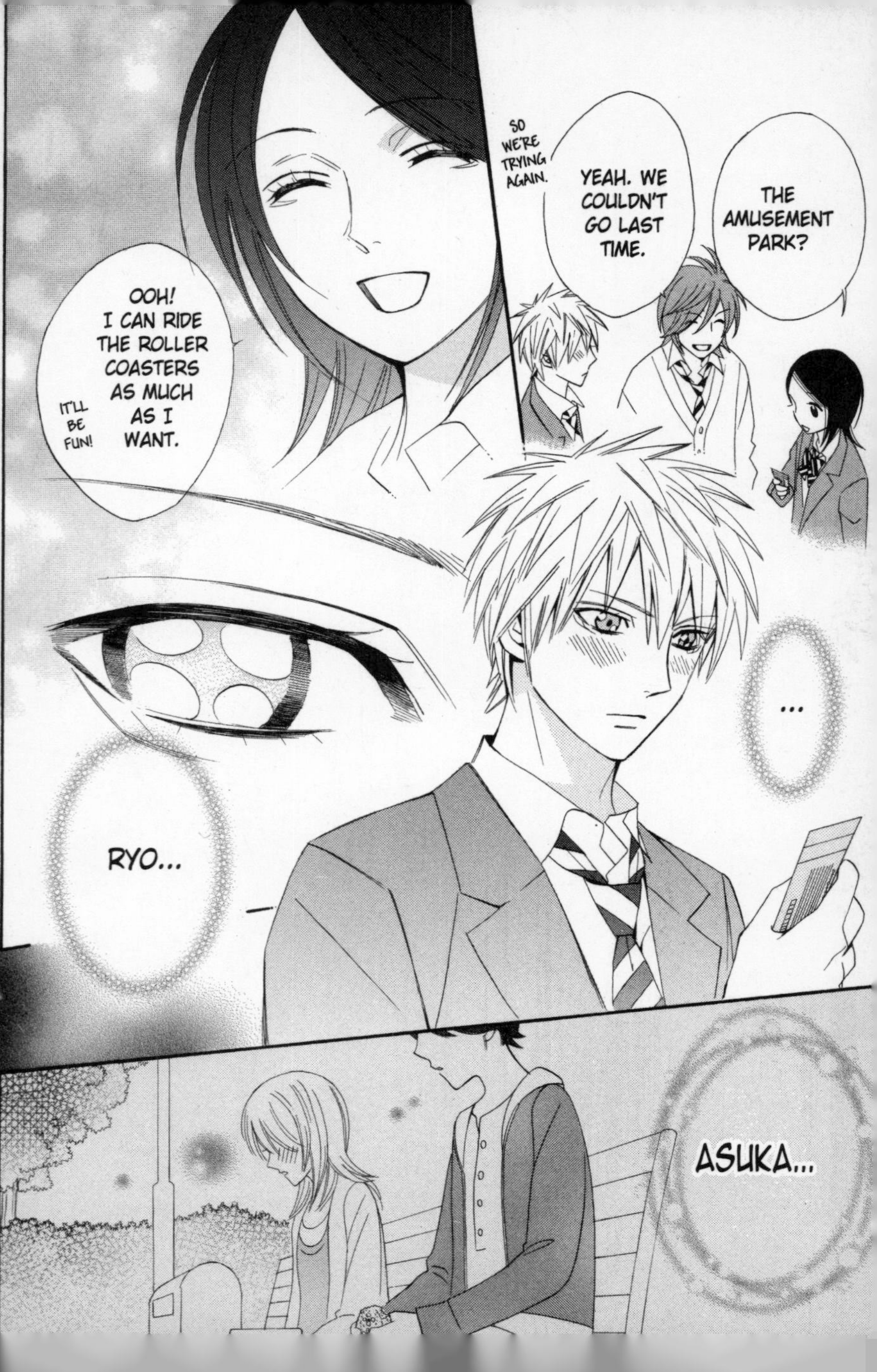
THE AMUSEMENT PARK?
YEAH. WE COULDN'T GO LAST TIME.
SO WE'RE TRYING AGAIN.
OOH! I CAN RIDE THE ROLLER COASTERS AS MUCH AS I WANT.
IT'LL BE FUN!
...
RYO...
ASUKA...

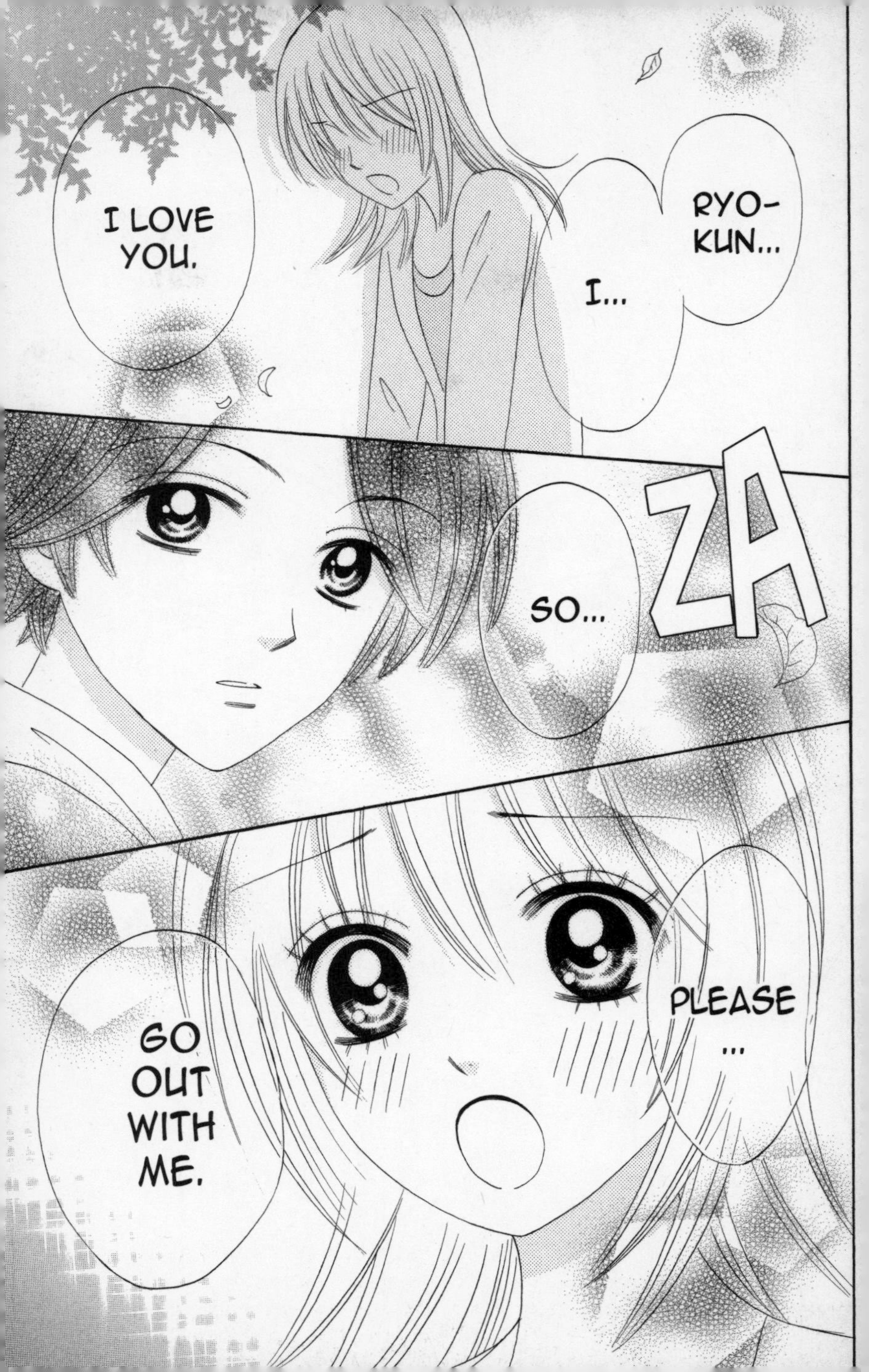
RYO-KUN... I...
I LOVE YOU.
ZA
SO...
PLEASE ...
GO OUT WITH ME.

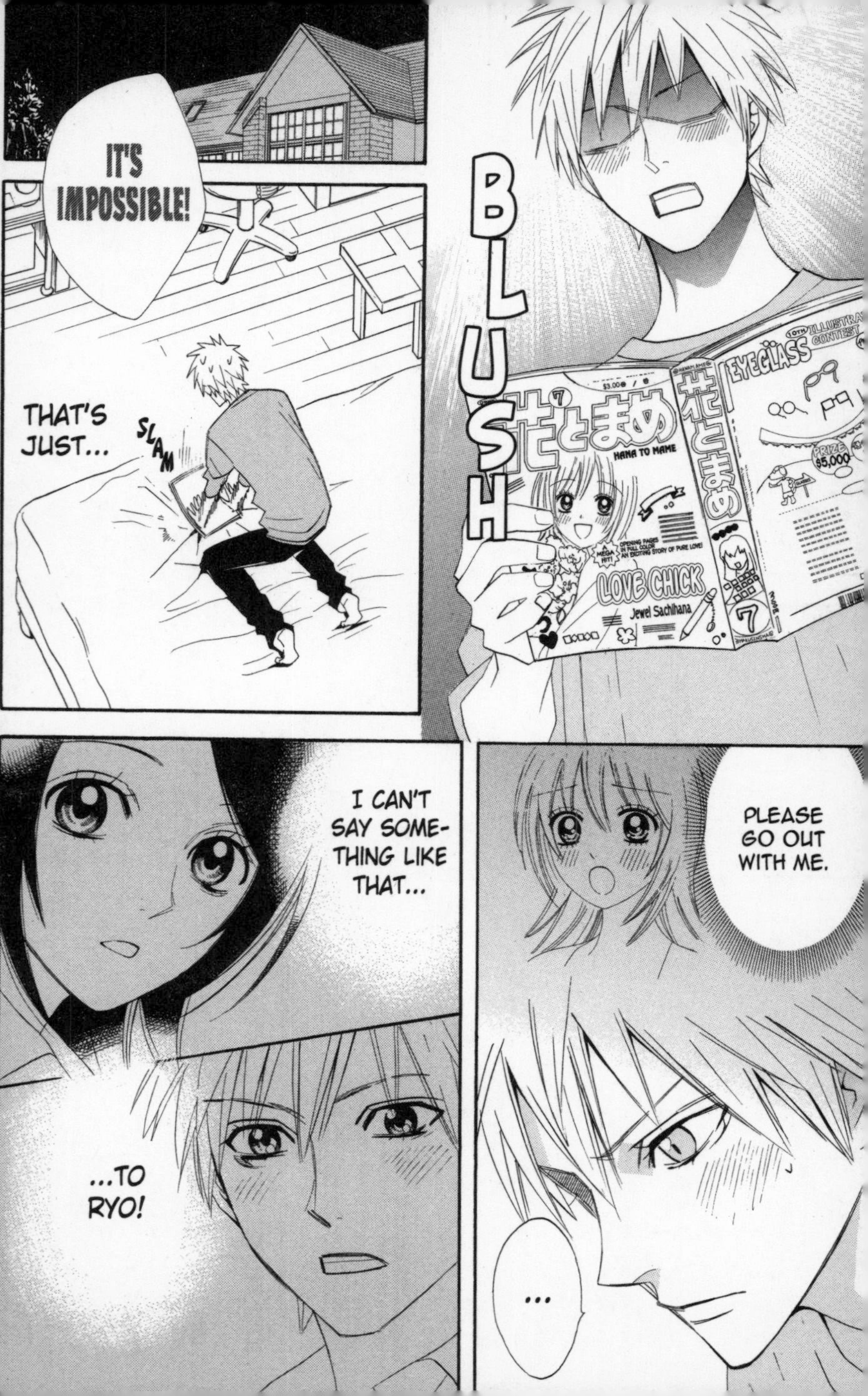
BLUSH
花とまめ
HANA TO MAME
LOVE CHICK
Jewel Sachihana
EYEGLASS
PRIZE $5,000
IT'S IMPOSSIBLE!
THAT'S JUST...
SLAM
PLEASE GO OUT WITH ME.
...
I CAN'T SAY SOME-THING LIKE THAT...
...TO RYO!

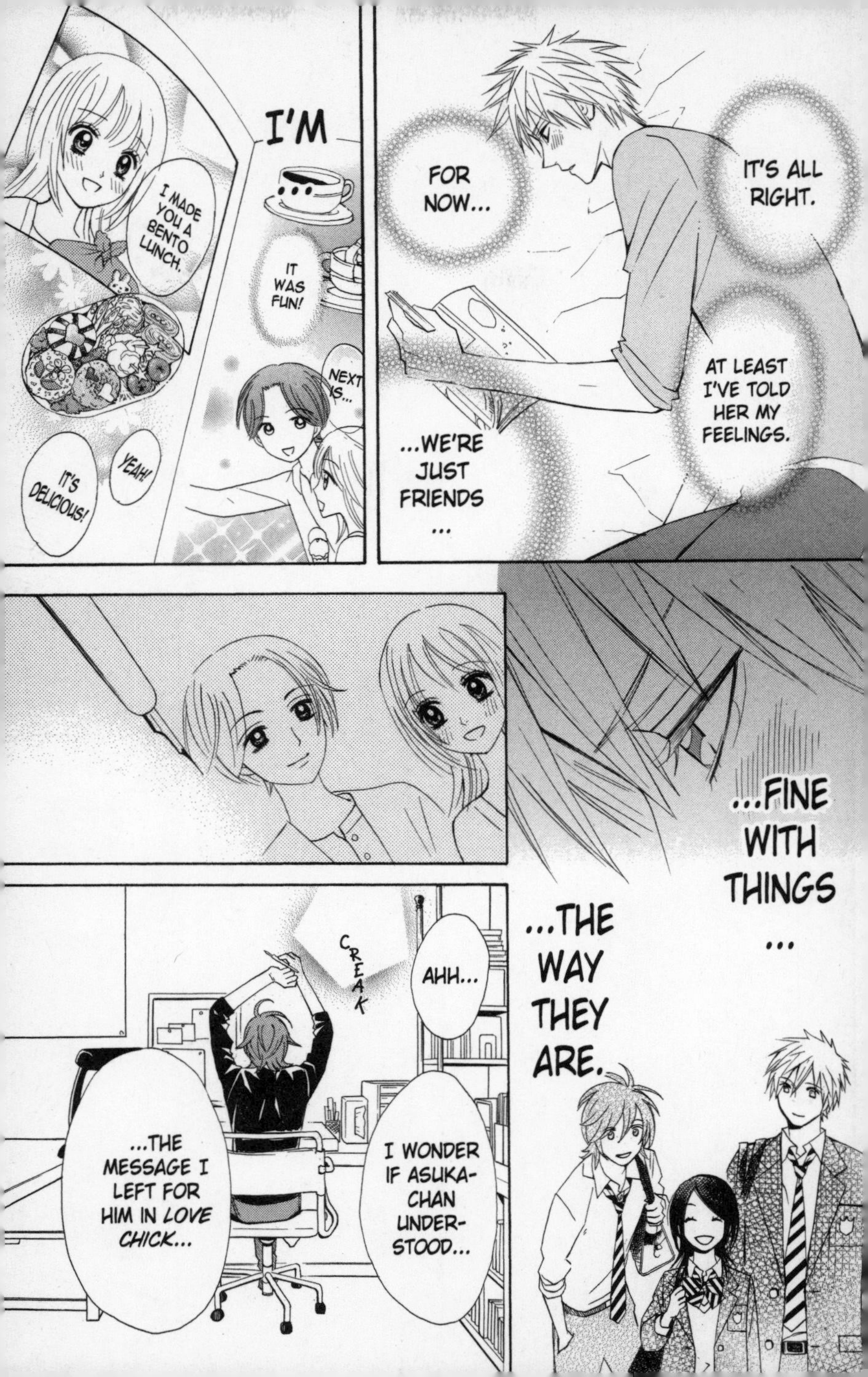
IT'S ALL RIGHT.
AT LEAST I'VE TOLD HER MY FEELINGS.
FOR NOW...
...WE'RE JUST FRIENDS...
I'M
I MADE YOU A BENTO LUNCH.
IT WAS FUN!
NEXT IS...
YEAH!
IT'S DELICIOUS!
...FINE WITH THINGS...
...THE WAY THEY ARE.
CREAK
AHH...
I WONDER IF ASUKA-CHAN UNDERSTOOD...
...THE MESSAGE I LEFT FOR HIM IN *LOVE CHICK*...

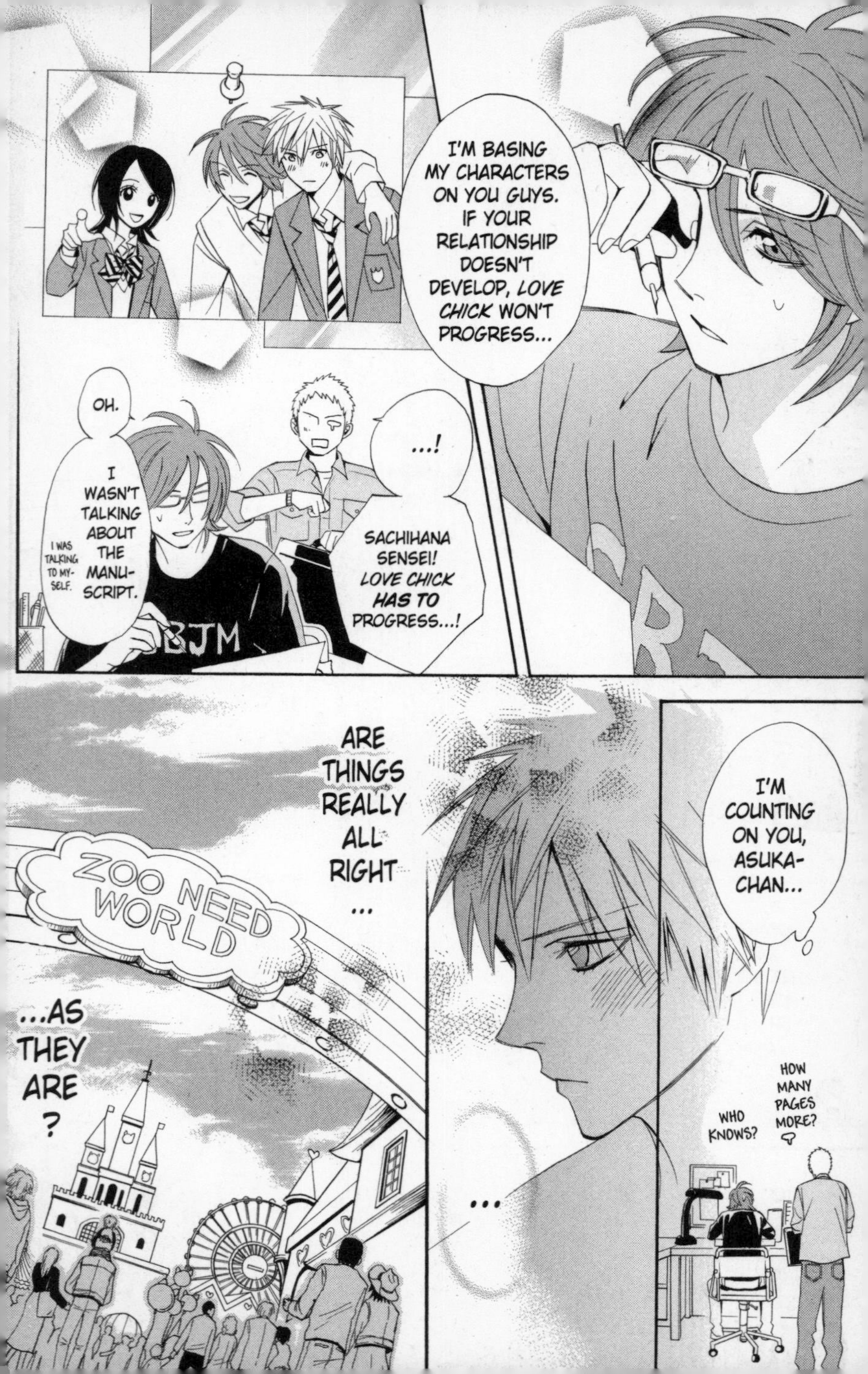
I'M BASING MY CHARACTERS ON YOU GUYS. IF YOUR RELATIONSHIP DOESN'T DEVELOP, *LOVE CHICK* WON'T PROGRESS...
...!
SACHIHANA SENSEI! *LOVE CHICK* **HAS TO** PROGRESS...!
OH.
I WASN'T TALKING ABOUT THE MANU-SCRIPT.
I WAS TALKING TO MY-SELF.
BJM
I'M COUNTING ON YOU, ASUKA-CHAN...
HOW MANY PAGES MORE?
WHO KNOWS?
...
ARE THINGS REALLY ALL RIGHT...
...AS THEY ARE?
ZOO NEED WORLD

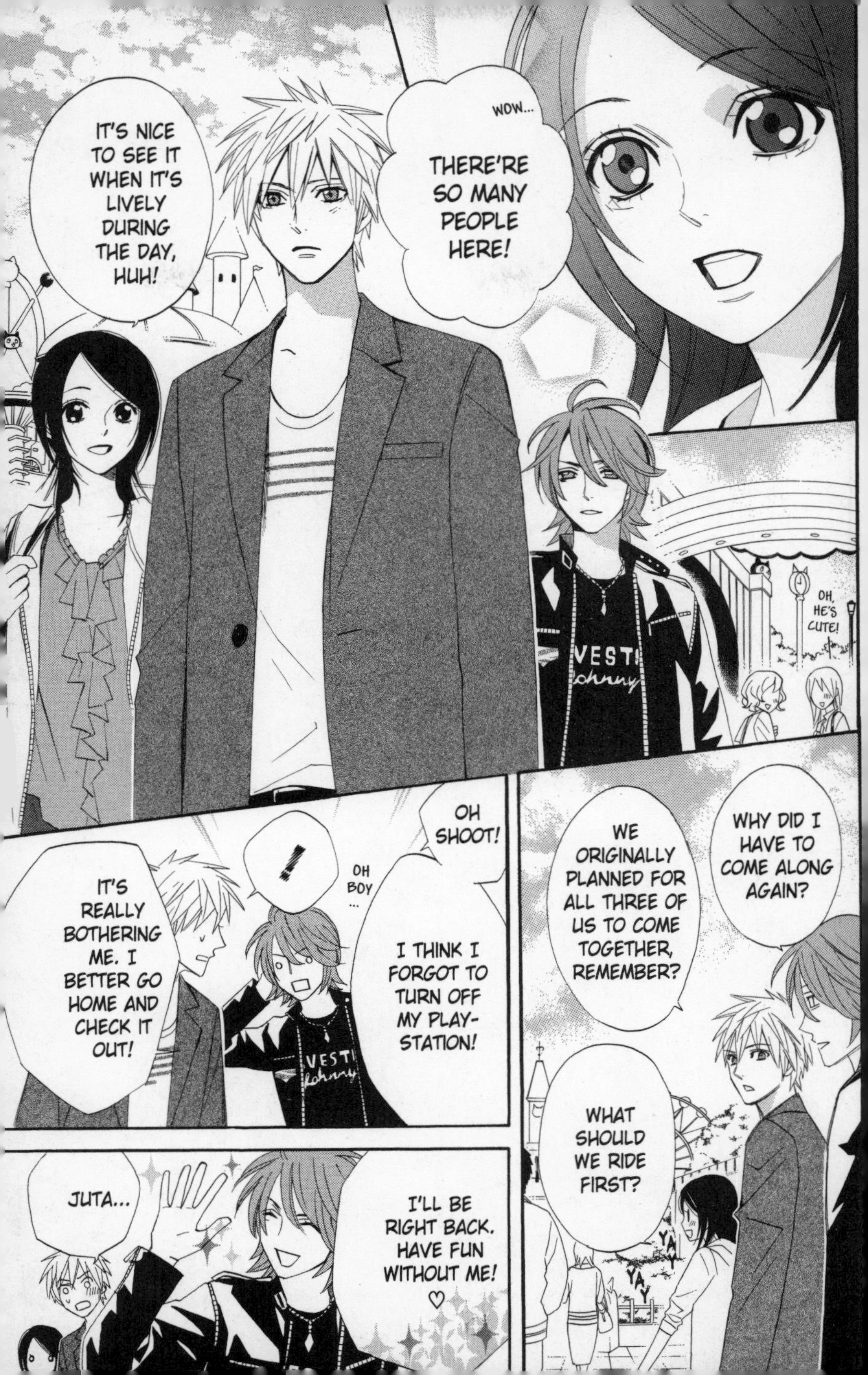
WOW...
THERE'RE SO MANY PEOPLE HERE!
OH, HE'S CUTE!
IT'S NICE TO SEE IT WHEN IT'S LIVELY DURING THE DAY, HUH!
WHY DID I HAVE TO COME ALONG AGAIN?
WE ORIGINALLY PLANNED FOR ALL THREE OF US TO COME TOGETHER, REMEMBER?
WHAT SHOULD WE RIDE FIRST?
YAY
YAY
OH SHOOT!
I THINK I FORGOT TO TURN OFF MY PLAY-STATION!
!
OH BOY ...
IT'S REALLY BOTHERING ME. I BETTER GO HOME AND CHECK IT OUT!
I'LL BE RIGHT BACK. HAVE FUN WITHOUT ME! ♡
JUTA...

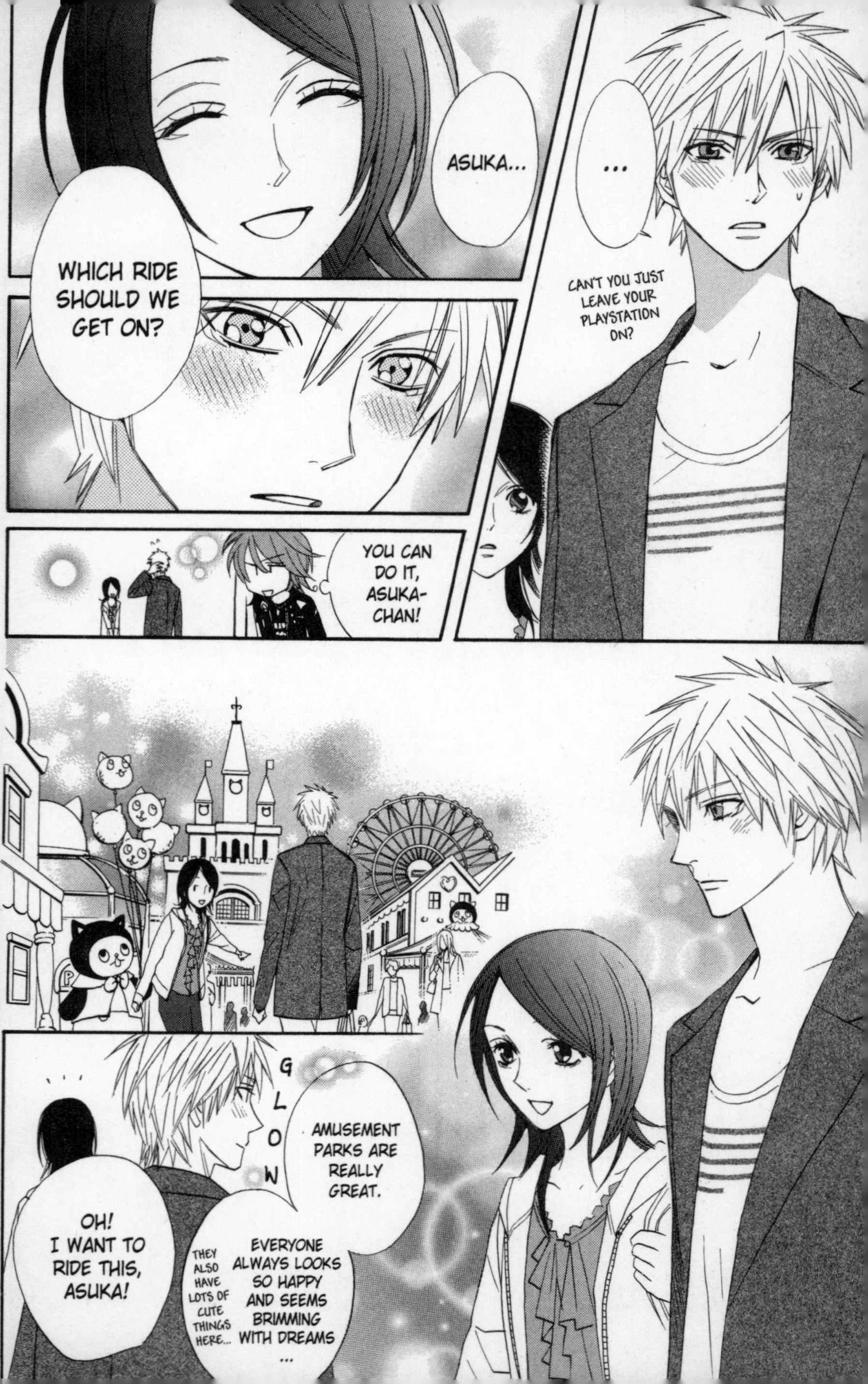
...
CAN'T YOU JUST LEAVE YOUR PLAYSTATION ON?
ASUKA...
WHICH RIDE SHOULD WE GET ON?
YOU CAN DO IT, ASUKA-CHAN!
GLOW
AMUSEMENT PARKS ARE REALLY GREAT.
EVERYONE ALWAYS LOOKS SO HAPPY AND SEEMS BRIMMING WITH DREAMS...
THEY ALSO HAVE LOTS OF CUTE THINGS HERE...
OH! I WANT TO RIDE THIS, ASUKA!

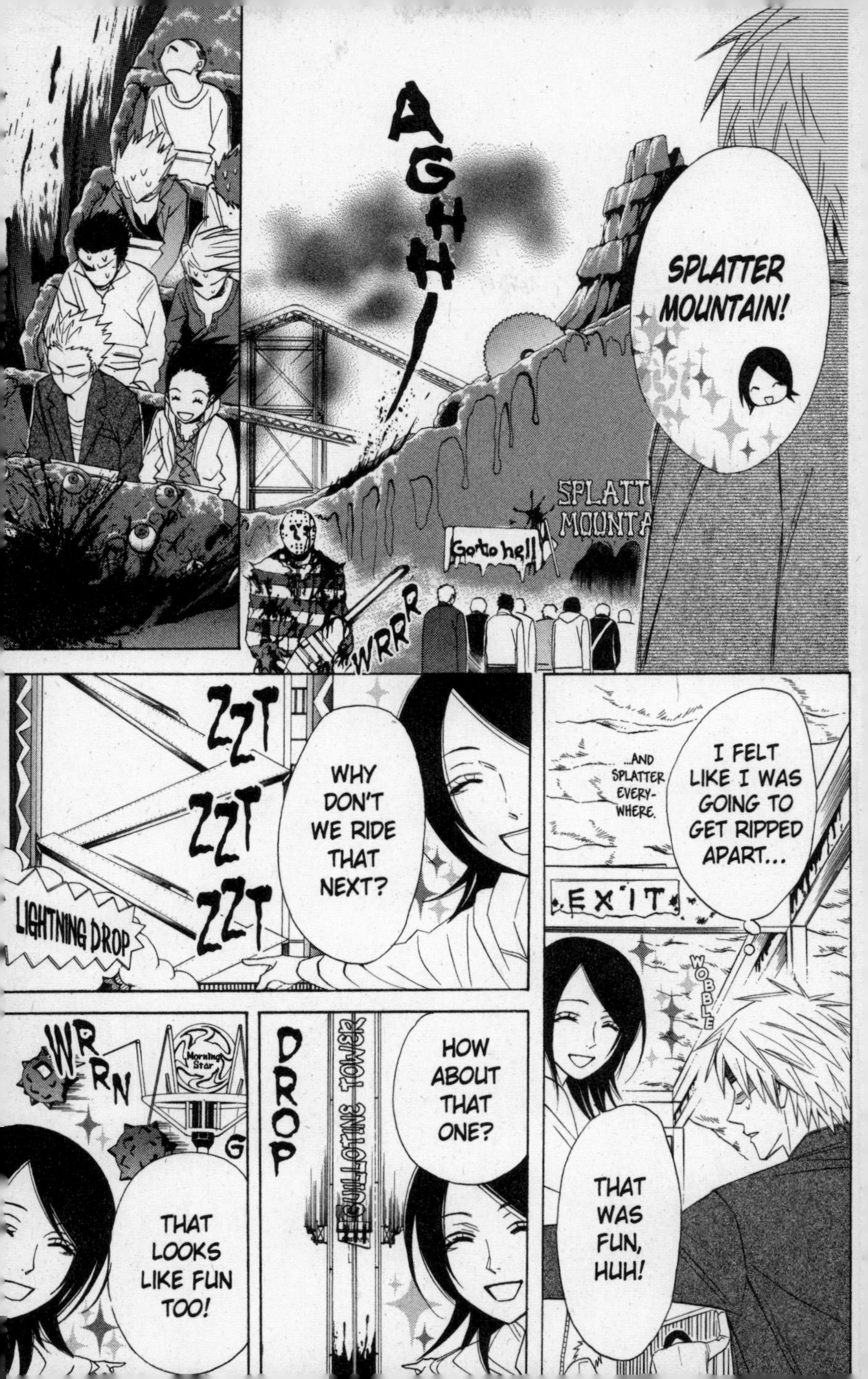
SPLATTER MOUNTAIN!
AGHH!
SPLATT MOUNTA
Go to hell
WRRR
I FELT LIKE I WAS GOING TO GET RIPPED APART...
...AND SPLATTER EVERY-WHERE.
EXIT
WOBBLE
THAT WAS FUN, HUH!
WHY DON'T WE RIDE THAT NEXT?
ZZT
ZZT
ZZT
LIGHTNING DROP
HOW ABOUT THAT ONE?
DROP
GUILLOTINE TOWER
WRRRN
Morning Star
G
THAT LOOKS LIKE FUN TOO!

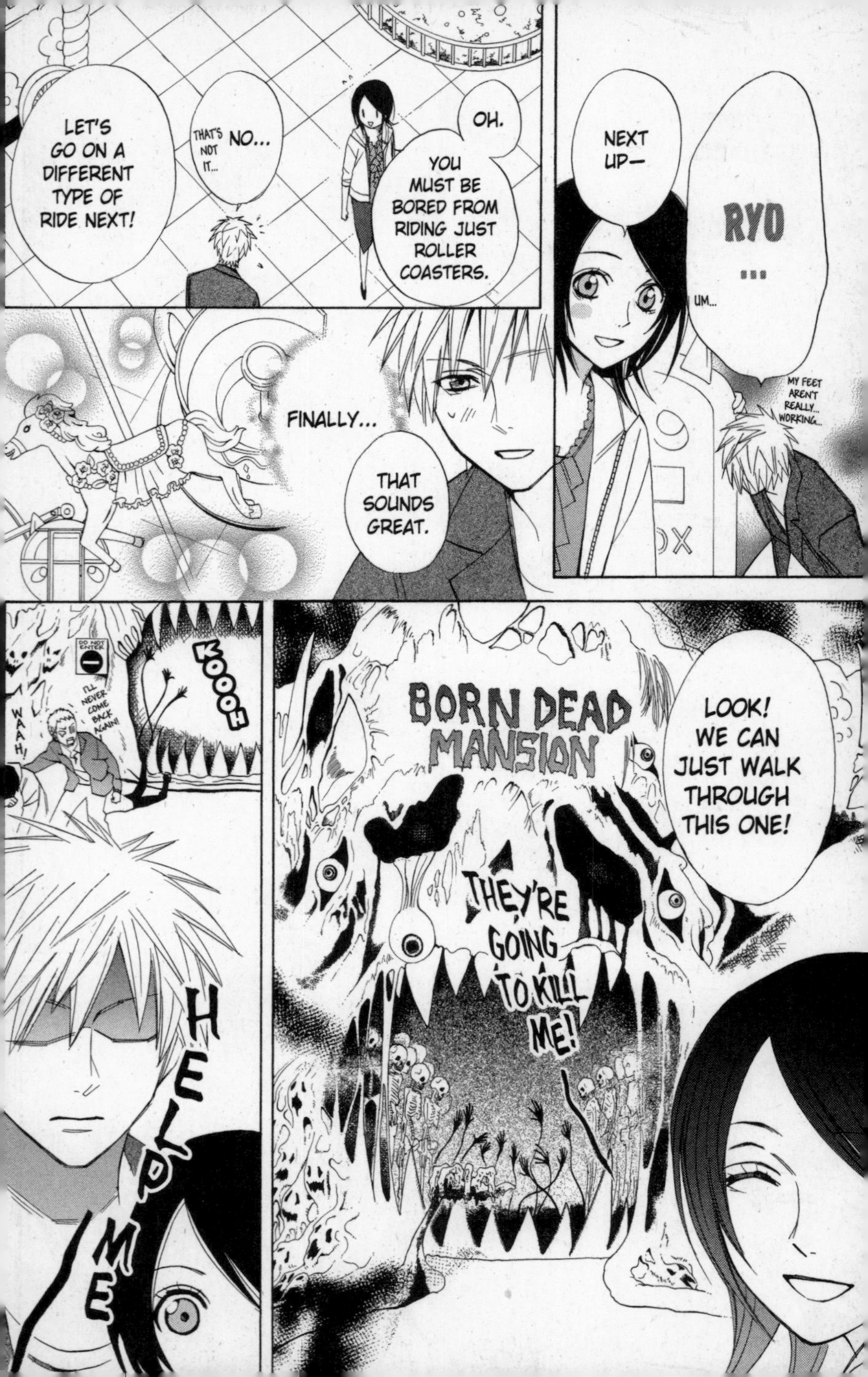
NEXT UP—
RYO ...
UM...
MY FEET AREN'T REALLY... WORKING...
OH.
YOU MUST BE BORED FROM RIDING JUST ROLLER COASTERS.
THAT'S NOT IT...
NO...
LET'S GO ON A DIFFERENT TYPE OF RIDE NEXT!
FINALLY...
THAT SOUNDS GREAT.
LOOK! WE CAN JUST WALK THROUGH THIS ONE!
BORN DEAD MANSION
THEY'RE GOING TO KILL ME!
KOOOH
DO NOT ENTER
I'LL NEVER COME BACK AGAIN!
WAAAH!
HELP ME

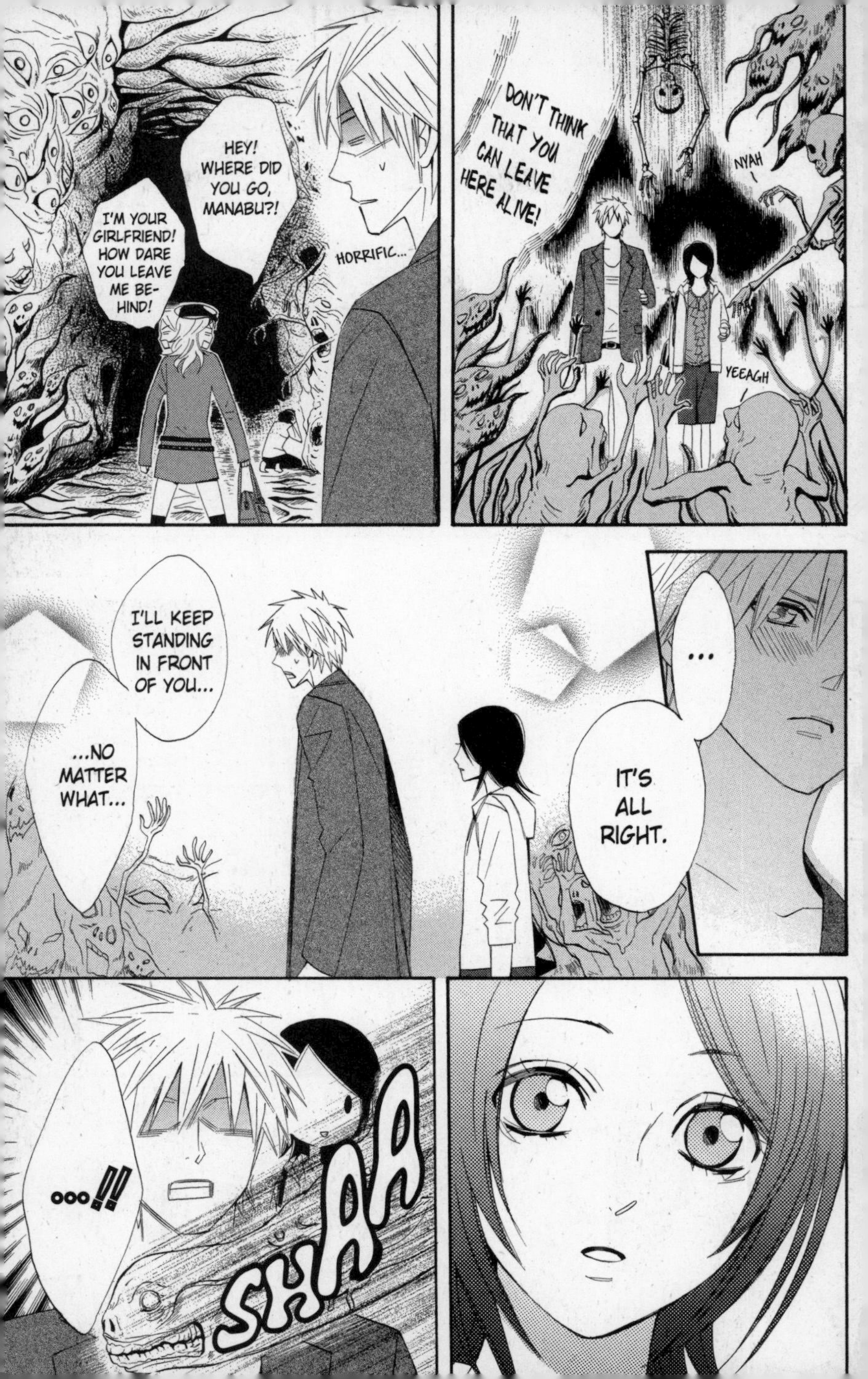
DON'T THINK THAT YOU CAN LEAVE HERE ALIVE!
NYAH
YEEAGH
HEY! WHERE DID YOU GO, MANABU?!
I'M YOUR GIRLFRIEND! HOW DARE YOU LEAVE ME BE-HIND!
HORRIFIC...
...
IT'S ALL RIGHT.
I'LL KEEP STANDING IN FRONT OF YOU...
...NO MATTER WHAT...
SHAA
ooo!!

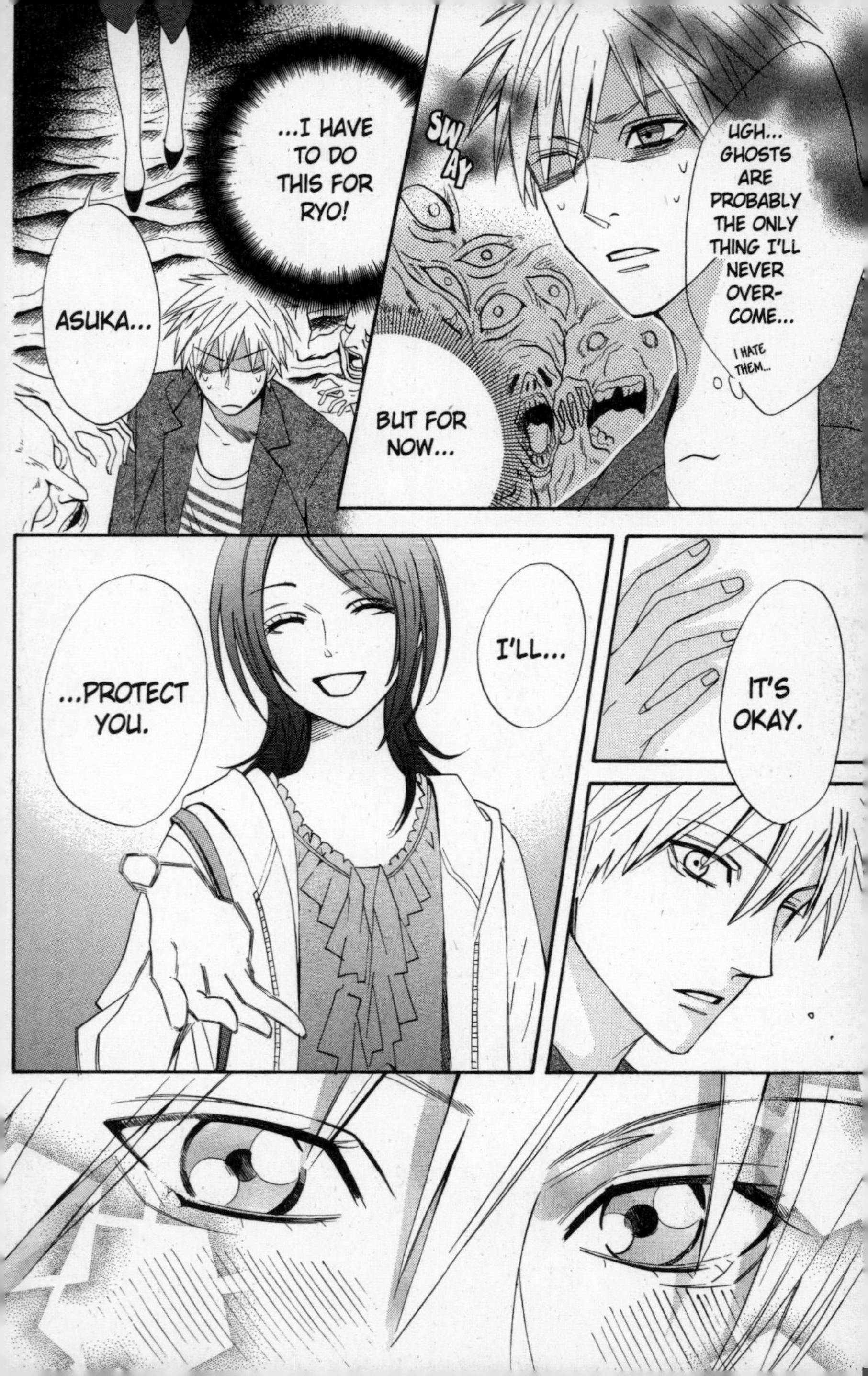
UGH... GHOSTS ARE PROBABLY THE ONLY THING I'LL NEVER OVER-COME...
SWAY
I HATE THEM...
BUT FOR NOW...
...I HAVE TO DO THIS FOR RYO!
ASUKA...
IT'S OKAY.
I'LL...
...PROTECT YOU.

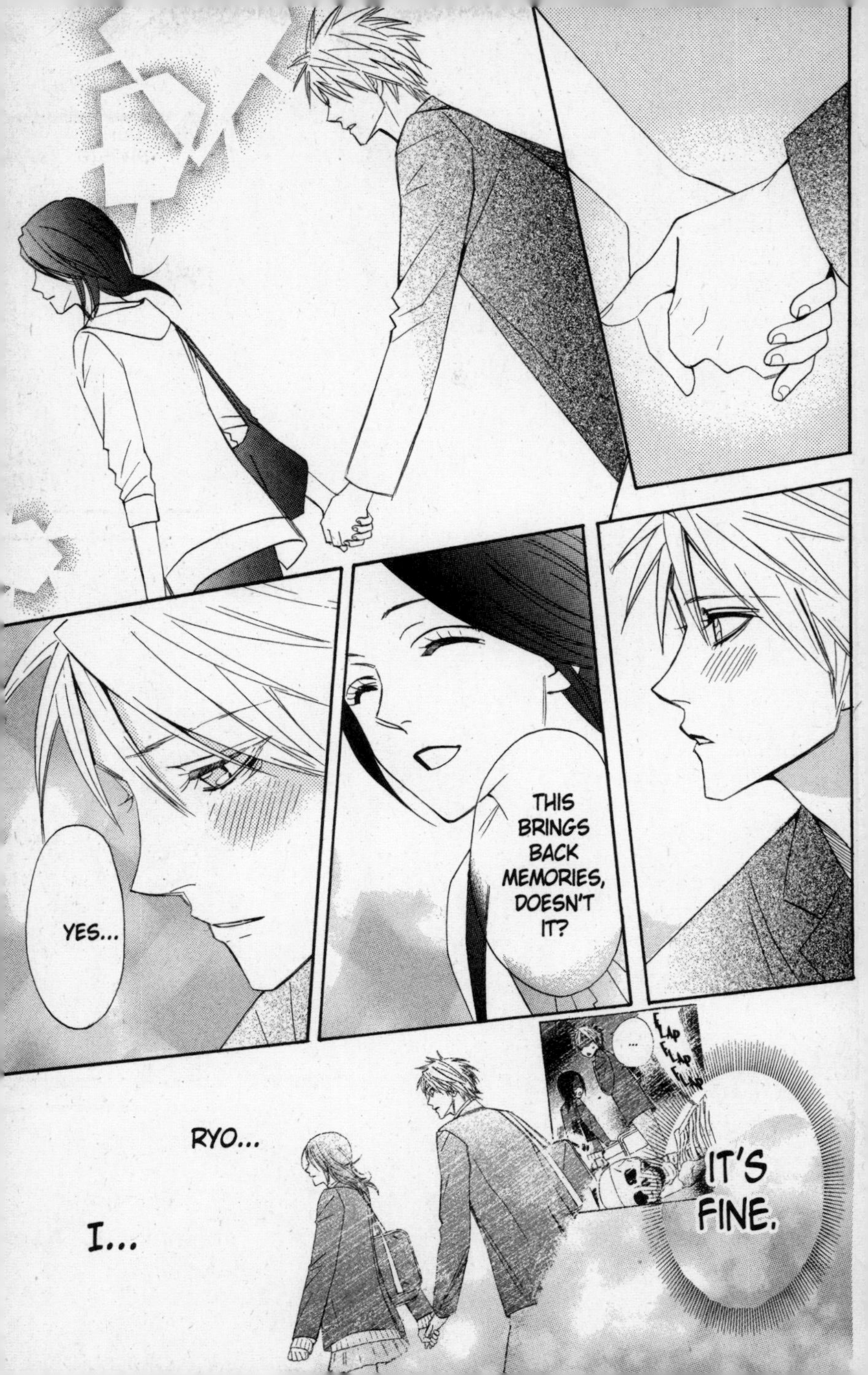
THIS BRINGS BACK MEMORIES, DOESN'T IT?
YES...
...
FLAP FLAP FLAP
IT'S FINE.
RYO...
I...

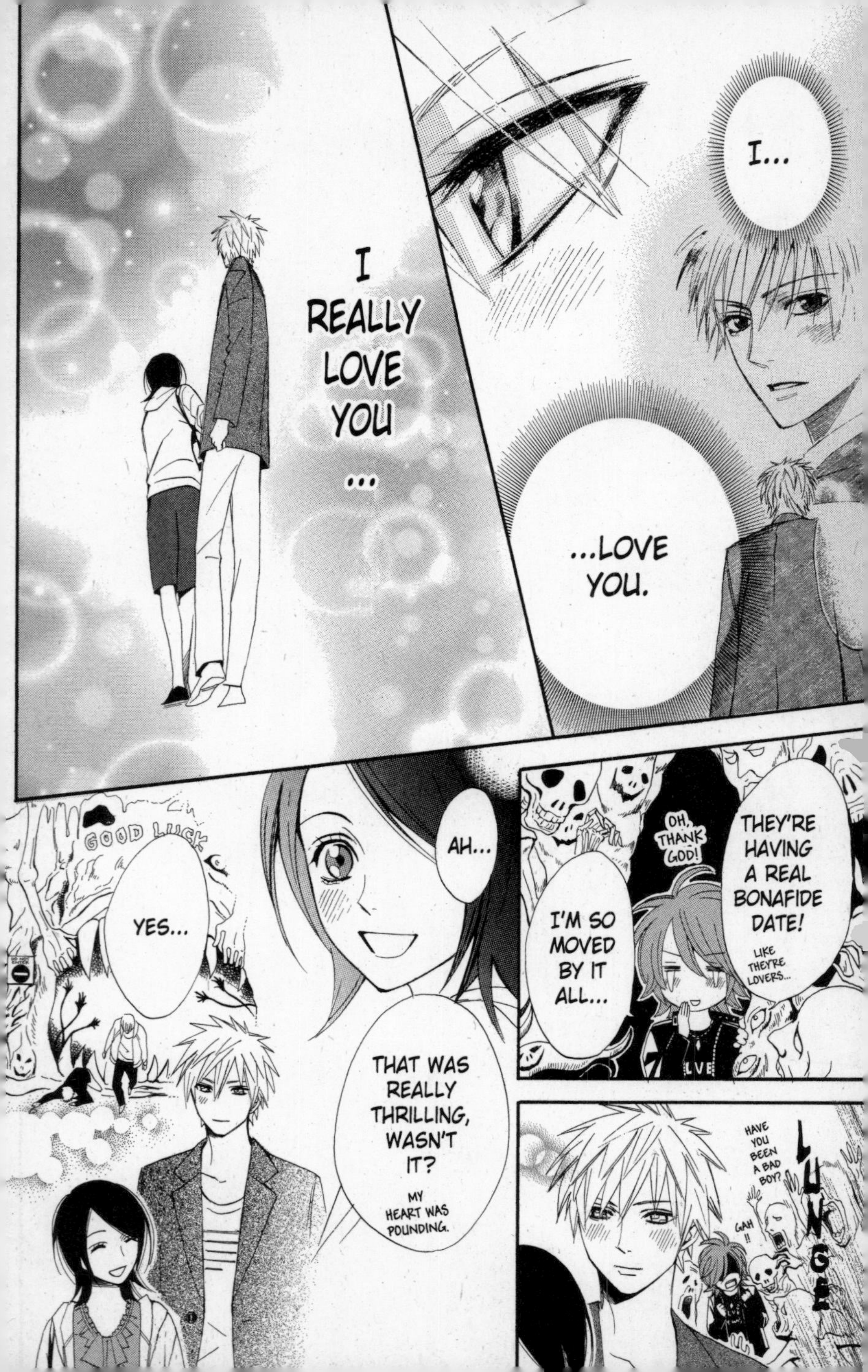
I...
...LOVE YOU.
I REALLY LOVE YOU...
THEY'RE HAVING A REAL BONAFIDE DATE!
LIKE THEY'RE LOVERS...
OH, THANK GOD!
I'M SO MOVED BY IT ALL...
HAVE YOU BEEN A BAD BOY?
LUNGE
GAH!!
AH...
THAT WAS REALLY THRILLING, WASN'T IT?
MY HEART WAS POUNDING.
YES...
GOOD LUCK

I DON'T LIKE HAUNTED HOUSES... BUT BEING TOGETHER WITH RYO...
...MADE IT FUN...
WHAT SHALL WE TRY NEXT?
YOO-HOO!
SWEET LOVERS!
WHAT TIME IS IT RIGHT NOW?
HEY...
I'M TALKING TO YOU HERE!

Zoo Need World once again. The male mascot is Zooni and the female one is Zukki. At amusement parks, I like the haunted houses and the free fall rides. (I don't like the spinning ones. I get motion sickness.) While I wrote this chapter, I thought about how wonderful it would be if Splatter Mountain really existed. I think that a completely horror-themed amusement park would be pretty popular if it was around...

I remember it was a lot of fun drawing the bushy-haired bespectacled man who appears in this chapter. Characters like him are more fun than handsome ones... Superficial men and men with shaved heads are also a lot of fun.

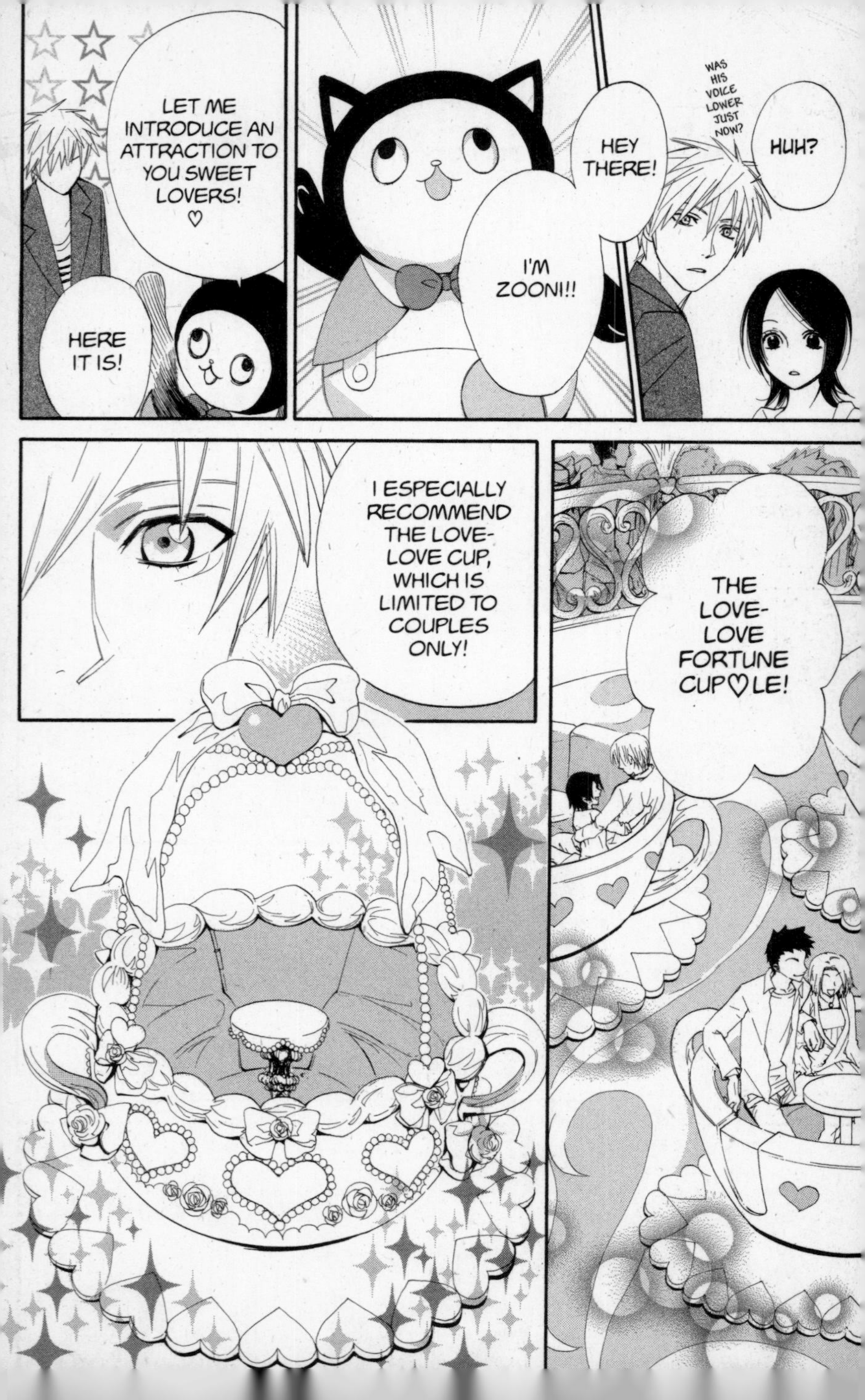
HUH?
WAS HIS VOICE LOWER JUST NOW?
HEY THERE!
I'M ZOONI!!
LET ME INTRODUCE AN ATTRACTION TO YOU SWEET LOVERS! ♡
HERE IT IS!
THE LOVE-LOVE FORTUNE CUP♡LE!
I ESPECIALLY RECOMMEND THE LOVE-LOVE CUP, WHICH IS LIMITED TO COUPLES ONLY!

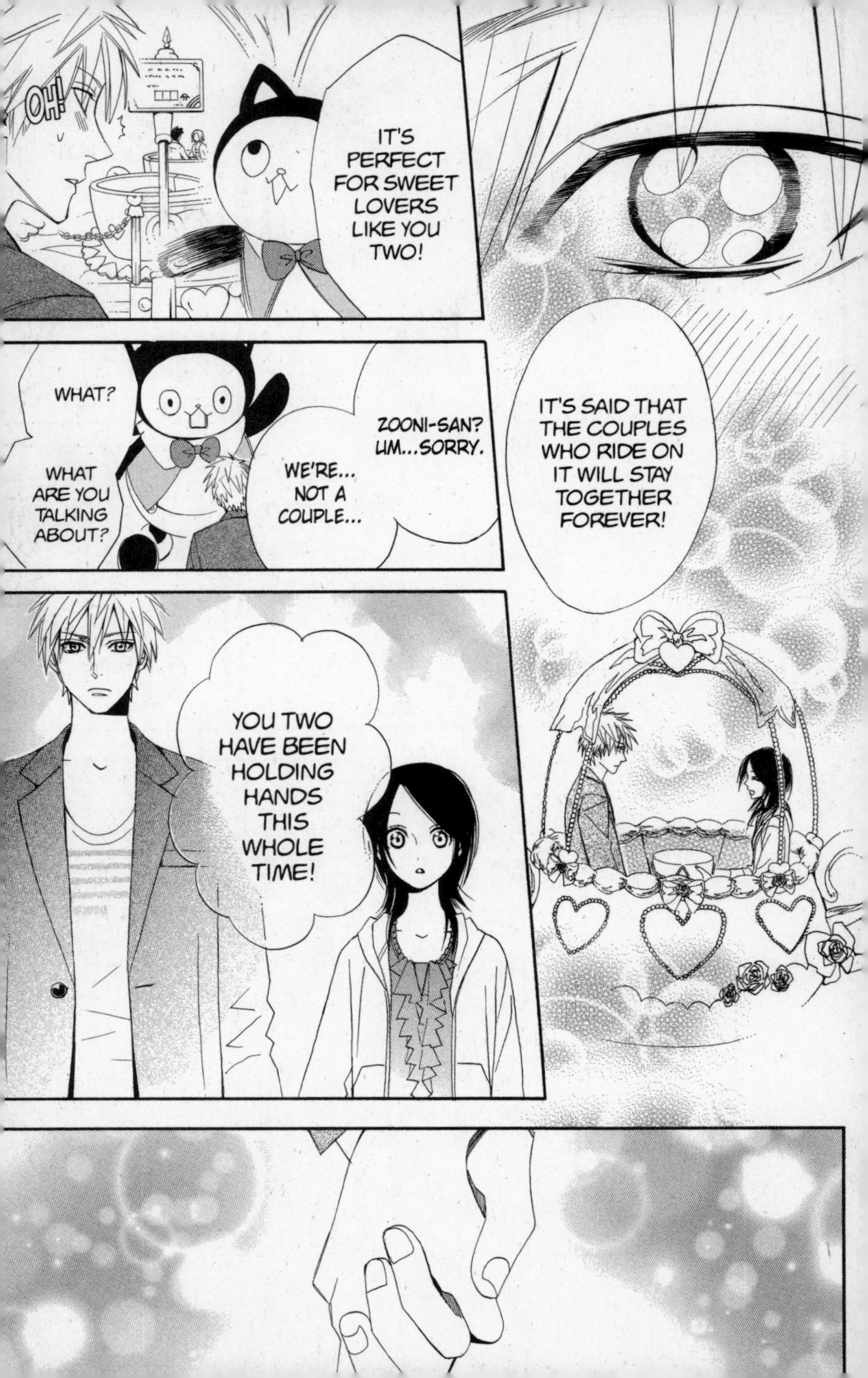
IT'S SAID THAT THE COUPLES WHO RIDE ON IT WILL STAY TOGETHER FOREVER!
OH!
IT'S PERFECT FOR SWEET LOVERS LIKE YOU TWO!
ZOONI-SAN? UM...SORRY.
WE'RE... NOT A COUPLE...
WHAT?
WHAT ARE YOU TALKING ABOUT?
YOU TWO HAVE BEEN HOLDING HANDS THIS WHOLE TIME!

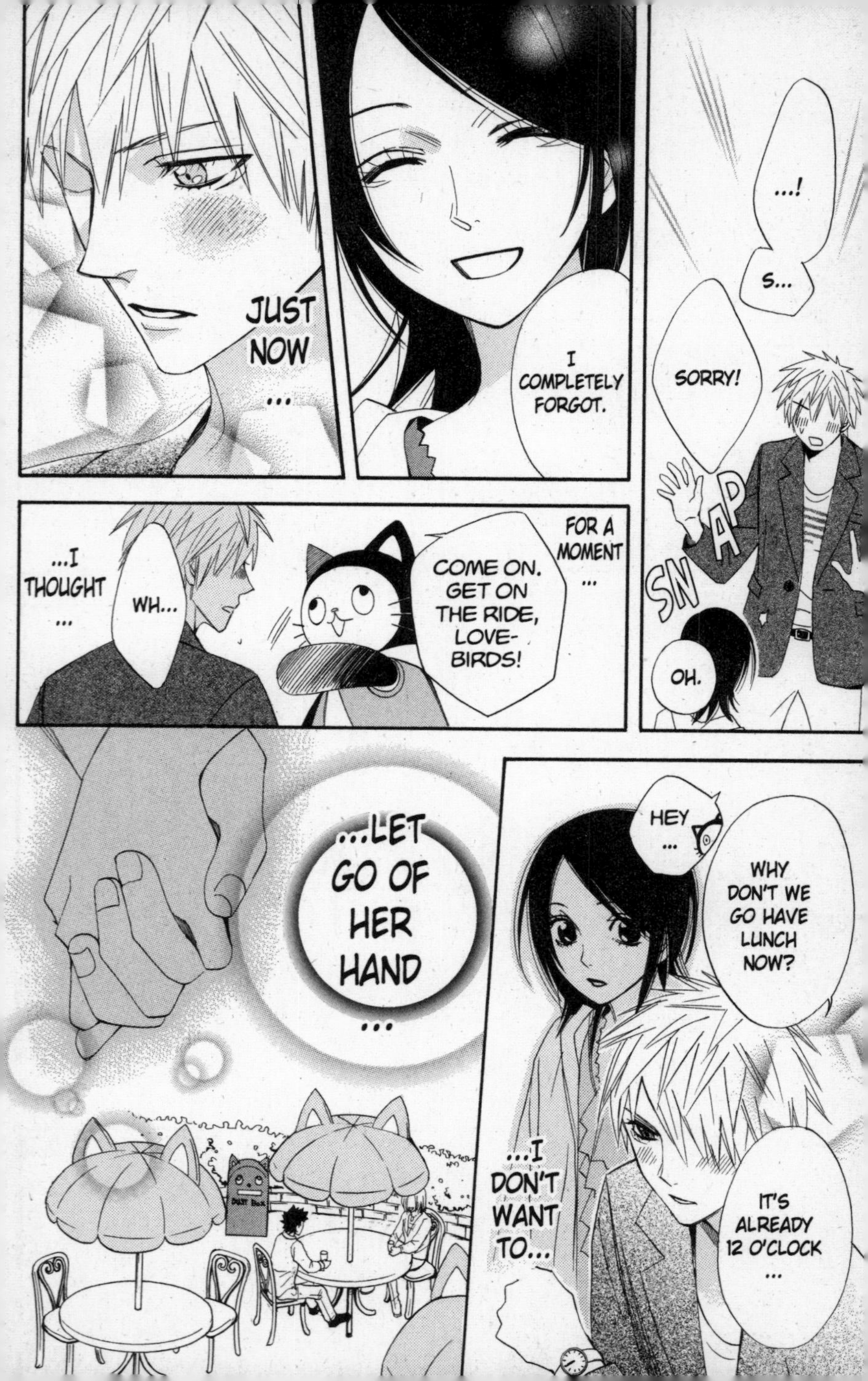
...!
S...
SORRY!
SNAP
OH.
I COMPLETELY FORGOT.
JUST NOW ...
FOR A MOMENT ...
COME ON. GET ON THE RIDE, LOVE-BIRDS!
WH...
...I THOUGHT ...
HEY ...
WHY DON'T WE GO HAVE LUNCH NOW?
IT'S ALREADY 12 O'CLOCK ...
...I DON'T WANT TO...
...LET GO OF HER HAND ...

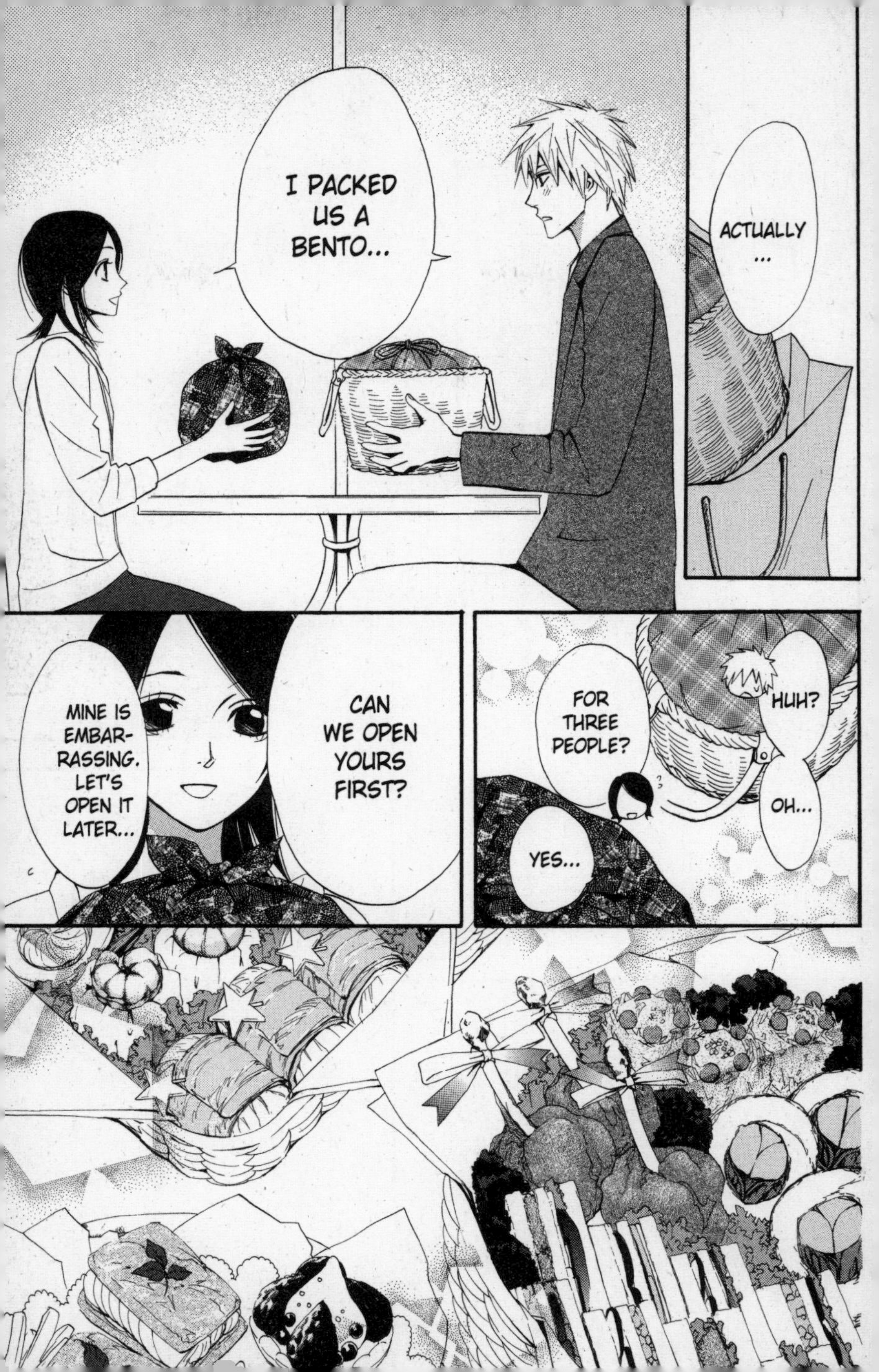
ACTUALLY ...
I PACKED US A BENTO...
HUH?
FOR THREE PEOPLE?
OH...
YES...
CAN WE OPEN YOURS FIRST?
MINE IS EMBAR-RASSING. LET'S OPEN IT LATER...

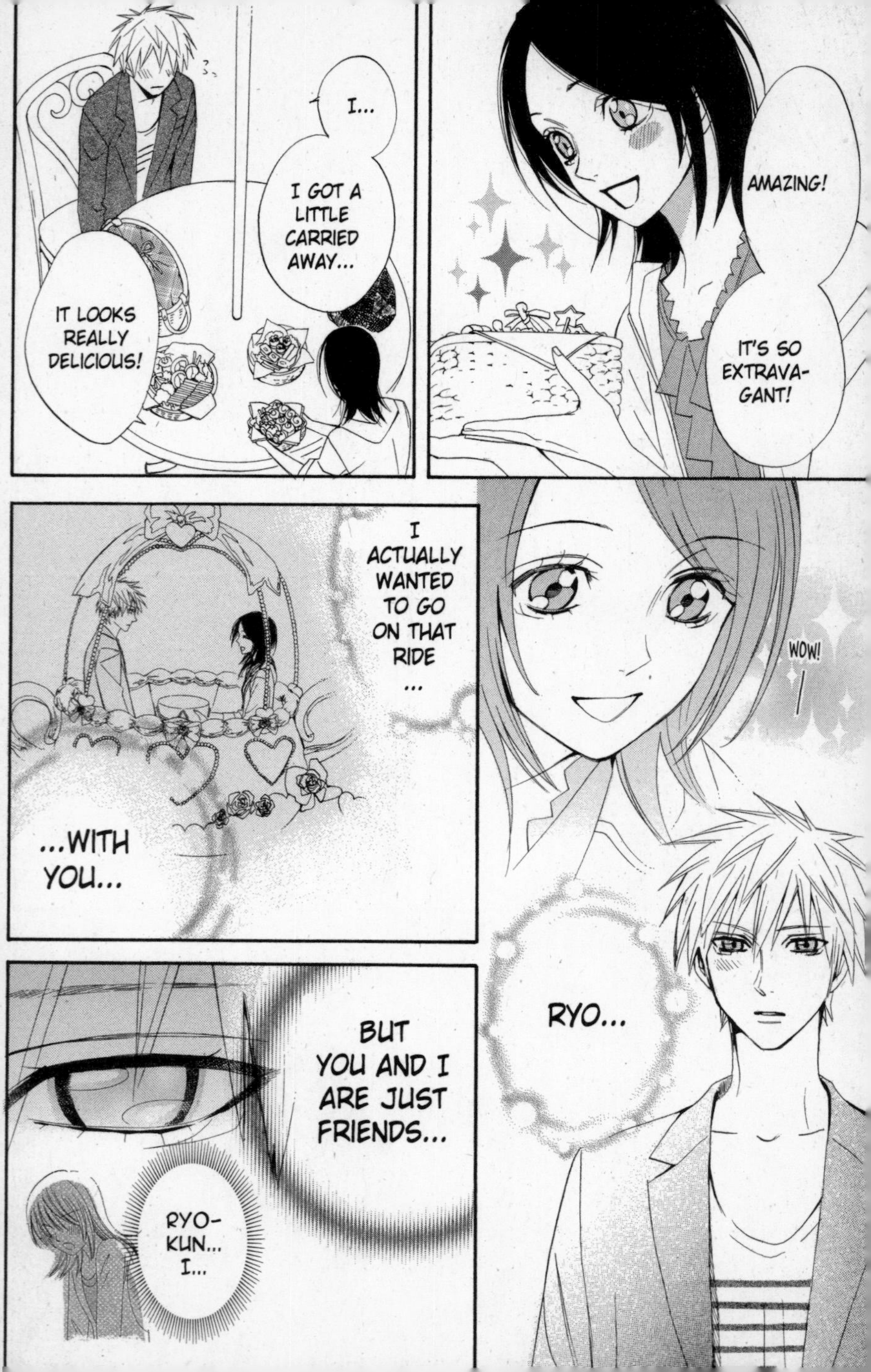
AMAZING!
IT'S SO EXTRAVA-GANT!
I...
I GOT A LITTLE CARRIED AWAY...
IT LOOKS REALLY DELICIOUS!
WOW!
RYO...
I ACTUALLY WANTED TO GO ON THAT RIDE...
...WITH YOU...
BUT YOU AND I ARE JUST FRIENDS...
RYO-KUN... I...

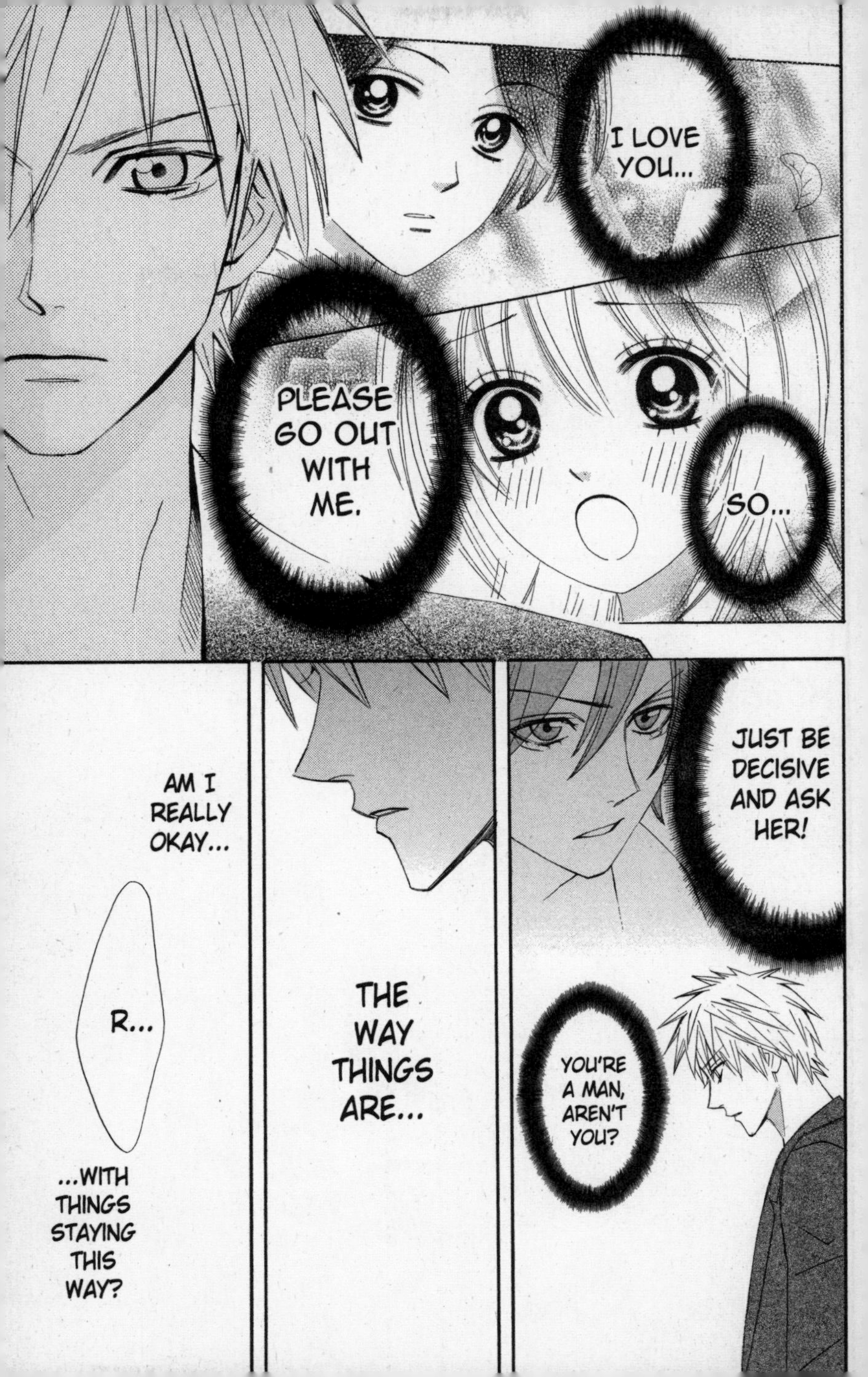
I LOVE YOU...
SO...
PLEASE GO OUT WITH ME.
JUST BE DECISIVE AND ASK HER!
YOU'RE A MAN, AREN'T YOU?
THE WAY THINGS ARE...
AM I REALLY OKAY...
R...
...WITH THINGS STAYING THIS WAY?

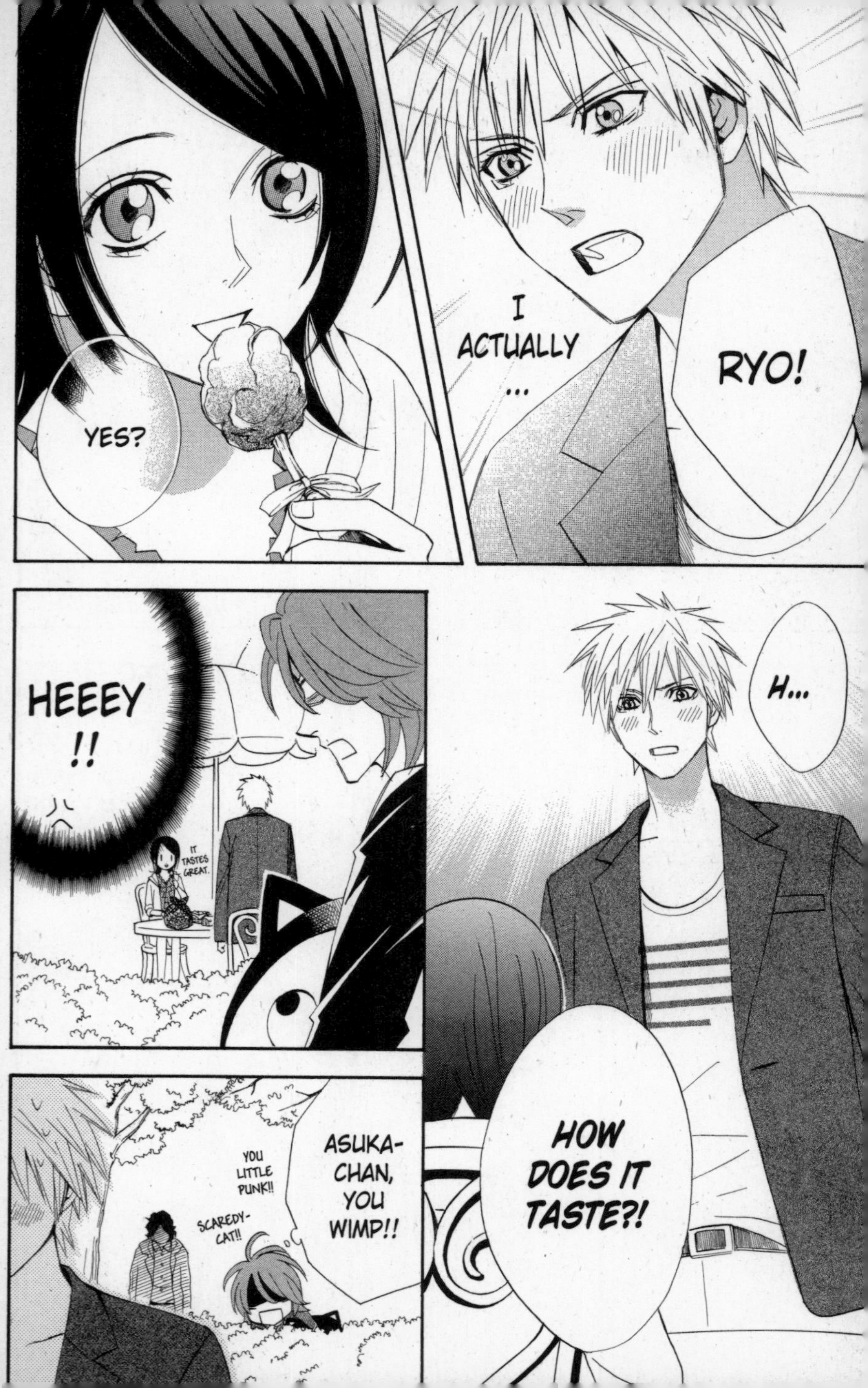
RYO!
I ACTUALLY ...
YES?
H...
HOW DOES IT TASTE?!
HEEEY !!
IT TASTES GREAT.
ASUKA-CHAN, YOU WIMP!!
YOU LITTLE PUNK!!
SCAREDY-CAT!!

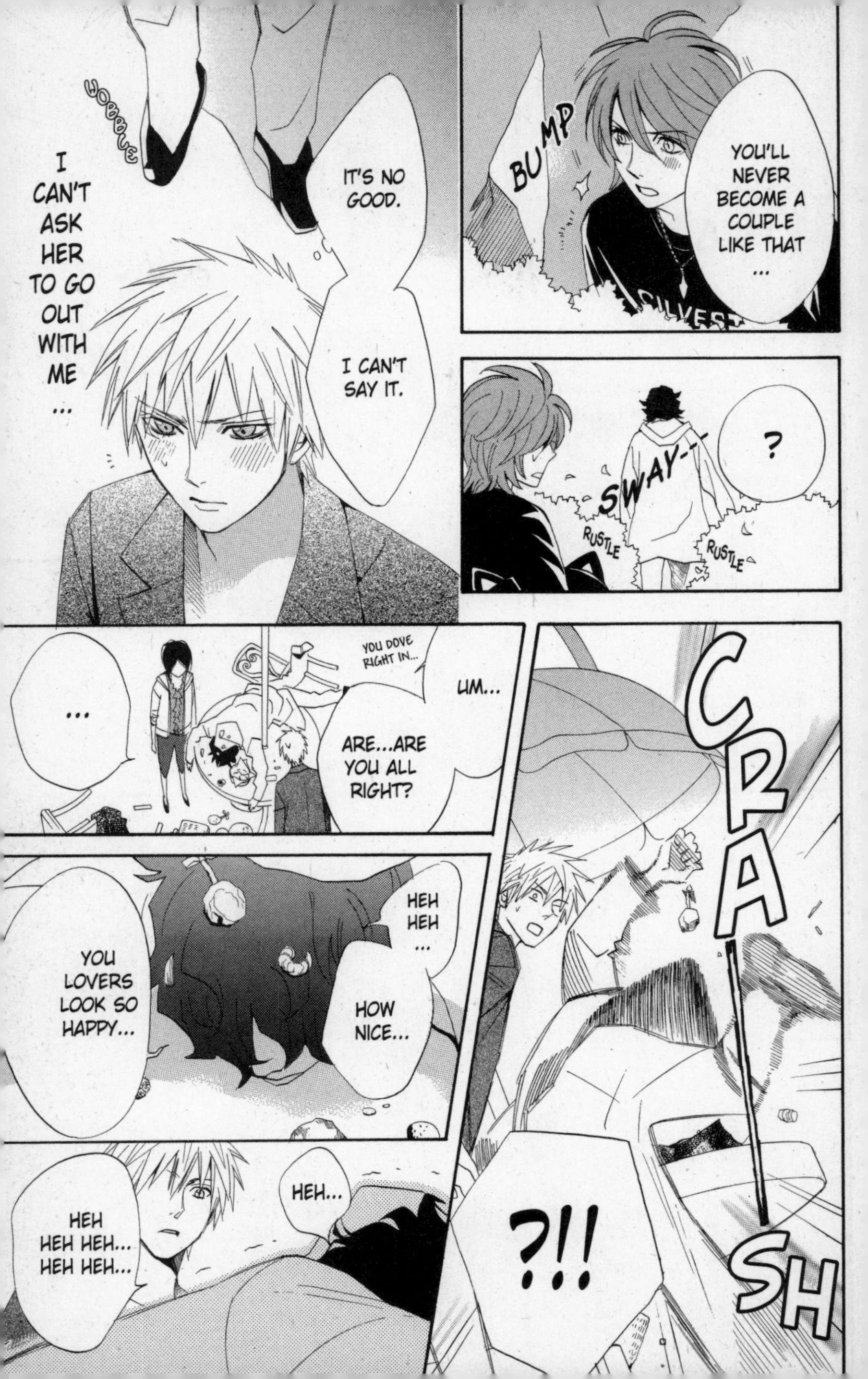
BUMP
YOU'LL NEVER BECOME A COUPLE LIKE THAT ...
SWAY
RUSTLE
?
RUSTLE
WOBBLE
IT'S NO GOOD.
I CAN'T SAY IT.
I CAN'T ASK HER TO GO OUT WITH ME ...
CRASH
?!!
UM...
ARE...ARE YOU ALL RIGHT?
YOU DOVE RIGHT IN...
...
HEH HEH ...
HOW NICE...
YOU LOVERS LOOK SO HAPPY...
HEH...
HEH HEH HEH... HEH HEH...

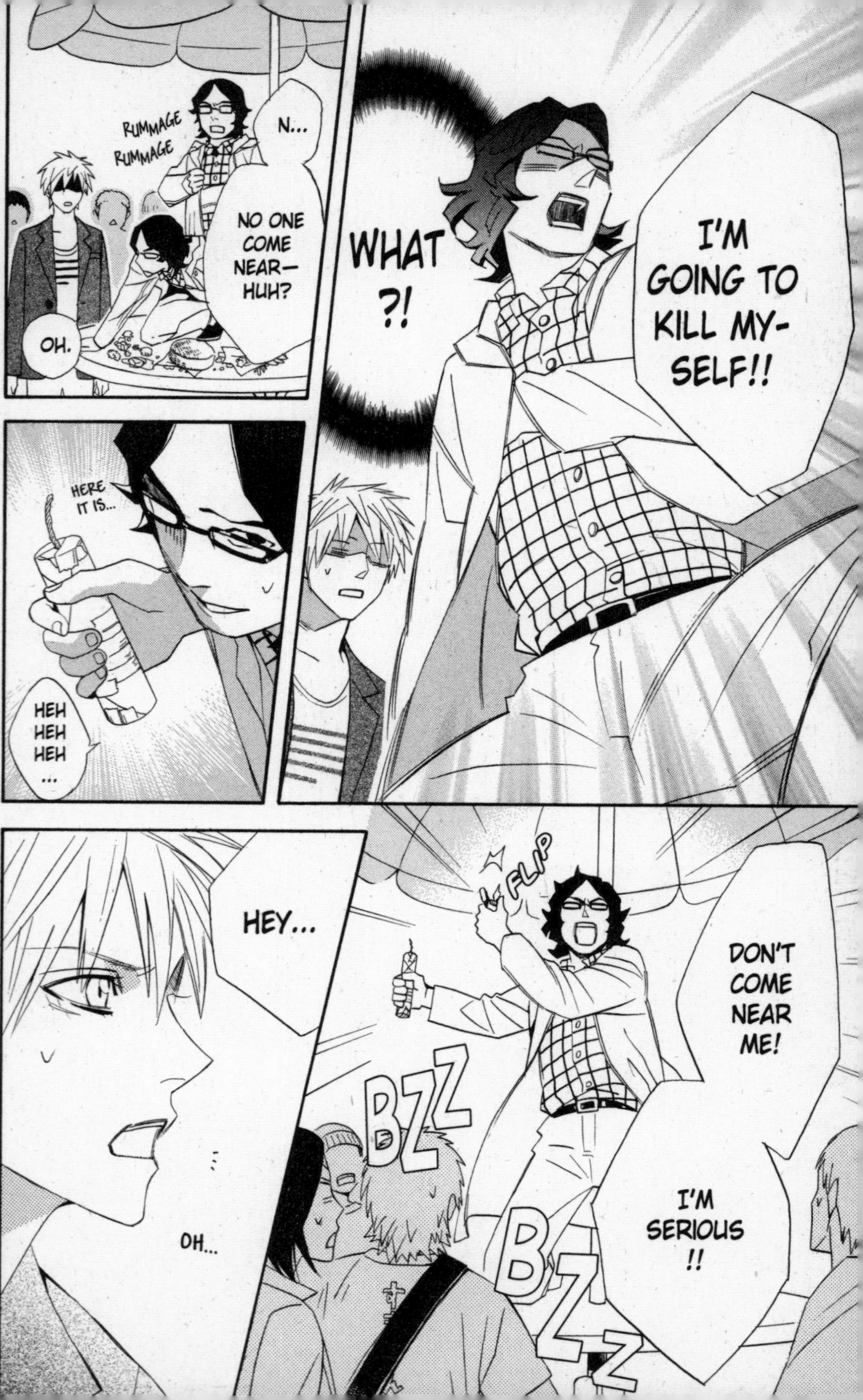
WHAT ?!
I'M GOING TO KILL MY-SELF!!
N...
RUMMAGE RUMMAGE
NO ONE COME NEAR— HUH?
OH.
HERE IT IS...
HEH HEH HEH ...
FLIP
DON'T COME NEAR ME!
I'M SERIOUS !!
BZZ
BZZ
HEY...
OH...

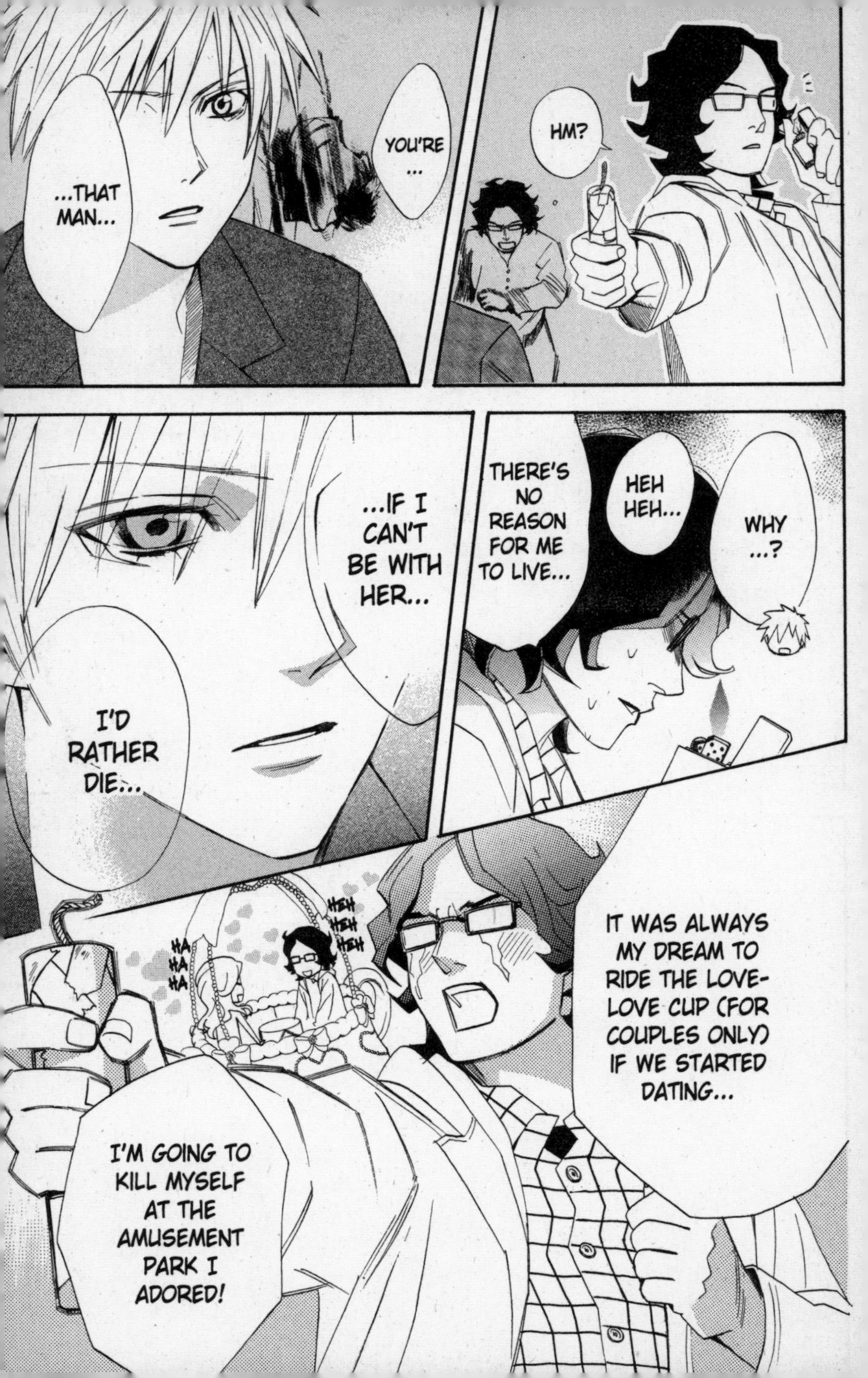
HM?
YOU'RE ...
...THAT MAN...
WHY ...?
HEH HEH...
THERE'S NO REASON FOR ME TO LIVE...
...IF I CAN'T BE WITH HER...
I'D RATHER DIE...
IT WAS ALWAYS MY DREAM TO RIDE THE LOVE-LOVE CUP (FOR COUPLES ONLY) IF WE STARTED DATING...
HEH HEH HEH
HA HA HA
I'M GOING TO KILL MYSELF AT THE AMUSEMENT PARK I ADORED!

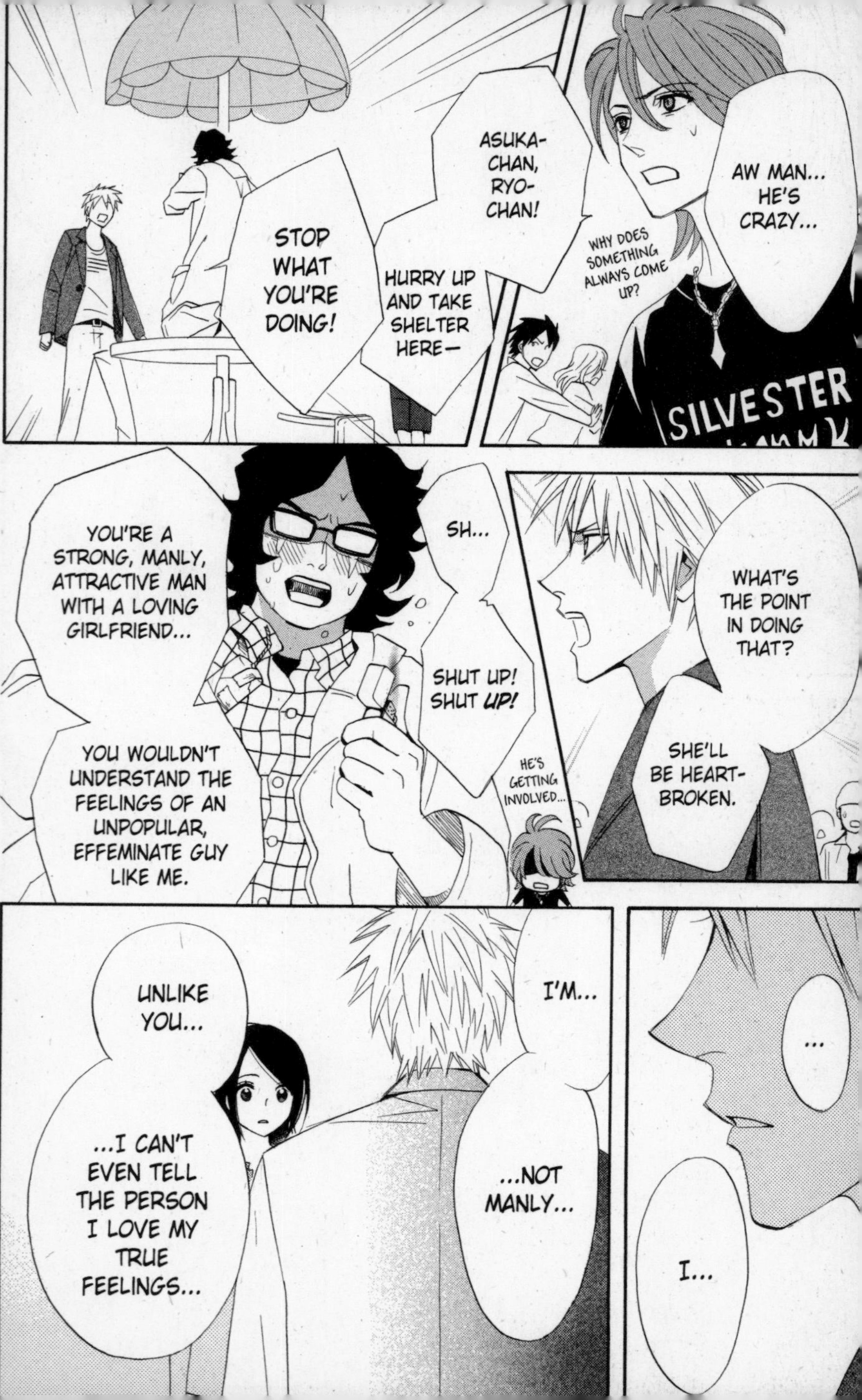
AW MAN... HE'S CRAZY...
WHY DOES SOMETHING ALWAYS COME UP?
SILVESTER
ASUKA-CHAN, RYO-CHAN!
HURRY UP AND TAKE SHELTER HERE—
STOP WHAT YOU'RE DOING!
WHAT'S THE POINT IN DOING THAT?
SHE'LL BE HEART-BROKEN.
SH...
SHUT UP! SHUT *UP!*
HE'S GETTING INVOLVED...
YOU'RE A STRONG, MANLY, ATTRACTIVE MAN WITH A LOVING GIRLFRIEND...
YOU WOULDN'T UNDERSTAND THE FEELINGS OF AN UNPOPULAR, EFFEMINATE GUY LIKE ME.
...
I...
I'M...
...NOT MANLY...
UNLIKE YOU...
...I CAN'T EVEN TELL THE PERSON I LOVE MY TRUE FEELINGS...

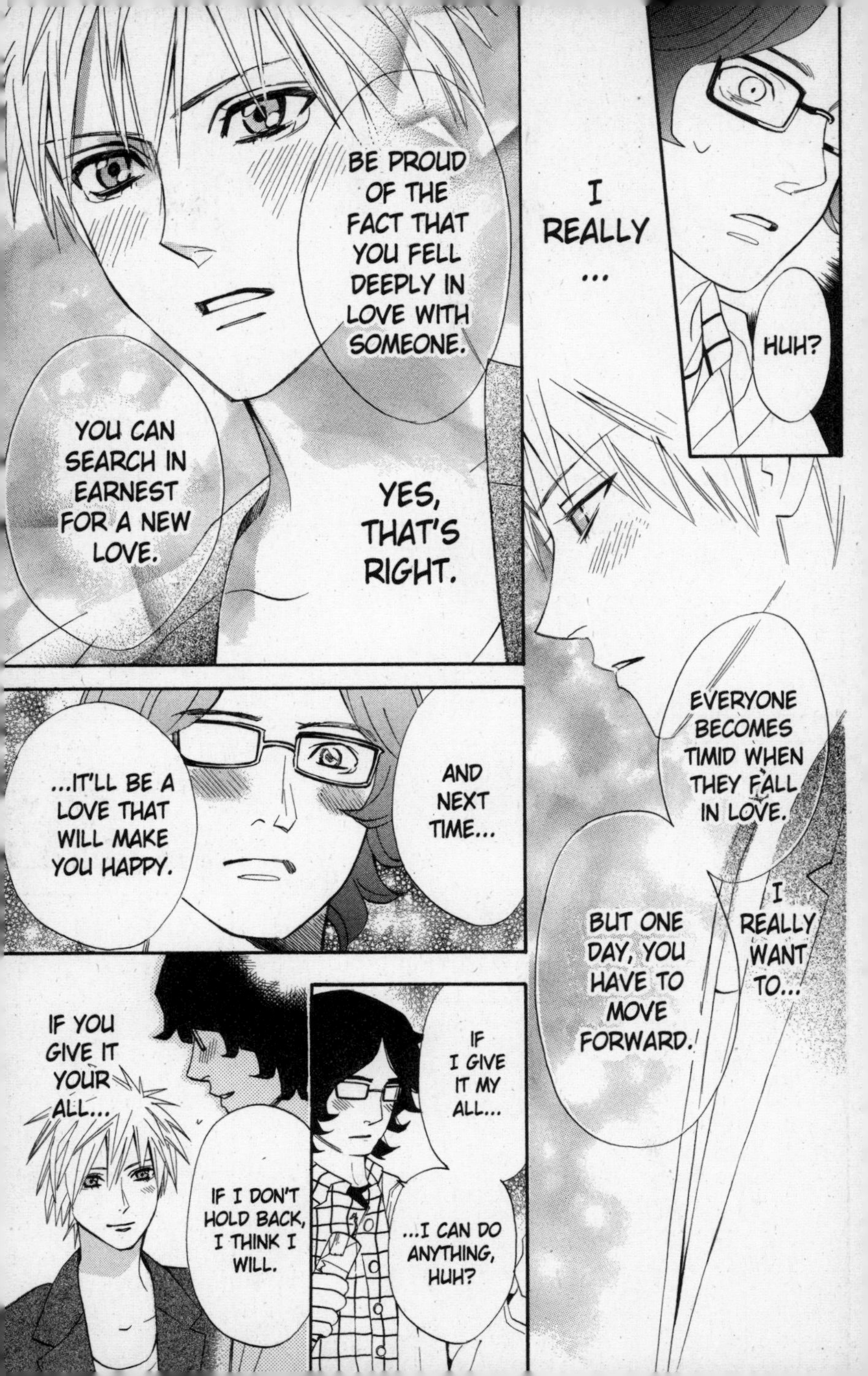
I REALLY ...
HUH?
EVERYONE BECOMES TIMID WHEN THEY FALL IN LOVE.
I REALLY WANT TO...
BUT ONE DAY, YOU HAVE TO MOVE FORWARD.
BE PROUD OF THE FACT THAT YOU FELL DEEPLY IN LOVE WITH SOMEONE.
YES, THAT'S RIGHT.
YOU CAN SEARCH IN EARNEST FOR A NEW LOVE.
AND NEXT TIME...
...IT'LL BE A LOVE THAT WILL MAKE YOU HAPPY.
IF I GIVE IT MY ALL...
...I CAN DO ANYTHING, HUH?
IF YOU GIVE IT YOUR ALL...
IF I DON'T HOLD BACK, I THINK I WILL.

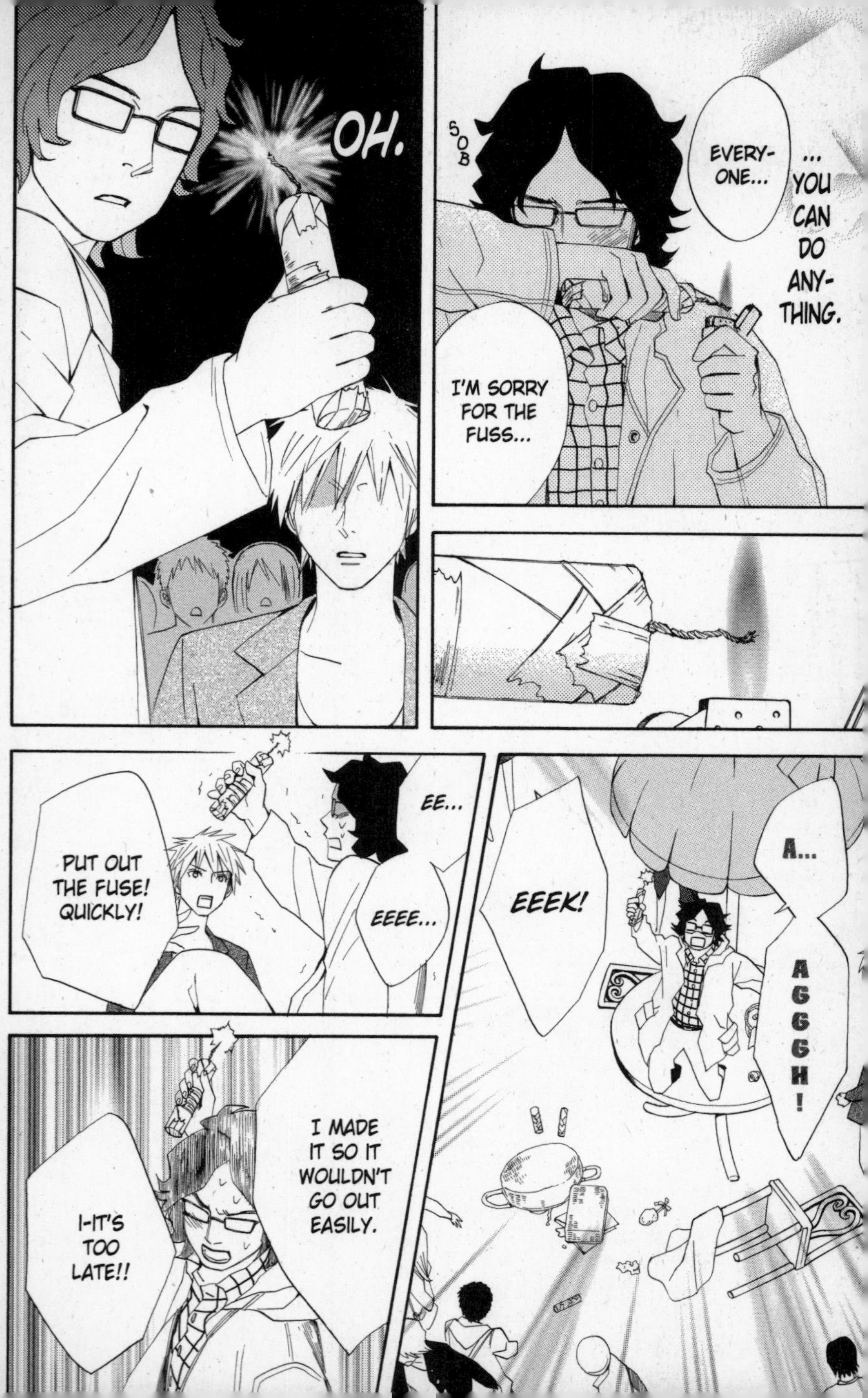
SOB
EVERY-ONE...
... YOU CAN DO ANY-THING.
I'M SORRY FOR THE FUSS...
OH.
A... AGGGH!
EEEK!
EE...
EEEE...
PUT OUT THE FUSE! QUICKLY!
I MADE IT SO IT WOULDN'T GO OUT EASILY.
I-IT'S TOO LATE!!

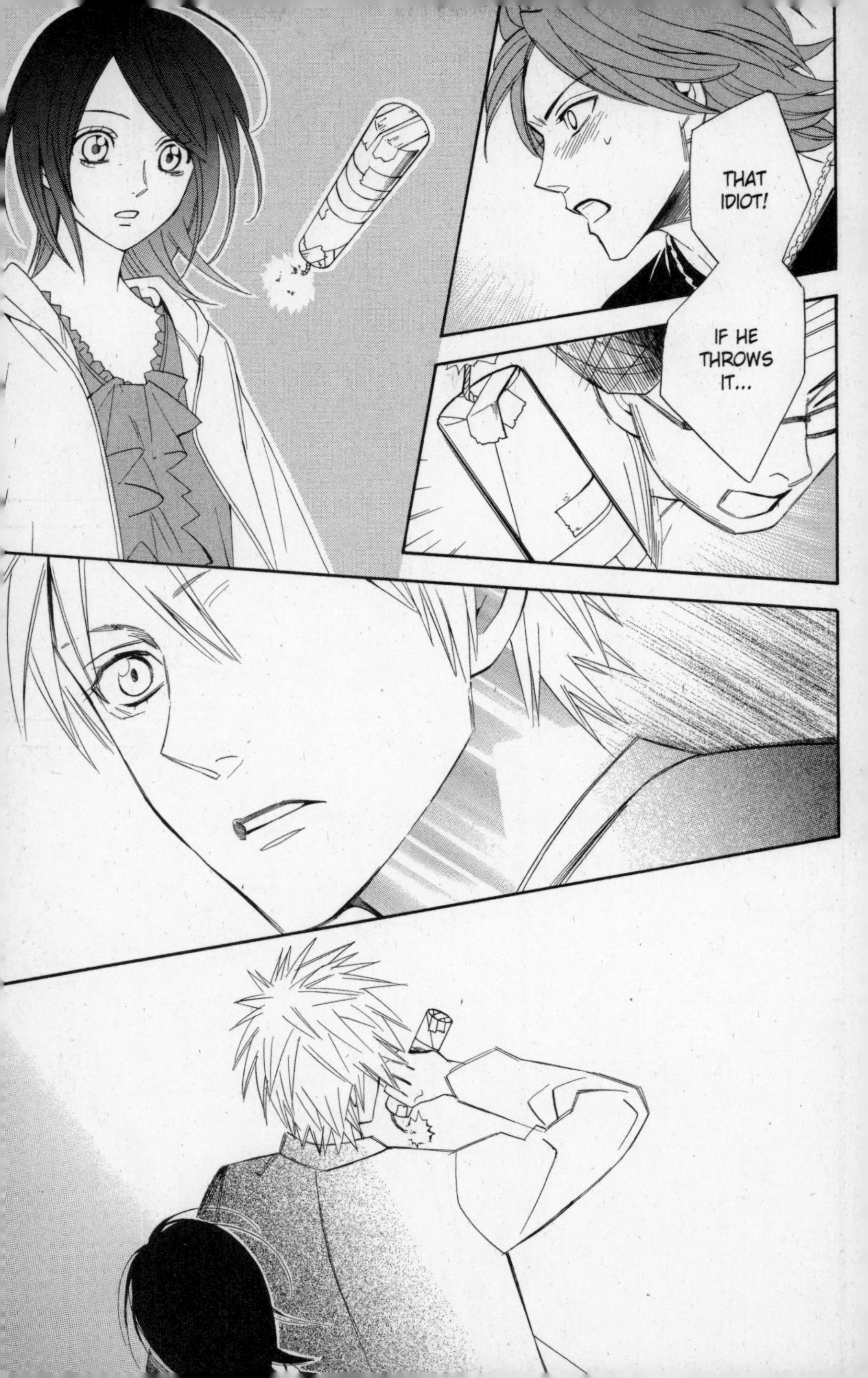
THAT IDIOT!
IF HE THROWS IT...

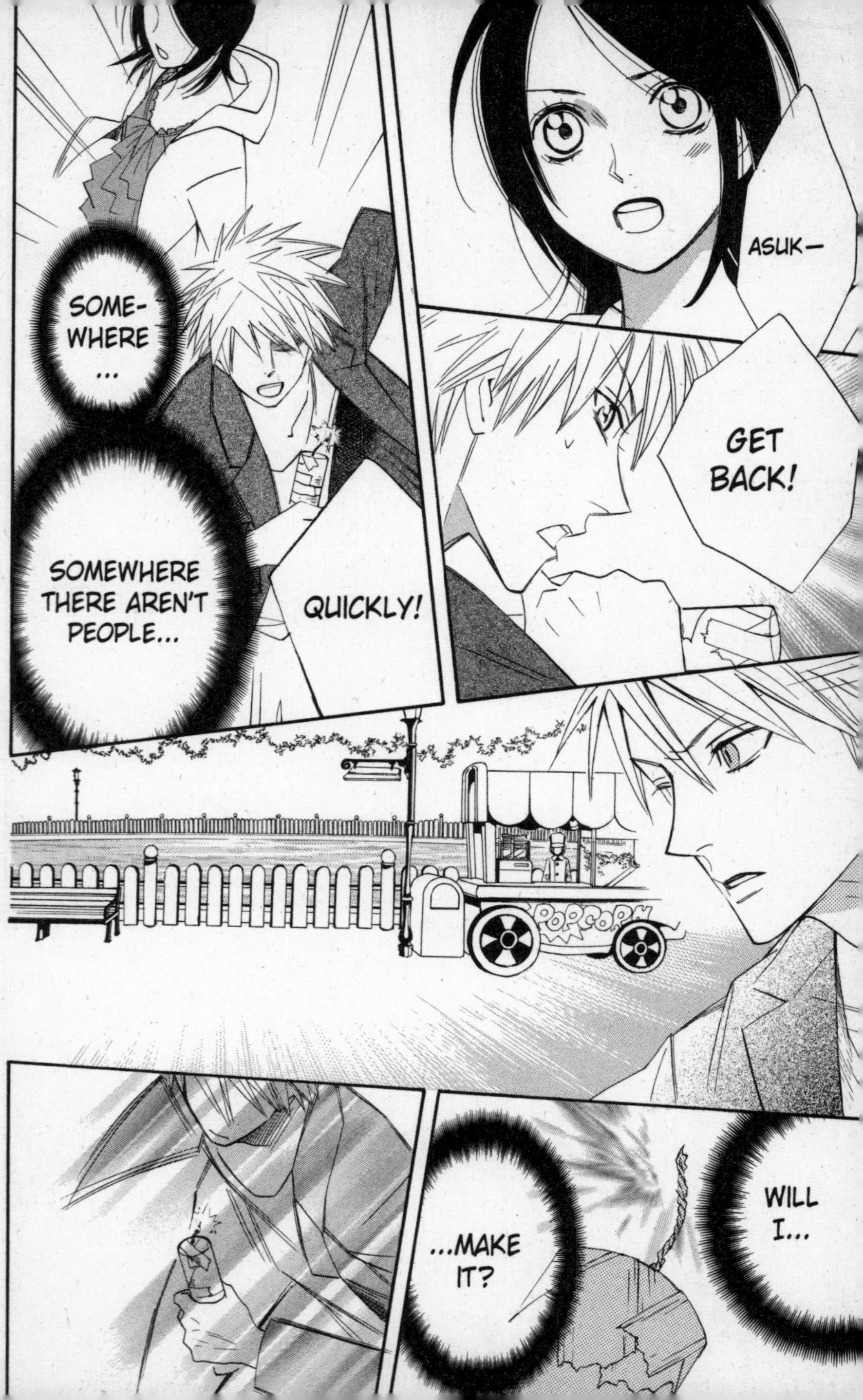
ASUK—
GET BACK!
SOME-WHERE...
QUICKLY!
SOMEWHERE THERE AREN'T PEOPLE...
WILL I...
...MAKE IT?

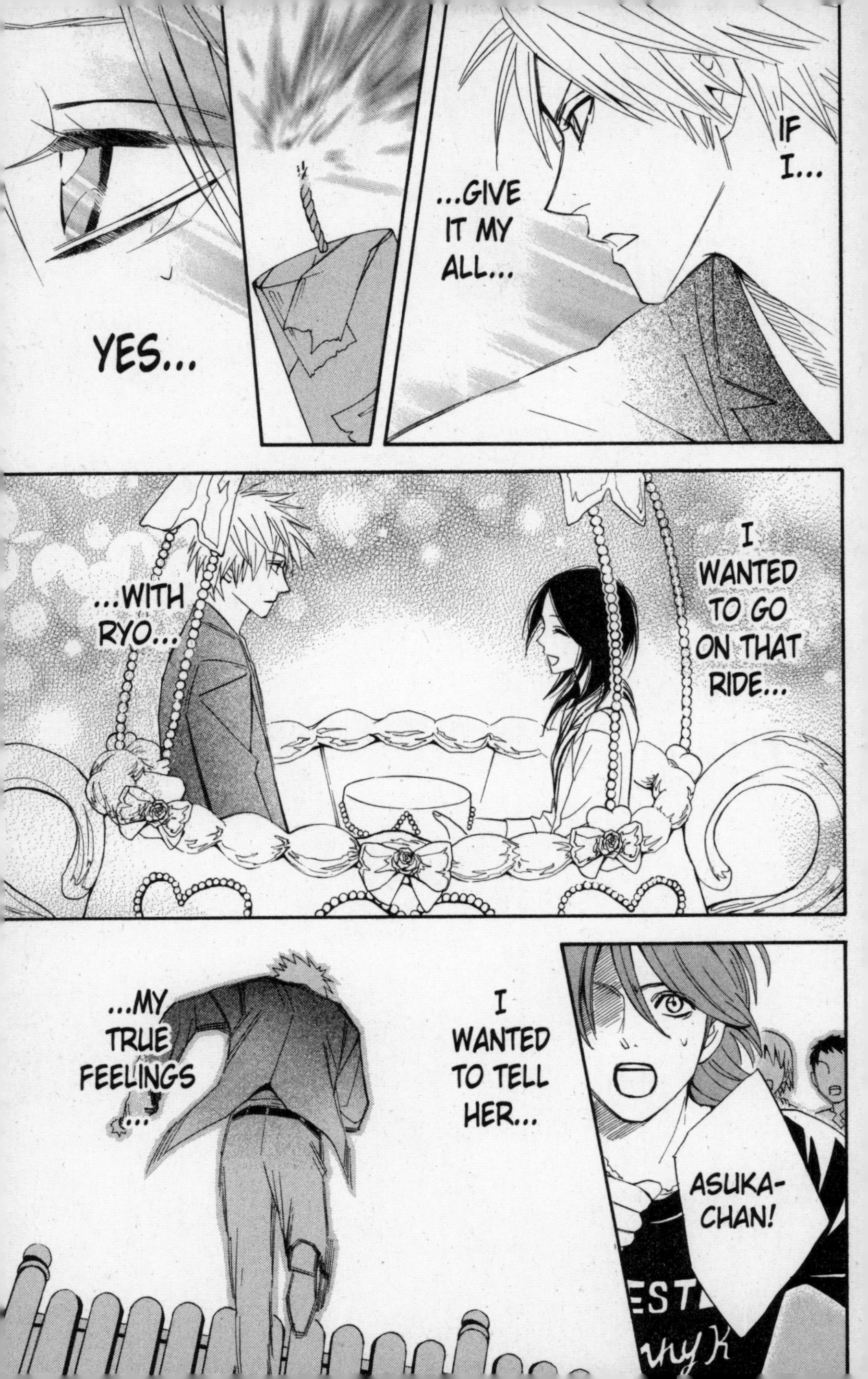
IF I...
...GIVE IT MY ALL...
YES...
I WANTED TO GO ON THAT RIDE...
...WITH RYO...
ASUKA-CHAN!
I WANTED TO TELL HER...
...MY TRUE FEELINGS...

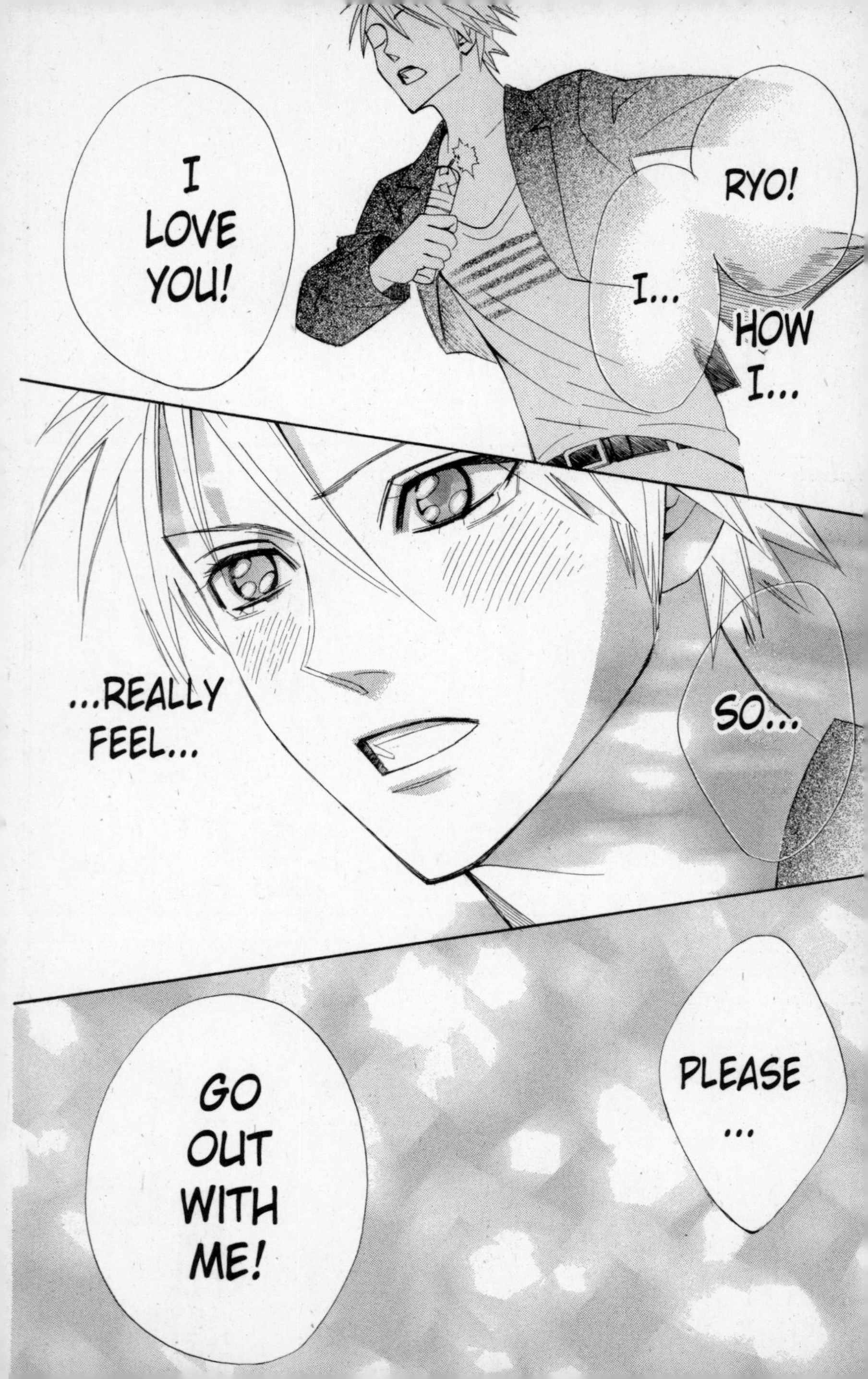
RYO!
I...
HOW I...
I LOVE YOU!
...REALLY FEEL...
SO...
PLEASE ...
GO OUT WITH ME!

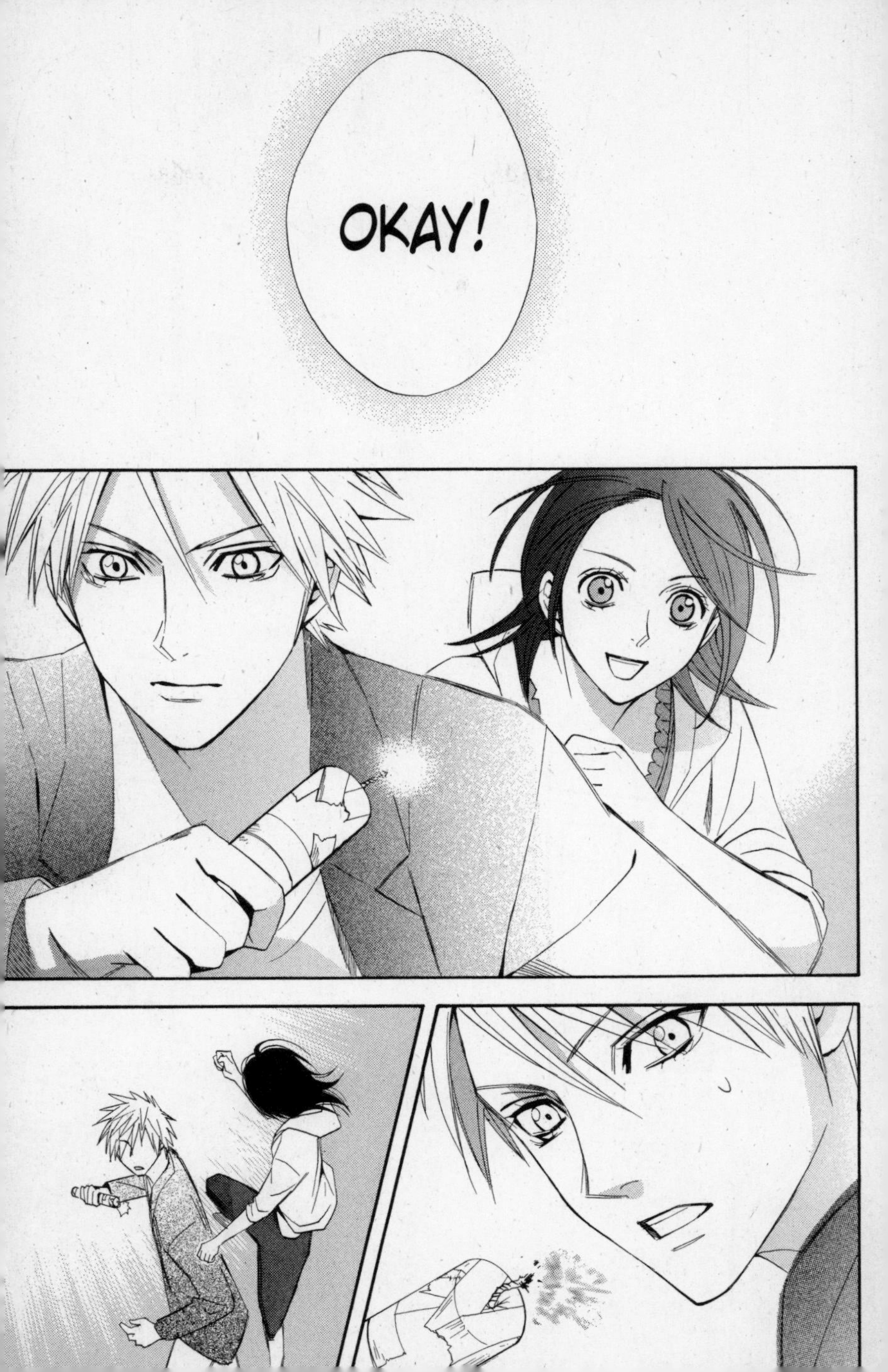
OKAY!

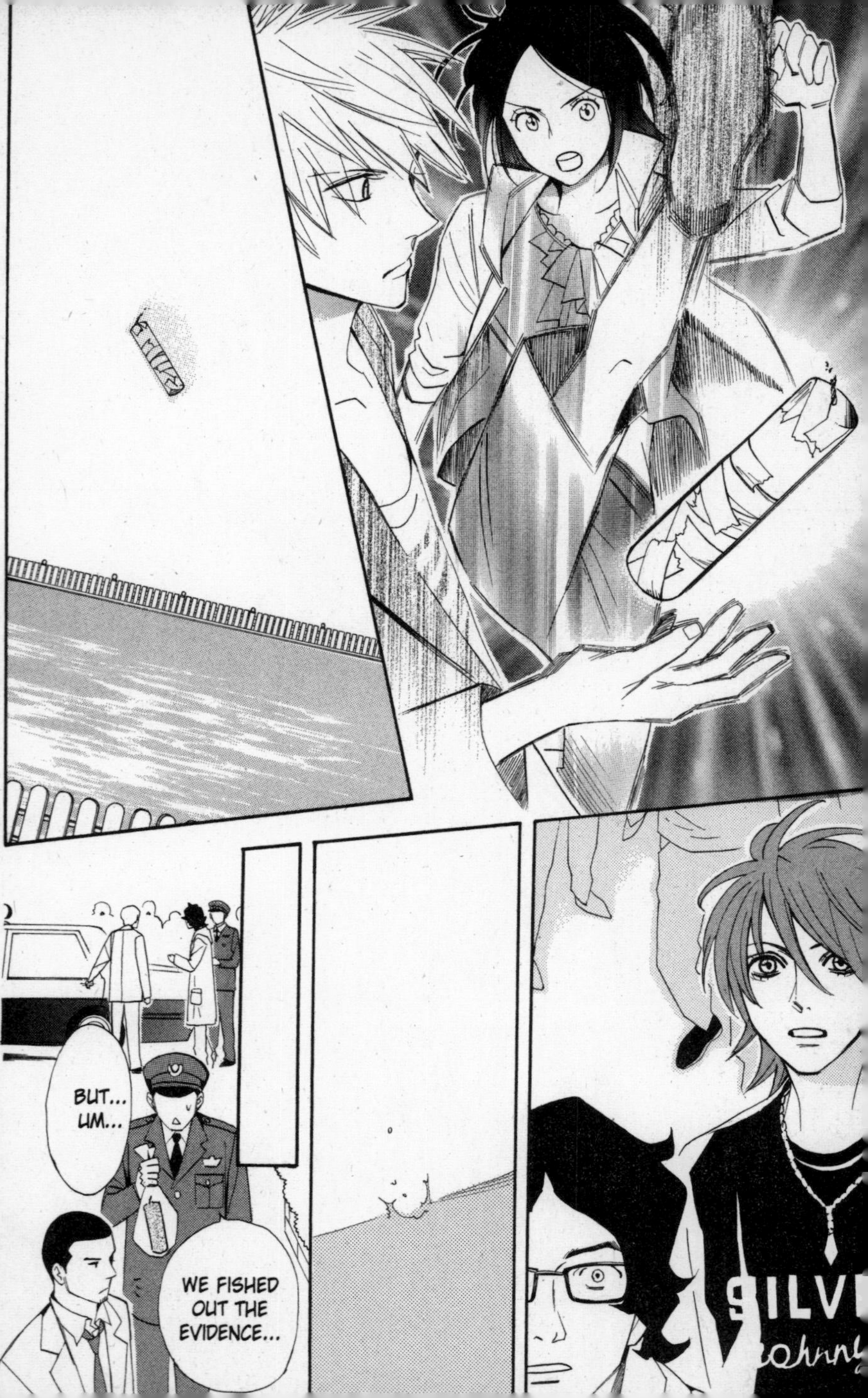
BUT... UM...
WE FISHED OUT THE EVIDENCE...

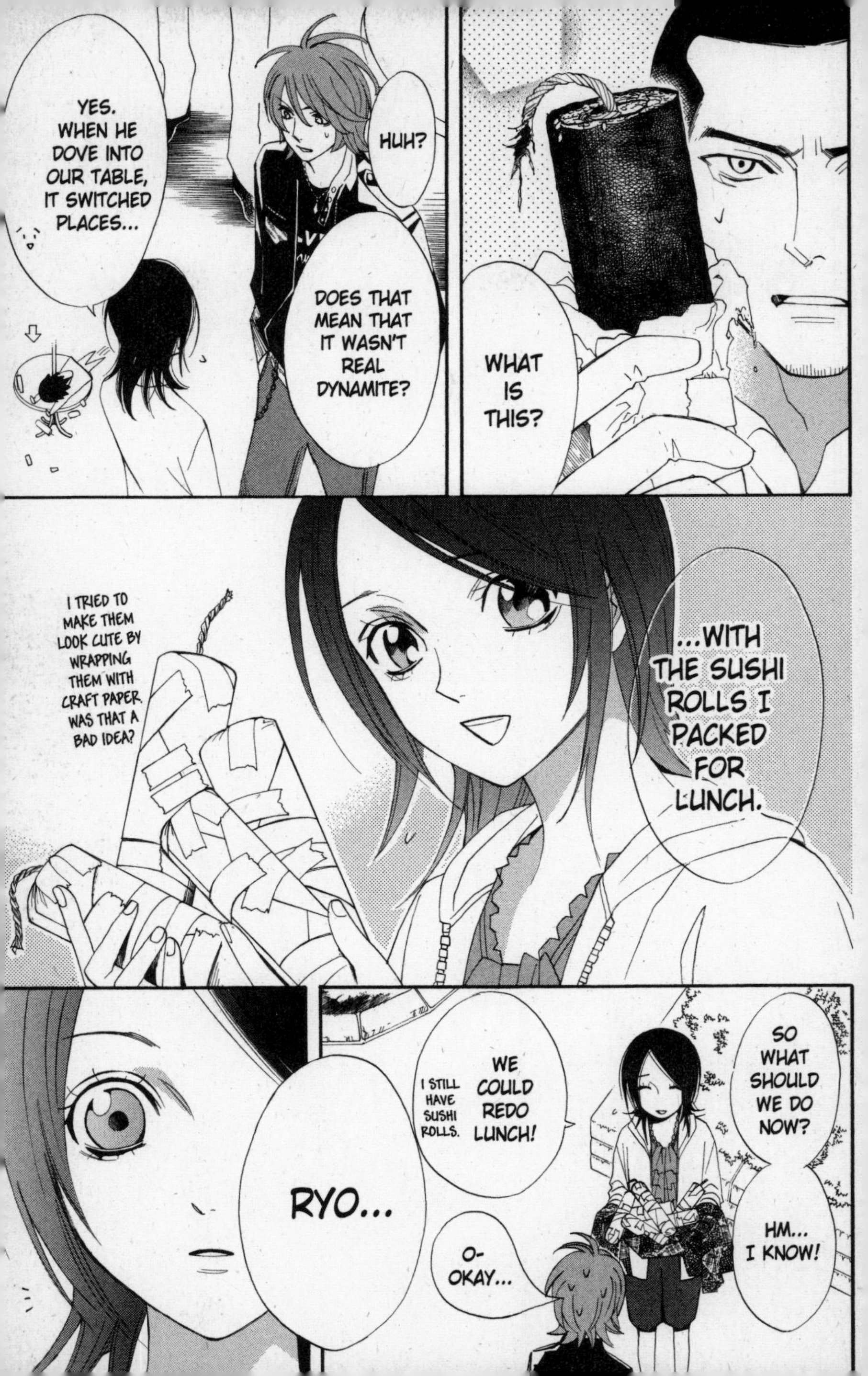

WHAT IS THIS?
HUH?
DOES THAT MEAN THAT IT WASN'T REAL DYNAMITE?
YES. WHEN HE DOVE INTO OUR TABLE, IT SWITCHED PLACES...
...WITH THE SUSHI ROLLS I PACKED FOR LUNCH.
I TRIED TO MAKE THEM LOOK CUTE BY WRAPPING THEM WITH CRAFT PAPER. WAS THAT A BAD IDEA?
SO WHAT SHOULD WE DO NOW?
HM... I KNOW!
WE COULD REDO LUNCH!
I STILL HAVE SUSHI ROLLS.
O-OKAY...
RYO...

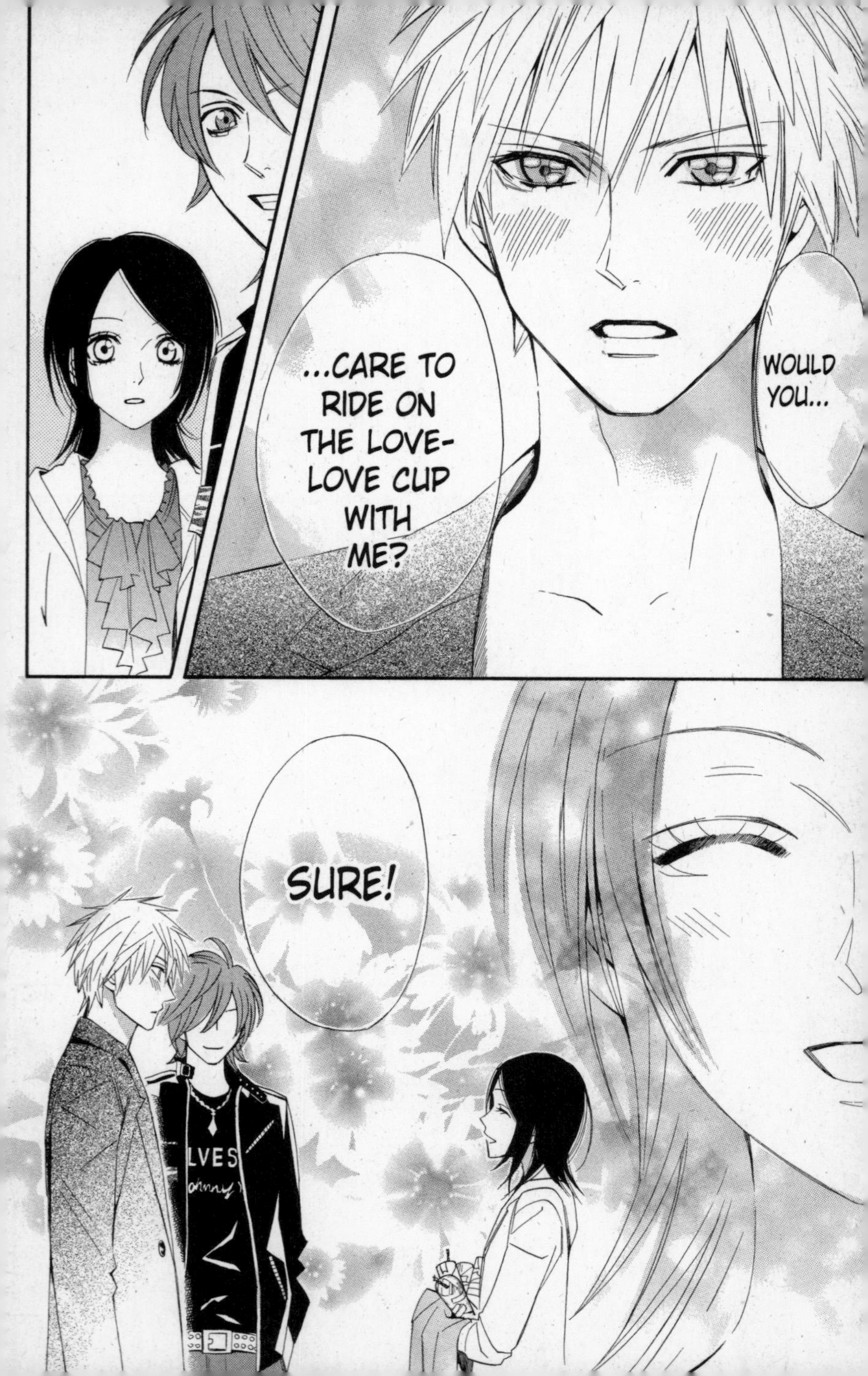
WOULD YOU...
...CARE TO RIDE ON THE LOVE-LOVE CUP WITH ME?
SURE!

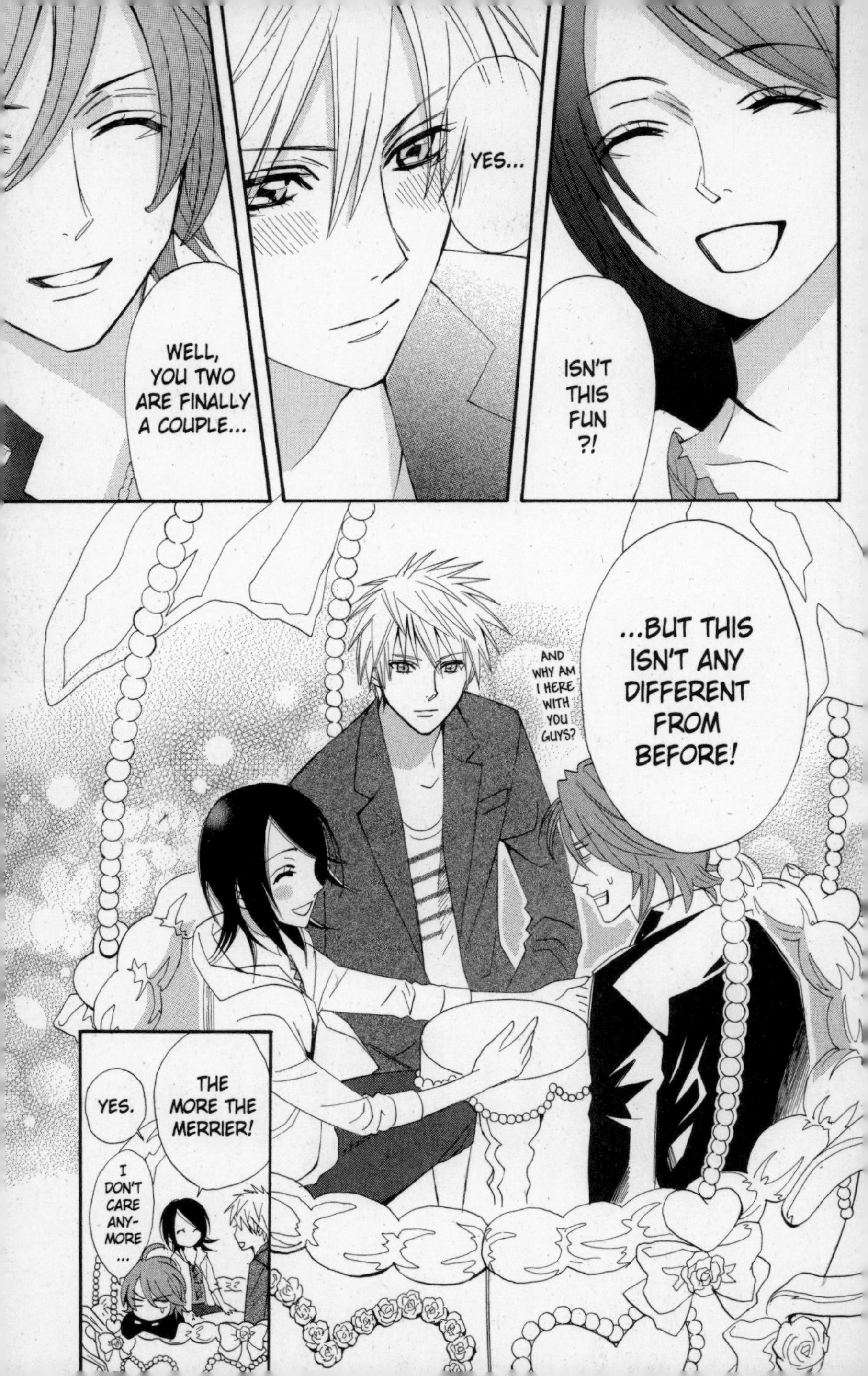
ISN'T THIS FUN ?!
YES...
WELL, YOU TWO ARE FINALLY A COUPLE...
...BUT THIS ISN'T ANY DIFFERENT FROM BEFORE!
AND WHY AM I HERE WITH YOU GUYS?
THE MORE THE MERRIER!
YES.
I DON'T CARE ANY-MORE ...

OTOMEN

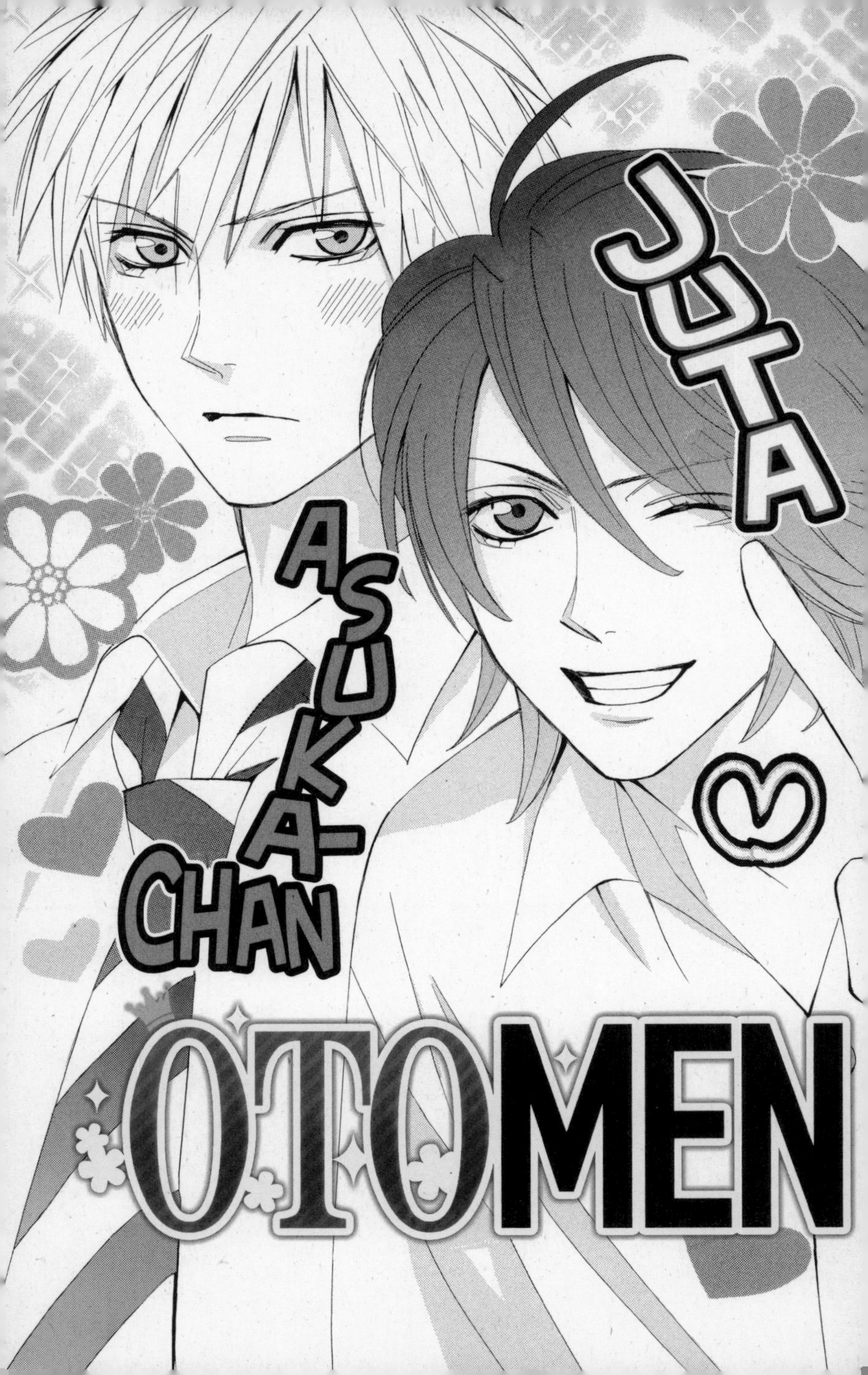
JUTA
ASUKA-CHAN
OTOMEN

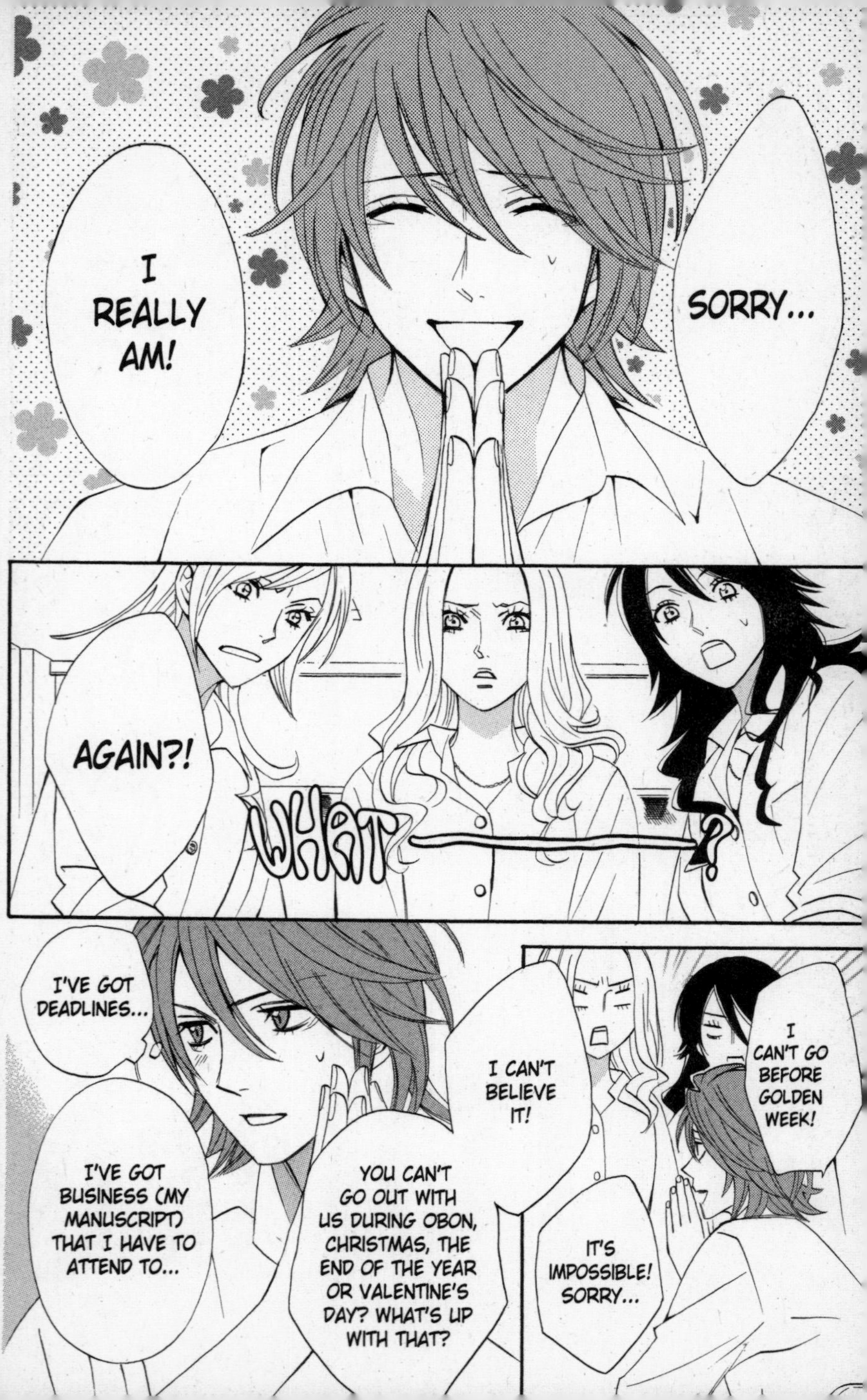
SORRY...
I REALLY AM!
WHAT——?
AGAIN?!
I CAN'T GO BEFORE GOLDEN WEEK!
I CAN'T BELIEVE IT!
IT'S IMPOSSIBLE! SORRY...
YOU CAN'T GO OUT WITH US DURING OBON, CHRISTMAS, THE END OF THE YEAR OR VALENTINE'S DAY? WHAT'S UP WITH THAT?
I'VE GOT DEADLINES...
I'VE GOT BUSINESS (MY MANUSCRIPT) THAT I HAVE TO ATTEND TO...

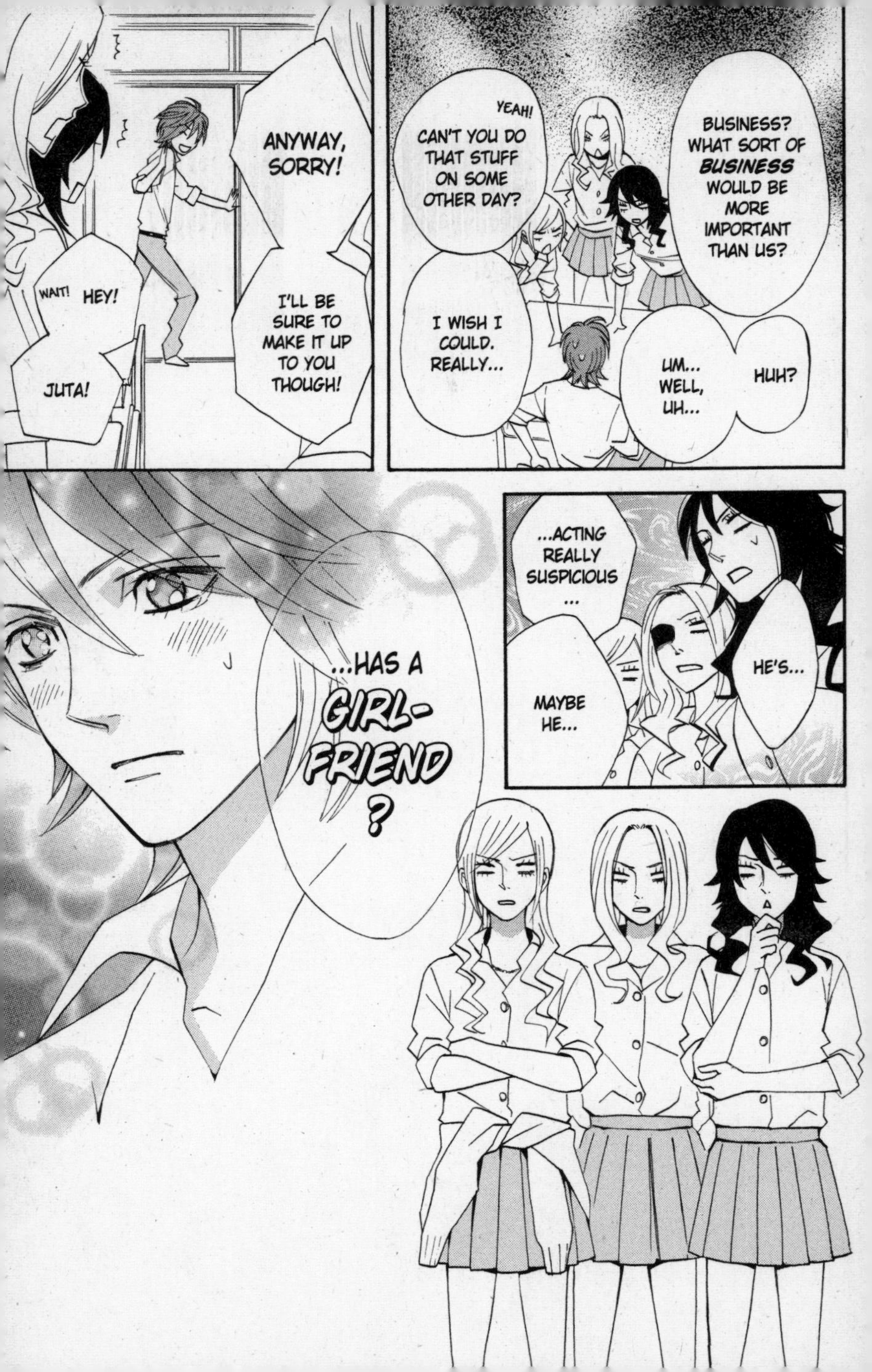
BUSINESS? WHAT SORT OF *BUSINESS* WOULD BE MORE IMPORTANT THAN US?
YEAH!
CAN'T YOU DO THAT STUFF ON SOME OTHER DAY?
HUH?
UM... WELL, UH...
I WISH I COULD. REALLY...
ANYWAY, SORRY!
I'LL BE SURE TO MAKE IT UP TO YOU THOUGH!
HEY!
WAIT!
JUTA!
HE'S...
...ACTING REALLY SUSPICIOUS ...
MAYBE HE...
...HAS A GIRL-FRIEND ?

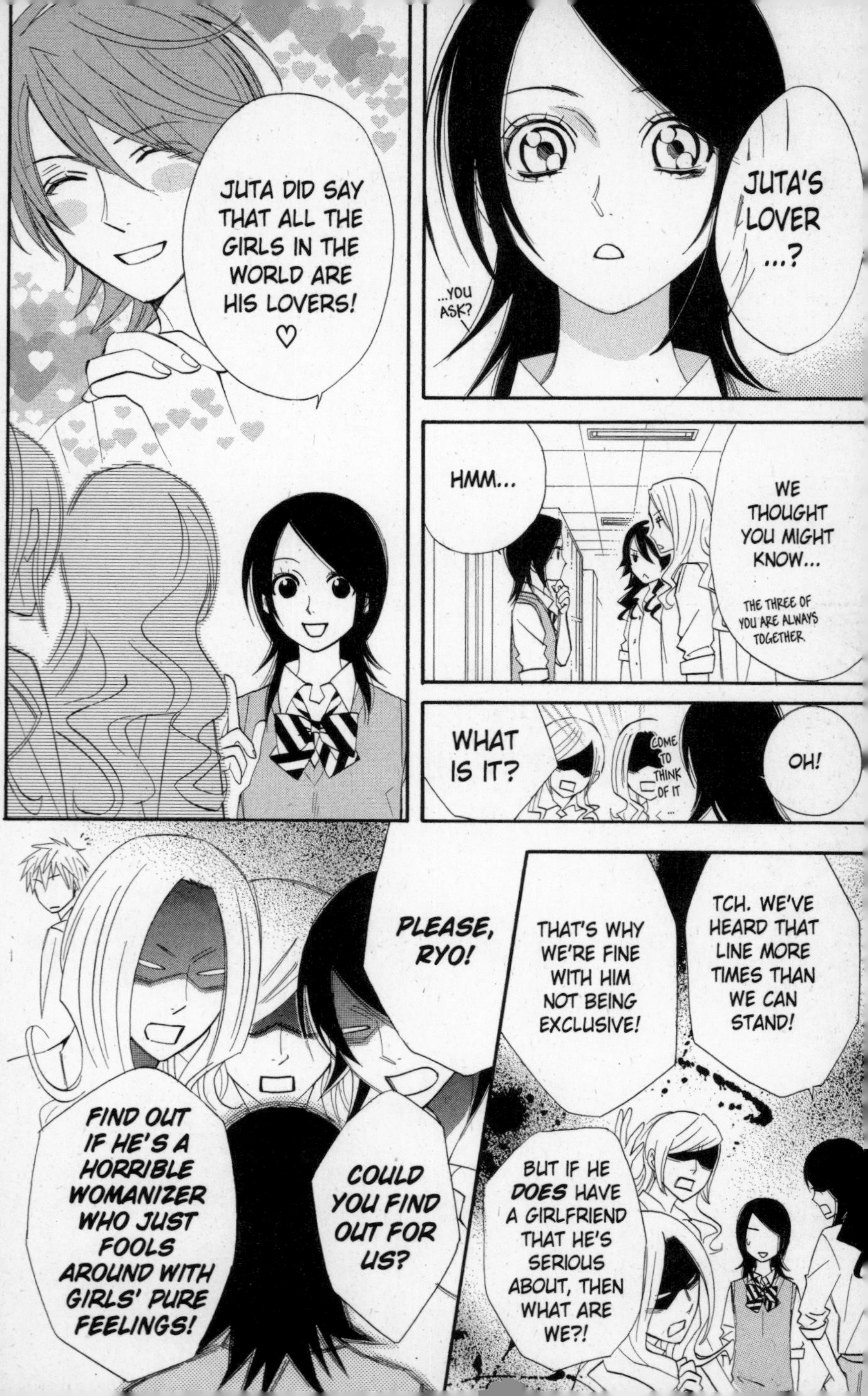
JUTA'S LOVER ...?
...YOU ASK?
WE THOUGHT YOU MIGHT KNOW...
THE THREE OF YOU ARE ALWAYS TOGETHER
HMM...
OH!
COME TO THINK OF IT ...
WHAT IS IT?
JUTA DID SAY THAT ALL THE GIRLS IN THE WORLD ARE HIS LOVERS! ♡
TCH. WE'VE HEARD THAT LINE MORE TIMES THAN WE CAN STAND!
THAT'S WHY WE'RE FINE WITH HIM NOT BEING EXCLUSIVE!
BUT IF HE *DOES* HAVE A GIRLFRIEND THAT HE'S SERIOUS ABOUT, THEN WHAT ARE WE?!
PLEASE, RYO!
COULD YOU FIND OUT FOR US?
FIND OUT IF HE'S A HORRIBLE WOMANIZER WHO JUST FOOLS AROUND WITH GIRLS' PURE FEELINGS!

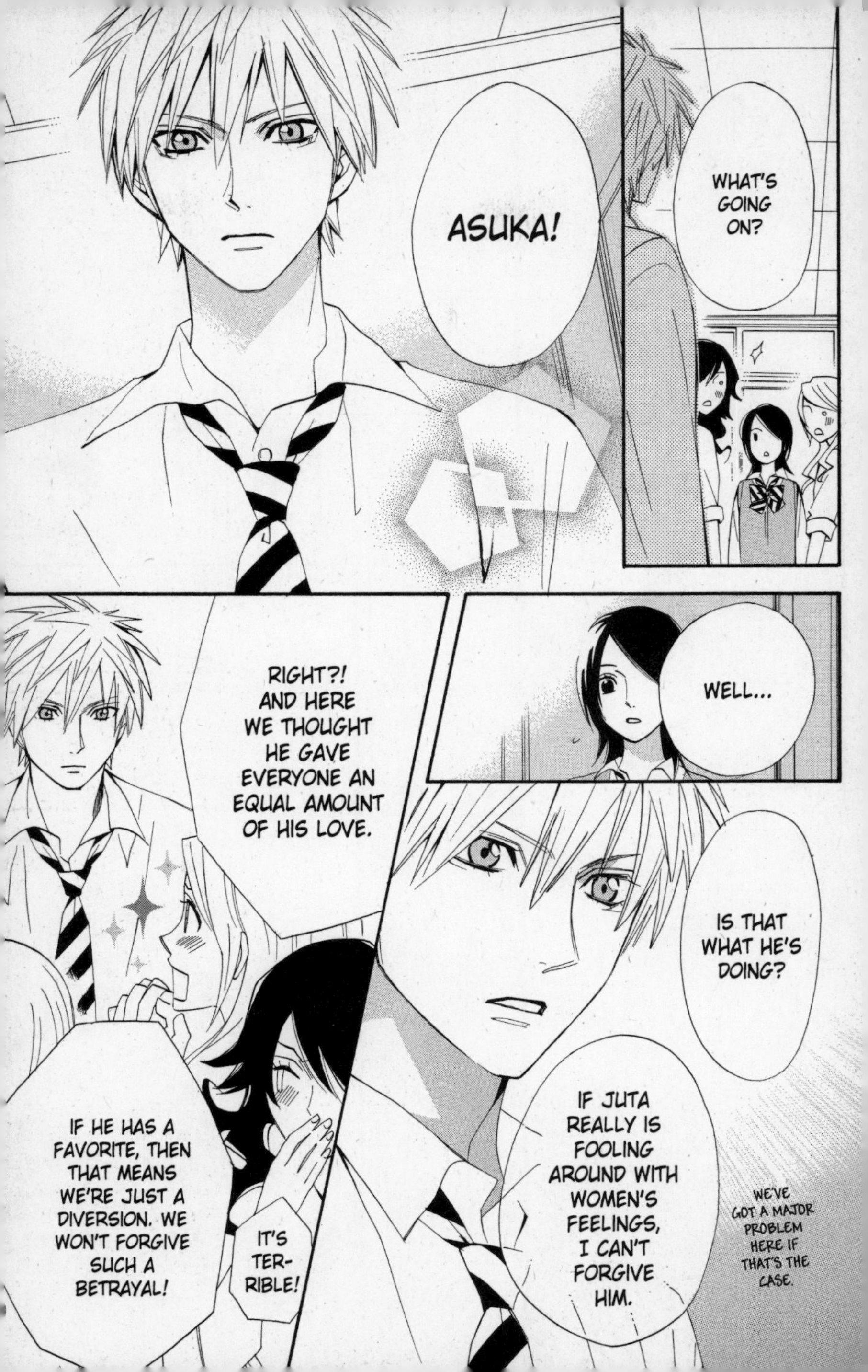
WHAT'S GOING ON?
ASUKA!
WELL...
RIGHT?! AND HERE WE THOUGHT HE GAVE EVERYONE AN EQUAL AMOUNT OF HIS LOVE.
IF HE HAS A FAVORITE, THEN THAT MEANS WE'RE JUST A DIVERSION. WE WON'T FORGIVE SUCH A BETRAYAL!
IT'S TER-RIBLE!
IS THAT WHAT HE'S DOING?
IF JUTA REALLY IS FOOLING AROUND WITH WOMEN'S FEELINGS, I CAN'T FORGIVE HIM.
WE'VE GOT A MAJOR PROBLEM HERE IF THAT'S THE CASE.

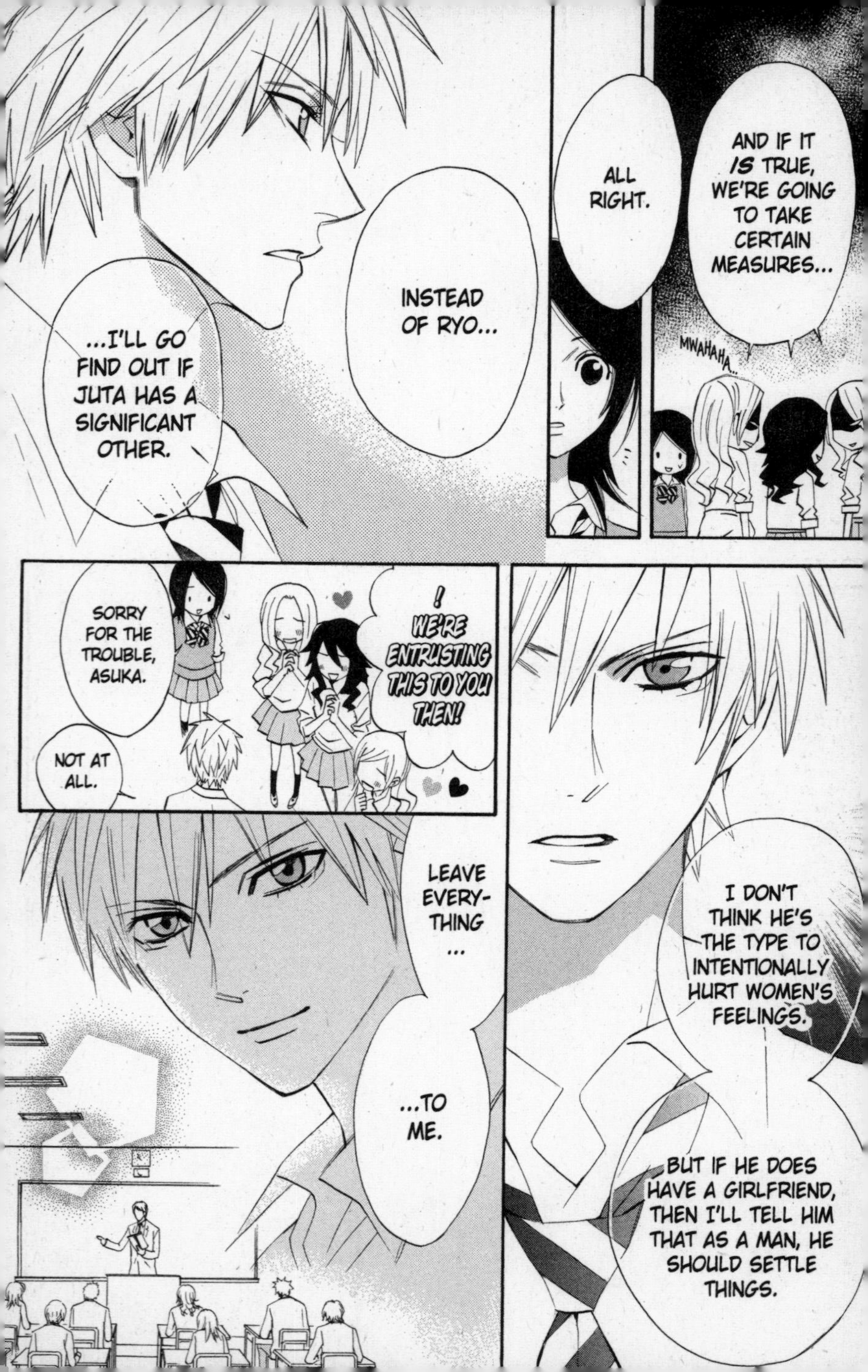
AND IF IT IS TRUE, WE'RE GOING TO TAKE CERTAIN MEASURES...
MWAHAHA...
ALL RIGHT.
INSTEAD OF RYO...
...I'LL GO FIND OUT IF JUTA HAS A SIGNIFICANT OTHER.
I DON'T THINK HE'S THE TYPE TO INTENTIONALLY HURT WOMEN'S FEELINGS.
BUT IF HE DOES HAVE A GIRLFRIEND, THEN I'LL TELL HIM THAT AS A MAN, HE SHOULD SETTLE THINGS.
! WE'RE ENTRUSTING THIS TO YOU THEN!
SORRY FOR THE TROUBLE, ASUKA.
NOT AT ALL.
LEAVE EVERY-THING...
...TO ME.

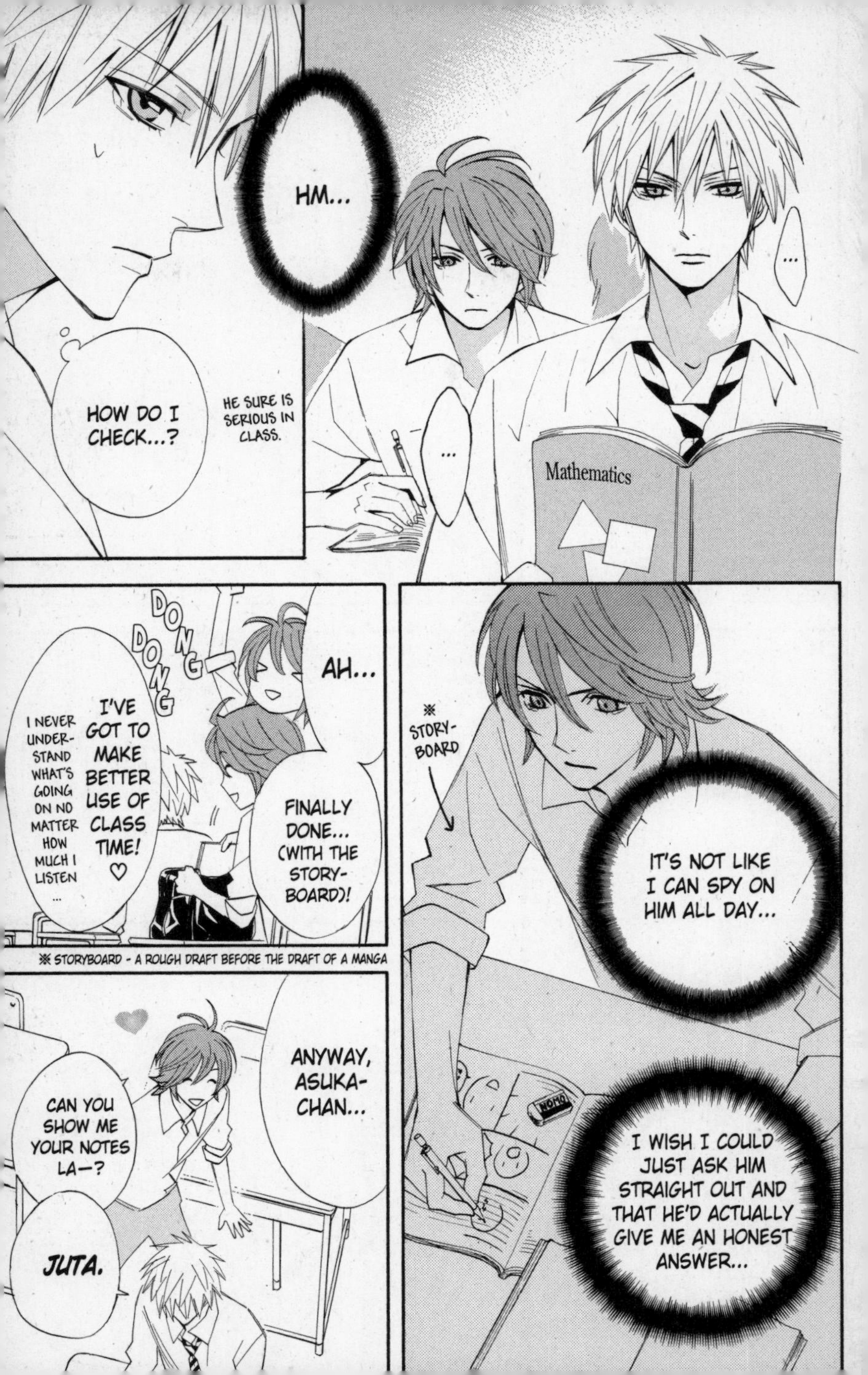
...
HM...
Mathematics
...
HE SURE IS SERIOUS IN CLASS.
HOW DO I CHECK...?
※ STORY-BOARD
IT'S NOT LIKE I CAN SPY ON HIM ALL DAY...
NOMO
I WISH I COULD JUST ASK HIM STRAIGHT OUT AND THAT HE'D ACTUALLY GIVE ME AN HONEST ANSWER...
AH...
FINALLY DONE... (WITH THE STORY-BOARD)!
DONG DONG
I'VE GOT TO MAKE BETTER USE OF CLASS TIME! ♡
I NEVER UNDER-STAND WHAT'S GOING ON NO MATTER HOW MUCH I LISTEN ...
※ STORYBOARD - A ROUGH DRAFT BEFORE THE DRAFT OF A MANGA
ANYWAY, ASUKA-CHAN...
CAN YOU SHOW ME YOUR NOTES LA—?
JUTA.

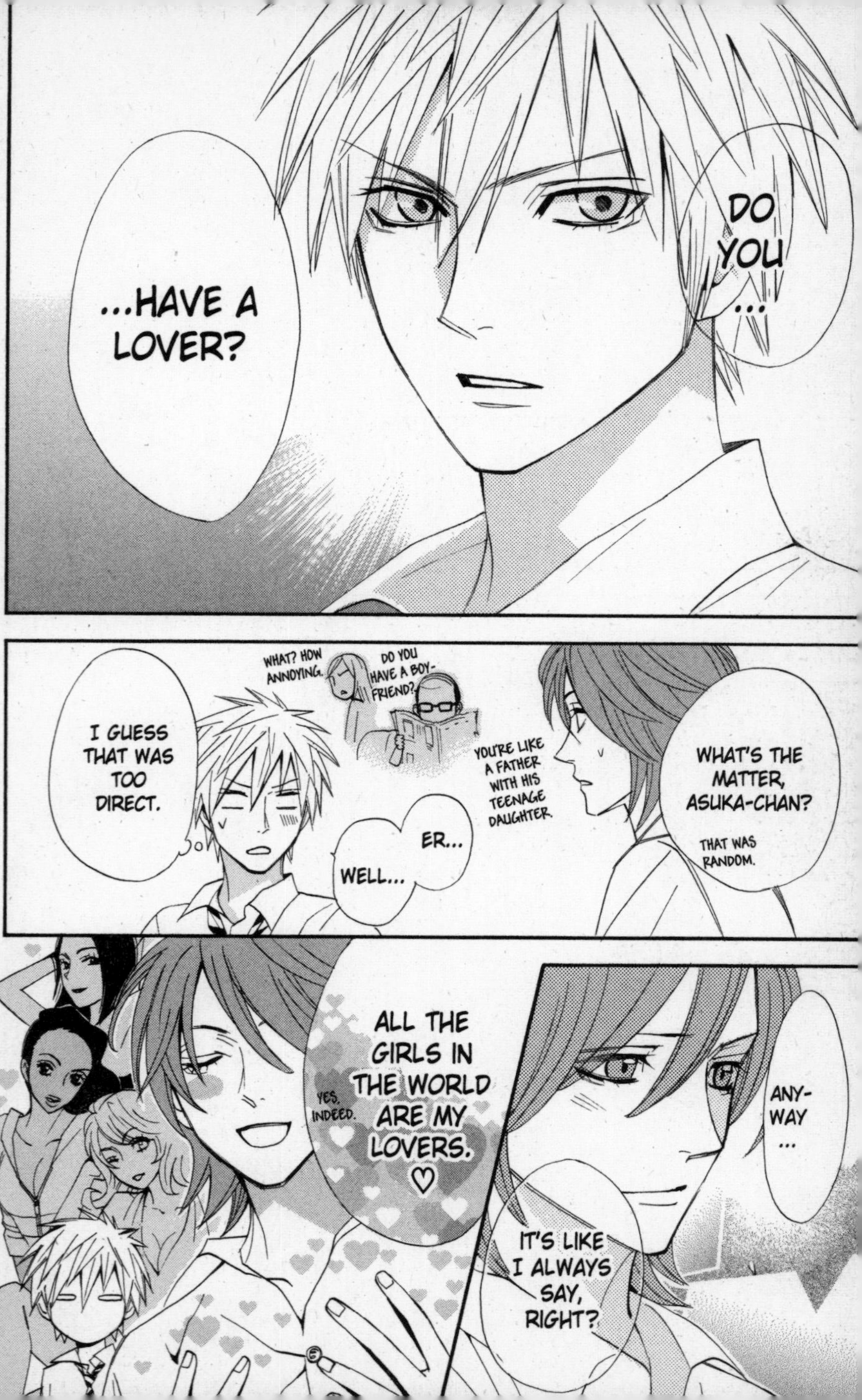
DO YOU ...
...HAVE A LOVER?
WHAT'S THE MATTER, ASUKA-CHAN?
THAT WAS RANDOM.
YOU'RE LIKE A FATHER WITH HIS TEENAGE DAUGHTER.
DO YOU HAVE A BOY-FRIEND?
WHAT? HOW ANNOYING.
ER... WELL...
I GUESS THAT WAS TOO DIRECT.
ANY-WAY ...
IT'S LIKE I ALWAYS SAY, RIGHT?
ALL THE GIRLS IN THE WORLD ARE MY LOVERS. ♡
YES, INDEED.

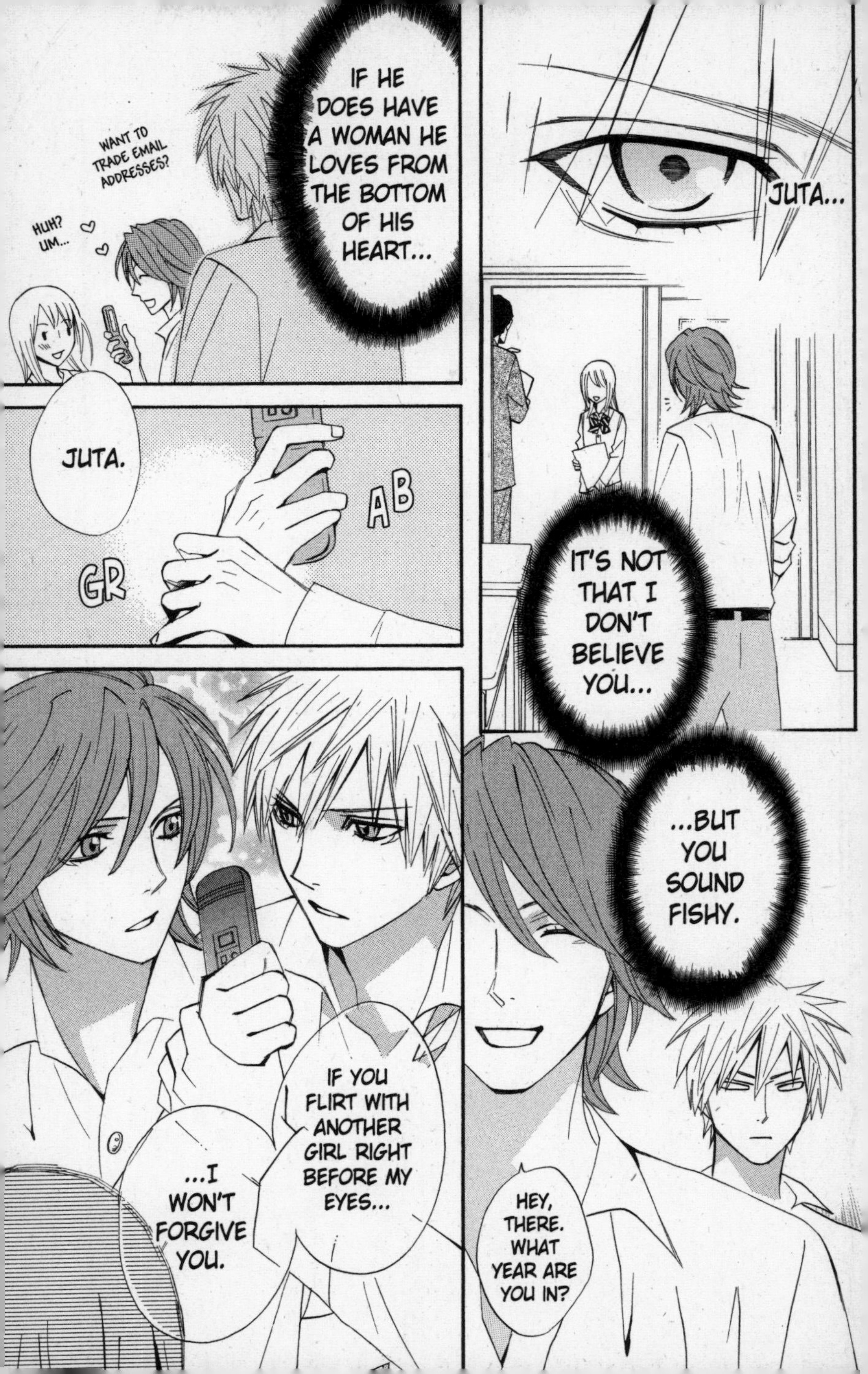
JUTA...
IT'S NOT THAT I DON'T BELIEVE YOU...
...BUT YOU SOUND FISHY.
HEY, THERE. WHAT YEAR ARE YOU IN?
IF HE DOES HAVE A WOMAN HE LOVES FROM THE BOTTOM OF HIS HEART...
WANT TO TRADE EMAIL ADDRESSES?
HUH? UM...
AB
JUTA.
GR
IF YOU FLIRT WITH ANOTHER GIRL RIGHT BEFORE MY EYES...
...I WON'T FORGIVE YOU.

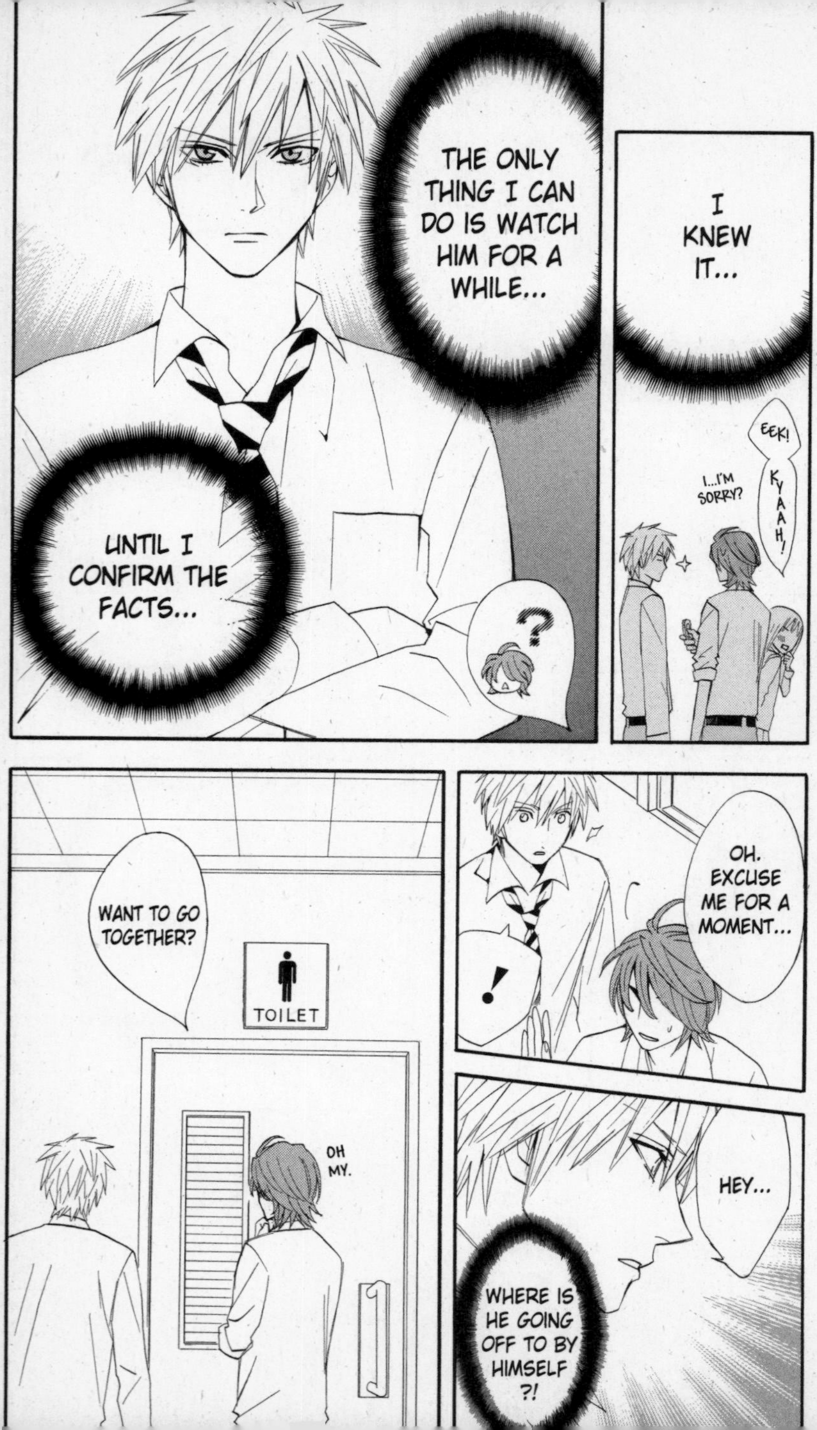
I KNEW IT...
EEK!
KYAAH!
I...I'M SORRY?
THE ONLY THING I CAN DO IS WATCH HIM FOR A WHILE...
UNTIL I CONFIRM THE FACTS...
?
OH. EXCUSE ME FOR A MOMENT...
!
HEY...
WHERE IS HE GOING OFF TO BY HIMSELF ?!
WANT TO GO TOGETHER?
TOILET
OH MY.

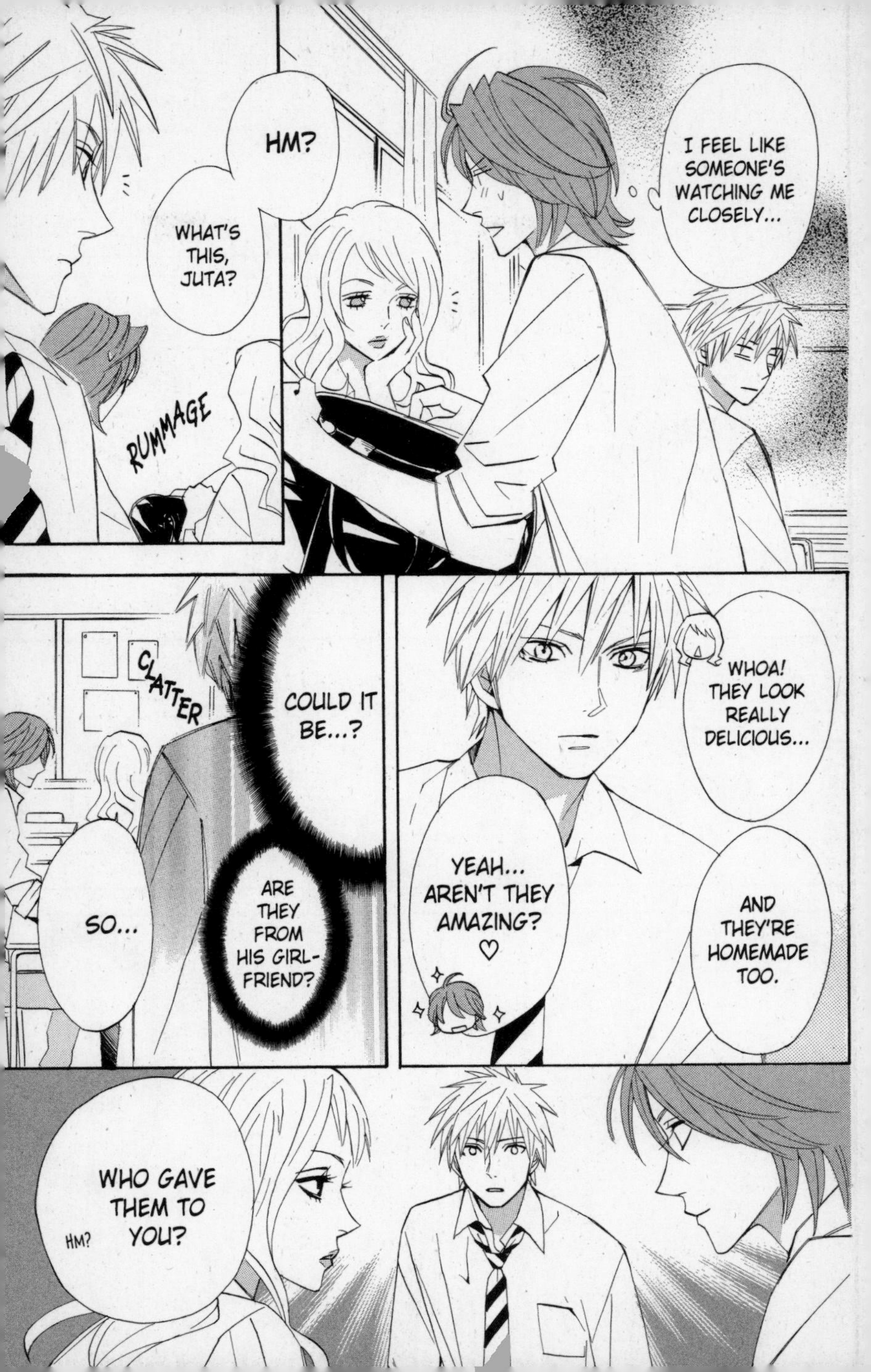
I FEEL LIKE SOMEONE'S WATCHING ME CLOSELY...
HM?
WHAT'S THIS, JUTA?
RUMMAGE
WHOA! THEY LOOK REALLY DELICIOUS...
YEAH... AREN'T THEY AMAZING? ♡
AND THEY'RE HOMEMADE TOO.
CLATTER
COULD IT BE...?
ARE THEY FROM HIS GIRL-FRIEND?
SO...
WHO GAVE THEM TO YOU?
HM?

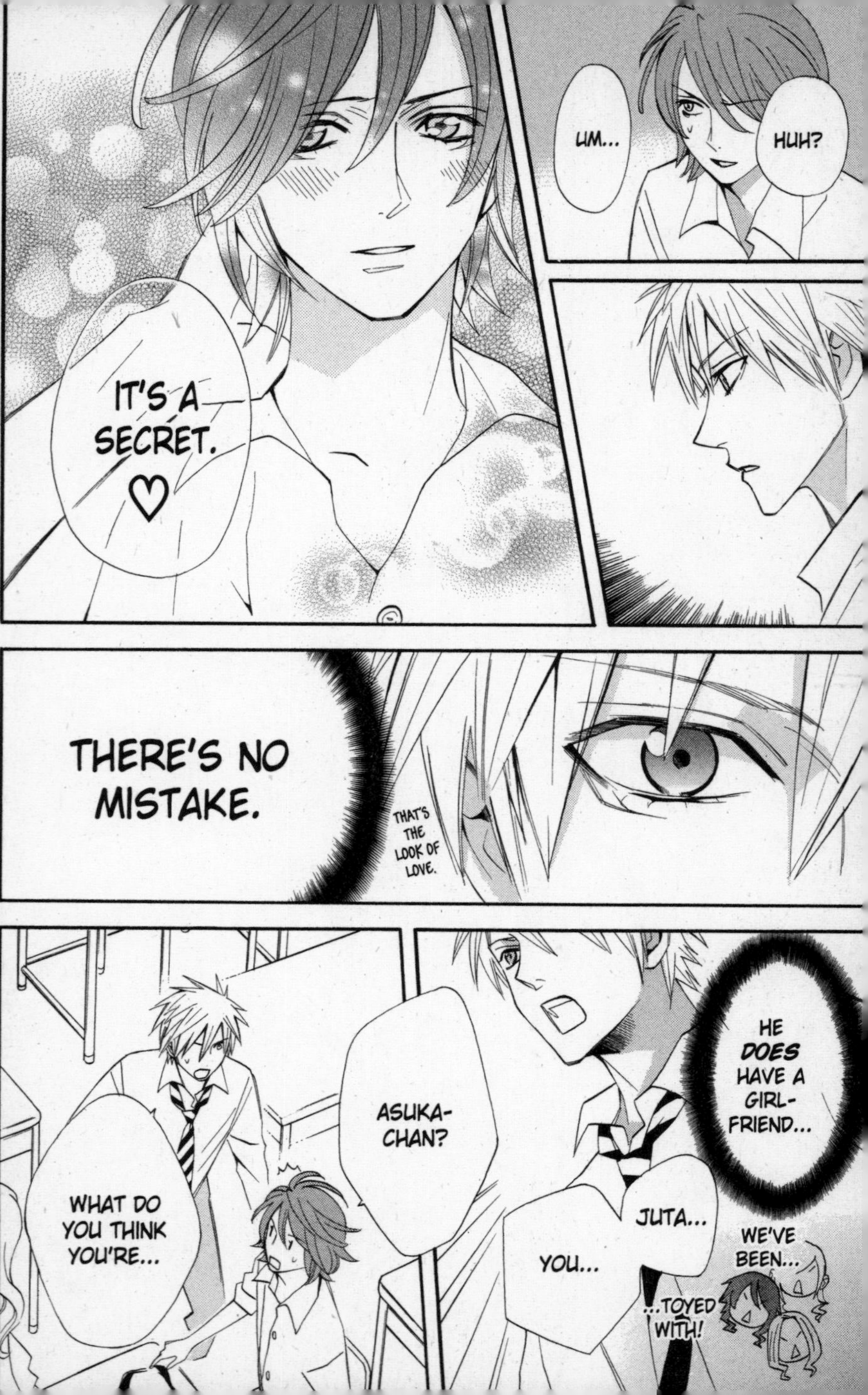
HUH?
UM...
IT'S A SECRET. ♡
THERE'S NO MISTAKE.
THAT'S THE LOOK OF LOVE.
HE *DOES* HAVE A GIRL-FRIEND...
ASUKA-CHAN?
WE'VE BEEN...
...TOYED WITH!
JUTA...
YOU...
WHAT DO YOU THINK YOU'RE...

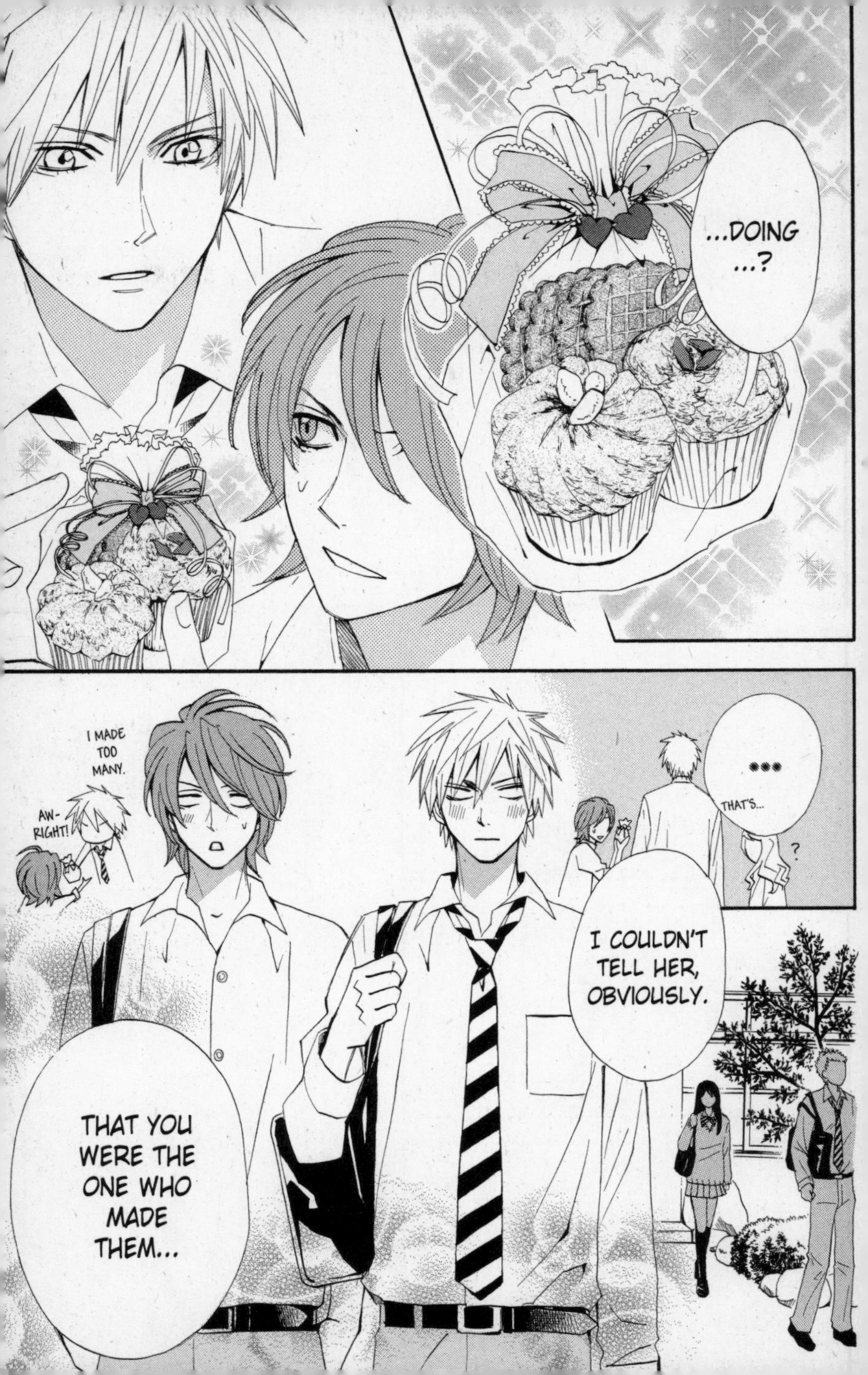
...DOING ...?
...
THAT'S...
?
I COULDN'T TELL HER, OBVIOUSLY.
I MADE TOO MANY.
AW-RIGHT!
THAT YOU WERE THE ONE WHO MADE THEM...

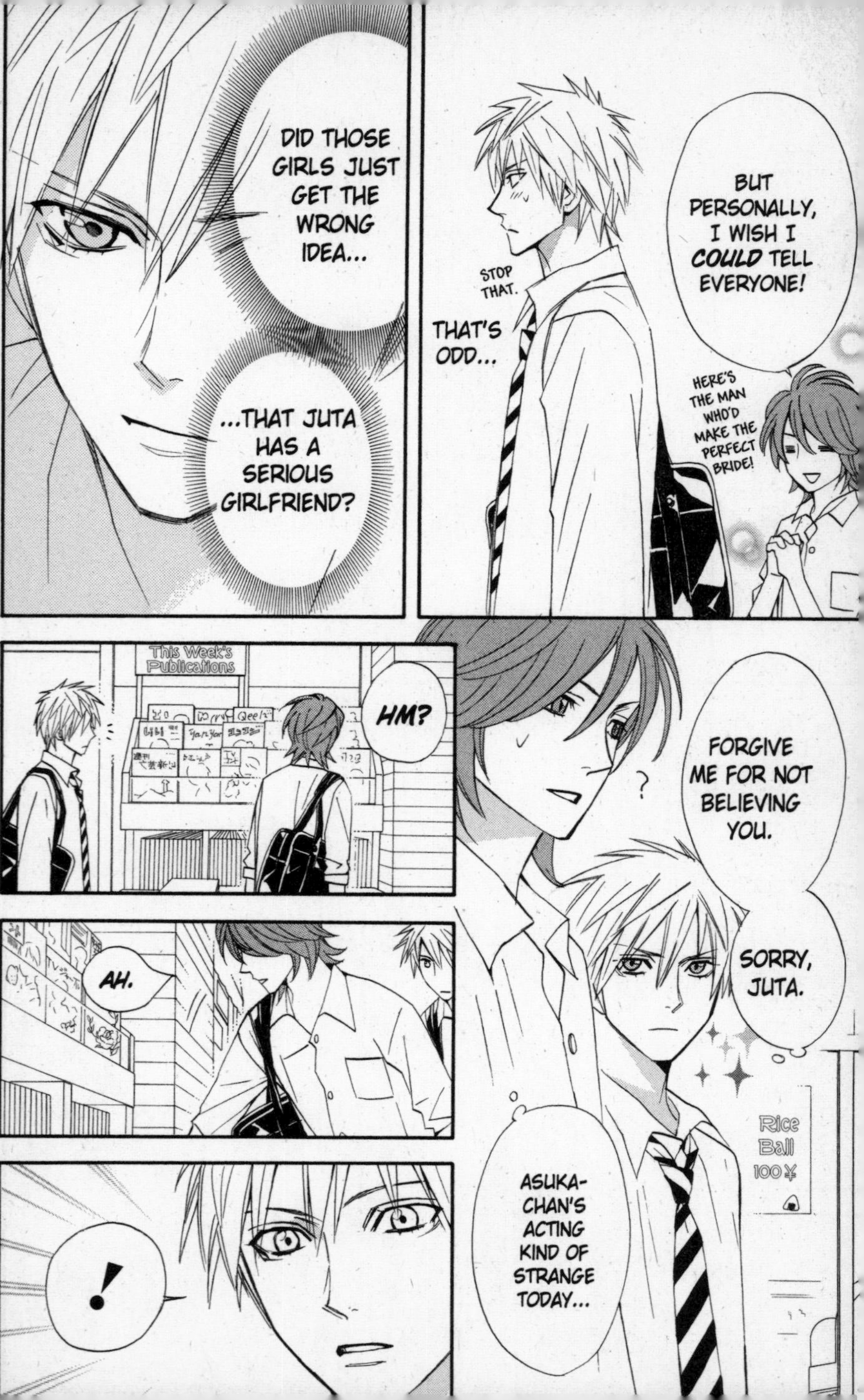
BUT PERSONALLY, I WISH I ***COULD*** TELL EVERYONE!
HERE'S THE MAN WHO'D MAKE THE PERFECT BRIDE!
STOP THAT.
THAT'S ODD...
DID THOSE GIRLS JUST GET THE WRONG IDEA...
...THAT JUTA HAS A SERIOUS GIRLFRIEND?
?
FORGIVE ME FOR NOT BELIEVING YOU.
SORRY, JUTA.
ASUKA-CHAN'S ACTING KIND OF STRANGE TODAY...
Rice Ball 100¥
This Week's Publications
HM?
AH.
!

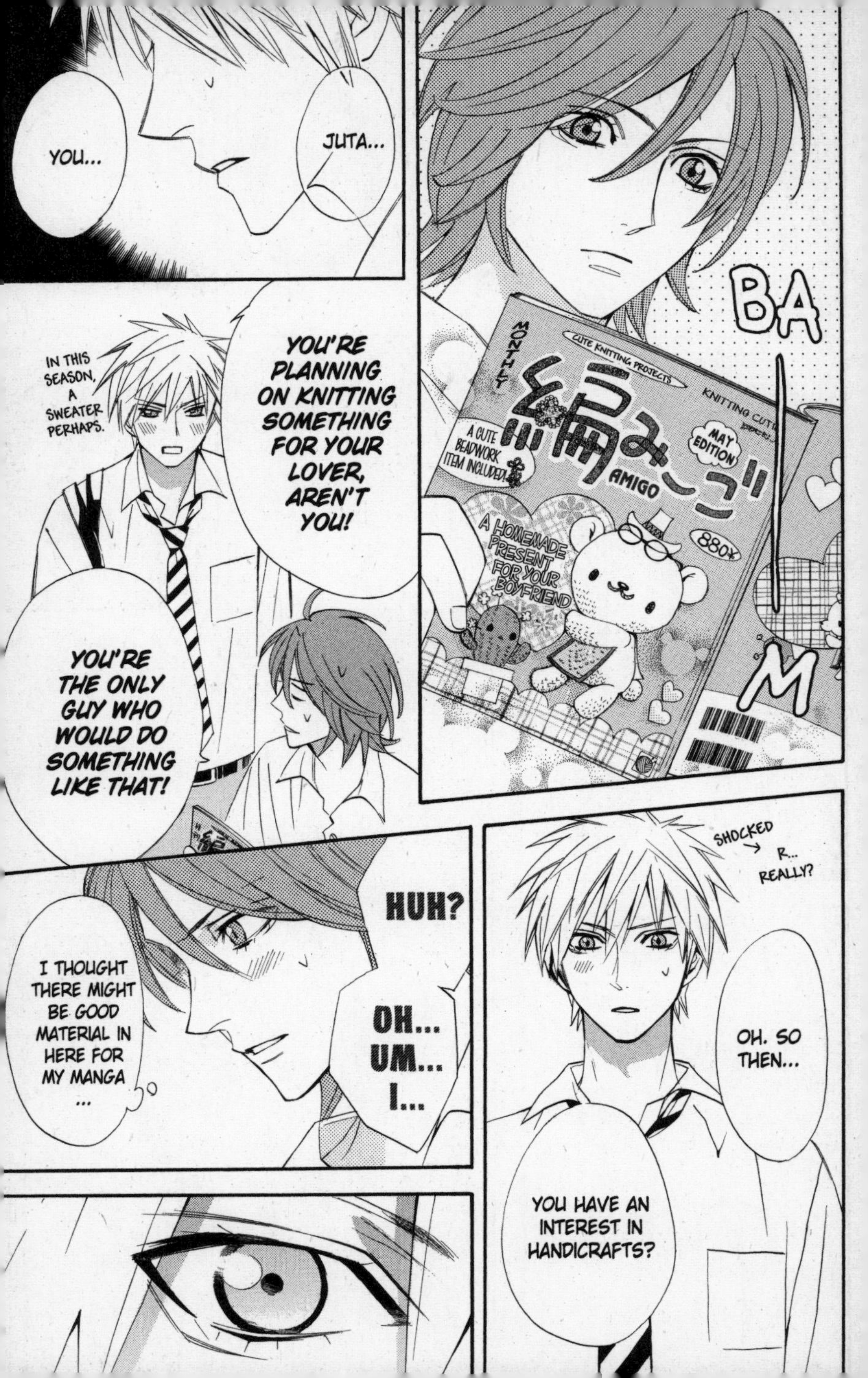
BA
M
MONTHLY
CUTE KNITTING PROJECTS
KNITTING CUTE
AMIGO
MAY EDITION
A CUTE BEADWORK ITEM INCLUDED!
A HOMEMADE PRESENT FOR YOUR BOYFRIEND
880¥
JUTA...
YOU...
YOU'RE PLANNING ON KNITTING SOMETHING FOR YOUR LOVER, AREN'T YOU!
IN THIS SEASON, A SWEATER PERHAPS.
YOU'RE THE ONLY GUY WHO WOULD DO SOMETHING LIKE THAT!
SHOCKED →
R... REALLY?
OH. SO THEN...
YOU HAVE AN INTEREST IN HANDICRAFTS?
HUH?
OH... UM... I...
I THOUGHT THERE MIGHT BE GOOD MATERIAL IN HERE FOR MY MANGA ...

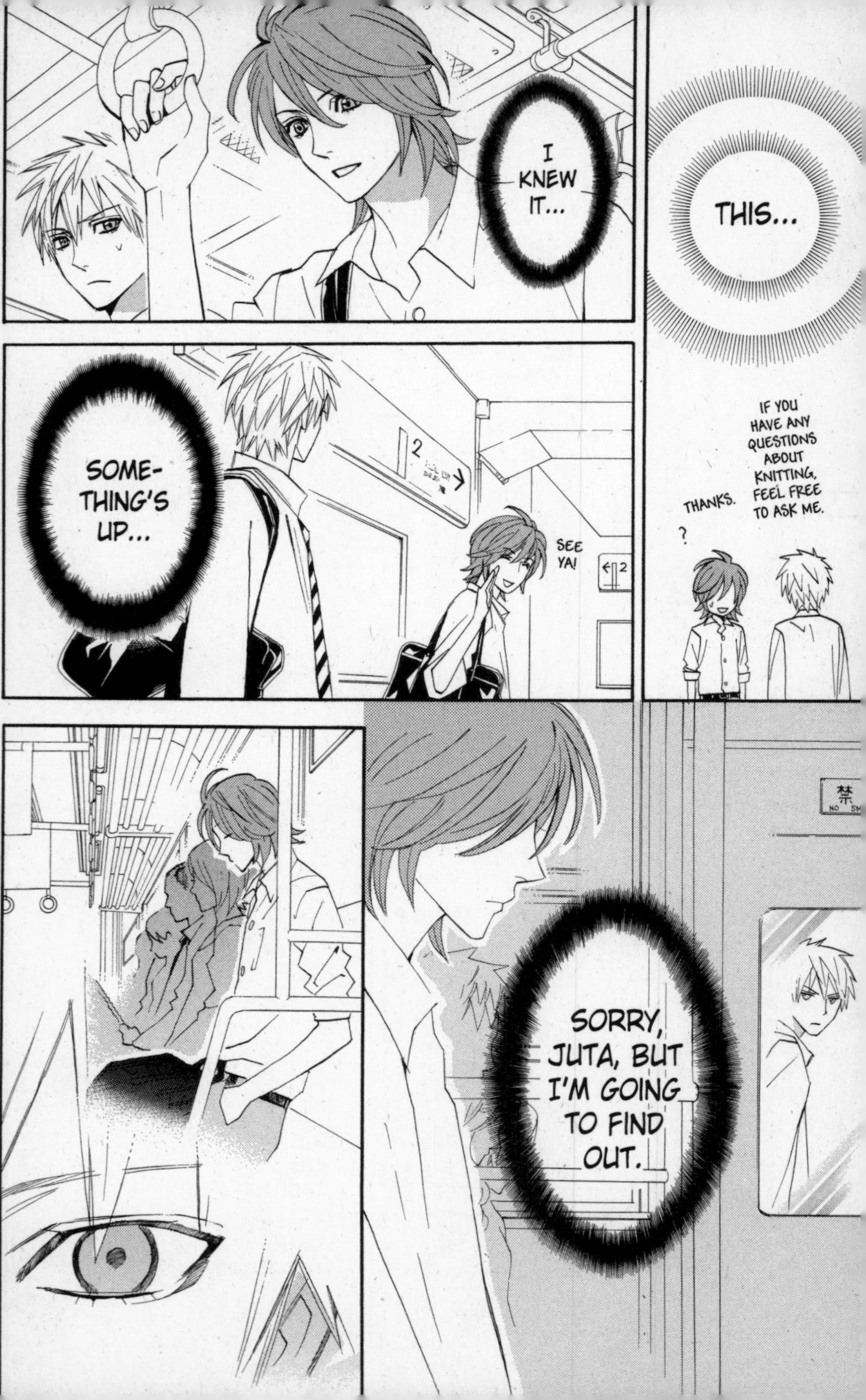
THIS...
I KNEW IT...
IF YOU HAVE ANY QUESTIONS ABOUT KNITTING, FEEL FREE TO ASK ME.
THANKS.
?
SEE YA!
SOME-THING'S UP...
禁
SORRY, JUTA, BUT I'M GOING TO FIND OUT.

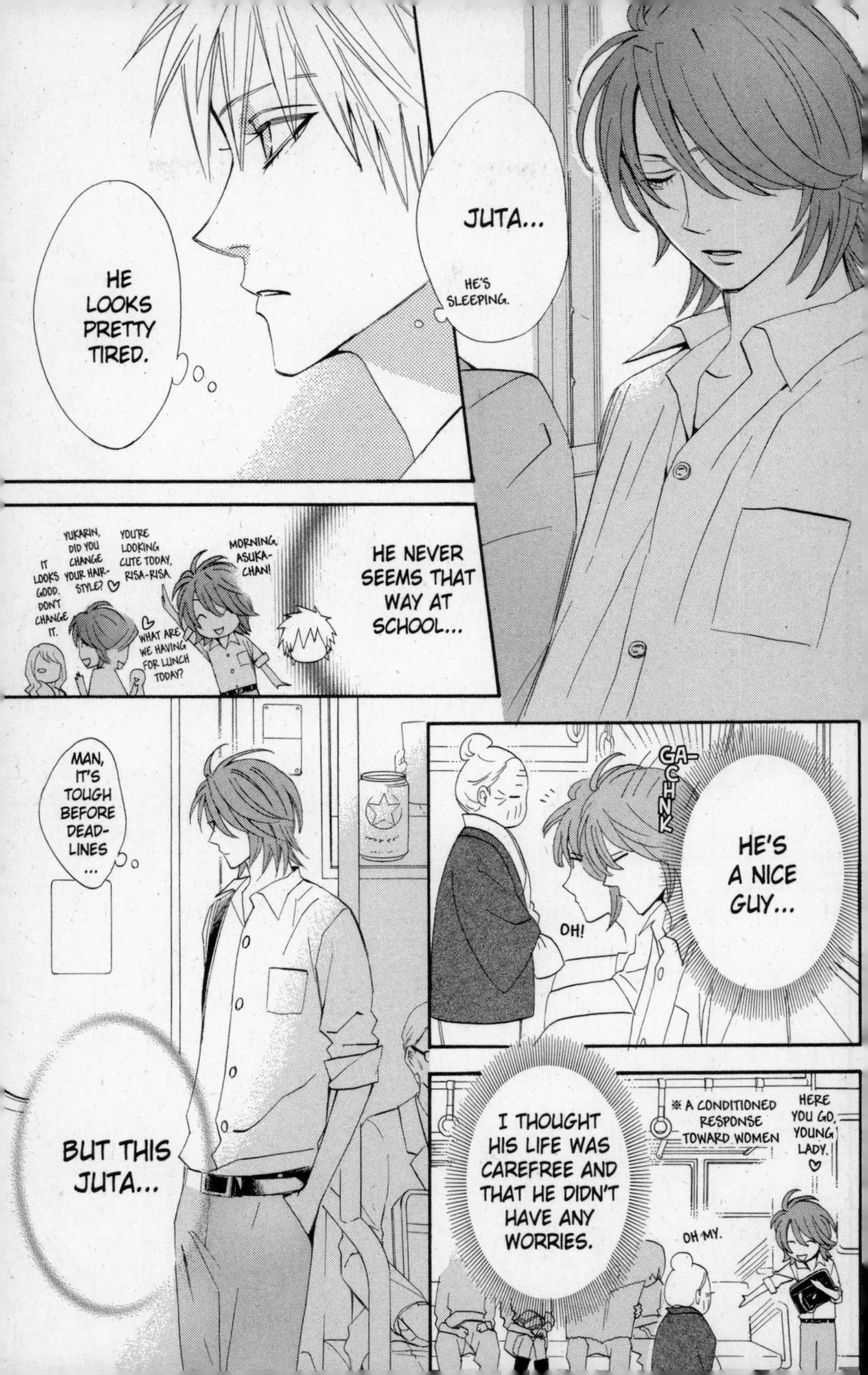
JUTA...
HE'S SLEEPING.
HE LOOKS PRETTY TIRED.
HE NEVER SEEMS THAT WAY AT SCHOOL...
MORNING, ASUKA-CHAN!
YOU'RE LOOKING CUTE TODAY, RISA-RISA.
WHAT ARE WE HAVING FOR LUNCH TODAY?
YUKARIN, DID YOU CHANGE YOUR HAIR-STYLE?
IT LOOKS GOOD. DON'T CHANGE IT.
GA-CHNK
HE'S A NICE GUY...
OH!
HERE YOU GO, YOUNG LADY.
※ A CONDITIONED RESPONSE TOWARD WOMEN
I THOUGHT HIS LIFE WAS CAREFREE AND THAT HE DIDN'T HAVE ANY WORRIES.
OH MY.
MAN, IT'S TOUGH BEFORE DEAD-LINES...
BUT THIS JUTA...

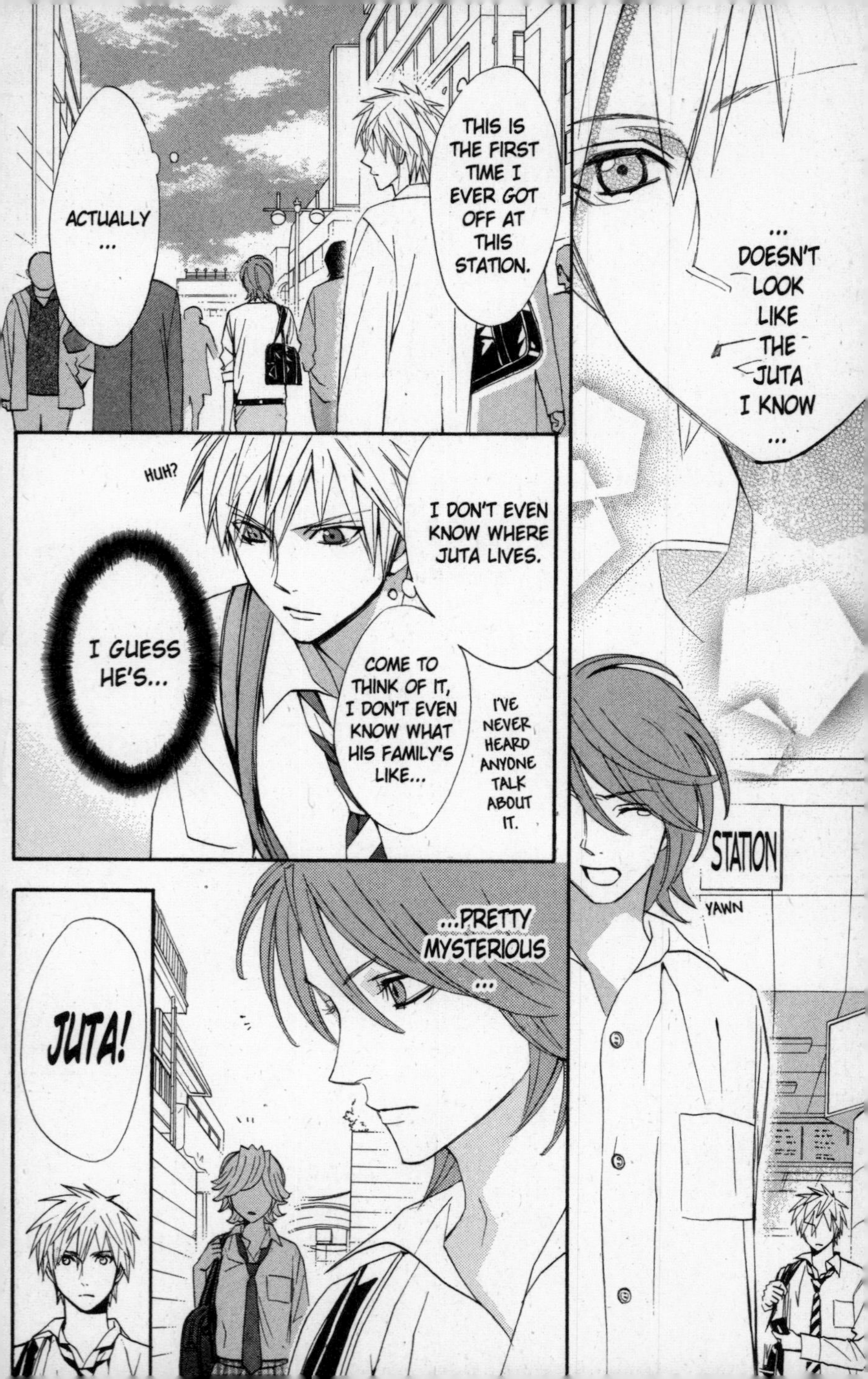
... DOESN'T LOOK LIKE THE JUTA I KNOW ...
STATION
YAWN
THIS IS THE FIRST TIME I EVER GOT OFF AT THIS STATION.
ACTUALLY ...
I DON'T EVEN KNOW WHERE JUTA LIVES.
HUH?
COME TO THINK OF IT, I DON'T EVEN KNOW WHAT HIS FAMILY'S LIKE...
I'VE NEVER HEARD ANYONE TALK ABOUT IT.
I GUESS HE'S...
...PRETTY MYSTERIOUS ...
JUTA!

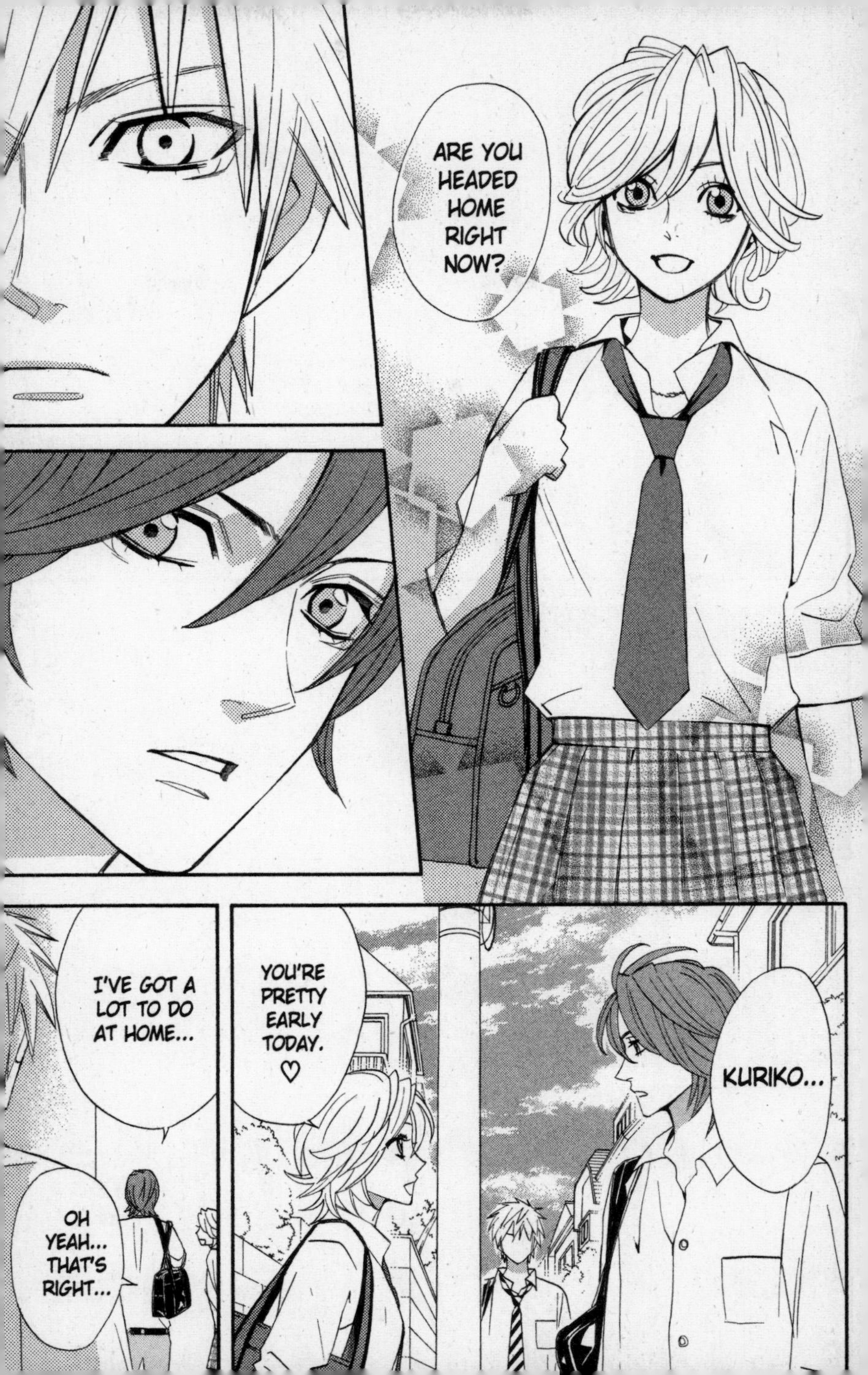
ARE YOU HEADED HOME RIGHT NOW?
KURIKO...
YOU'RE PRETTY EARLY TODAY. ♡
I'VE GOT A LOT TO DO AT HOME...
OH YEAH... THAT'S RIGHT...

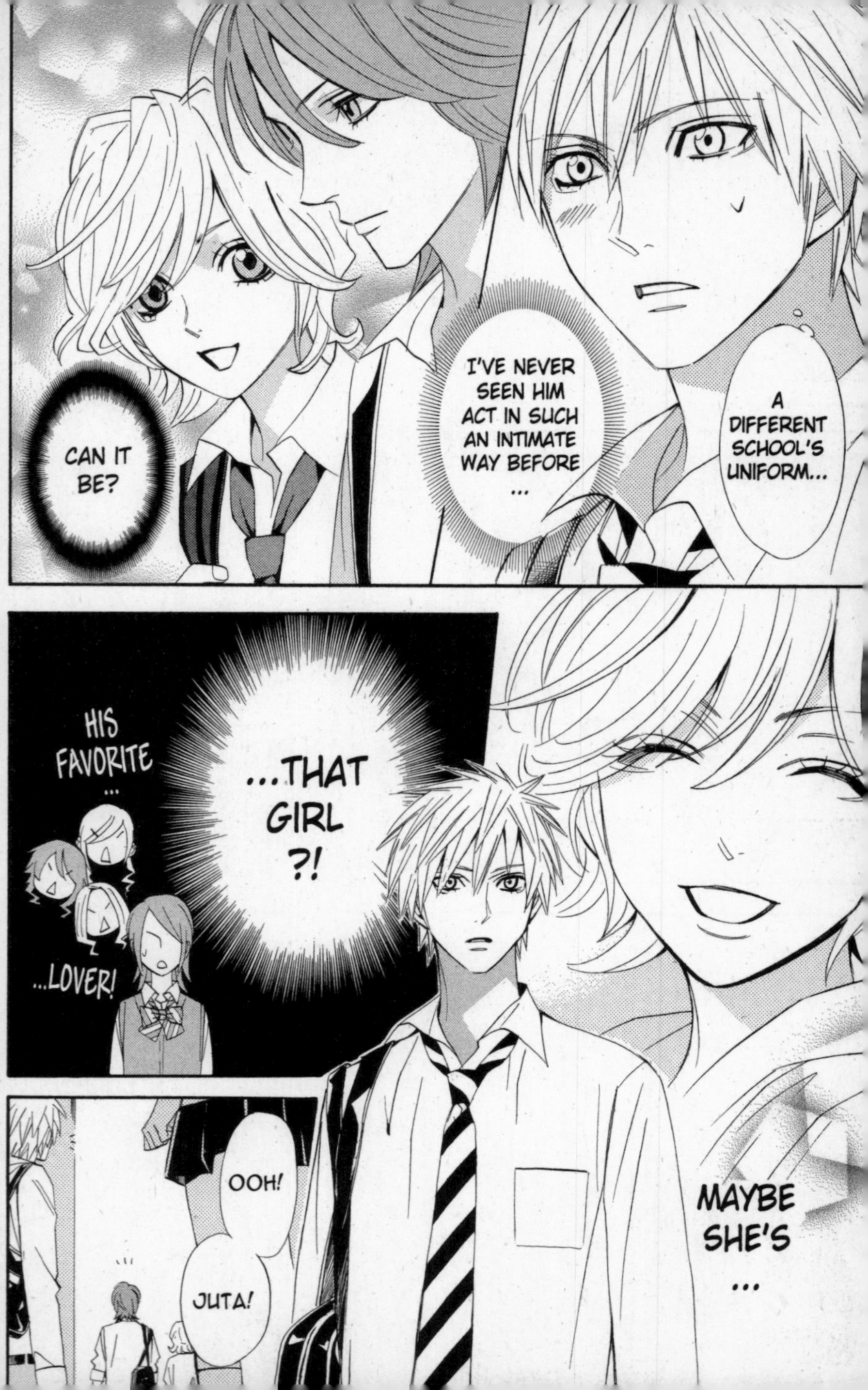
A DIFFERENT SCHOOL'S UNIFORM...
I'VE NEVER SEEN HIM ACT IN SUCH AN INTIMATE WAY BEFORE ...
CAN IT BE?
MAYBE SHE'S ...
...THAT GIRL ?!
HIS FAVORITE ...
...LOVER!
OOH!
JUTA!

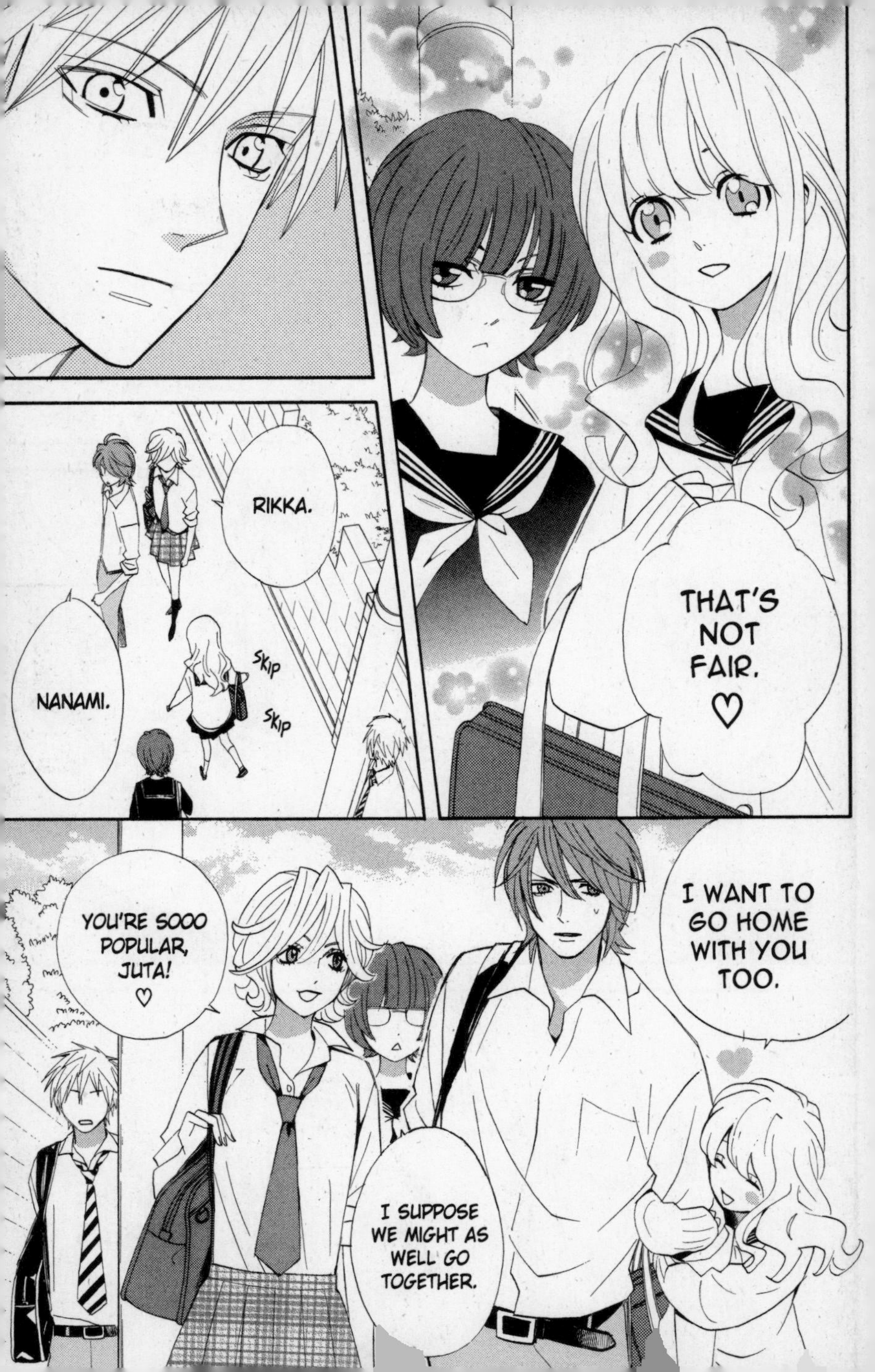
THAT'S NOT FAIR. ♡
RIKKA.
SKIP SKIP
NANAMI.
I WANT TO GO HOME WITH YOU TOO.
YOU'RE SOOO POPULAR, JUTA! ♡
I SUPPOSE WE MIGHT AS WELL GO TOGETHER.

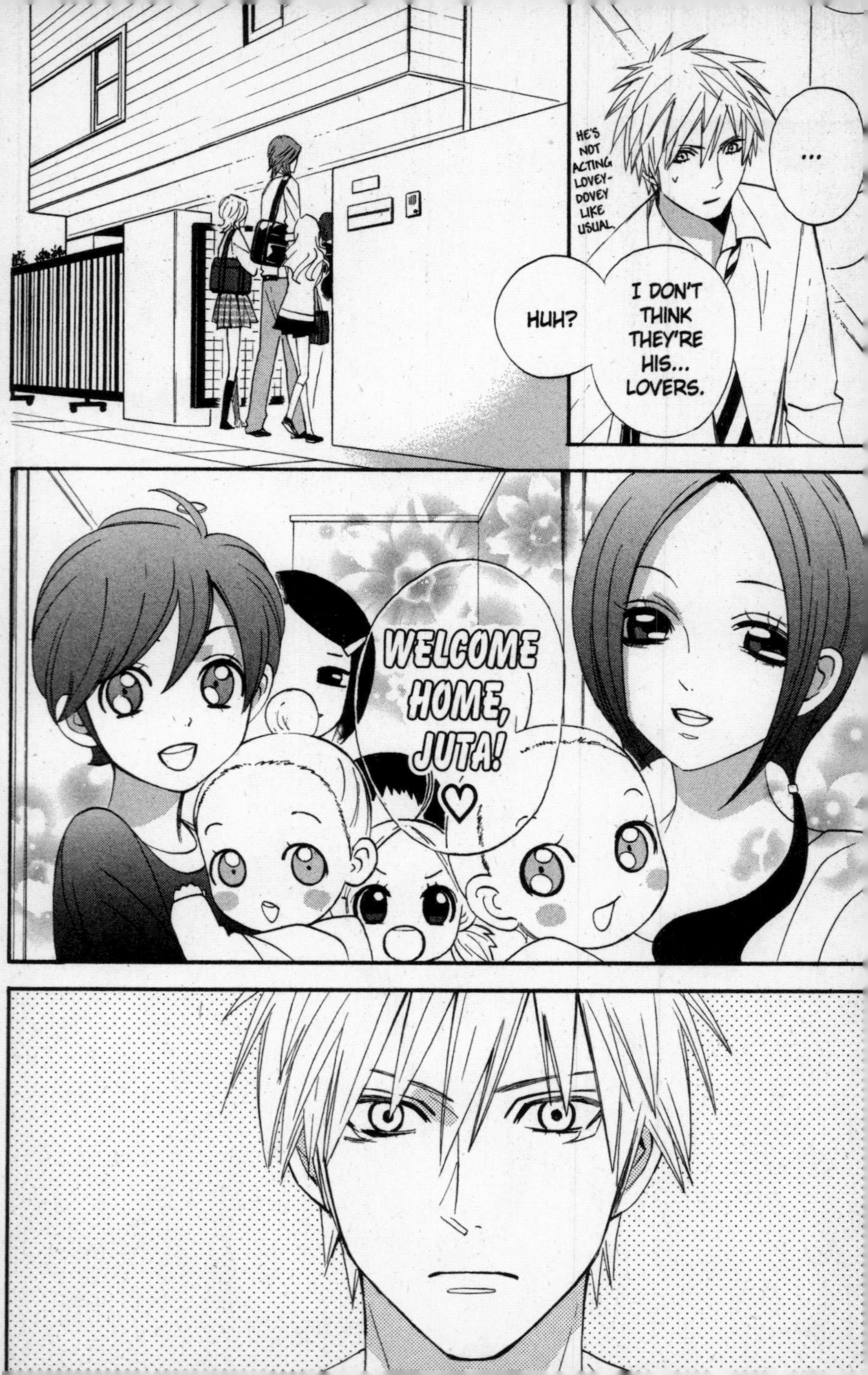
...
HE'S NOT ACTING LOVEY-DOVEY LIKE USUAL.
I DON'T THINK THEY'RE HIS... LOVERS.
HUH?
WELCOME HOME, JUTA! ♡

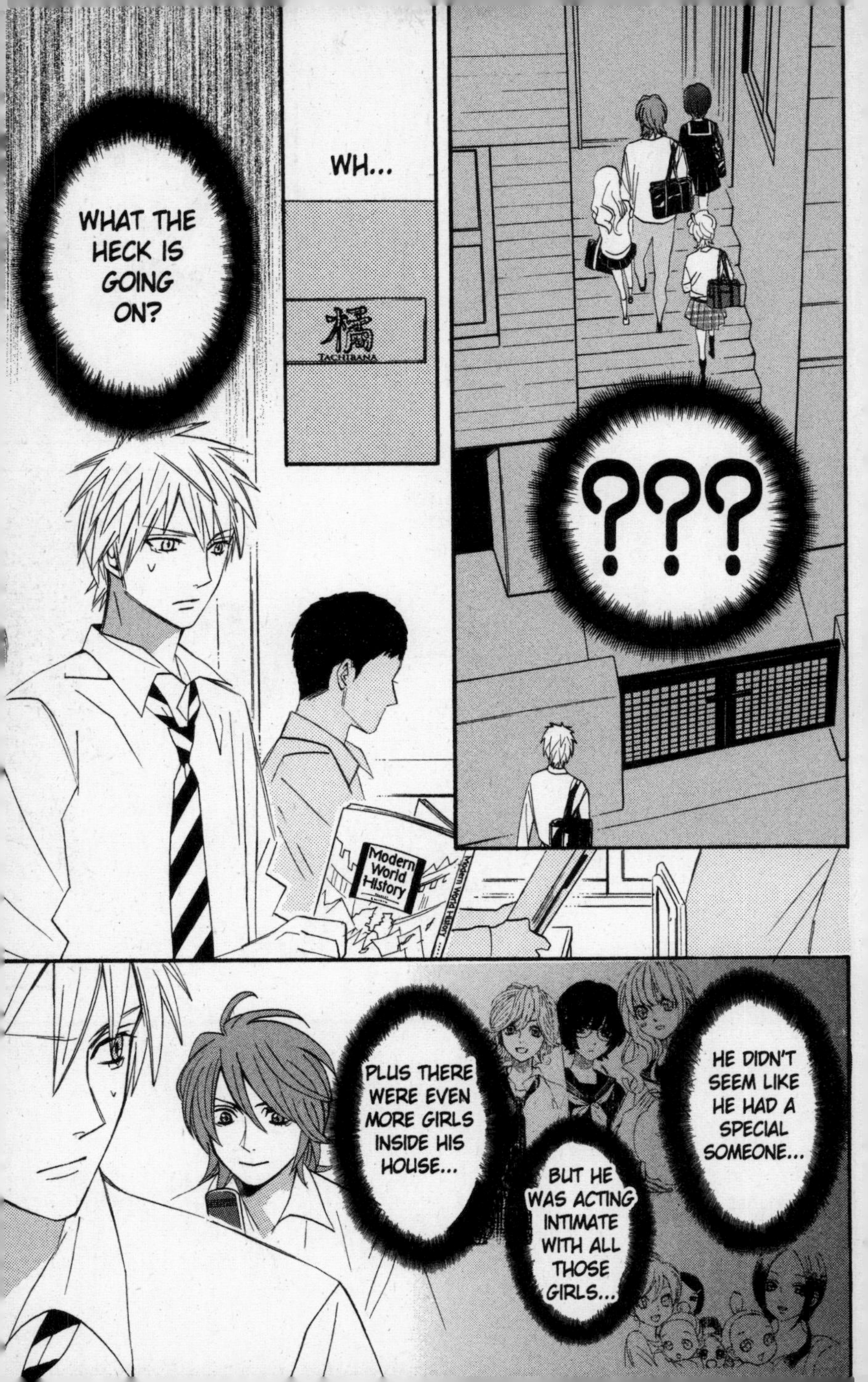
???
WH...
橘
TACHIBANA
WHAT THE HECK IS GOING ON?
Modern World History
Modern World History
HE DIDN'T SEEM LIKE HE HAD A SPECIAL SOMEONE...
BUT HE WAS ACTING INTIMATE WITH ALL THOSE GIRLS...
PLUS THERE WERE EVEN MORE GIRLS INSIDE HIS HOUSE...

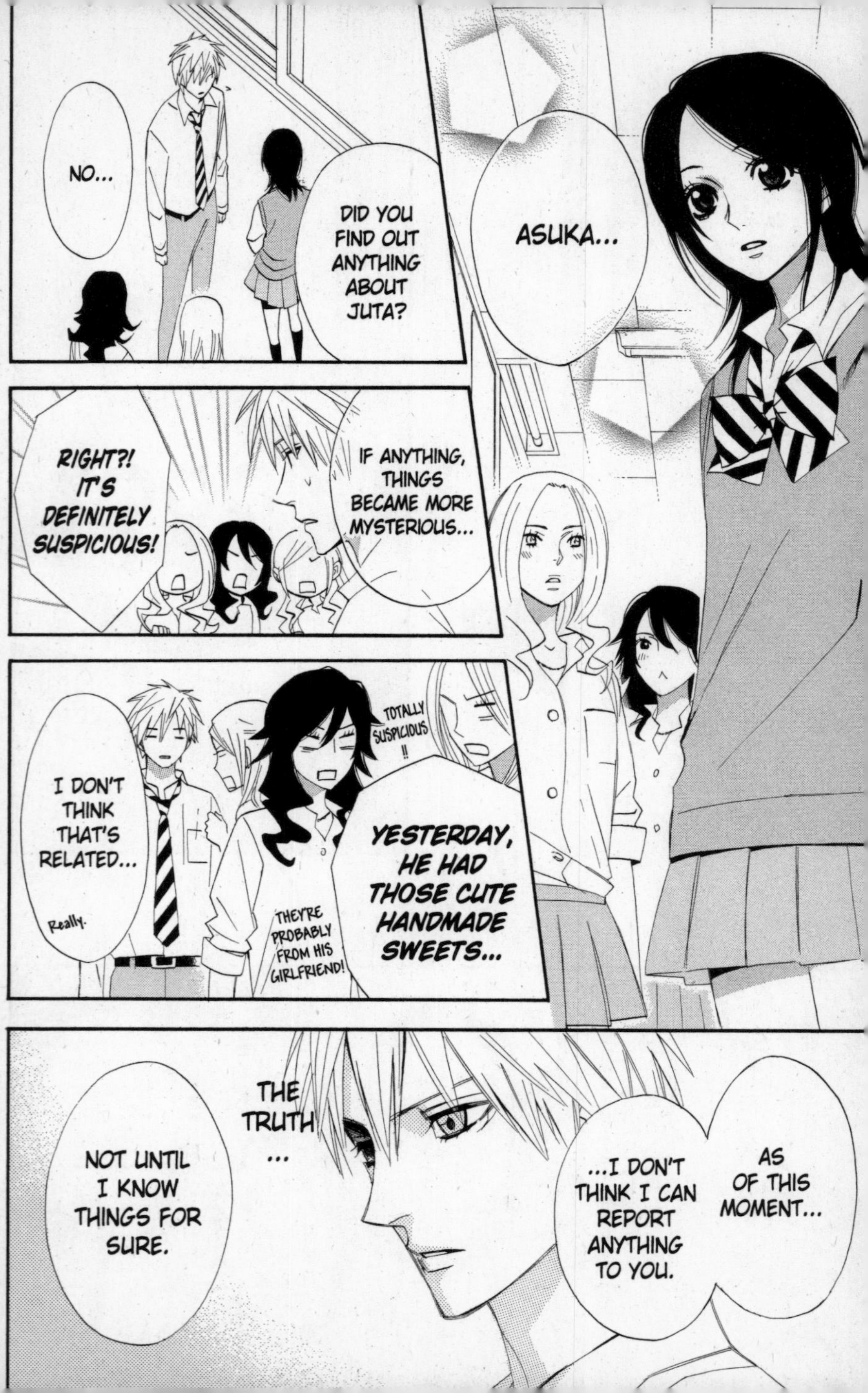
ASUKA...
DID YOU FIND OUT ANYTHING ABOUT JUTA?
NO...
IF ANYTHING, THINGS BECAME MORE MYSTERIOUS...
RIGHT?! IT'S DEFINITELY SUSPICIOUS!
TOTALLY SUSPICIOUS !!
YESTERDAY, HE HAD THOSE CUTE HANDMADE SWEETS...
THEY'RE PROBABLY FROM HIS GIRLFRIEND!
I DON'T THINK THAT'S RELATED...
Really.
AS OF THIS MOMENT...
...I DON'T THINK I CAN REPORT ANYTHING TO YOU.
THE TRUTH ...
NOT UNTIL I KNOW THINGS FOR SURE.

I'VE GOT TO FIND OUT...

...WHAT'S REALLY GOING ON...

AH-HA...

SO THAT'S WHY ASUKA-CHAN WAS ACTING THE WAY HE WAS...

HOW PROBLEM-ATIC...

I GET IT NOW.

NOW THEN...

JUTA...

WHAT SHOULD I DO?

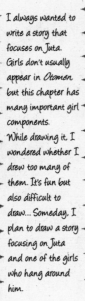

I always wanted to write a story that focuses on Juta. Girls don't usually appear in *Otomen* but this chapter has many important girl components. While drawing it, I wondered whether I drew too many of them. It's fun but also difficult to draw... Someday, I plan to draw a story focusing on Juta and one of the girls who hang around him.

In the next story, a new character I had always wanted to draw makes an appearance. He was far easier to shape than I'd anticipated, which made things very convenient.

I hope we meet again in volume 4

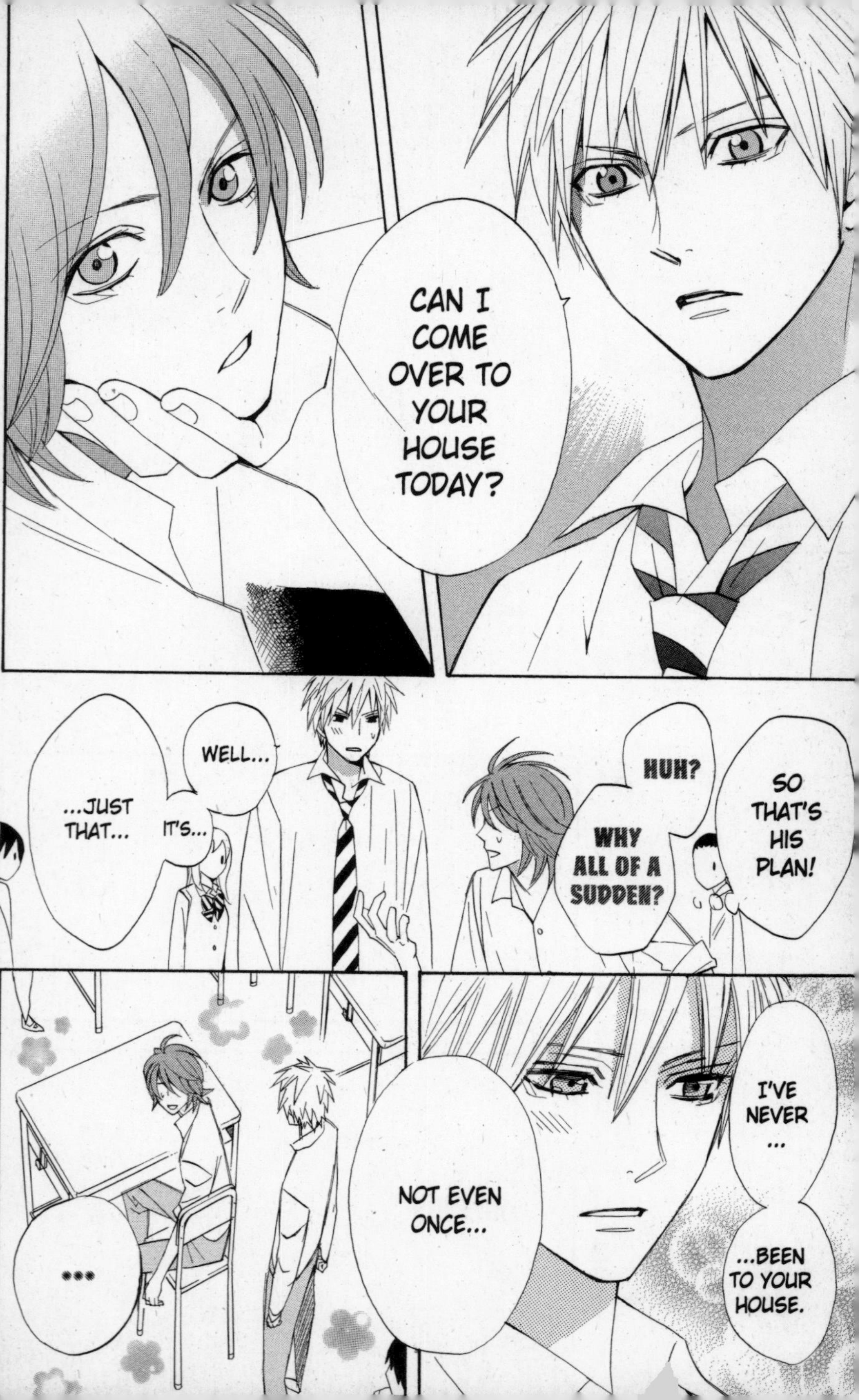
CAN I COME OVER TO YOUR HOUSE TODAY?
SO THAT'S HIS PLAN!
HUH?
WHY ALL OF A SUDDEN?
WELL...
IT'S...
...JUST THAT...
I'VE NEVER ...
...BEEN TO YOUR HOUSE.
NOT EVEN ONCE...
...

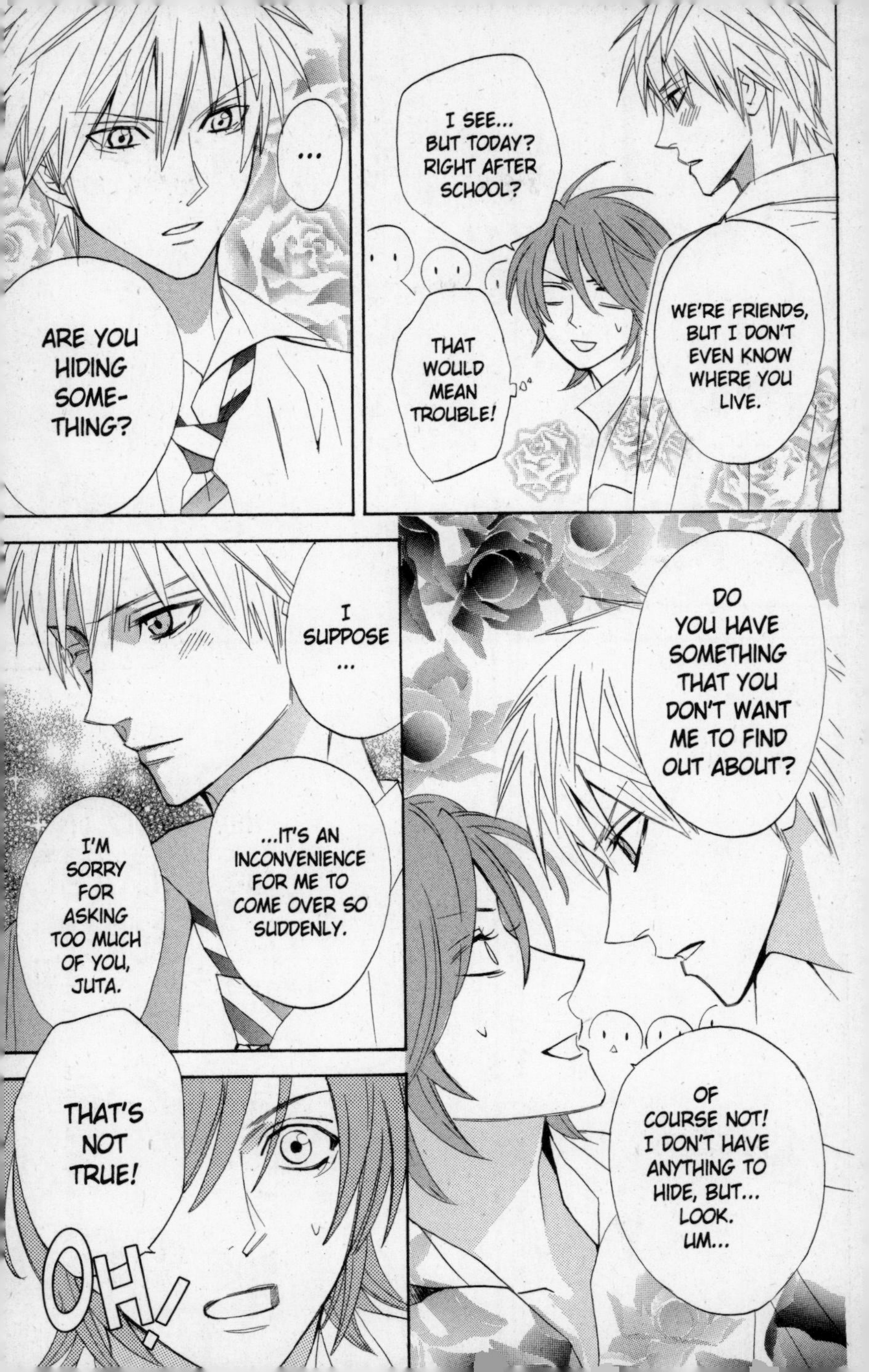
I SEE... BUT TODAY? RIGHT AFTER SCHOOL?
WE'RE FRIENDS, BUT I DON'T EVEN KNOW WHERE YOU LIVE.
THAT WOULD MEAN TROUBLE!
...
ARE YOU HIDING SOME-THING?
DO YOU HAVE SOMETHING THAT YOU DON'T WANT ME TO FIND OUT ABOUT?
OF COURSE NOT! I DON'T HAVE ANYTHING TO HIDE, BUT... LOOK. UM...
I SUPPOSE...
...IT'S AN INCONVENIENCE FOR ME TO COME OVER SO SUDDENLY.
I'M SORRY FOR ASKING TOO MUCH OF YOU, JUTA.
THAT'S NOT TRUE!
OH!

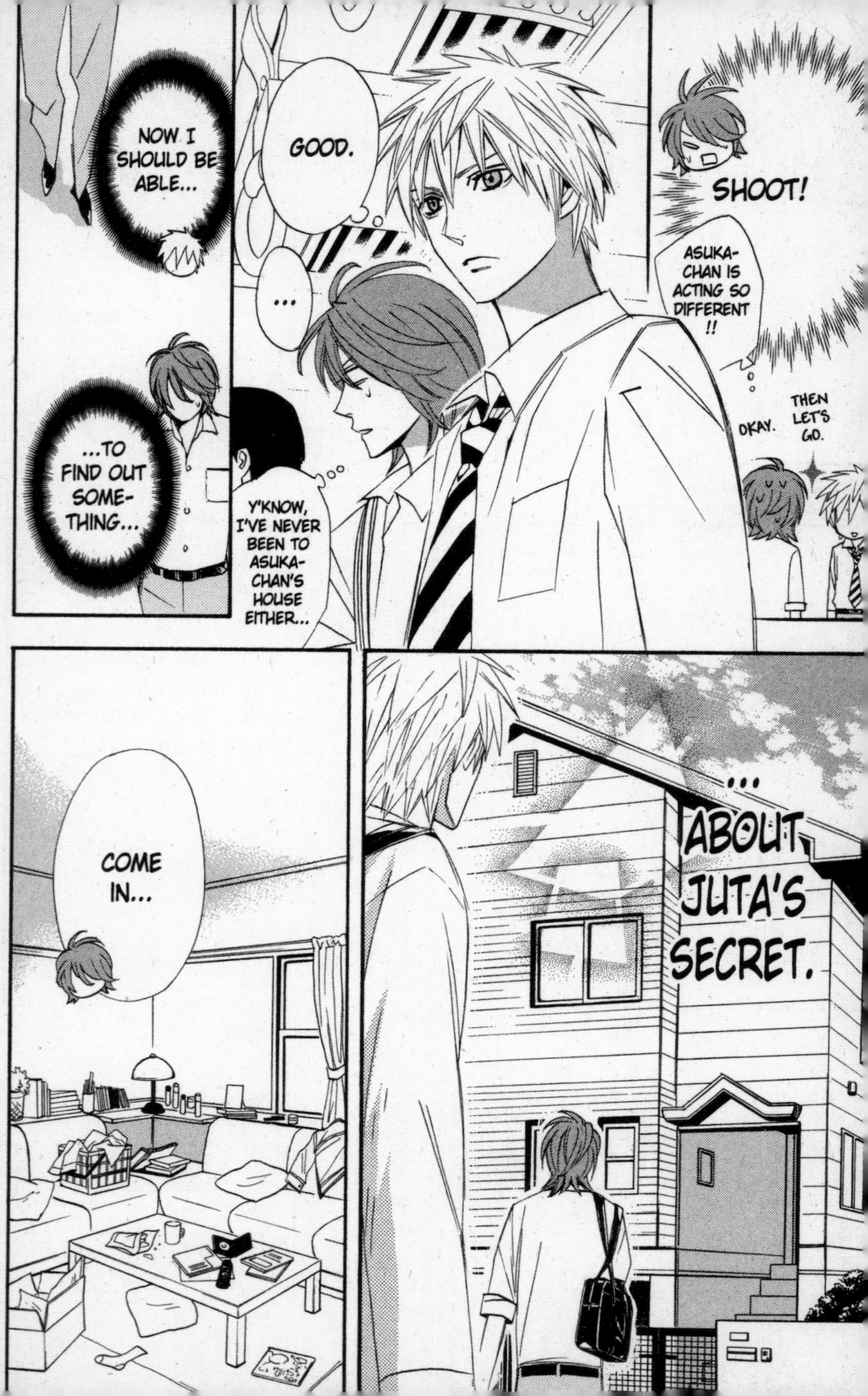
SHOOT!
ASUKA-CHAN IS ACTING SO DIFFERENT !!
THEN LET'S GO.
OKAY.
GOOD.
...
Y'KNOW, I'VE NEVER BEEN TO ASUKA-CHAN'S HOUSE EITHER...
NOW I SHOULD BE ABLE...
...TO FIND OUT SOME-THING...
...ABOUT JUTA'S SECRET.
COME IN...

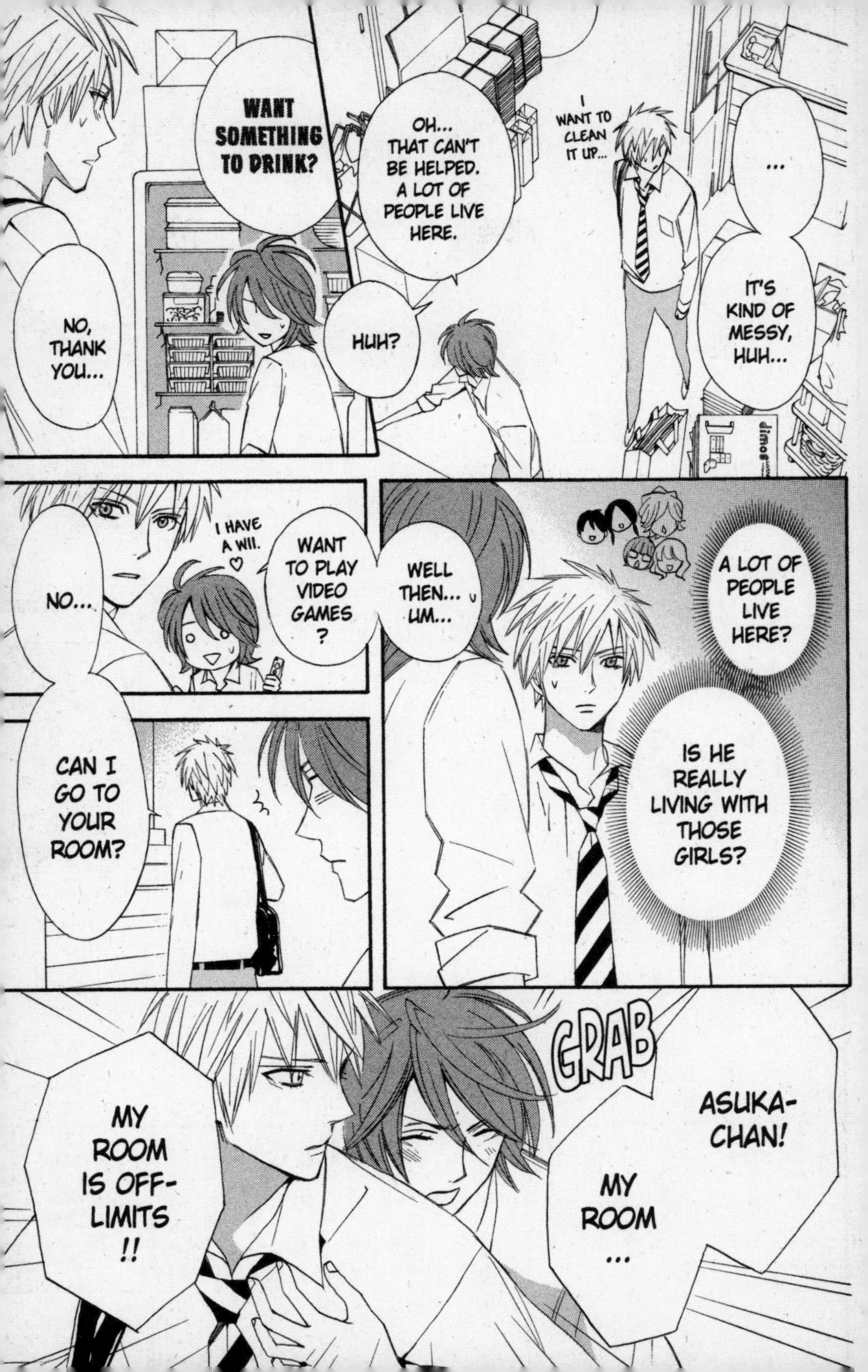
...
IT'S KIND OF MESSY, HUH...
I WANT TO CLEAN IT UP...
OH... THAT CAN'T BE HELPED. A LOT OF PEOPLE LIVE HERE.
HUH?
WANT SOMETHING TO DRINK?
NO, THANK YOU...
A LOT OF PEOPLE LIVE HERE?
IS HE REALLY LIVING WITH THOSE GIRLS?
WELL THEN... UM...
WANT TO PLAY VIDEO GAMES?
I HAVE A WII. ♡
NO...
CAN I GO TO YOUR ROOM?
GRAB
ASUKA-CHAN!
MY ROOM ...
MY ROOM IS OFF-LIMITS!!

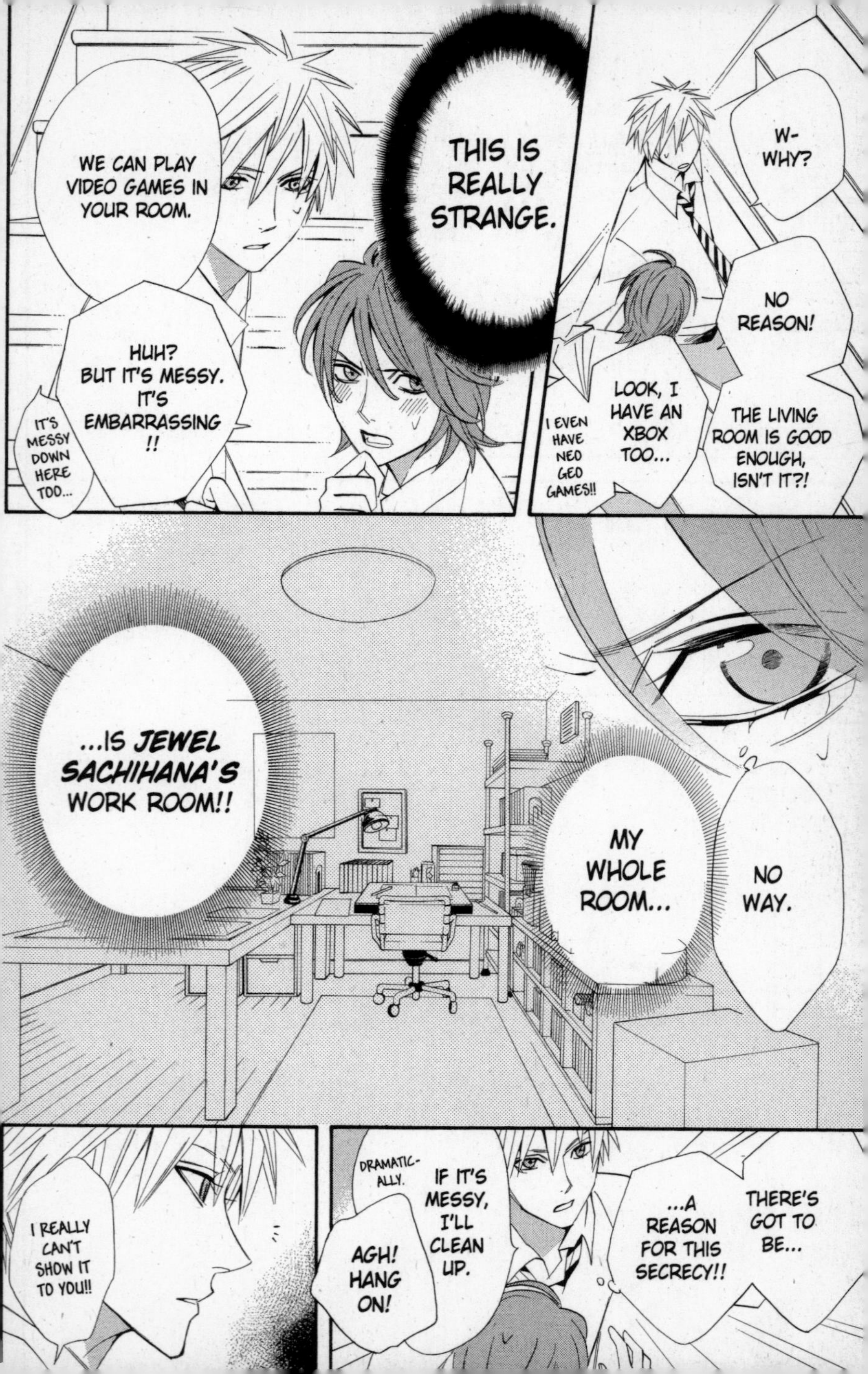
W-WHY?
NO REASON!
THE LIVING ROOM IS GOOD ENOUGH, ISN'T IT?!
LOOK, I HAVE AN XBOX TOO...
I EVEN HAVE NEO GEO GAMES!!
THIS IS REALLY STRANGE.
WE CAN PLAY VIDEO GAMES IN YOUR ROOM.
HUH? BUT IT'S MESSY. IT'S EMBARRASSING!!
IT'S MESSY DOWN HERE TOO...
NO WAY.
MY WHOLE ROOM...
...IS ***JEWEL SACHIHANA'S*** WORK ROOM!!
THERE'S GOT TO BE...
...A REASON FOR THIS SECRECY!!
IF IT'S MESSY, I'LL CLEAN UP.
DRAMATIC-ALLY.
AGH! HANG ON!
I REALLY CAN'T SHOW IT TO YOU!!

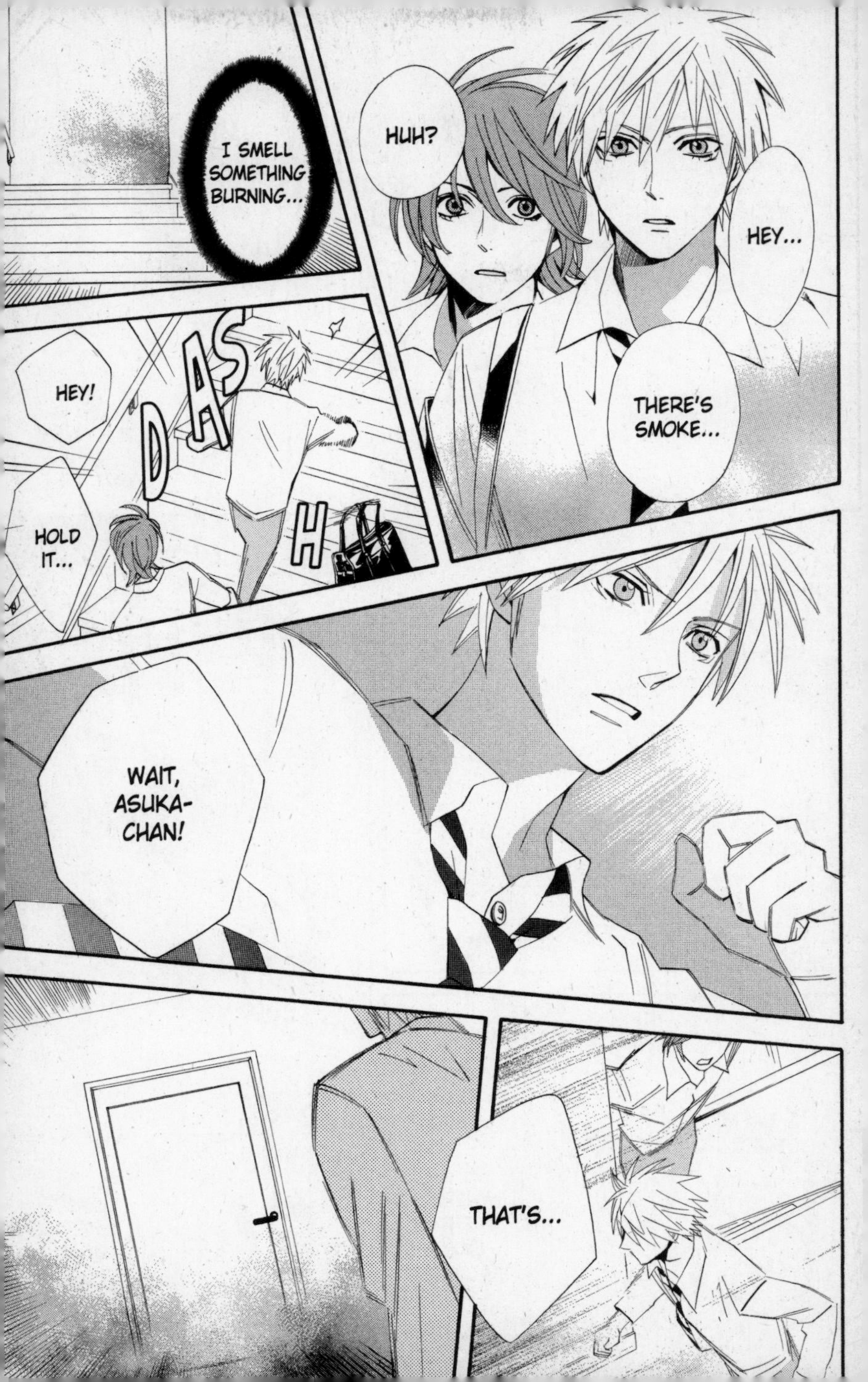
HUH?
HEY...
THERE'S SMOKE...
I SMELL SOMETHING BURNING...
DASH
HEY!
HOLD IT...
WAIT, ASUKA-CHAN!
THAT'S...

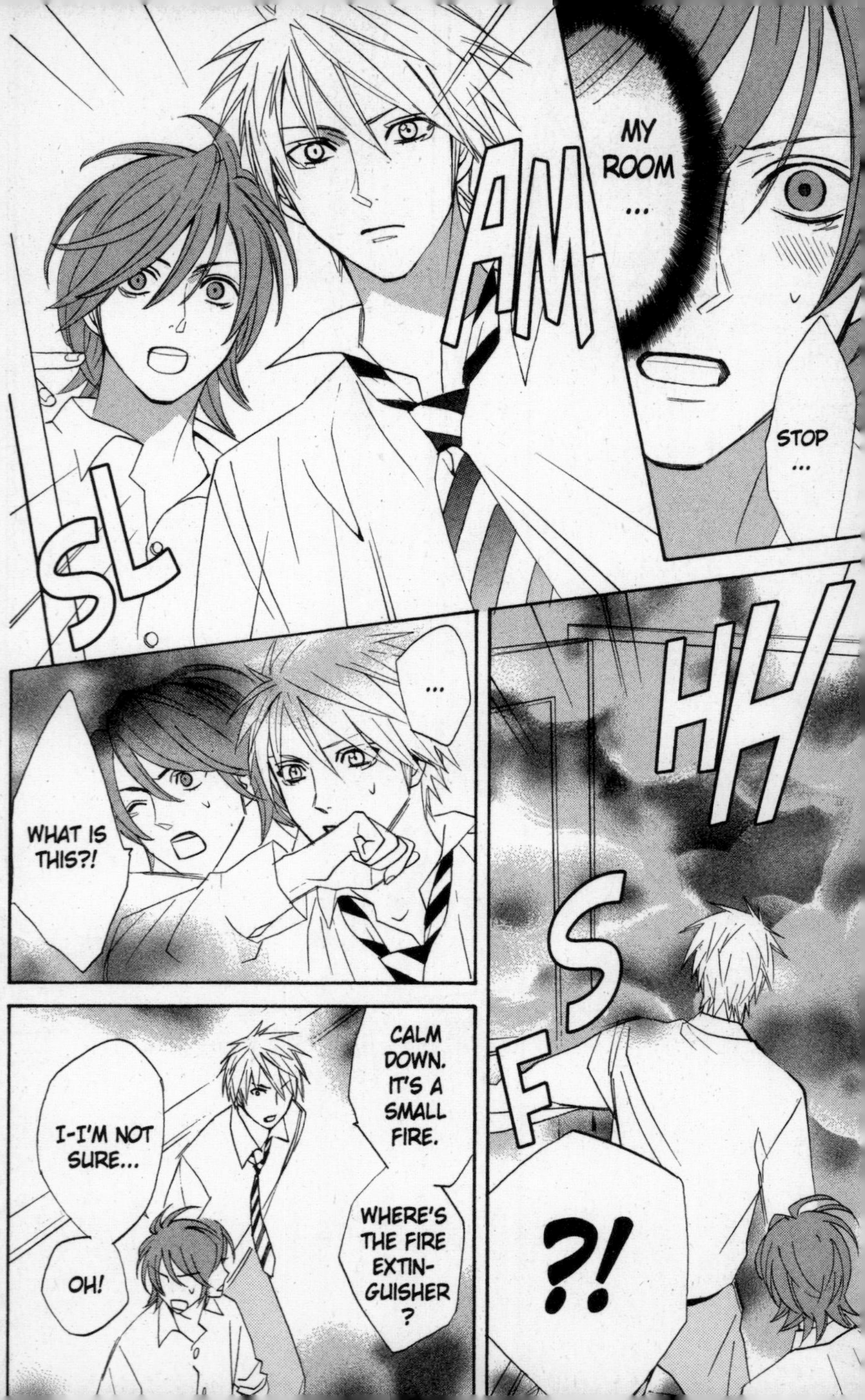
MY ROOM ...
STOP ...
SL
AM
HH
S
F
?!
...
WHAT IS THIS?!
CALM DOWN. IT'S A SMALL FIRE.
WHERE'S THE FIRE EXTIN-GUISHER?
I-I'M NOT SURE...
OH!

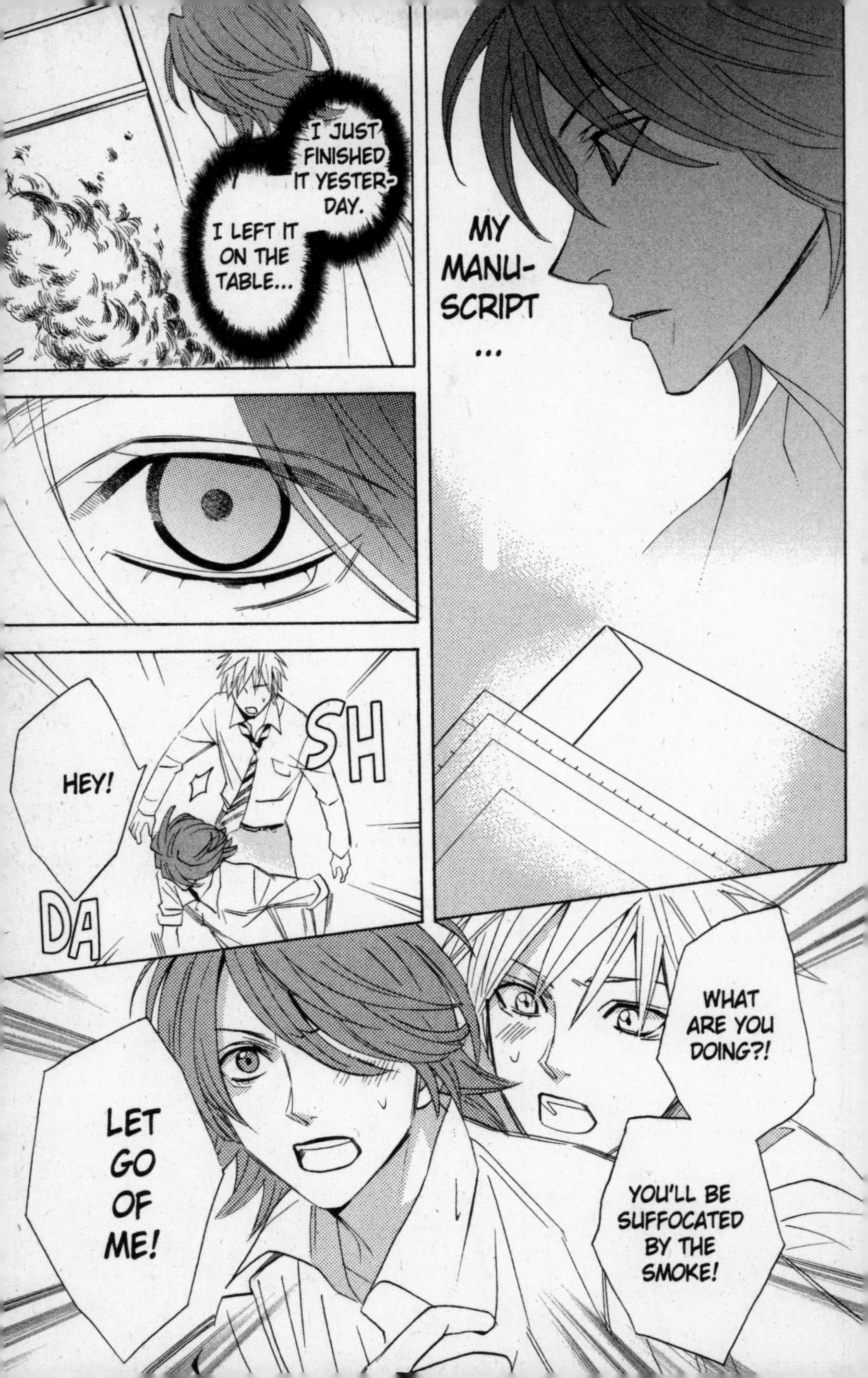
MY MANU-SCRIPT ...
I JUST FINISHED IT YESTER-DAY.
I LEFT IT ON THE TABLE...
SH
HEY!
DA
WHAT ARE YOU DOING?!
YOU'LL BE SUFFOCATED BY THE SMOKE!
LET GO OF ME!

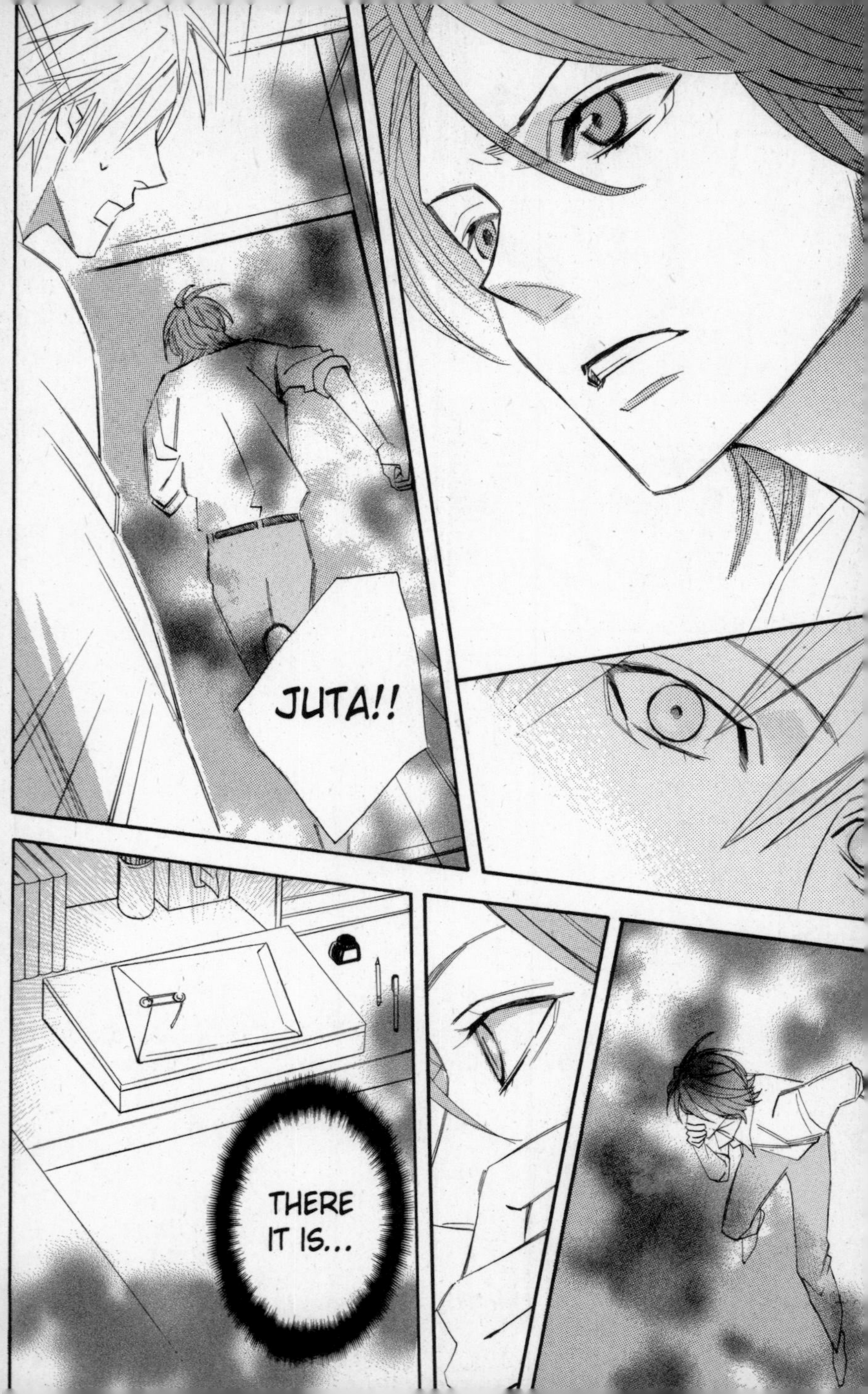
JUTA!!
THERE IT IS...

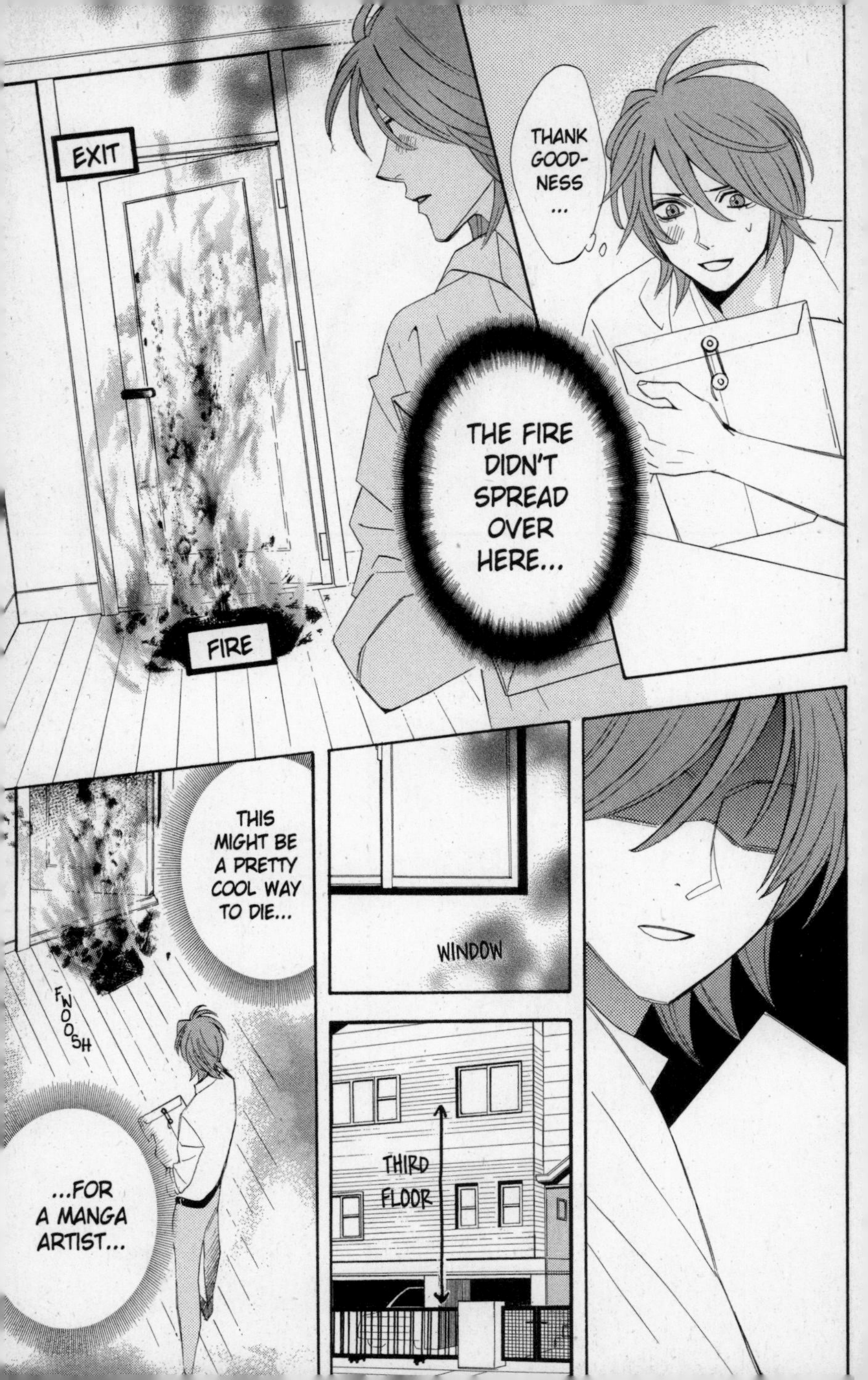
THANK GOODNESS...
THE FIRE DIDN'T SPREAD OVER HERE...
EXIT
FIRE
WINDOW
THIRD FLOOR
THIS MIGHT BE A PRETTY COOL WAY TO DIE...
FWOOSH
...FOR A MANGA ARTIST...

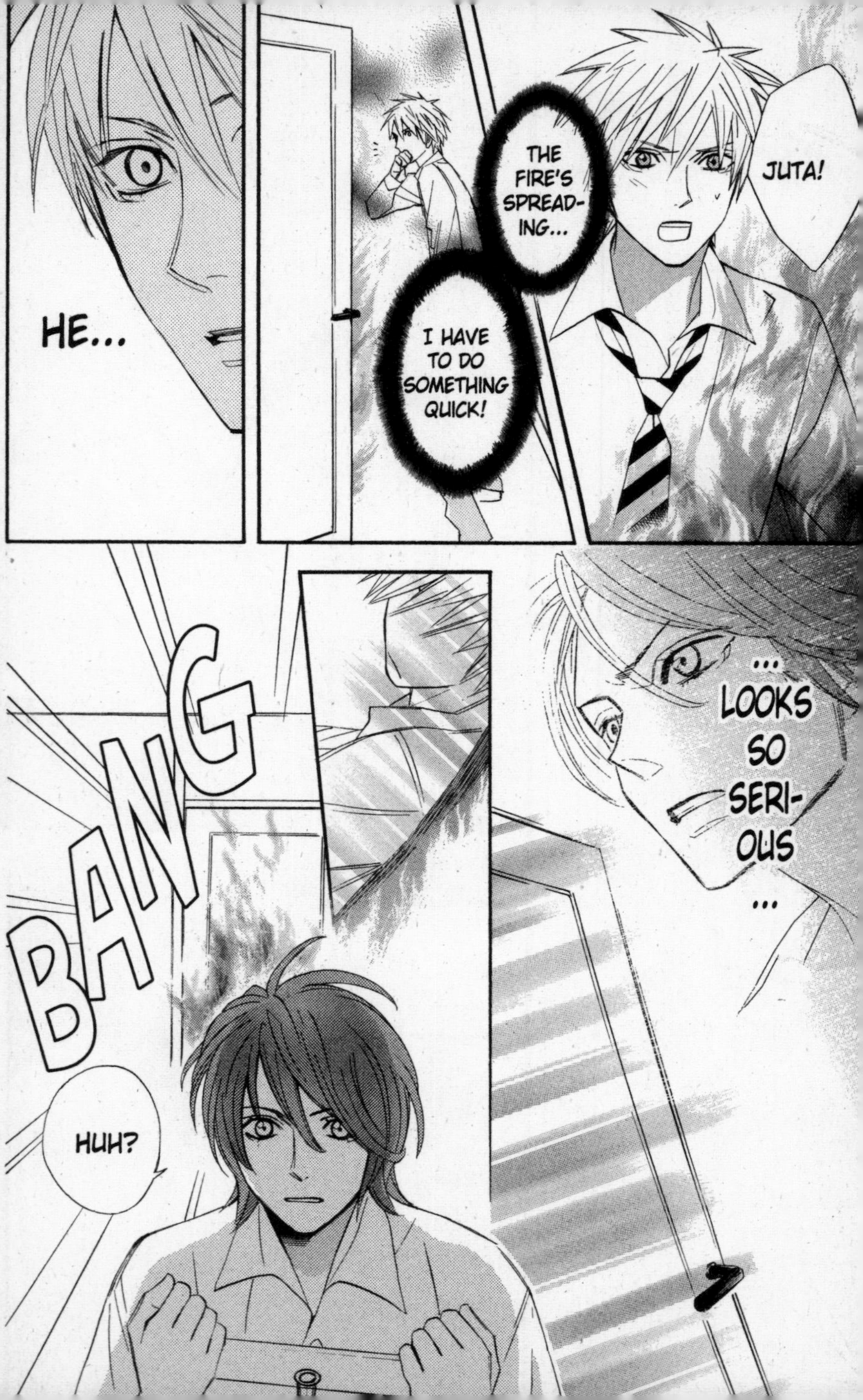
JUTA!
THE FIRE'S SPREADING...
I HAVE TO DO SOMETHING QUICK!
HE...
... LOOKS SO SERIOUS ...
BANG
HUH?

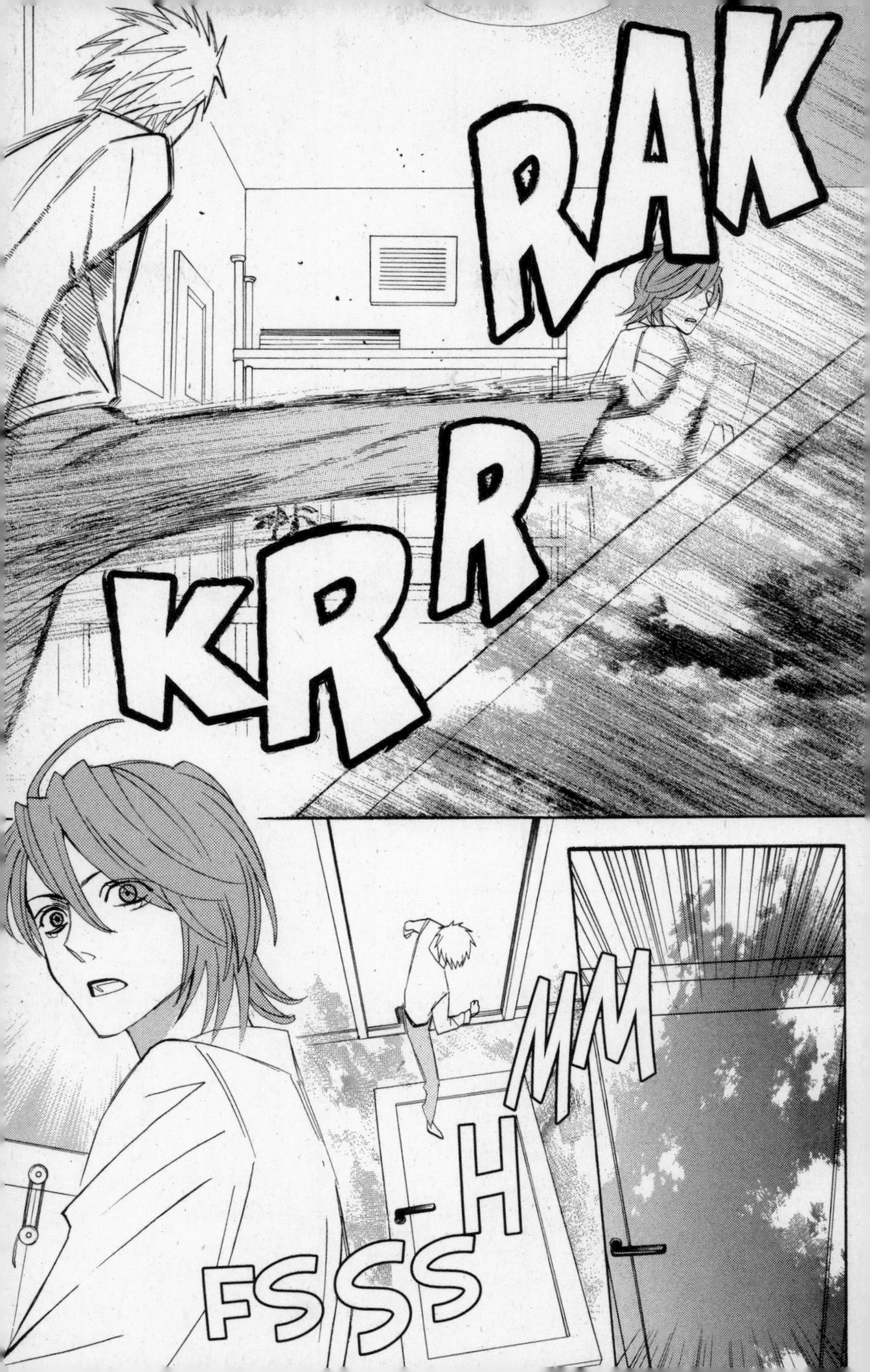
RAK
KRR
MM
H
FSSS

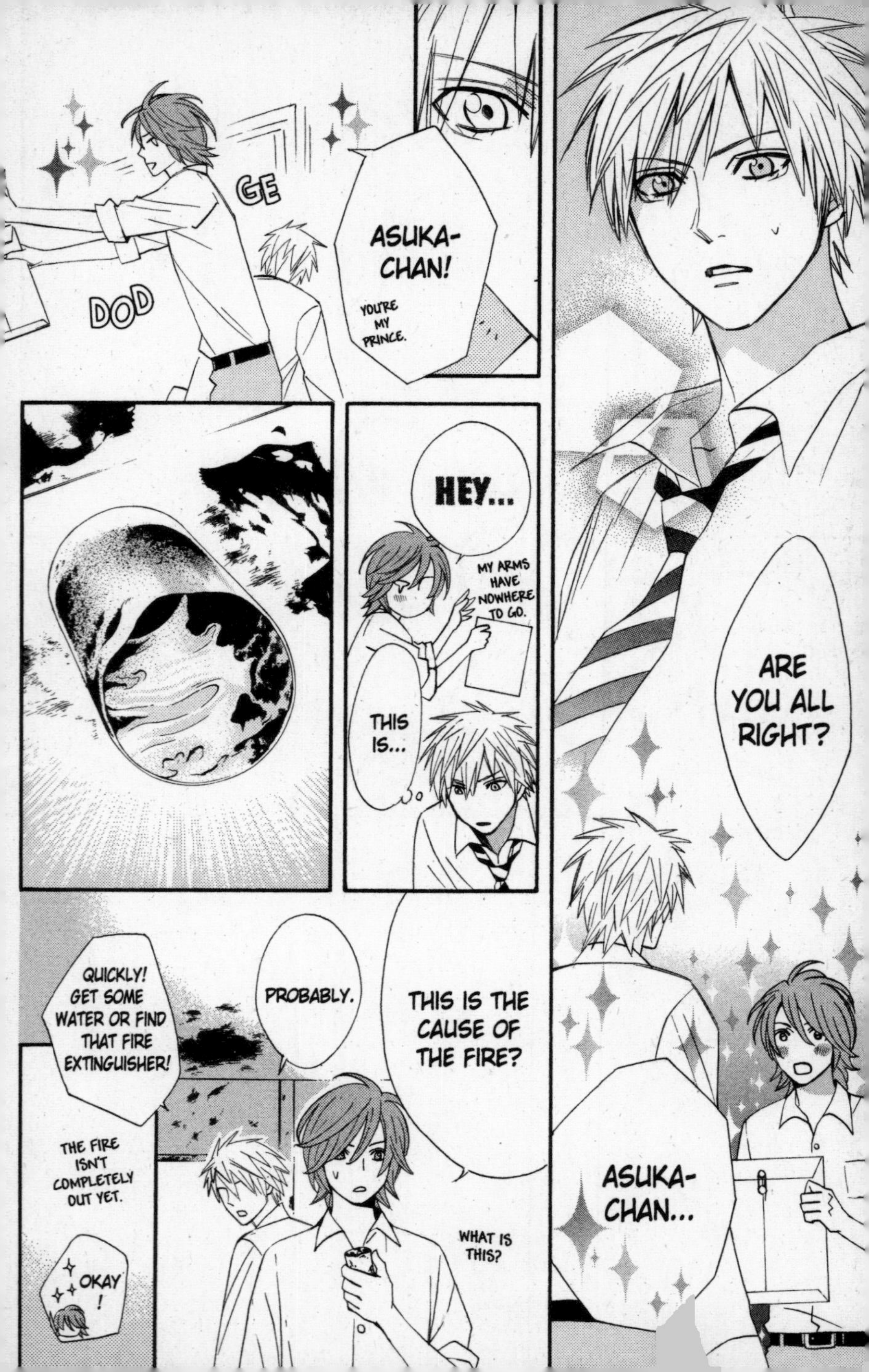
ARE YOU ALL RIGHT?
ASUKA-CHAN...
ASUKA-CHAN!
YOU'RE MY PRINCE.
GE
DOD
HEY...
MY ARMS HAVE NOWHERE TO GO.
THIS IS...
THIS IS THE CAUSE OF THE FIRE?
WHAT IS THIS?
PROBABLY.
QUICKLY! GET SOME WATER OR FIND THAT FIRE EXTINGUISHER!
THE FIRE ISN'T COMPLETELY OUT YET.
OKAY!

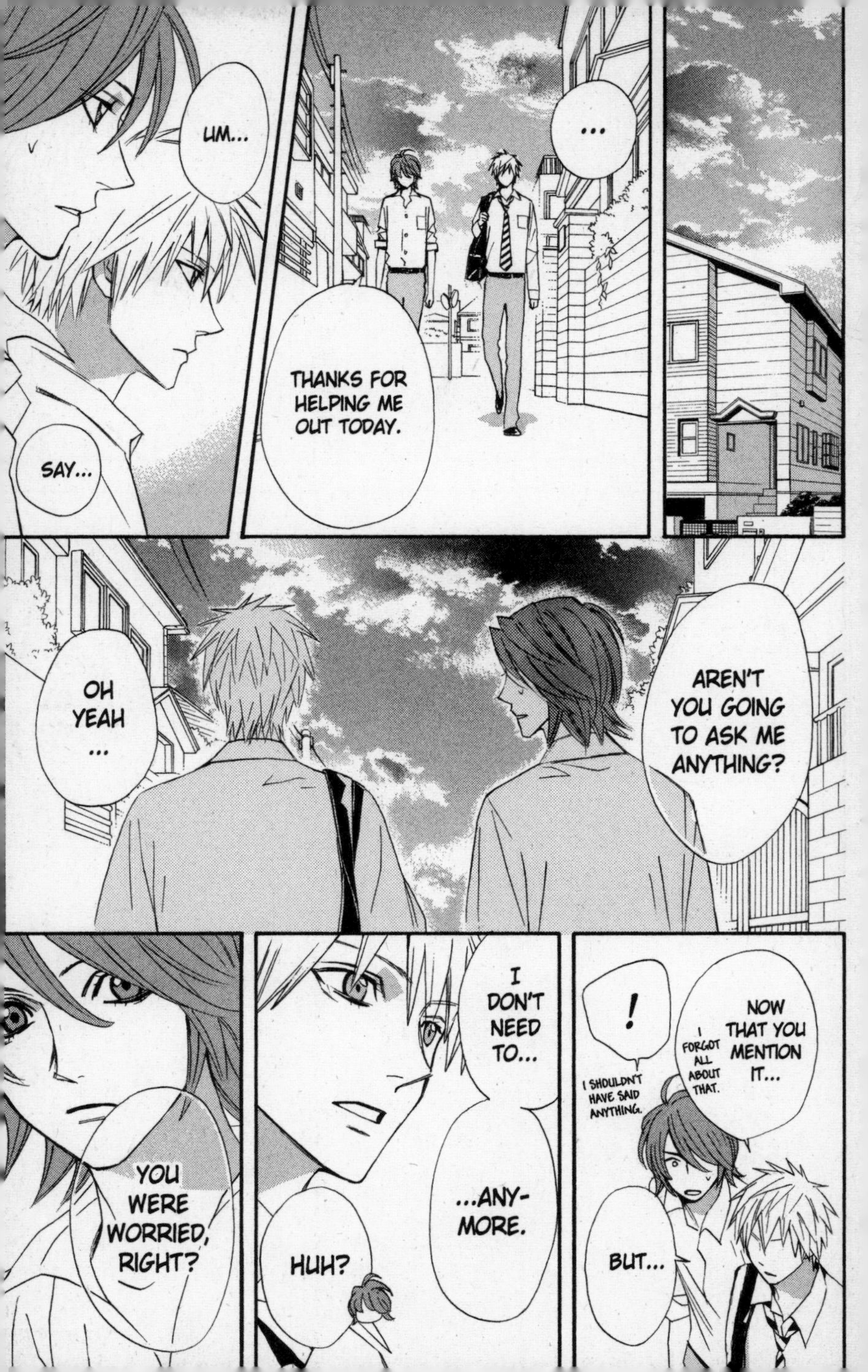
...
THANKS FOR HELPING ME OUT TODAY.
UM...
SAY...
AREN'T YOU GOING TO ASK ME ANYTHING?
OH YEAH ...
NOW THAT YOU MENTION IT...
I FORGOT ALL ABOUT THAT.
!
I SHOULDN'T HAVE SAID ANYTHING.
BUT...
I DON'T NEED TO...
...ANY-MORE.
HUH?
YOU WERE WORRIED, RIGHT?

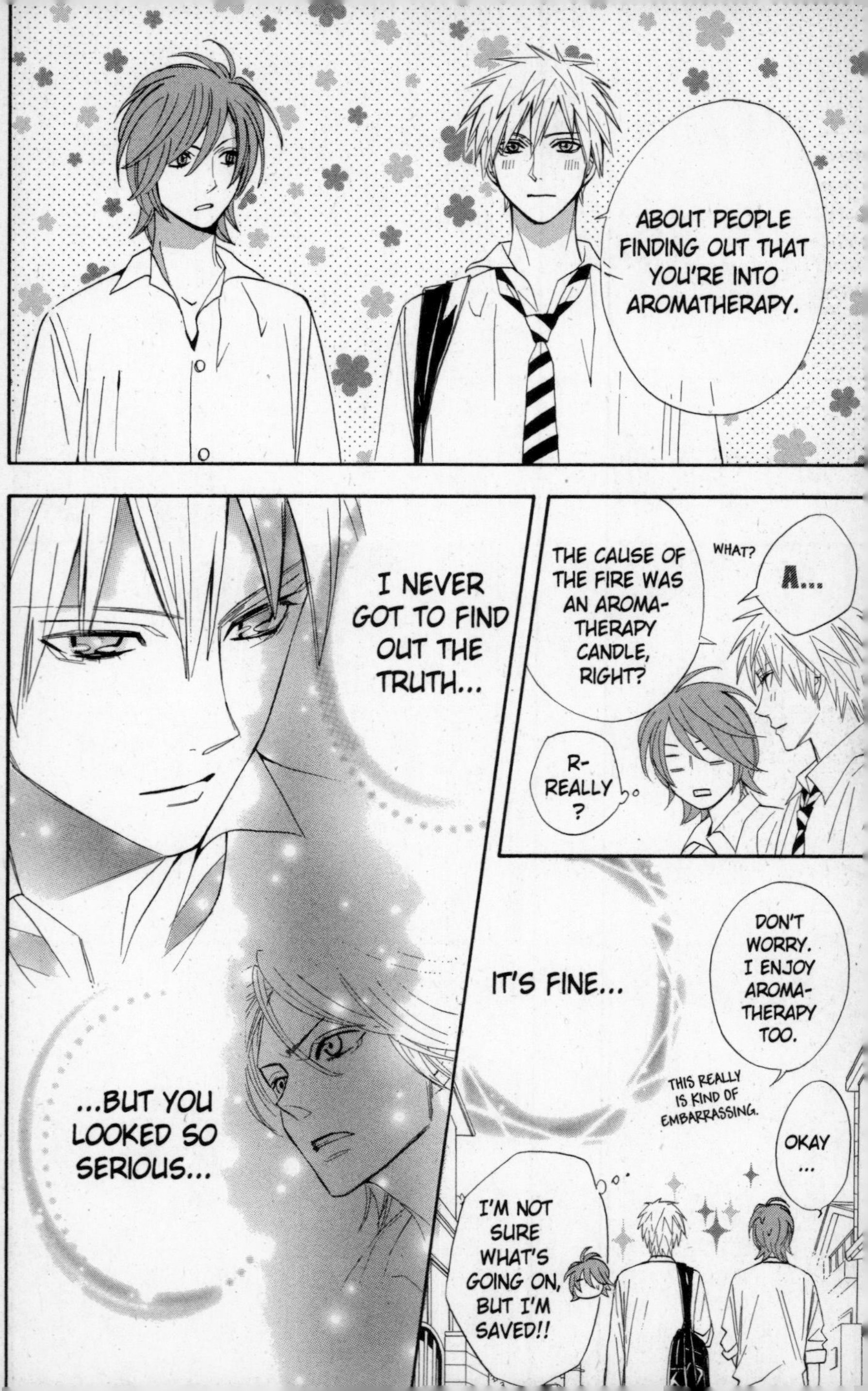
ABOUT PEOPLE FINDING OUT THAT YOU'RE INTO AROMATHERAPY.
A...
WHAT?
THE CAUSE OF THE FIRE WAS AN AROMA-THERAPY CANDLE, RIGHT?
R-REALLY?
DON'T WORRY. I ENJOY AROMA-THERAPY TOO.
OKAY...
THIS REALLY IS KIND OF EMBARRASSING.
IT'S FINE...
I'M NOT SURE WHAT'S GOING ON, BUT I'M SAVED!!
I NEVER GOT TO FIND OUT THE TRUTH...
...BUT YOU LOOKED SO SERIOUS...

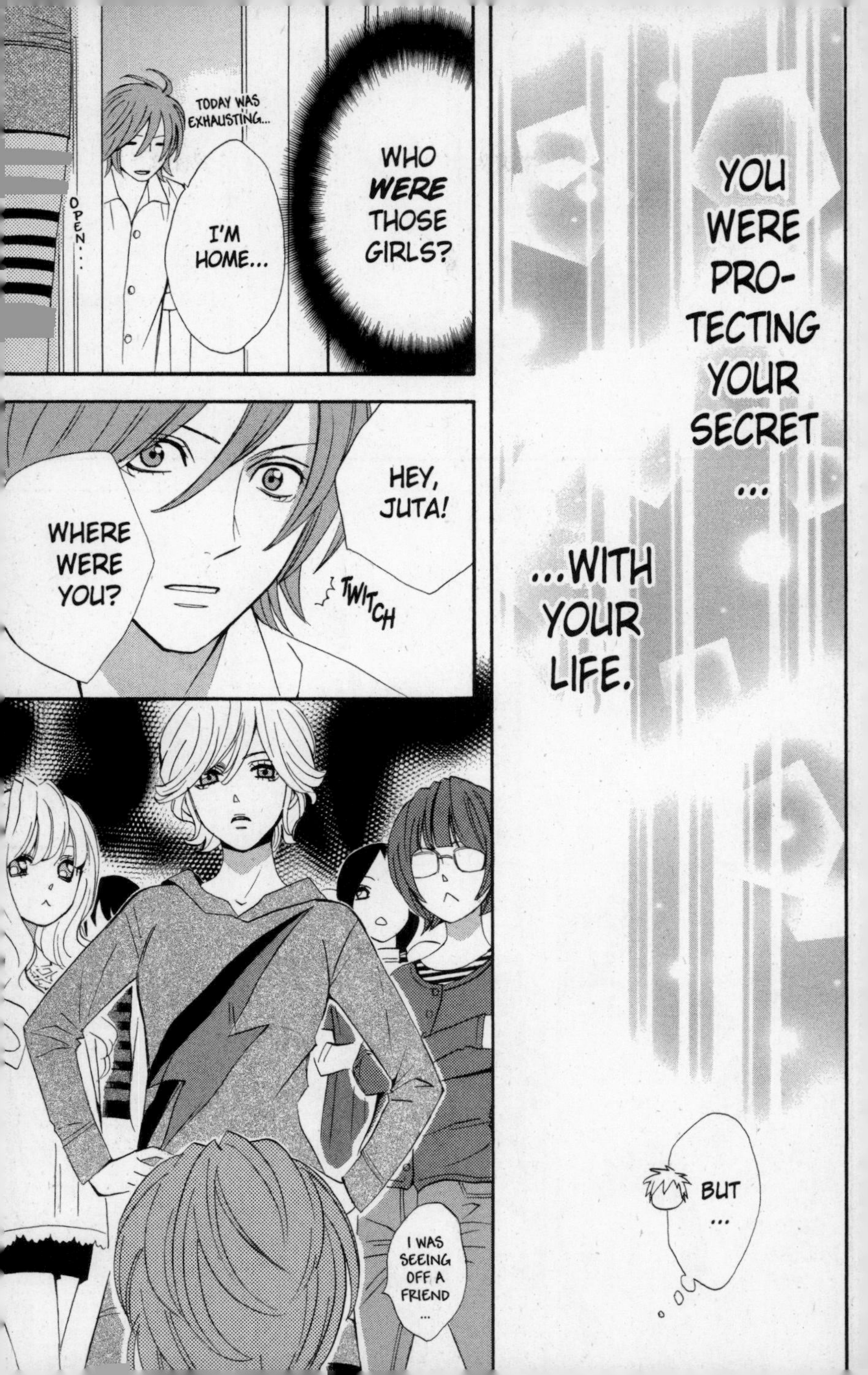
YOU WERE PRO-TECTING YOUR SECRET ...
...WITH YOUR LIFE.
BUT ...
WHO WERE THOSE GIRLS?
TODAY WAS EXHAUSTING...
I'M HOME...
OPEN...
HEY, JUTA!
TWITCH
WHERE WERE YOU?
I WAS SEEING OFF A FRIEND ...

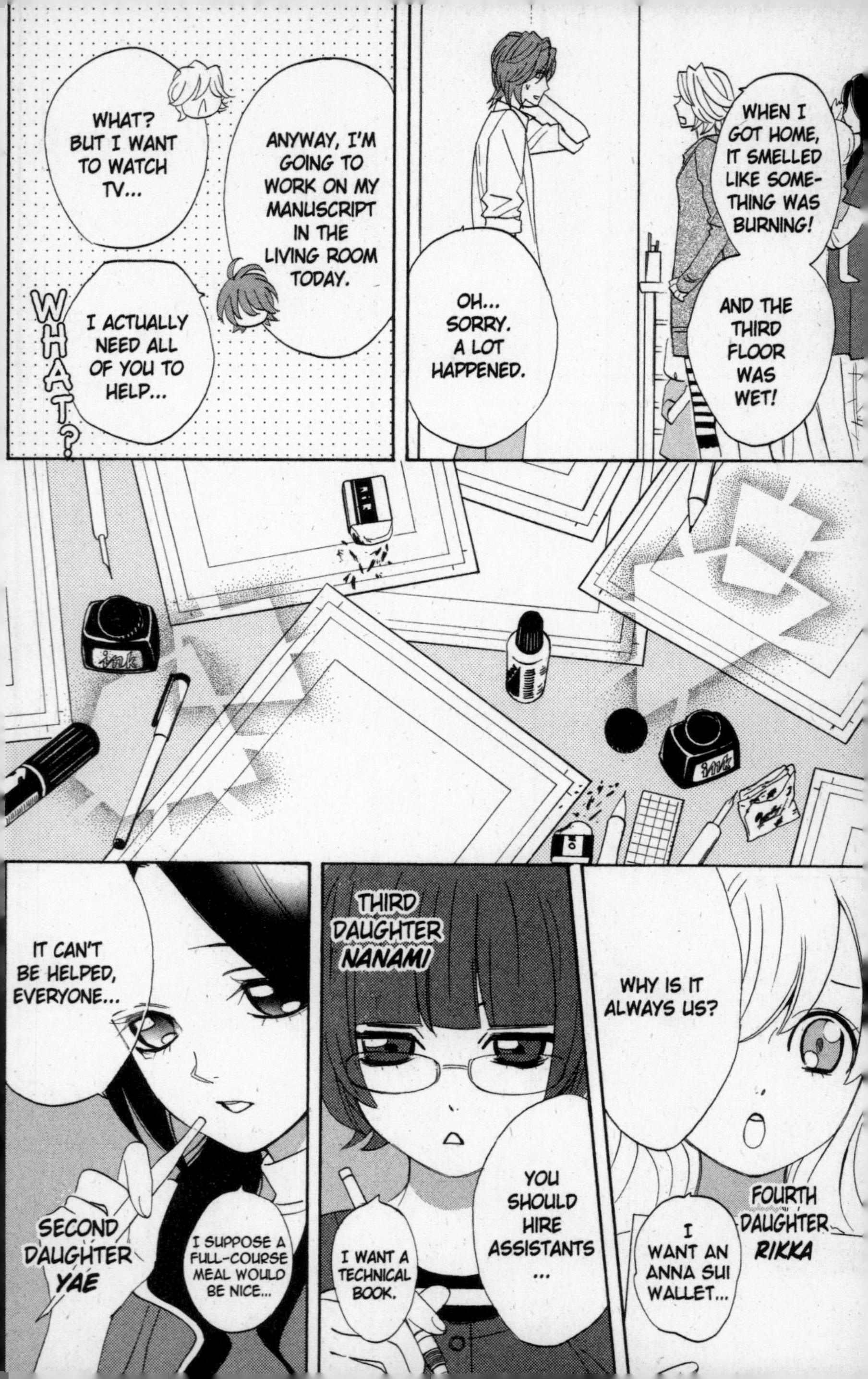
WHEN I GOT HOME, IT SMELLED LIKE SOMETHING WAS BURNING!
AND THE THIRD FLOOR WAS WET!
OH... SORRY. A LOT HAPPENED.
ANYWAY, I'M GOING TO WORK ON MY MANUSCRIPT IN THE LIVING ROOM TODAY.
WHAT? BUT I WANT TO WATCH TV...
I ACTUALLY NEED ALL OF YOU TO HELP...
WHAT?
WHY IS IT ALWAYS US?
FOURTH DAUGHTER RIKKA
I WANT AN ANNA SUI WALLET...
THIRD DAUGHTER NANAMI
YOU SHOULD HIRE ASSISTANTS ...
I WANT A TECHNICAL BOOK.
IT CAN'T BE HELPED, EVERYONE...
SECOND DAUGHTER YAE
I SUPPOSE A FULL-COURSE MEAL WOULD BE NICE...

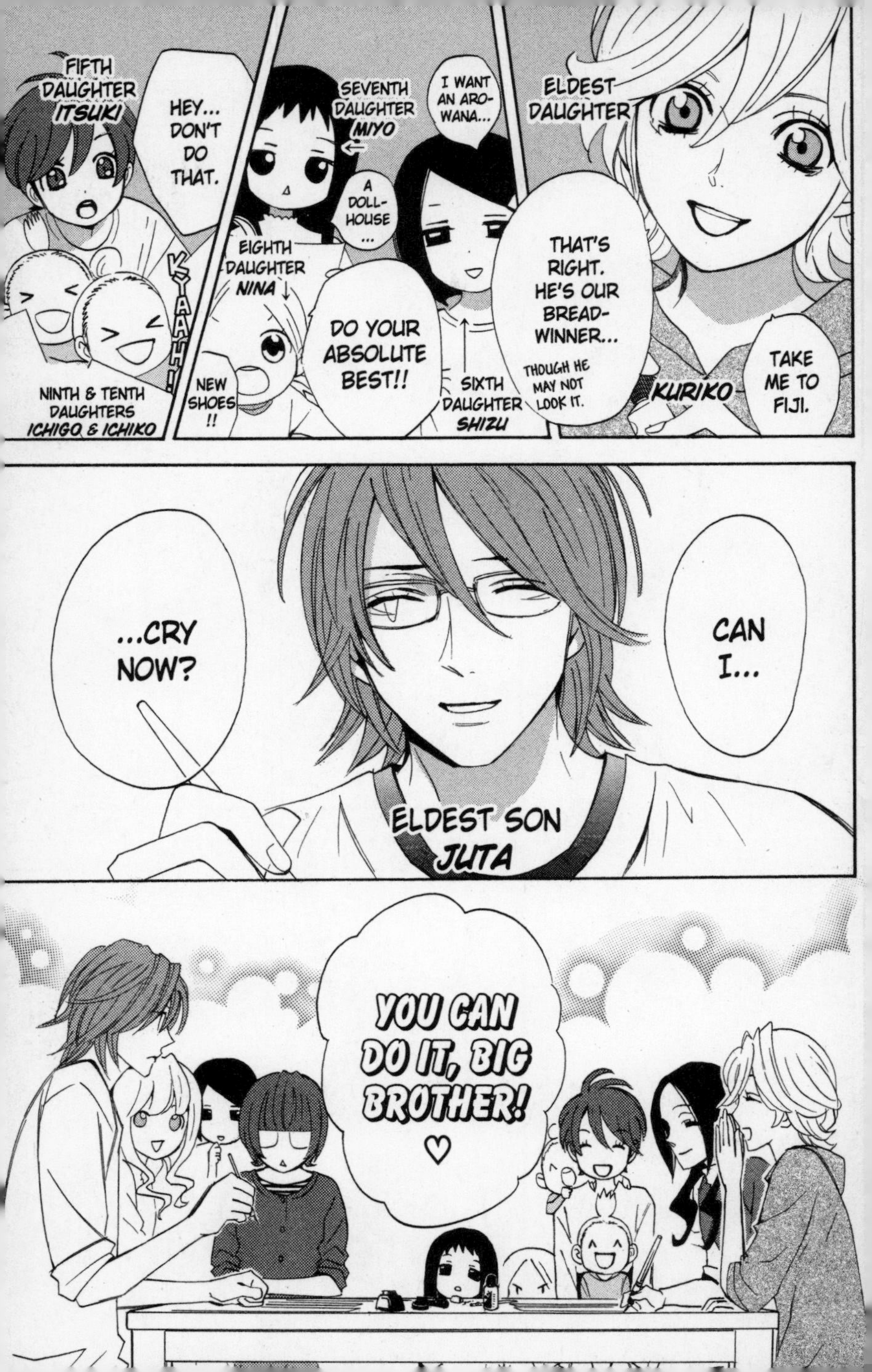

ELDEST DAUGHTER
THAT'S RIGHT. HE'S OUR BREAD-WINNER... THOUGH HE MAY NOT LOOK IT.
TAKE ME TO FIJI.
KURIKO
I WANT AN ARO-WANA...
SEVENTH DAUGHTER MIYO
A DOLL-HOUSE...
DO YOUR ABSOLUTE BEST!!
SIXTH DAUGHTER SHIZU
EIGHTH DAUGHTER NINA
NEW SHOES!!
HEY... DON'T DO THAT.
FIFTH DAUGHTER ITSUKI
KYAAAH!
NINTH & TENTH DAUGHTERS ICHIGO & ICHIKO
CAN I...
...CRY NOW?
ELDEST SON JUTA
YOU CAN DO IT, BIG BROTHER! ♥

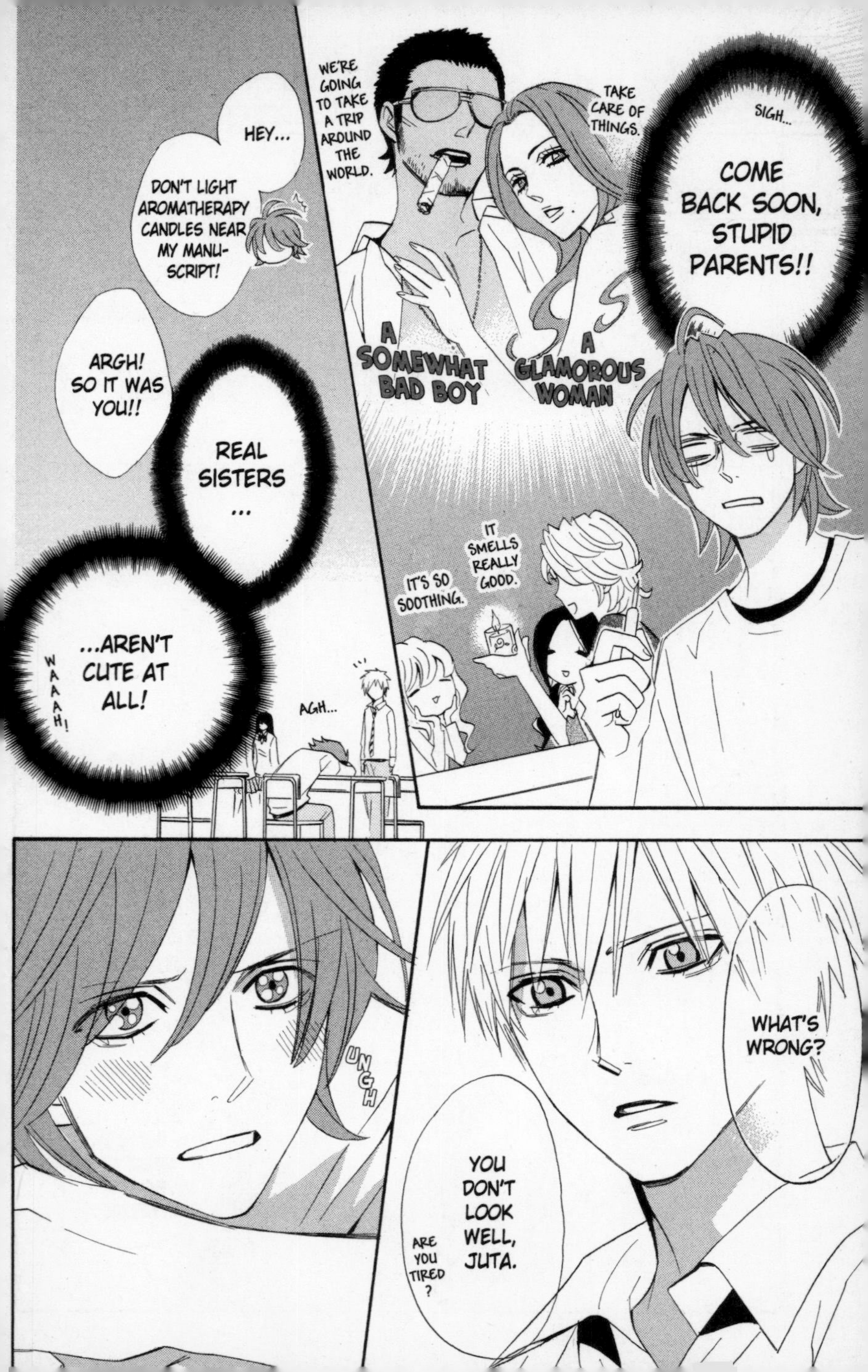
SIGH...
COME BACK SOON, STUPID PARENTS!!
TAKE CARE OF THINGS.
WE'RE GOING TO TAKE A TRIP AROUND THE WORLD.
A GLAMOROUS WOMAN
A SOMEWHAT BAD BOY
IT SMELLS REALLY GOOD.
IT'S SO SOOTHING.
HEY...
DON'T LIGHT AROMATHERAPY CANDLES NEAR MY MANU-SCRIPT!
ARGH! SO IT WAS YOU!!
REAL SISTERS ...
...AREN'T CUTE AT ALL!
WAAAAH!
AGH...
WHAT'S WRONG?
YOU DON'T LOOK WELL, JUTA.
ARE YOU TIRED?
UNGH

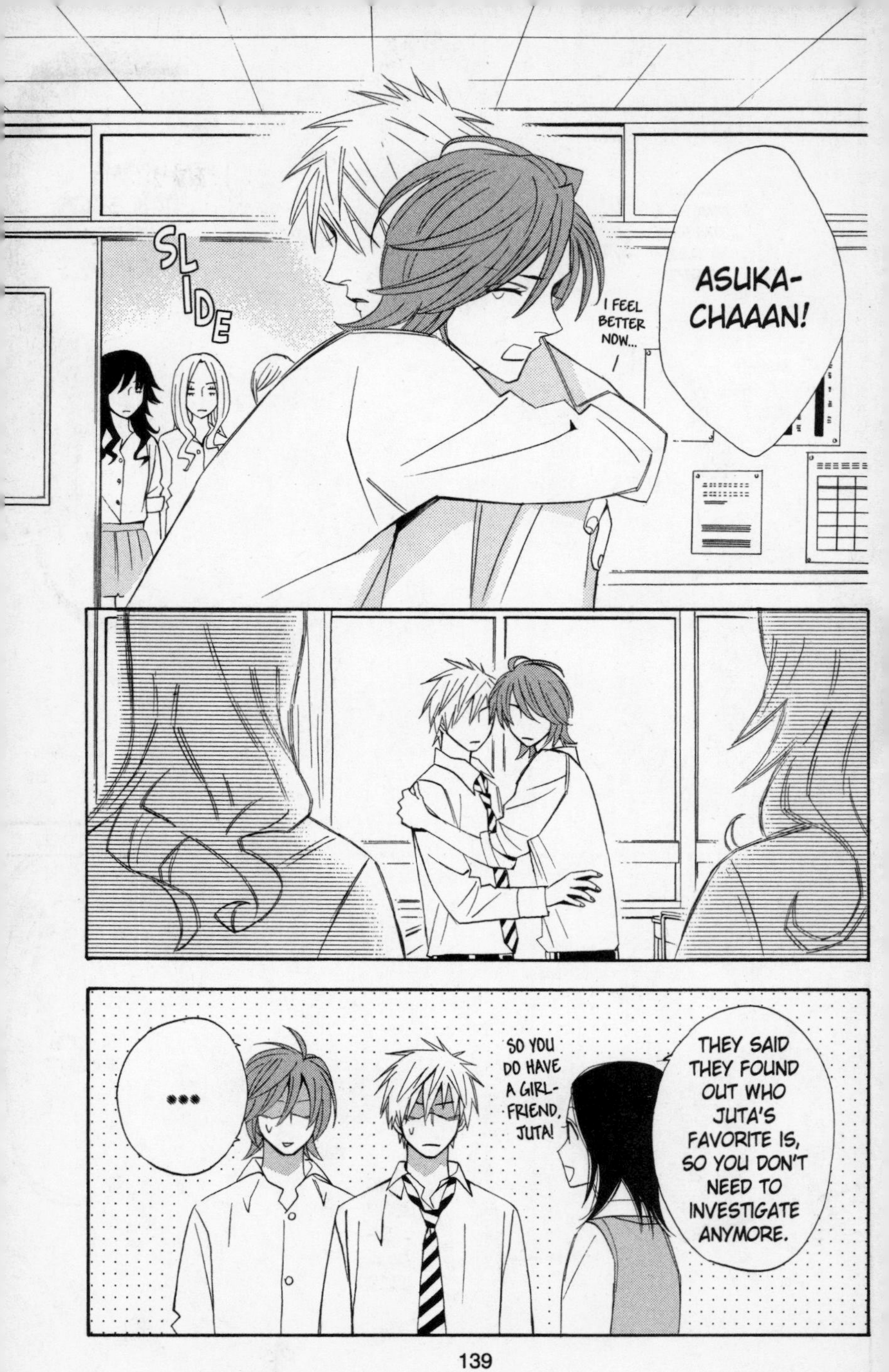
ASUKA-CHAAAN!
I FEEL BETTER NOW...
SLIDE
THEY SAID THEY FOUND OUT WHO JUTA'S FAVORITE IS, SO YOU DON'T NEED TO INVESTIGATE ANYMORE.
SO YOU DO HAVE A GIRL-FRIEND, JUTA!
...

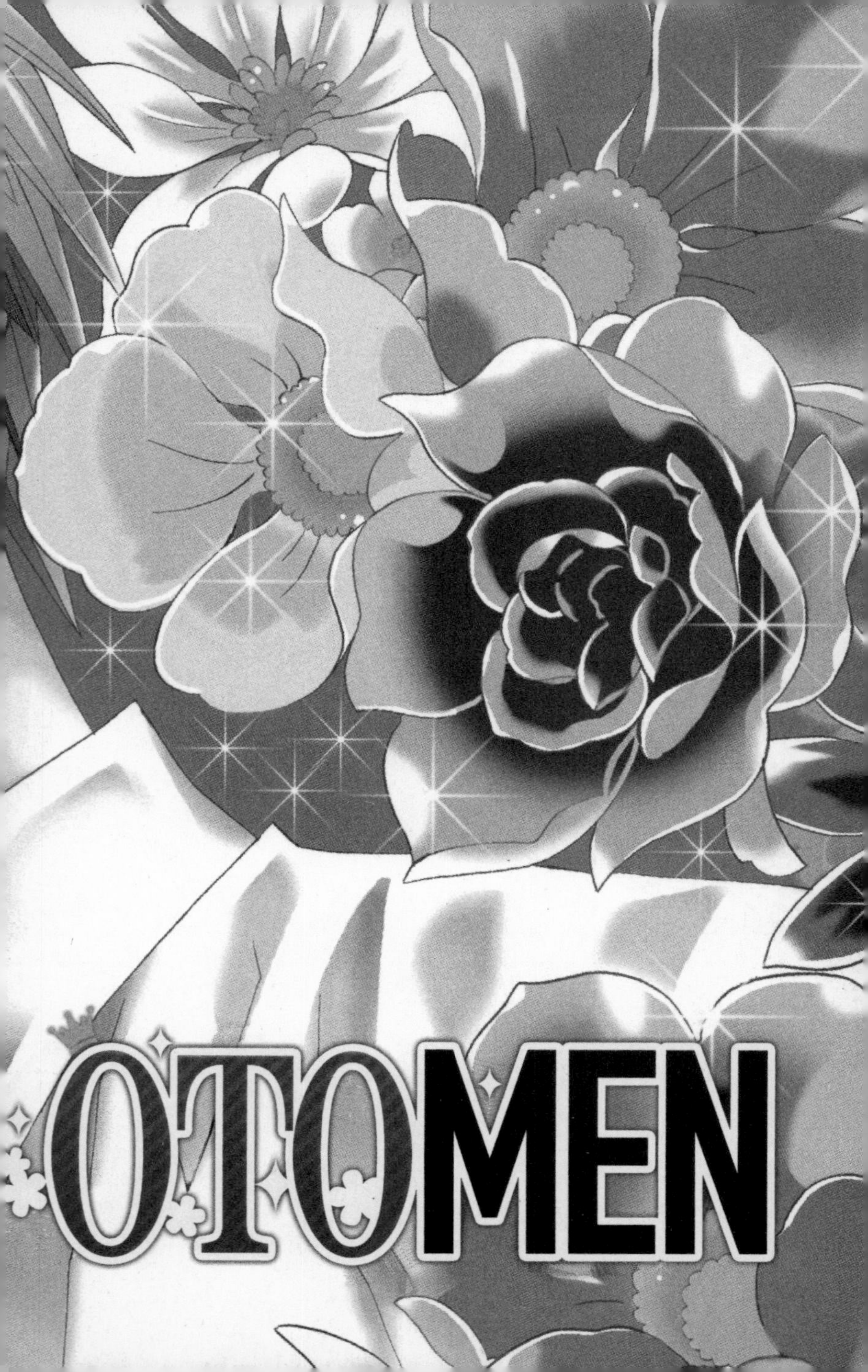
OTOMEN

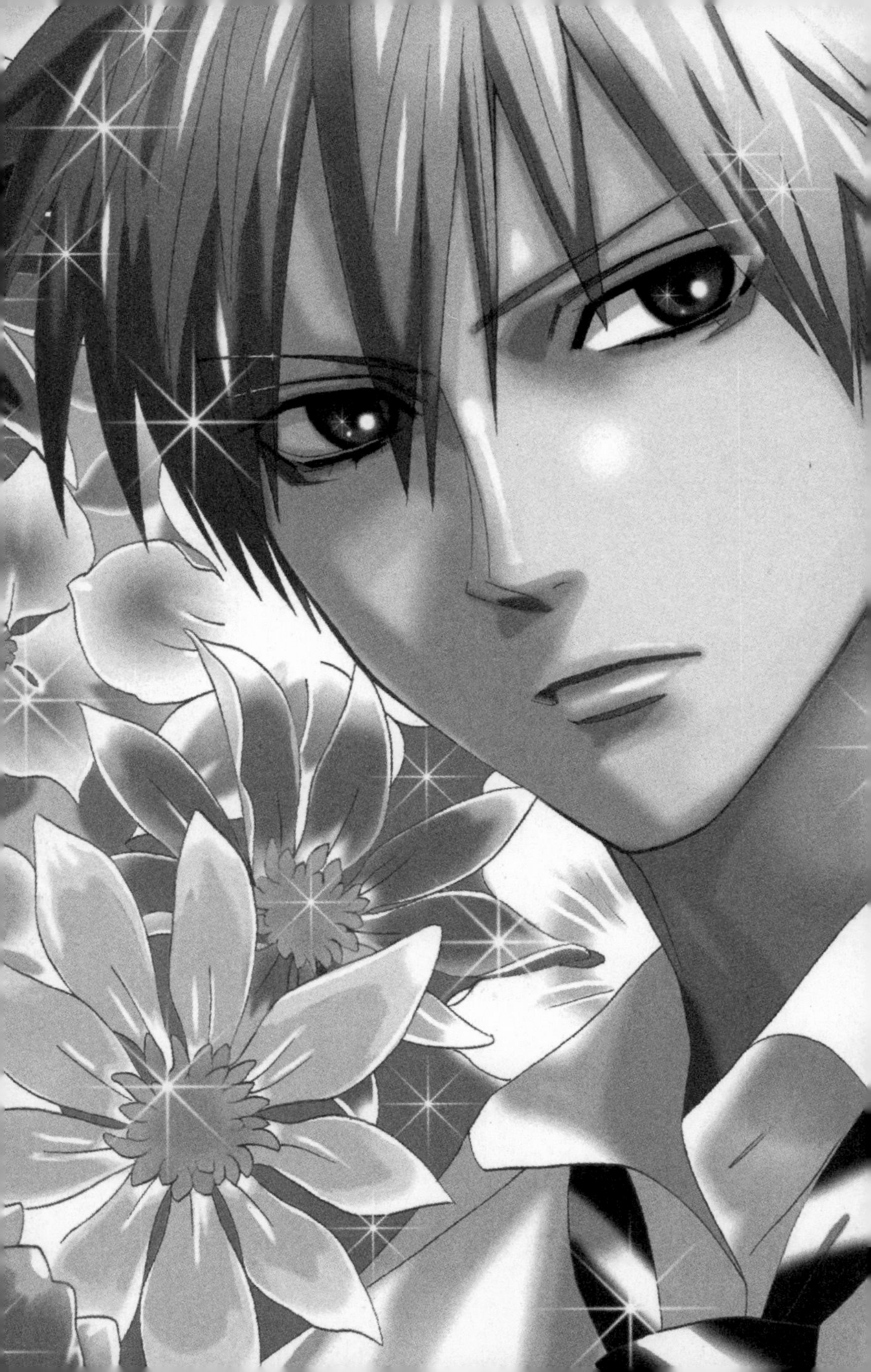

OTOMEN

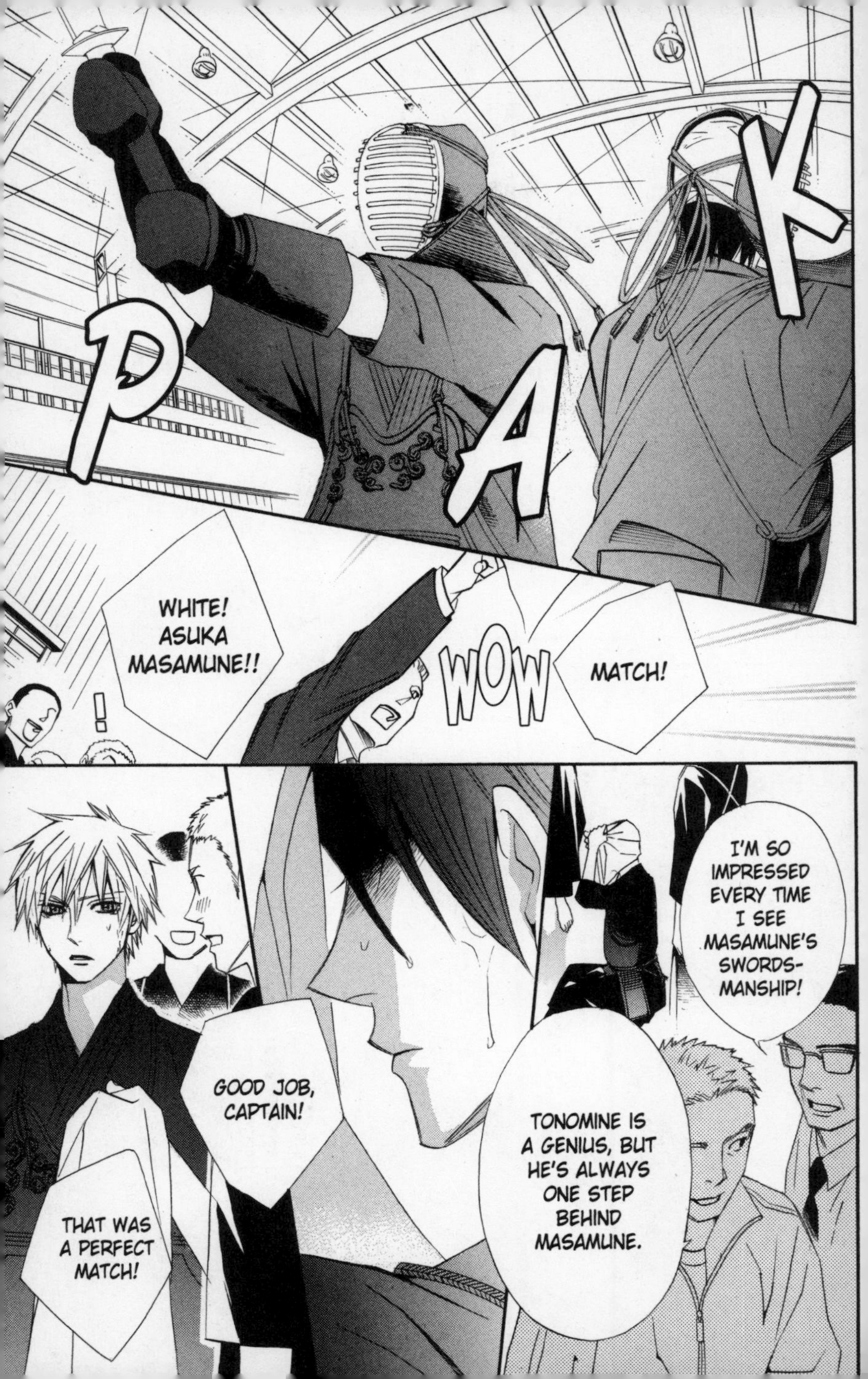
PAK
MATCH!
WOW
WHITE! ASUKA MASAMUNE!!
!
I'M SO IMPRESSED EVERY TIME I SEE MASAMUNE'S SWORDS-MANSHIP!
TONOMINE IS A GENIUS, BUT HE'S ALWAYS ONE STEP BEHIND MASAMUNE.
GOOD JOB, CAPTAIN!
THAT WAS A PERFECT MATCH!

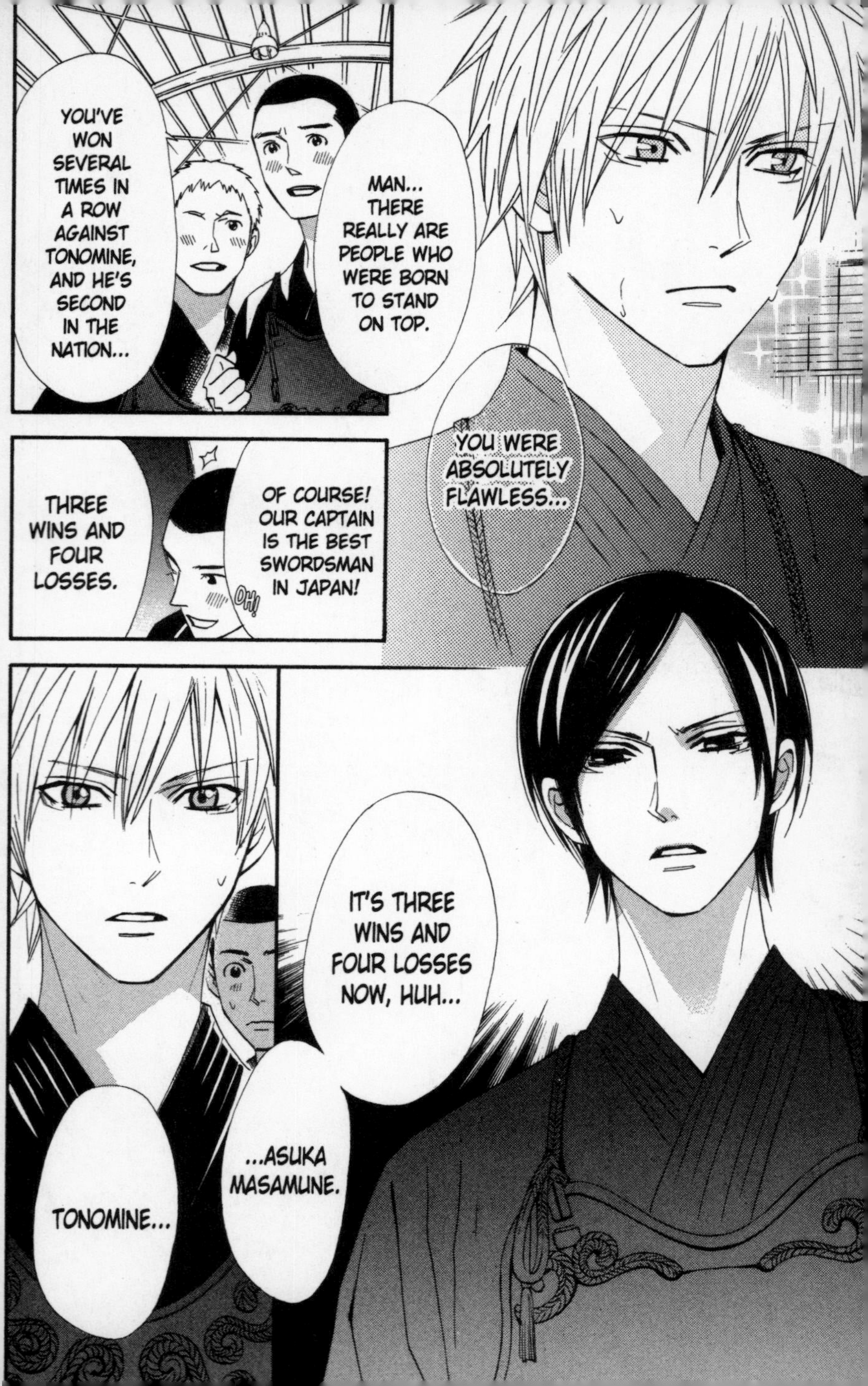

YOU WERE ABSOLUTELY FLAWLESS...
MAN... THERE REALLY ARE PEOPLE WHO WERE BORN TO STAND ON TOP.
YOU'VE WON SEVERAL TIMES IN A ROW AGAINST TONOMINE, AND HE'S SECOND IN THE NATION...
OF COURSE! OUR CAPTAIN IS THE BEST SWORDSMAN IN JAPAN!
OH!
THREE WINS AND FOUR LOSSES.
IT'S THREE WINS AND FOUR LOSSES NOW, HUH...
...ASUKA MASAMUNE.
TONOMINE...

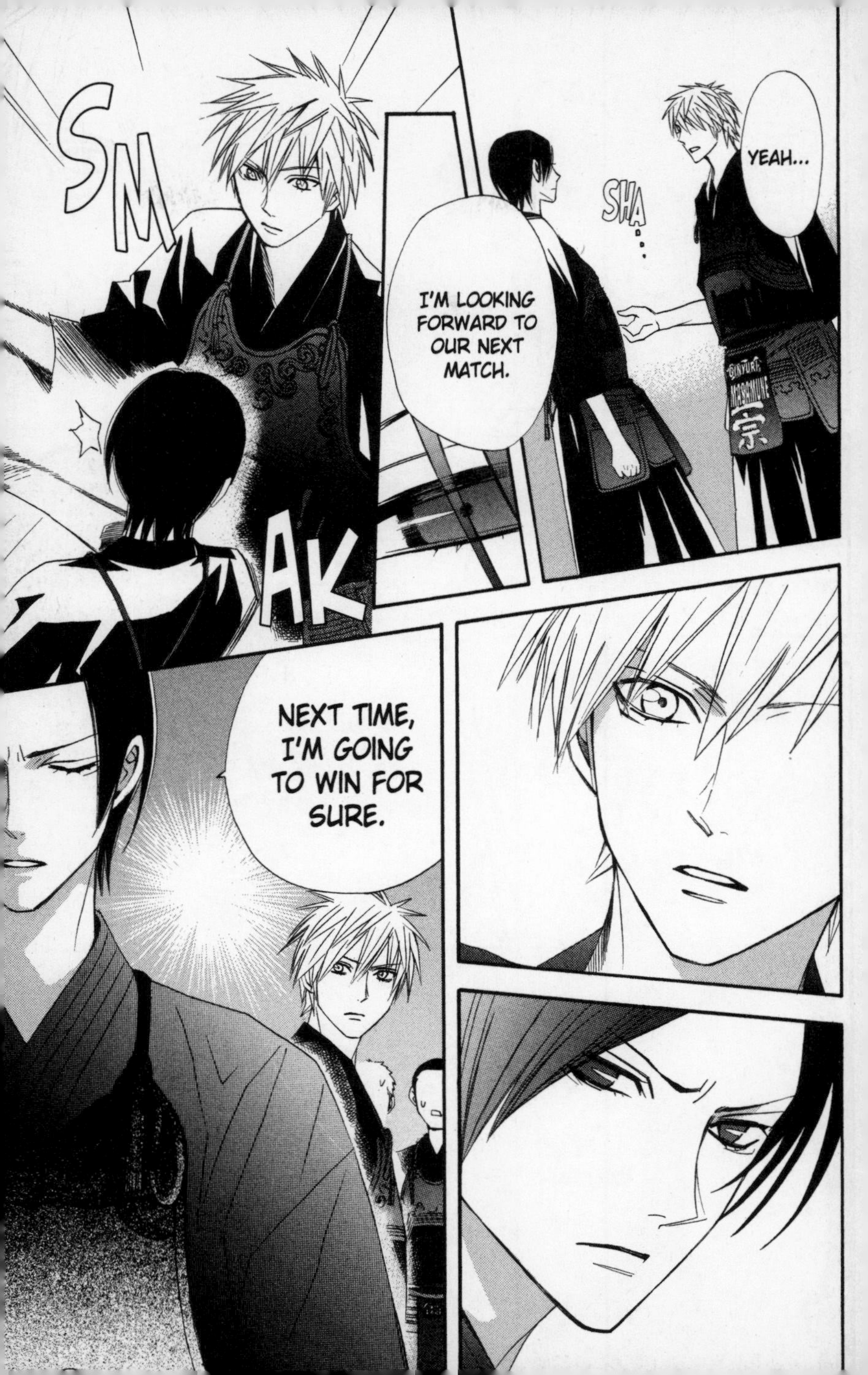
YEAH...
SHA...
I'M LOOKING FORWARD TO OUR NEXT MATCH.
SMAK
NEXT TIME, I'M GOING TO WIN FOR SURE.

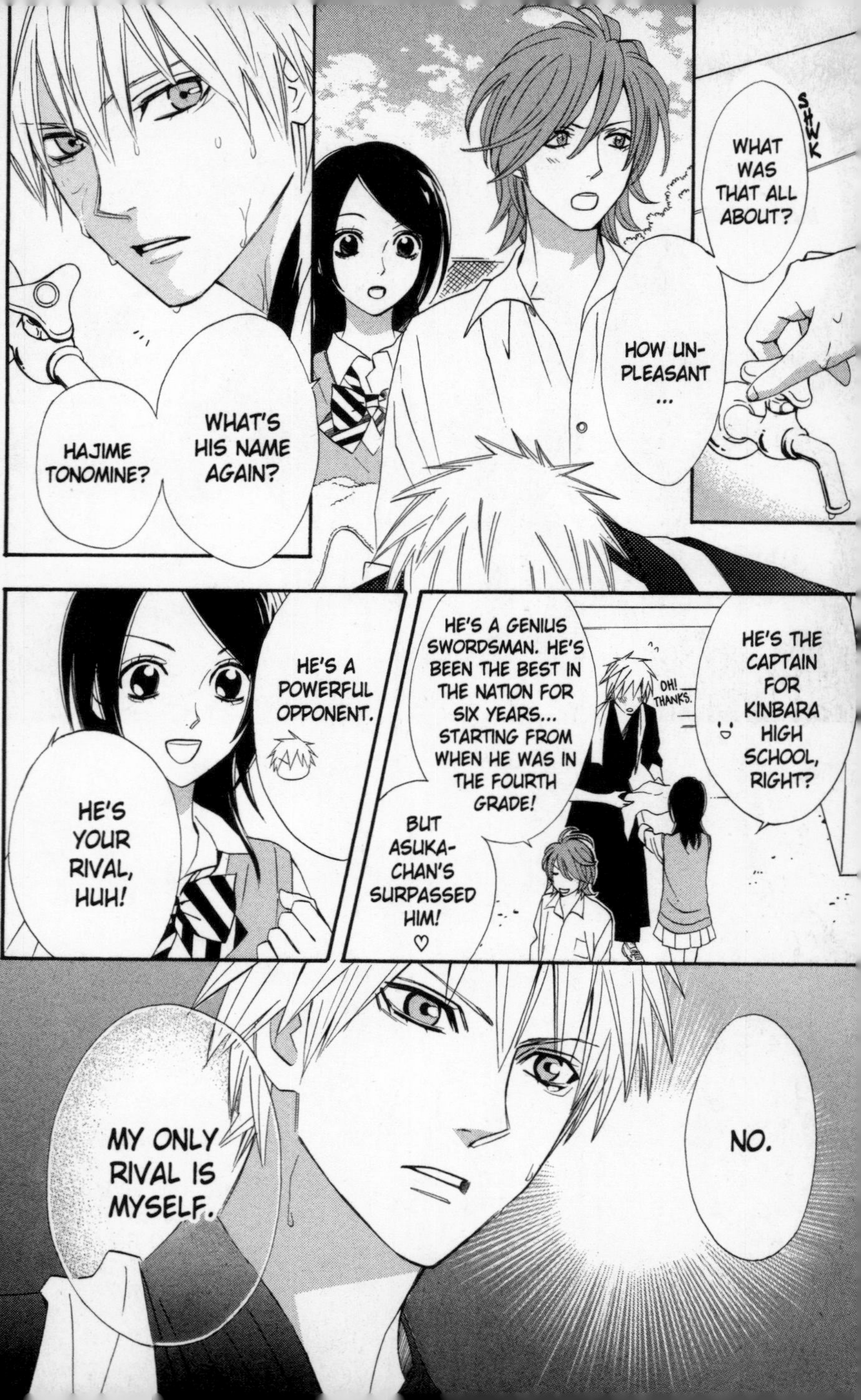
SHWK
WHAT WAS THAT ALL ABOUT?
HOW UN-PLEASANT ...
WHAT'S HIS NAME AGAIN?
HAJIME TONOMINE?
HE'S THE CAPTAIN FOR KINBARA HIGH SCHOOL, RIGHT?
OH! THANKS.
HE'S A GENIUS SWORDSMAN. HE'S BEEN THE BEST IN THE NATION FOR SIX YEARS... STARTING FROM WHEN HE WAS IN THE FOURTH GRADE!
BUT ASUKA-CHAN'S SURPASSED HIM! ♡
HE'S A POWERFUL OPPONENT.
HE'S YOUR RIVAL, HUH!
NO.
MY ONLY RIVAL IS MYSELF.

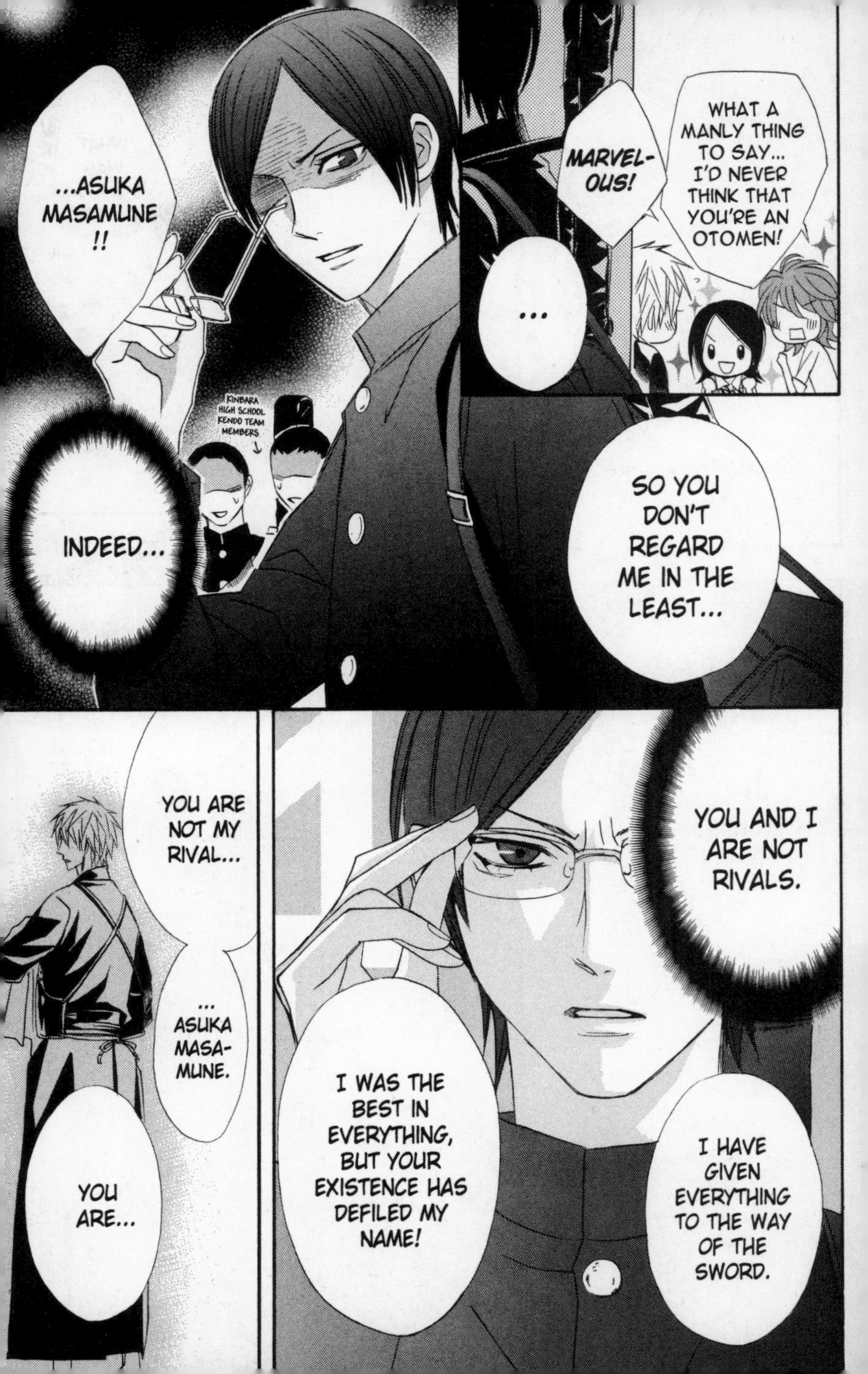
WHAT A MANLY THING TO SAY... I'D NEVER THINK THAT YOU'RE AN OTOMEN!
MARVEL-OUS!
...
...ASUKA MASAMUNE !!
SO YOU DON'T REGARD ME IN THE LEAST...
KINBARA HIGH SCHOOL KENDO TEAM MEMBERS
INDEED...
YOU AND I ARE NOT RIVALS.
I HAVE GIVEN EVERYTHING TO THE WAY OF THE SWORD.
I WAS THE BEST IN EVERYTHING, BUT YOUR EXISTENCE HAS DEFILED MY NAME!
YOU ARE NOT MY RIVAL...
... ASUKA MASA-MUNE.
YOU ARE...

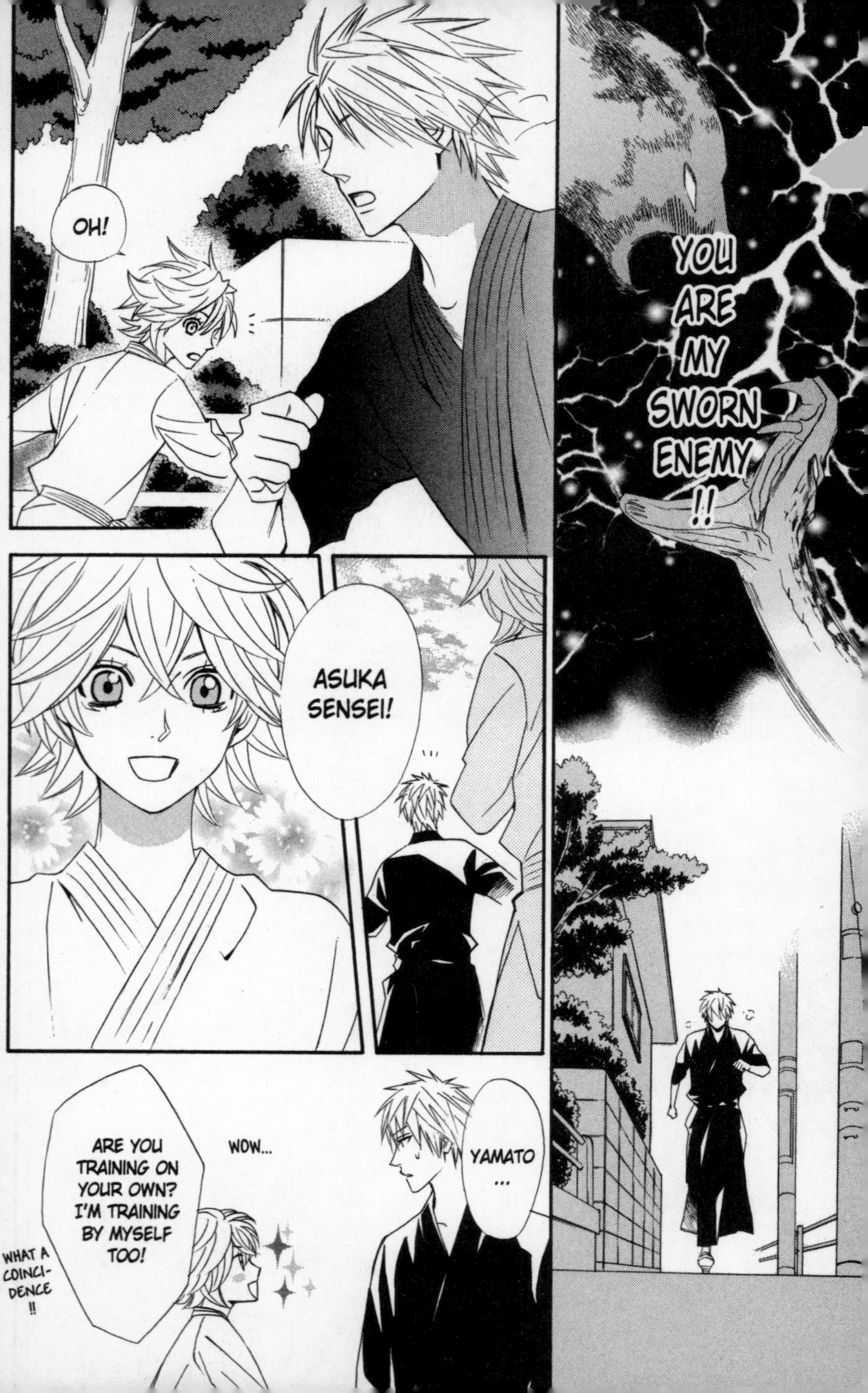
YOU ARE MY SWORN ENEMY !!
OH!
ASUKA SENSEI!
YAMATO ...
WOW...
ARE YOU TRAINING ON YOUR OWN? I'M TRAINING BY MYSELF TOO!
WHAT A COINCI-DENCE !!

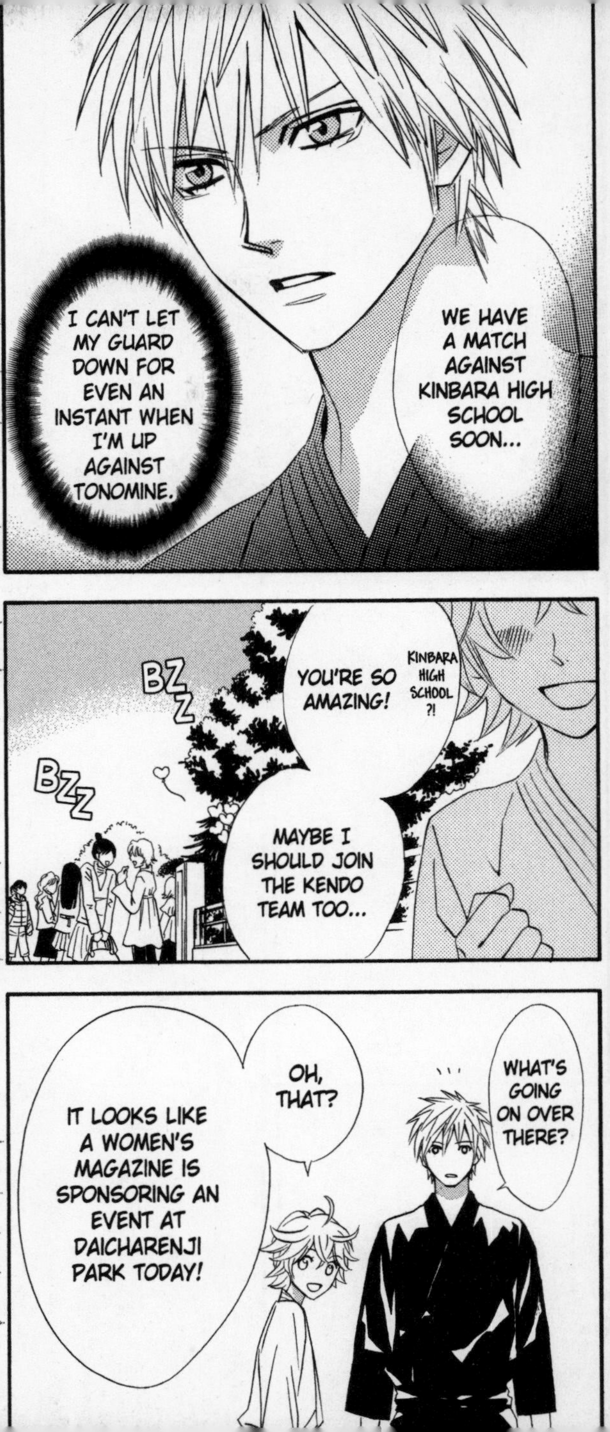
WE HAVE A MATCH AGAINST KINBARA HIGH SCHOOL SOON...
I CAN'T LET MY GUARD DOWN FOR EVEN AN INSTANT WHEN I'M UP AGAINST TONOMINE.
KINBARA HIGH SCHOOL ?!
YOU'RE SO AMAZING!
MAYBE I SHOULD JOIN THE KENDO TEAM TOO...
BZZ
BZZ
WHAT'S GOING ON OVER THERE?
OH, THAT?
IT LOOKS LIKE A WOMEN'S MAGAZINE IS SPONSORING AN EVENT AT DAICHARENJI PARK TODAY!

Production Assistance:

Shimada-san
Takowa-san
Kawashima-san
Sayaka-san
Kuwana-san
Tanaka-san
Nishizawa-san
Yone-san
Nakazawa-san
Sakurai-san

Special Thanks:

Prime Street
Harajuku Branch
Shogomama
Furuzuka-san
Abewo
Abe-san
All my readers

If you have any thoughts or opinions...
↓

Aya Kanno
c/o Otomen Editor
Viz Media
P.O. Box 77010
San Francisco, CA
94107

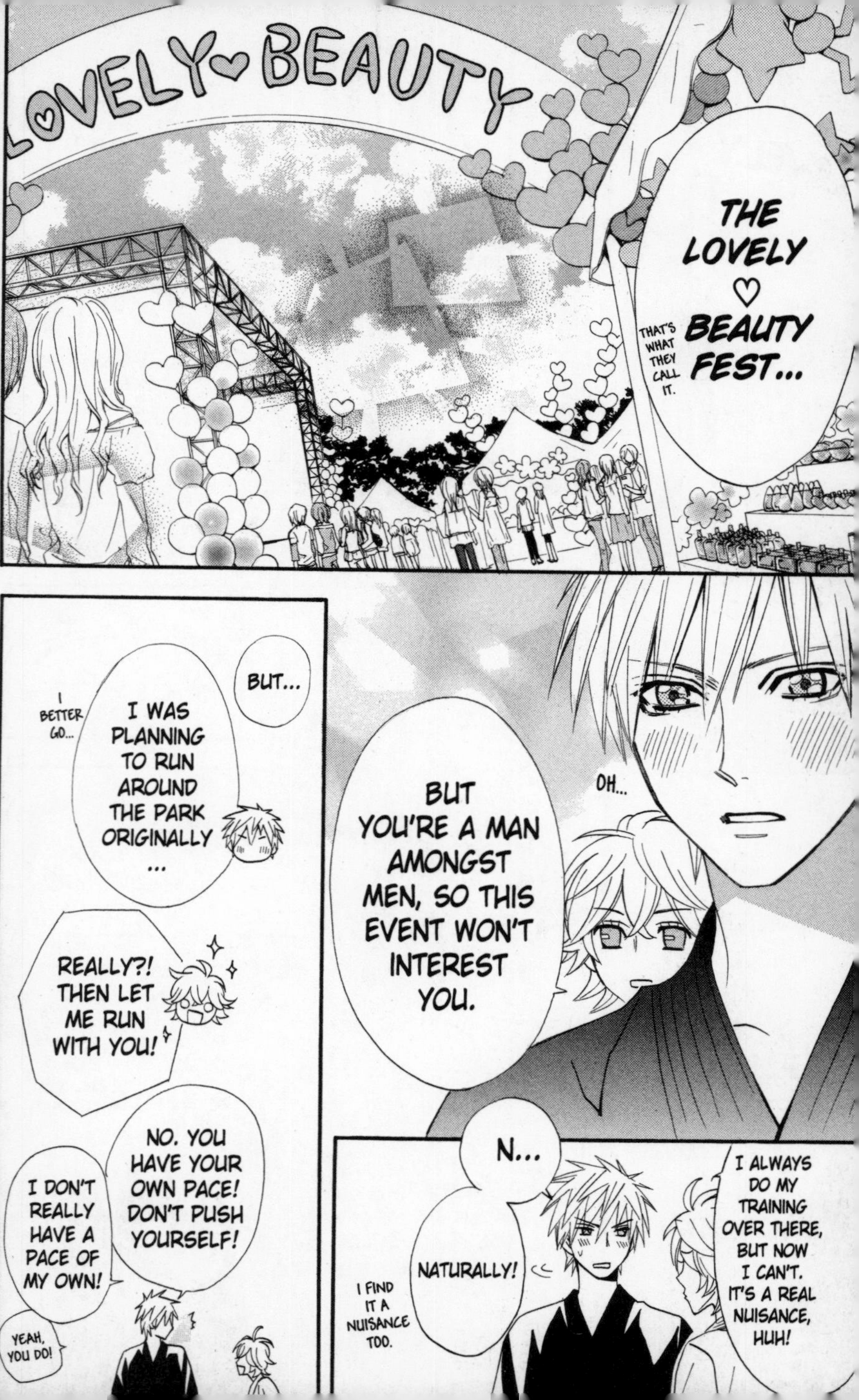
LOVELY♡BEAUTY
THE LOVELY ♡ BEAUTY FEST...
THAT'S WHAT THEY CALL IT.
OH...
BUT YOU'RE A MAN AMONGST MEN, SO THIS EVENT WON'T INTEREST YOU.
I ALWAYS DO MY TRAINING OVER THERE, BUT NOW I CAN'T. IT'S A REAL NUISANCE, HUH!
N...
NATURALLY!
I FIND IT A NUISANCE TOO.
BUT...
I WAS PLANNING TO RUN AROUND THE PARK ORIGINALLY...
I BETTER GO...
REALLY?! THEN LET ME RUN WITH YOU!
NO. YOU HAVE YOUR OWN PACE! DON'T PUSH YOURSELF!
I DON'T REALLY HAVE A PACE OF MY OWN!
YEAH, YOU DO!

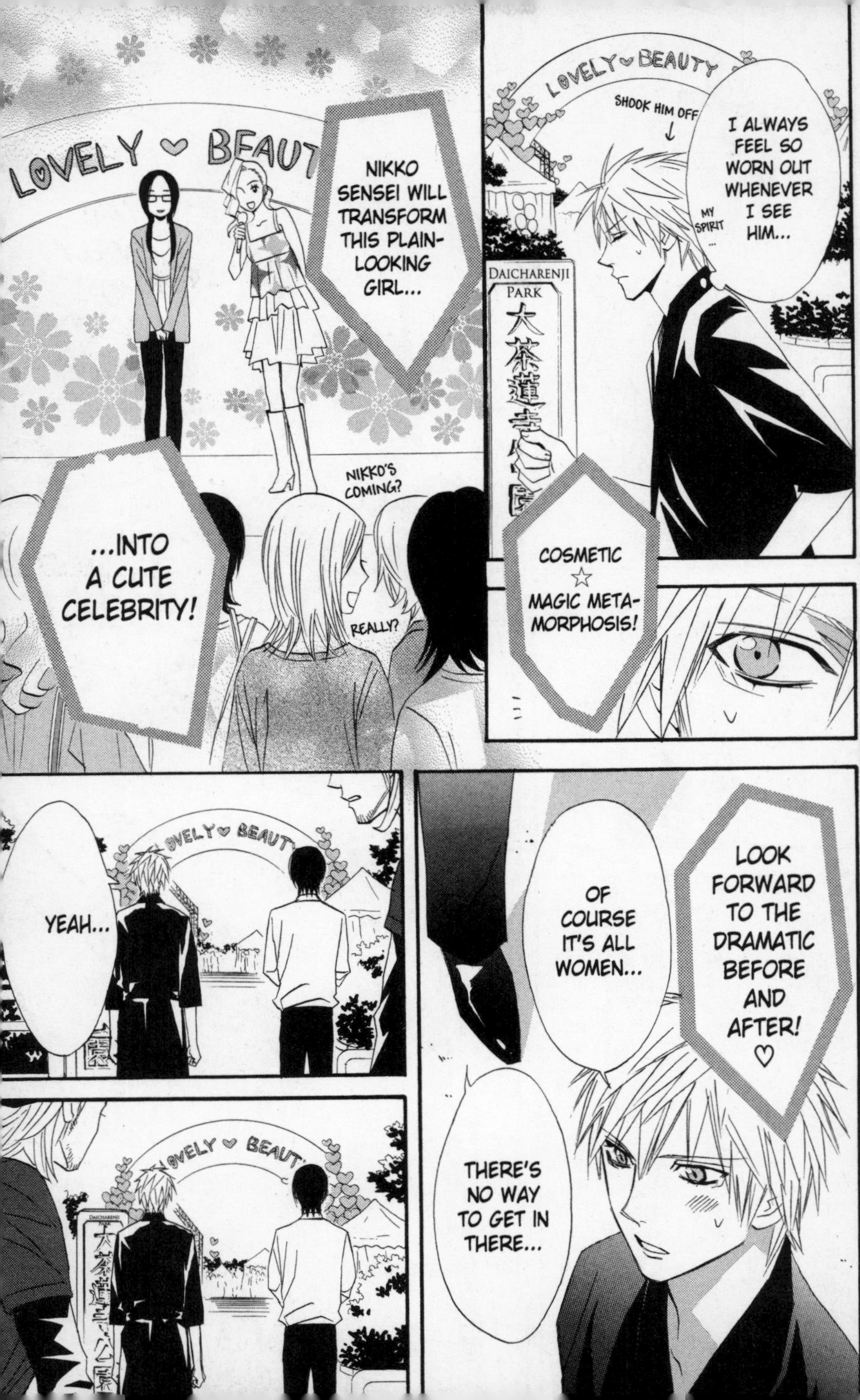
LOVELY ♥ BEAUTY
SHOOK HIM OFF
I ALWAYS FEEL SO WORN OUT WHENEVER I SEE HIM...
MY SPIRIT ...
DAICHARENJI PARK
大茶蓮寺公園
COSMETIC ☆ MAGIC META-MORPHOSIS!
LOVELY ♥ BEAUT
NIKKO SENSEI WILL TRANSFORM THIS PLAIN-LOOKING GIRL...
...INTO A CUTE CELEBRITY!
NIKKO'S COMING?
REALLY?
LOOK FORWARD TO THE DRAMATIC BEFORE AND AFTER! ♡
OF COURSE IT'S ALL WOMEN...
THERE'S NO WAY TO GET IN THERE...
LOVELY ♥ BEAUT
YEAH...
LOVELY ♥ BEAUT
DAICHARENJI PARK

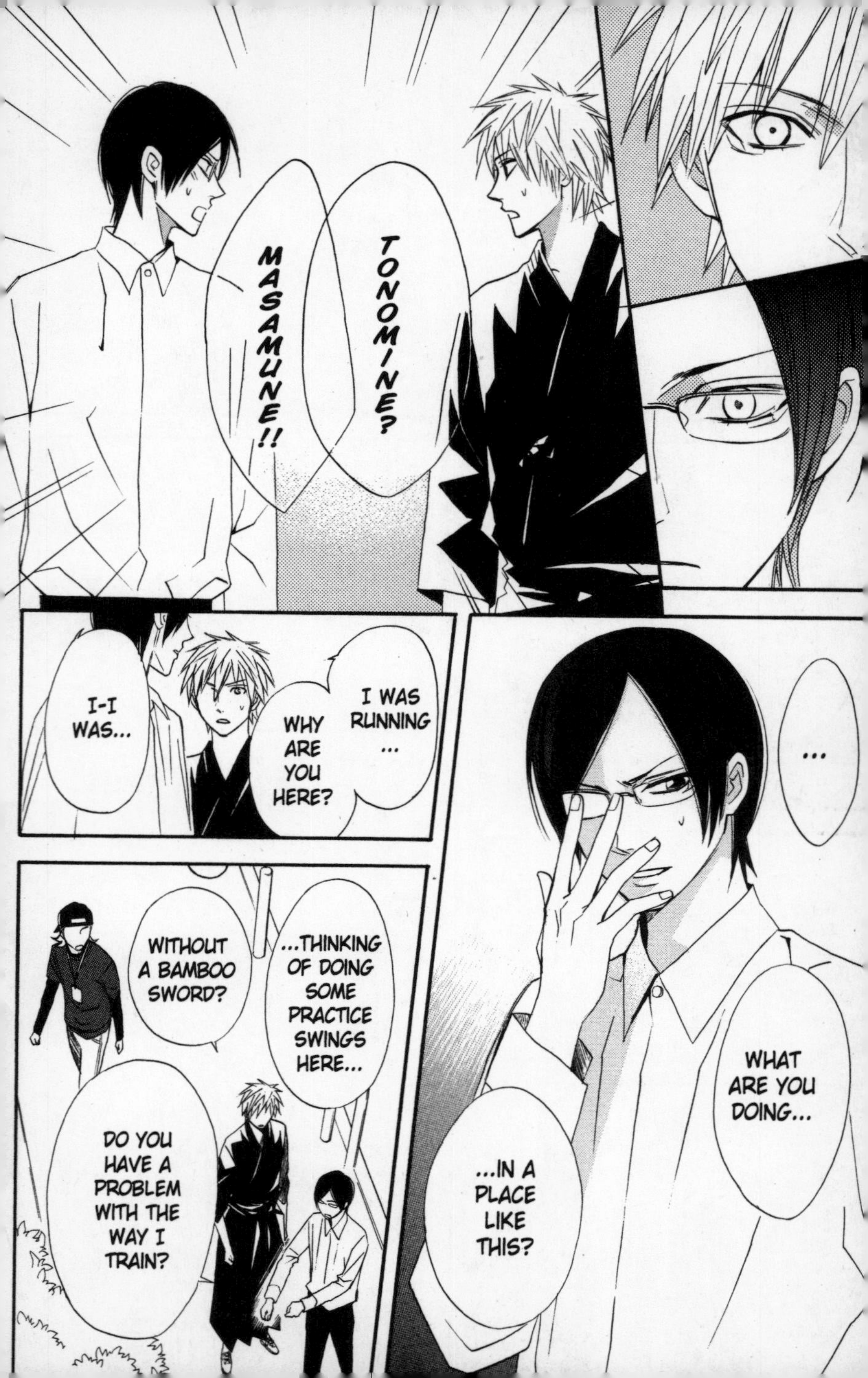
TONOMINE?
MASAMUNE!!
...
WHAT ARE YOU DOING...
...IN A PLACE LIKE THIS?
I WAS RUNNING ...
WHY ARE YOU HERE?
I-I WAS...
...THINKING OF DOING SOME PRACTICE SWINGS HERE...
WITHOUT A BAMBOO SWORD?
DO YOU HAVE A PROBLEM WITH THE WAY I TRAIN?

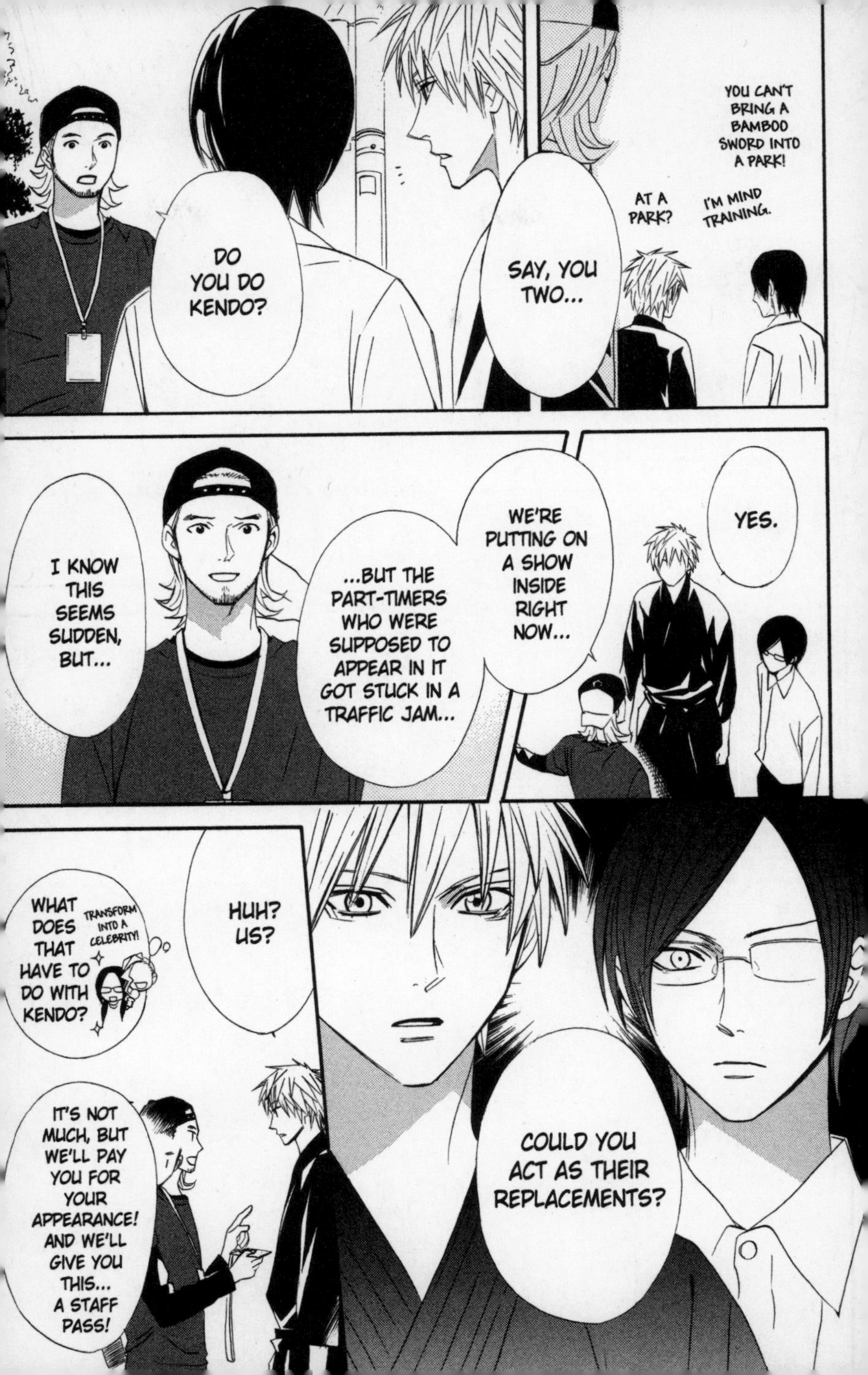
YOU CAN'T BRING A BAMBOO SWORD INTO A PARK!
I'M MIND TRAINING.
AT A PARK?
SAY, YOU TWO...
DO YOU DO KENDO?
YES.
WE'RE PUTTING ON A SHOW INSIDE RIGHT NOW...
...BUT THE PART-TIMERS WHO WERE SUPPOSED TO APPEAR IN IT GOT STUCK IN A TRAFFIC JAM...
I KNOW THIS SEEMS SUDDEN, BUT...
HUH? US?
WHAT DOES THAT HAVE TO DO WITH KENDO?
TRANSFORM INTO A CELEBRITY!
COULD YOU ACT AS THEIR REPLACEMENTS?
IT'S NOT MUCH, BUT WE'LL PAY YOU FOR YOUR APPEARANCE! AND WE'LL GIVE YOU THIS... A STAFF PASS!

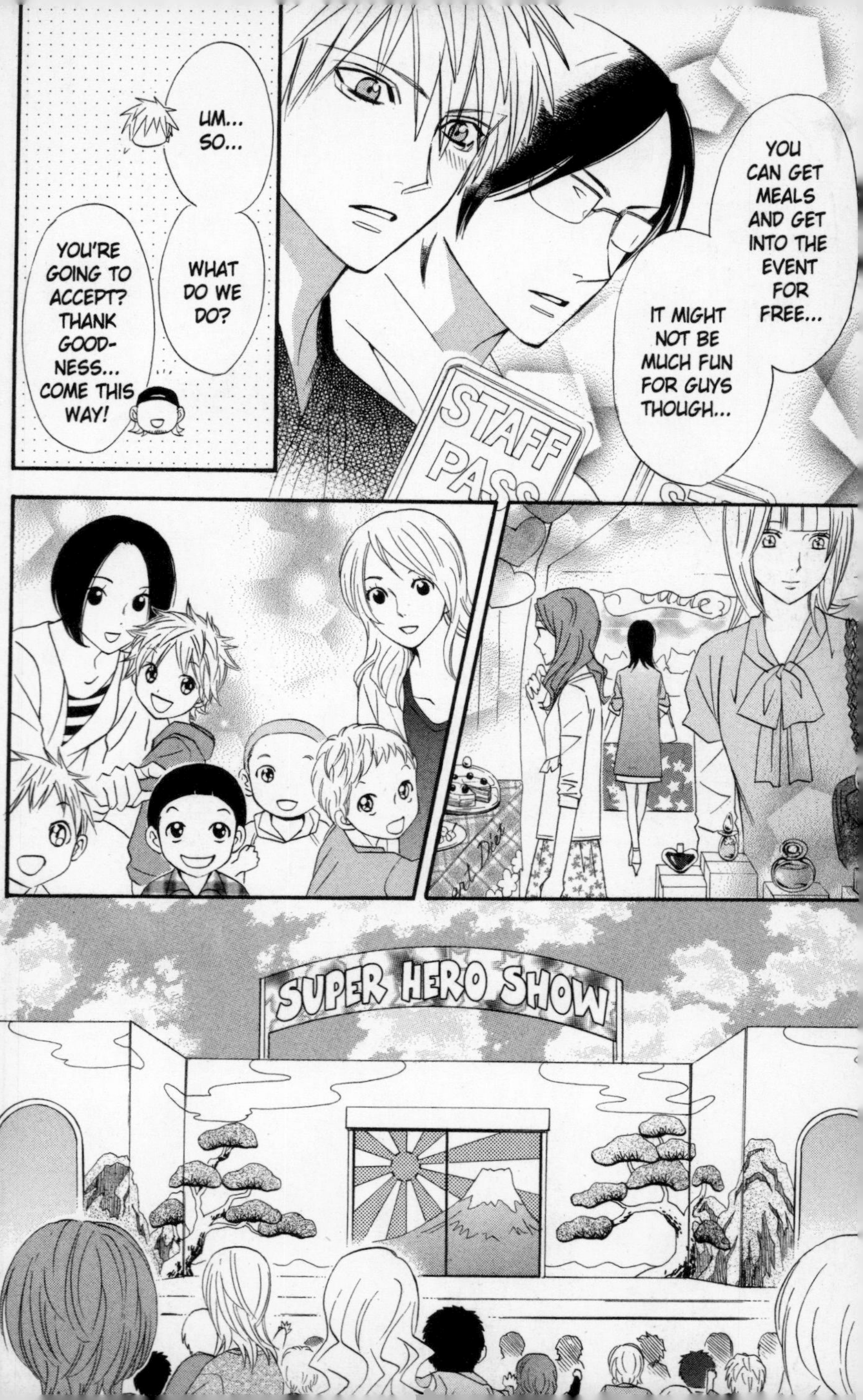
YOU CAN GET MEALS AND GET INTO THE EVENT FOR FREE...
IT MIGHT NOT BE MUCH FUN FOR GUYS THOUGH...
STAFF PASS
UM... SO...
WHAT DO WE DO?
YOU'RE GOING TO ACCEPT? THANK GOOD-NESS... COME THIS WAY!
SUPER HERO SHOW

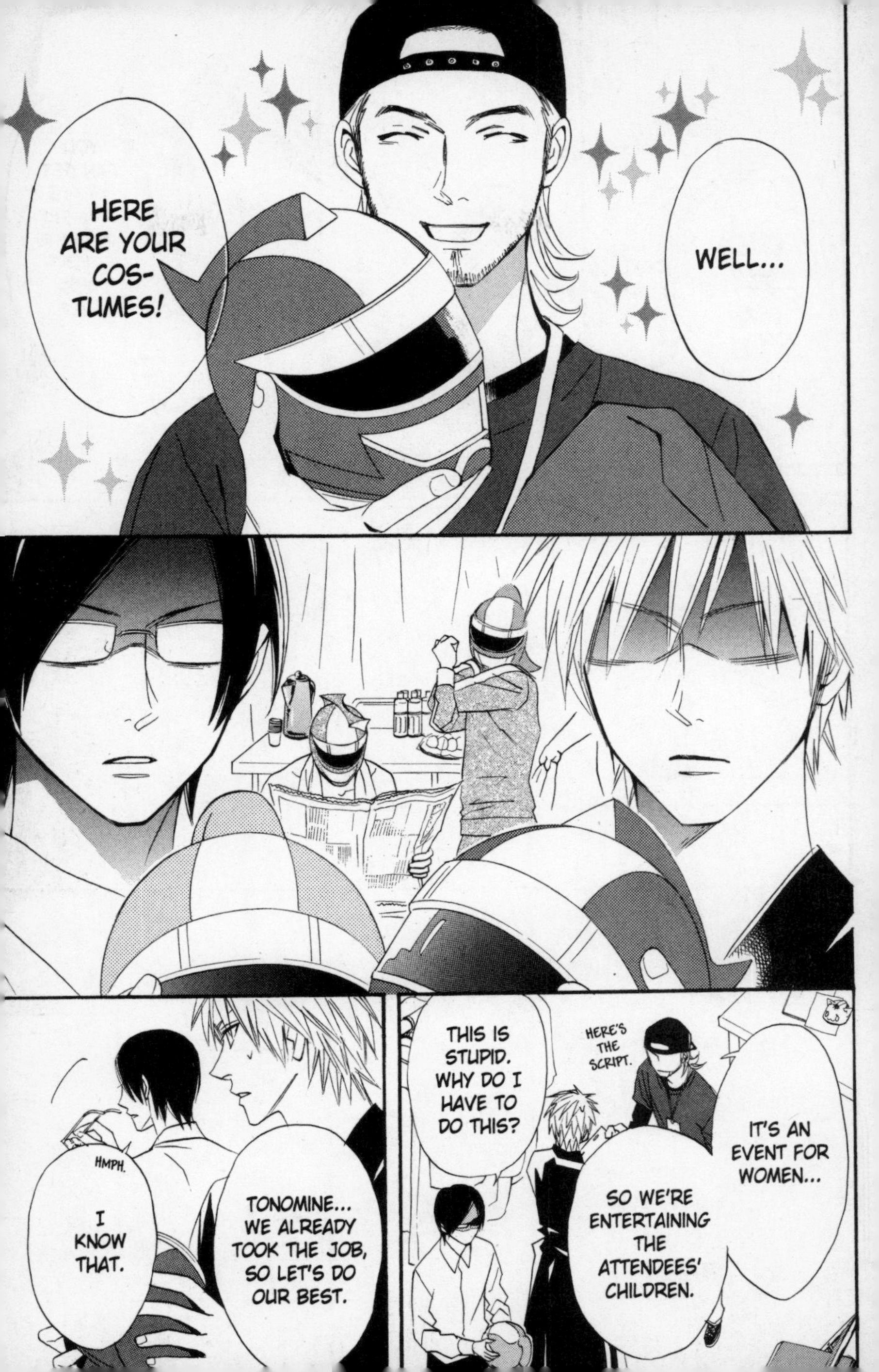
WELL...
HERE ARE YOUR COS-TUMES!
HERE'S THE SCRIPT.
THIS IS STUPID. WHY DO I HAVE TO DO THIS?
IT'S AN EVENT FOR WOMEN...
SO WE'RE ENTERTAINING THE ATTENDEES' CHILDREN.
TONOMINE... WE ALREADY TOOK THE JOB, SO LET'S DO OUR BEST.
HMPH.
I KNOW THAT.

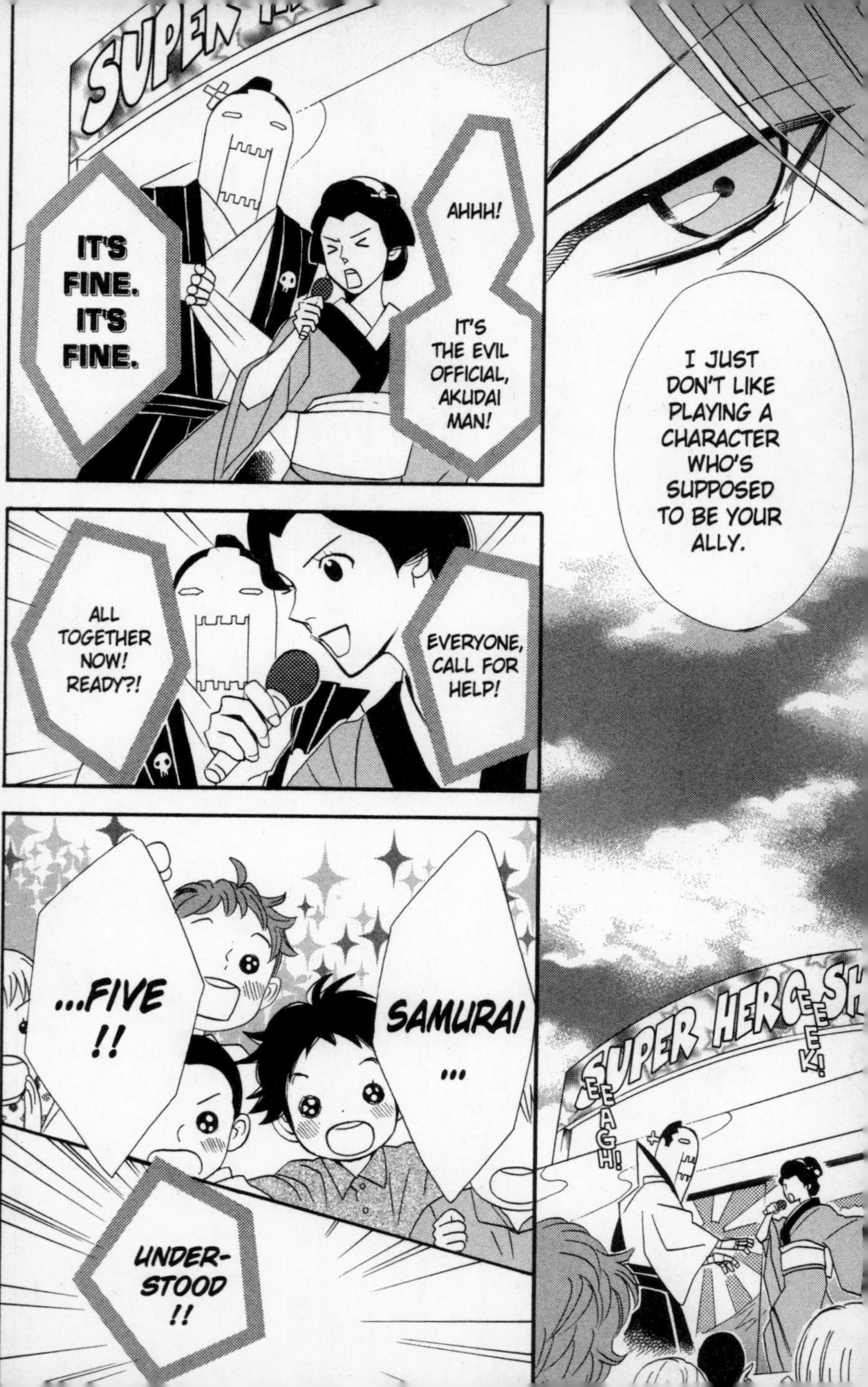

I JUST DON'T LIKE PLAYING A CHARACTER WHO'S SUPPOSED TO BE YOUR ALLY.
EEEK!
EEEAGH!
AHHH!
IT'S THE EVIL OFFICIAL, AKUDAI MAN!
IT'S FINE. IT'S FINE.
EVERYONE, CALL FOR HELP!
ALL TOGETHER NOW! READY?!
SAMURAI ...
...FIVE !!
UNDER-STOOD !!

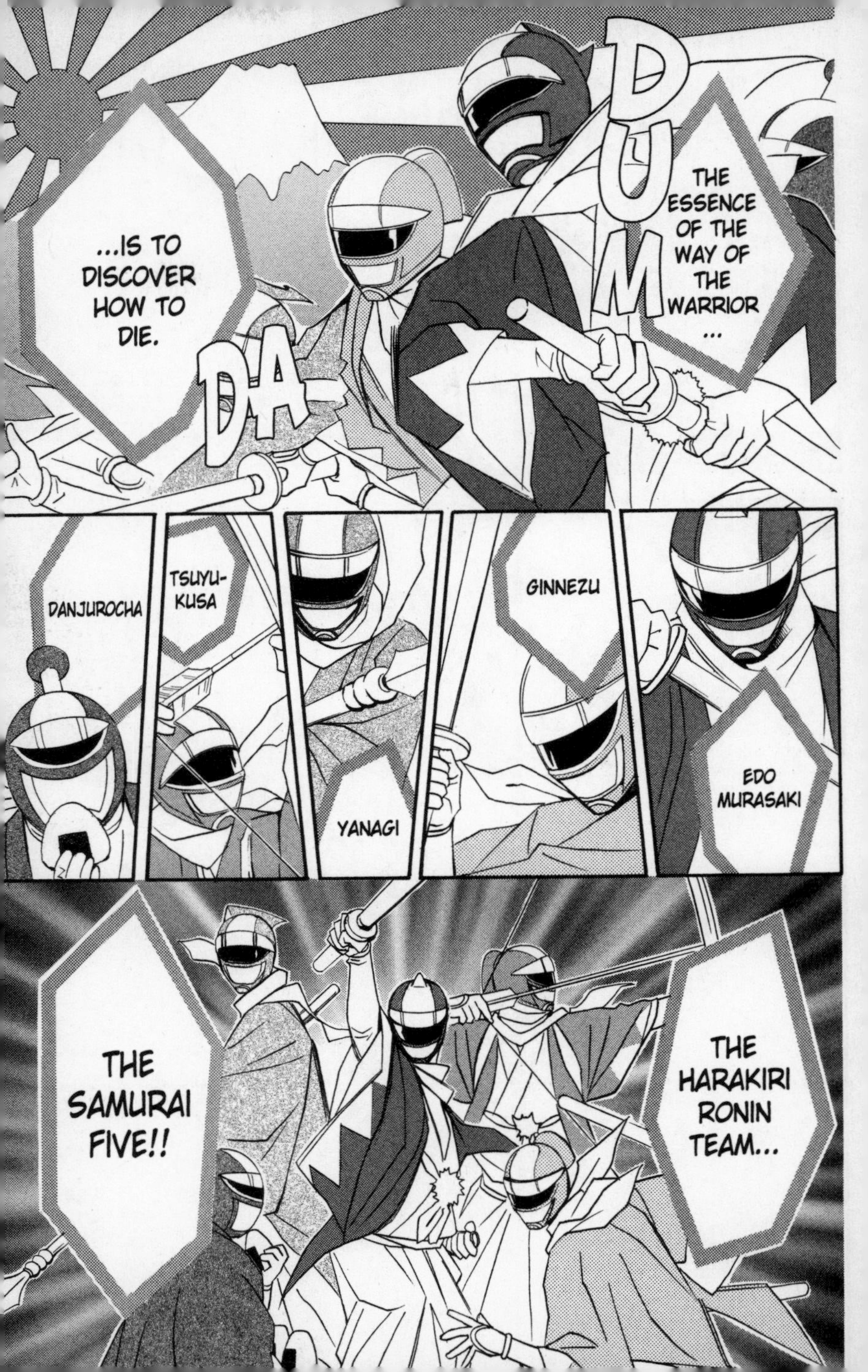
DUM
THE ESSENCE OF THE WAY OF THE WARRIOR...
...IS TO DISCOVER HOW TO DIE.
DA
EDO MURASAKI
GINNEZU
YANAGI
TSUYU-KUSA
DANJUROCHA
THE HARAKIRI RONIN TEAM...
THE SAMURAI FIVE!!

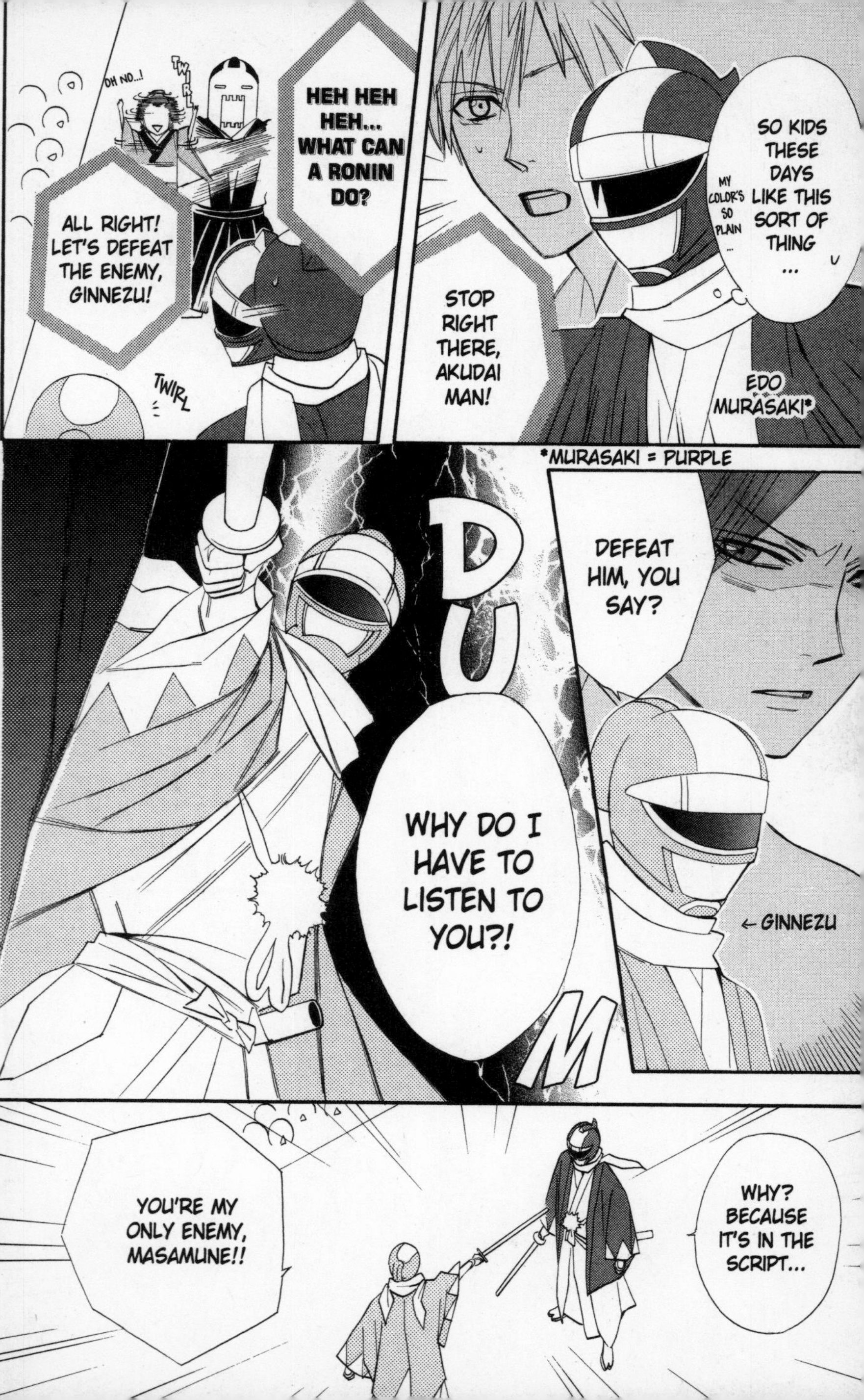
SO KIDS THESE DAYS LIKE THIS SORT OF THING ...
MY COLOR'S SO PLAIN ...
STOP RIGHT THERE, AKUDAI MAN!
EDO MURASAKI*
HEH HEH HEH... WHAT CAN A RONIN DO?
TWIRL
OH NO...!
ALL RIGHT! LET'S DEFEAT THE ENEMY, GINNEZU!
TWIRL
*MURASAKI = PURPLE
DEFEAT HIM, YOU SAY?
← GINNEZU
DUM
WHY DO I HAVE TO LISTEN TO YOU?!
WHY? BECAUSE IT'S IN THE SCRIPT...
YOU'RE MY ONLY ENEMY, MASAMUNE!!

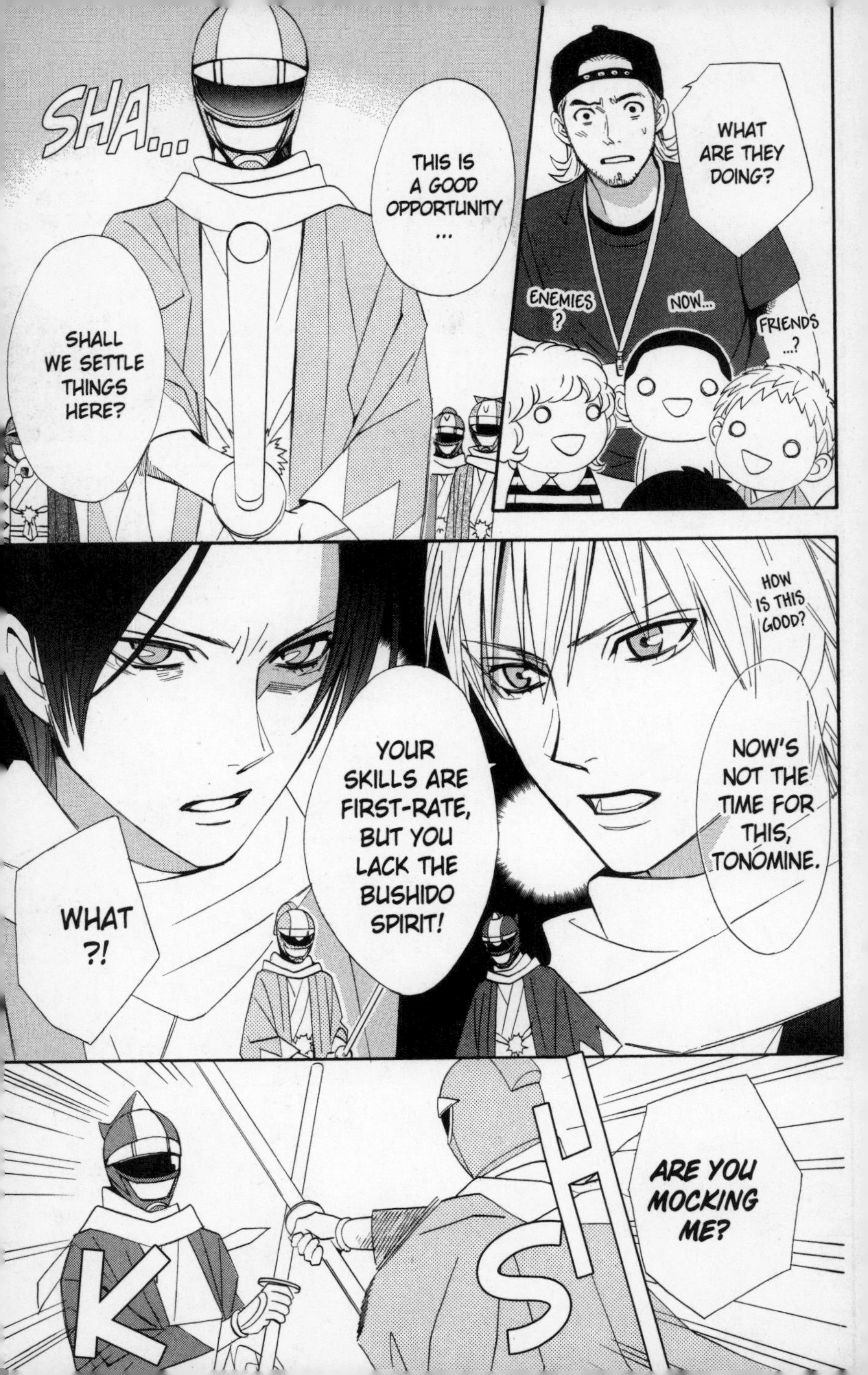
WHAT ARE THEY DOING?
ENEMIES ?
NOW...
FRIENDS ...?
THIS IS A GOOD OPPORTUNITY ...
SHALL WE SETTLE THINGS HERE?
SHA...
HOW IS THIS GOOD?
NOW'S NOT THE TIME FOR THIS, TONOMINE.
YOUR SKILLS ARE FIRST-RATE, BUT YOU LACK THE BUSHIDO SPIRIT!
WHAT ?!
ARE YOU MOCKING ME?
SH
K

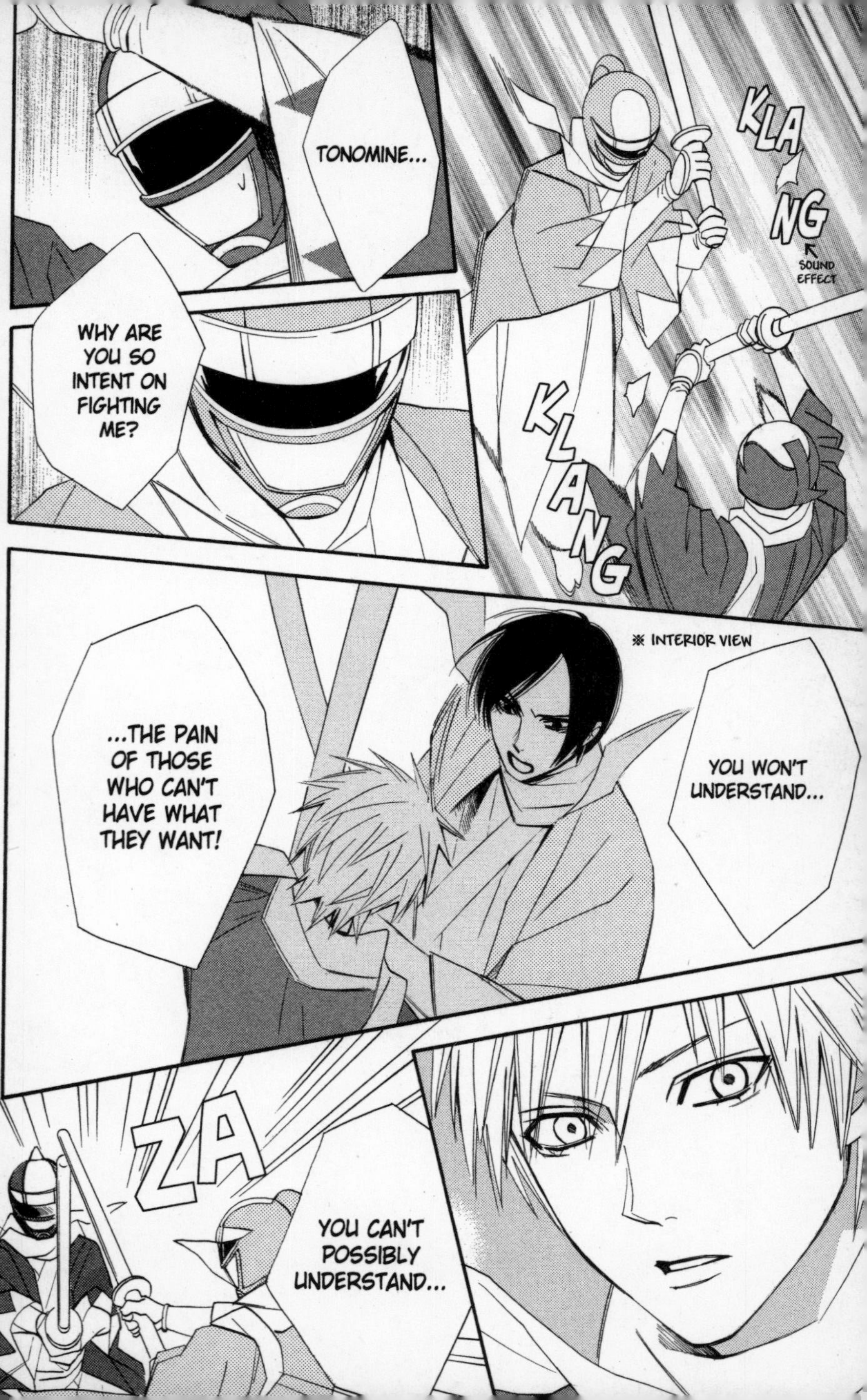
KLANG
SOUND EFFECT
KLANG
TONOMINE...
WHY ARE YOU SO INTENT ON FIGHTING ME?
※ INTERIOR VIEW
YOU WON'T UNDERSTAND...
...THE PAIN OF THOSE WHO CAN'T HAVE WHAT THEY WANT!
ZA
YOU CAN'T POSSIBLY UNDERSTAND...

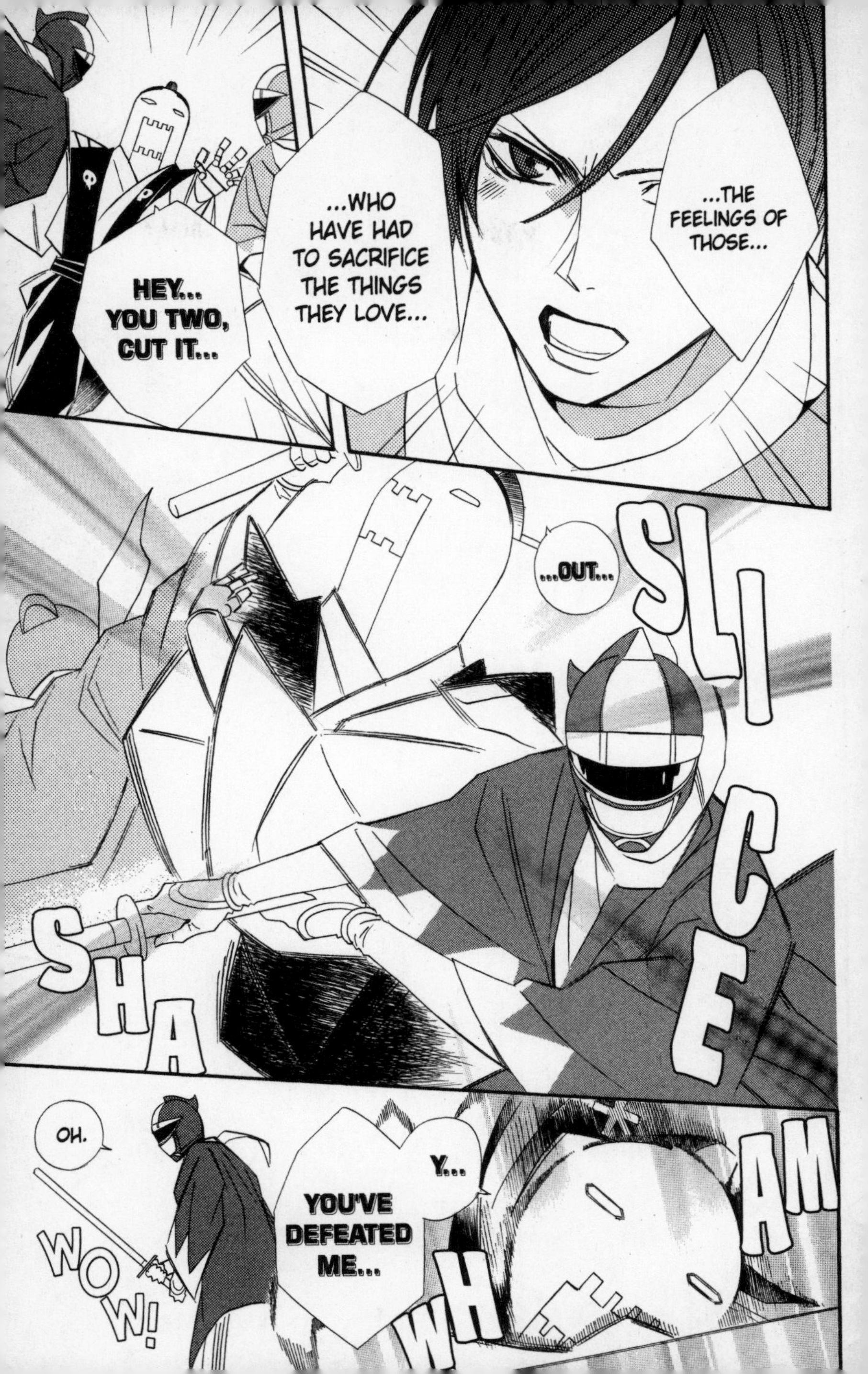
...THE FEELINGS OF THOSE...
...WHO HAVE HAD TO SACRIFICE THE THINGS THEY LOVE...
HEY... YOU TWO, CUT IT...
...OUT...
SLICE
SHA
WHAM
Y...
YOU'VE DEFEATED ME...
OH.
WOW!

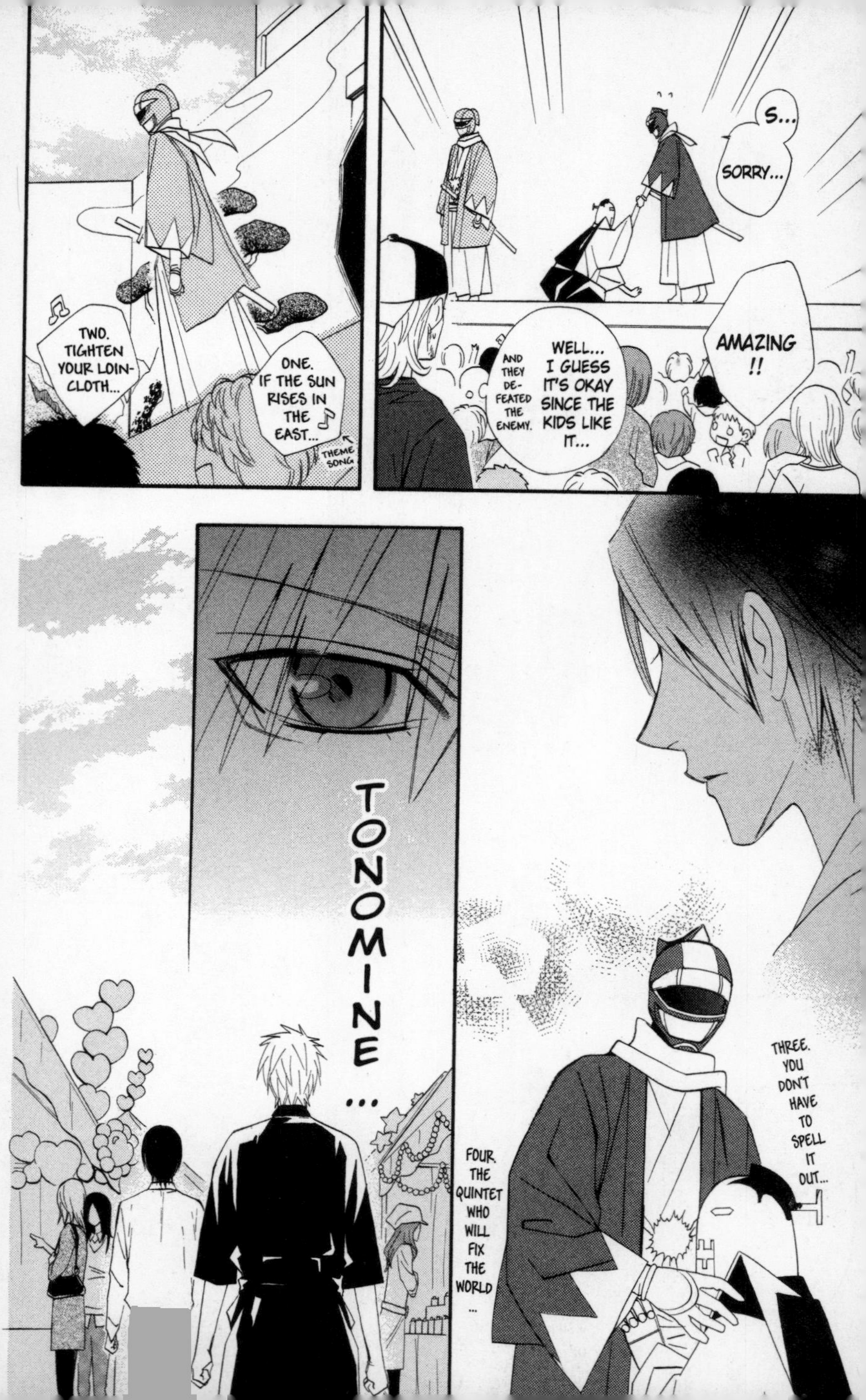
S... SORRY...
AMAZING!!
WELL... I GUESS IT'S OKAY SINCE THE KIDS LIKE IT...
AND THEY DEFEATED THE ENEMY.
ONE. IF THE SUN RISES IN THE EAST...
THEME SONG
TWO. TIGHTEN YOUR LOINCLOTH...
THREE. YOU DON'T HAVE TO SPELL IT OUT...
FOUR. THE QUINTET WHO WILL FIX THE WORLD...
TONOMINE...

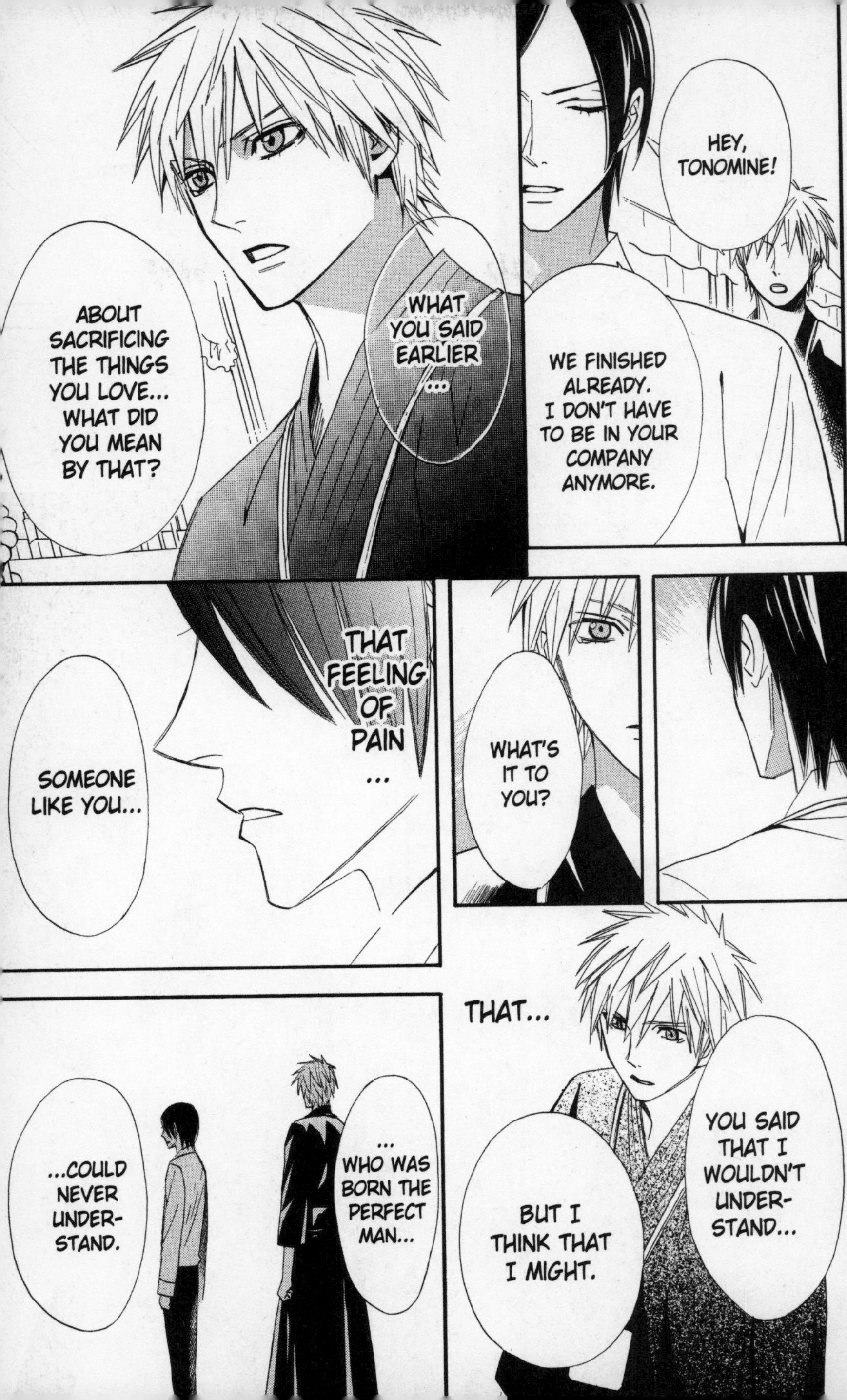
HEY, TONOMINE!
WE FINISHED ALREADY. I DON'T HAVE TO BE IN YOUR COMPANY ANYMORE.
WHAT YOU SAID EARLIER ...
ABOUT SACRIFICING THE THINGS YOU LOVE... WHAT DID YOU MEAN BY THAT?
WHAT'S IT TO YOU?
THAT FEELING OF PAIN ...
SOMEONE LIKE YOU...
THAT...
YOU SAID THAT I WOULDN'T UNDER-STAND...
BUT I THINK THAT I MIGHT.
... WHO WAS BORN THE PERFECT MAN...
...COULD NEVER UNDER-STAND.

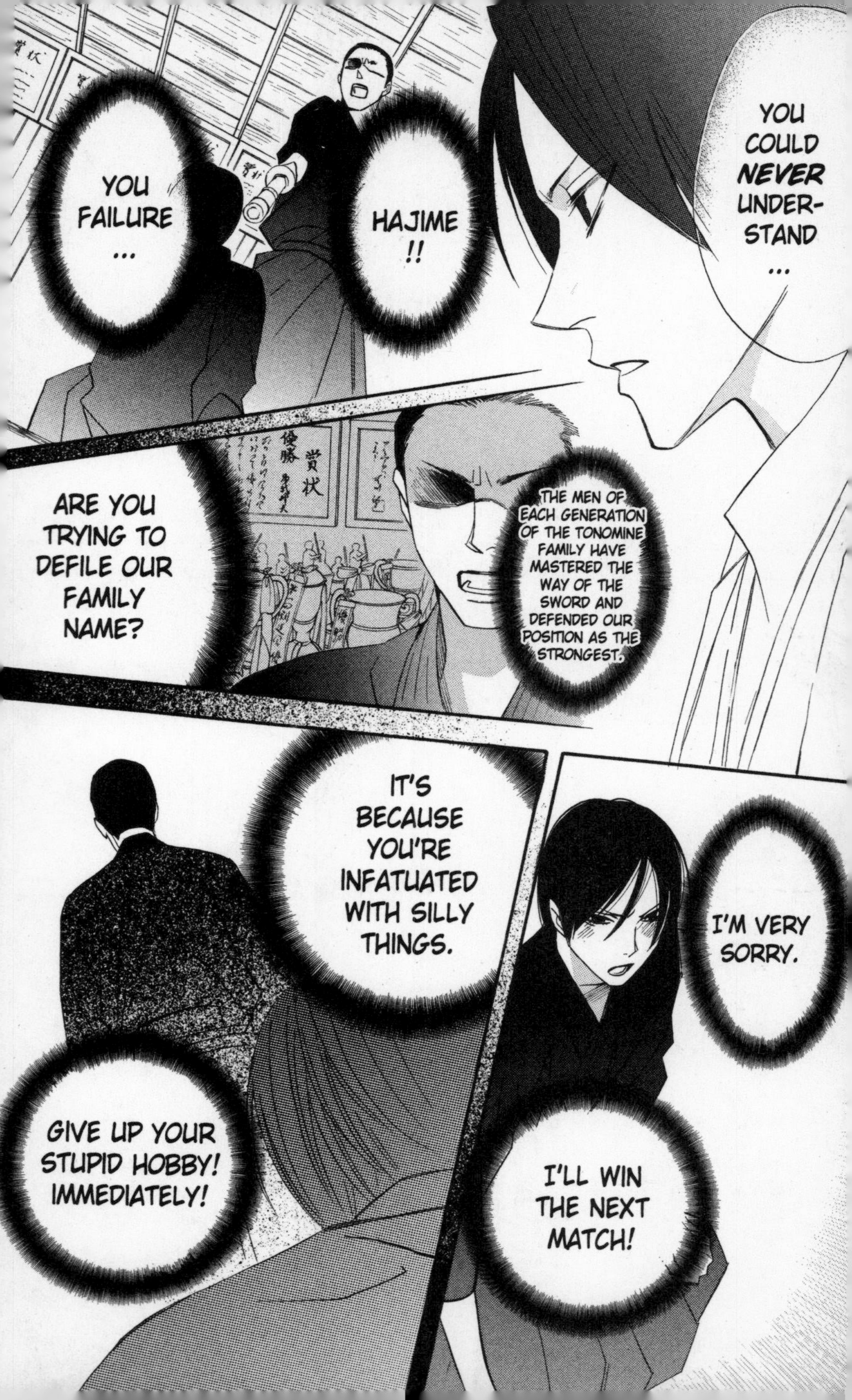
YOU COULD NEVER UNDER-STAND...
HAJIME!!
YOU FAILURE...
THE MEN OF EACH GENERATION OF THE TONOMINE FAMILY HAVE MASTERED THE WAY OF THE SWORD AND DEFENDED OUR POSITION AS THE STRONGEST.
ARE YOU TRYING TO DEFILE OUR FAMILY NAME?
I'M VERY SORRY.
I'LL WIN THE NEXT MATCH!
IT'S BECAUSE YOU'RE INFATUATED WITH SILLY THINGS.
GIVE UP YOUR STUPID HOBBY! IMMEDIATELY!

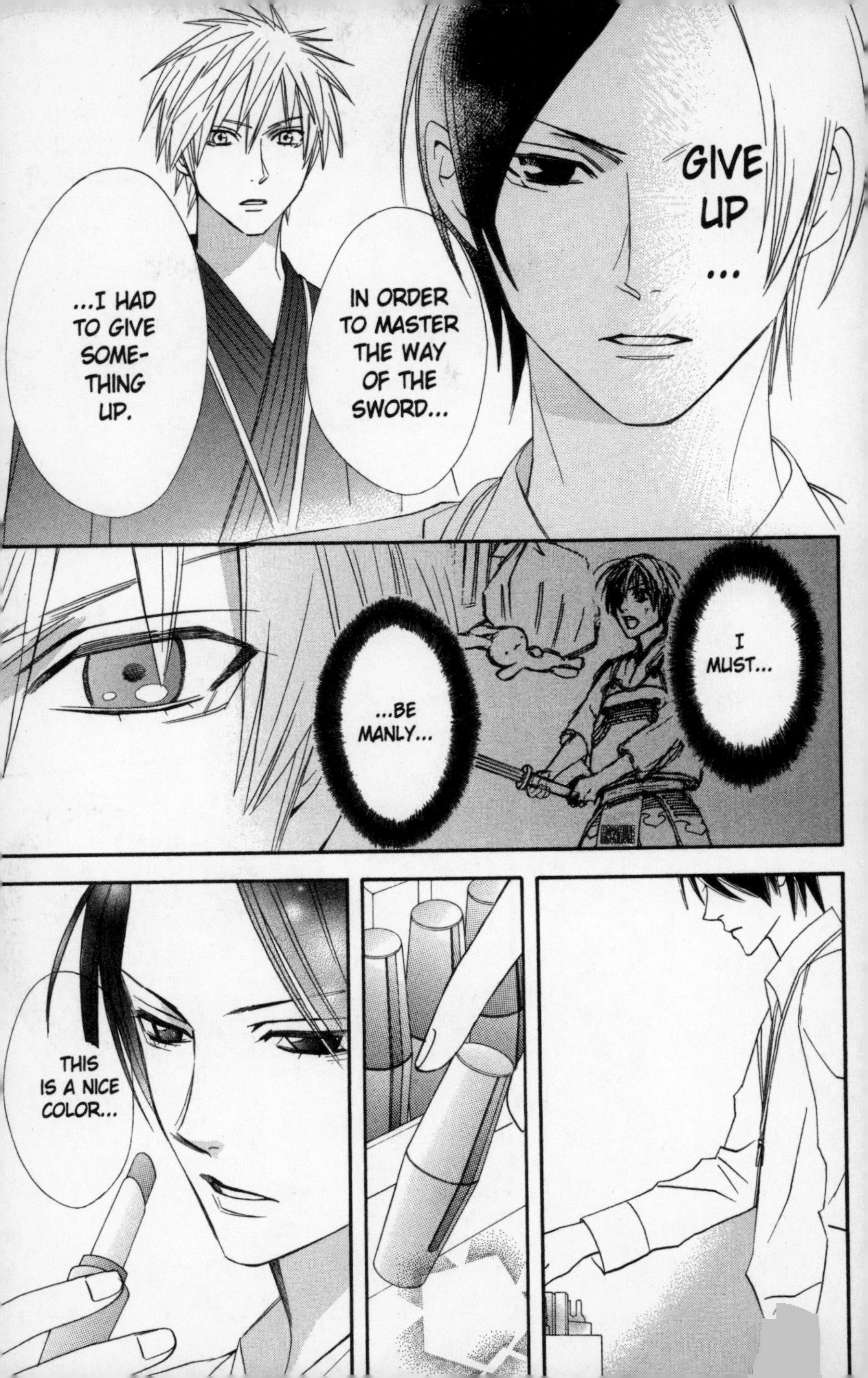
GIVE UP ...
IN ORDER TO MASTER THE WAY OF THE SWORD...
...I HAD TO GIVE SOME-THING UP.
I MUST...
...BE MANLY...
THIS IS A NICE COLOR...

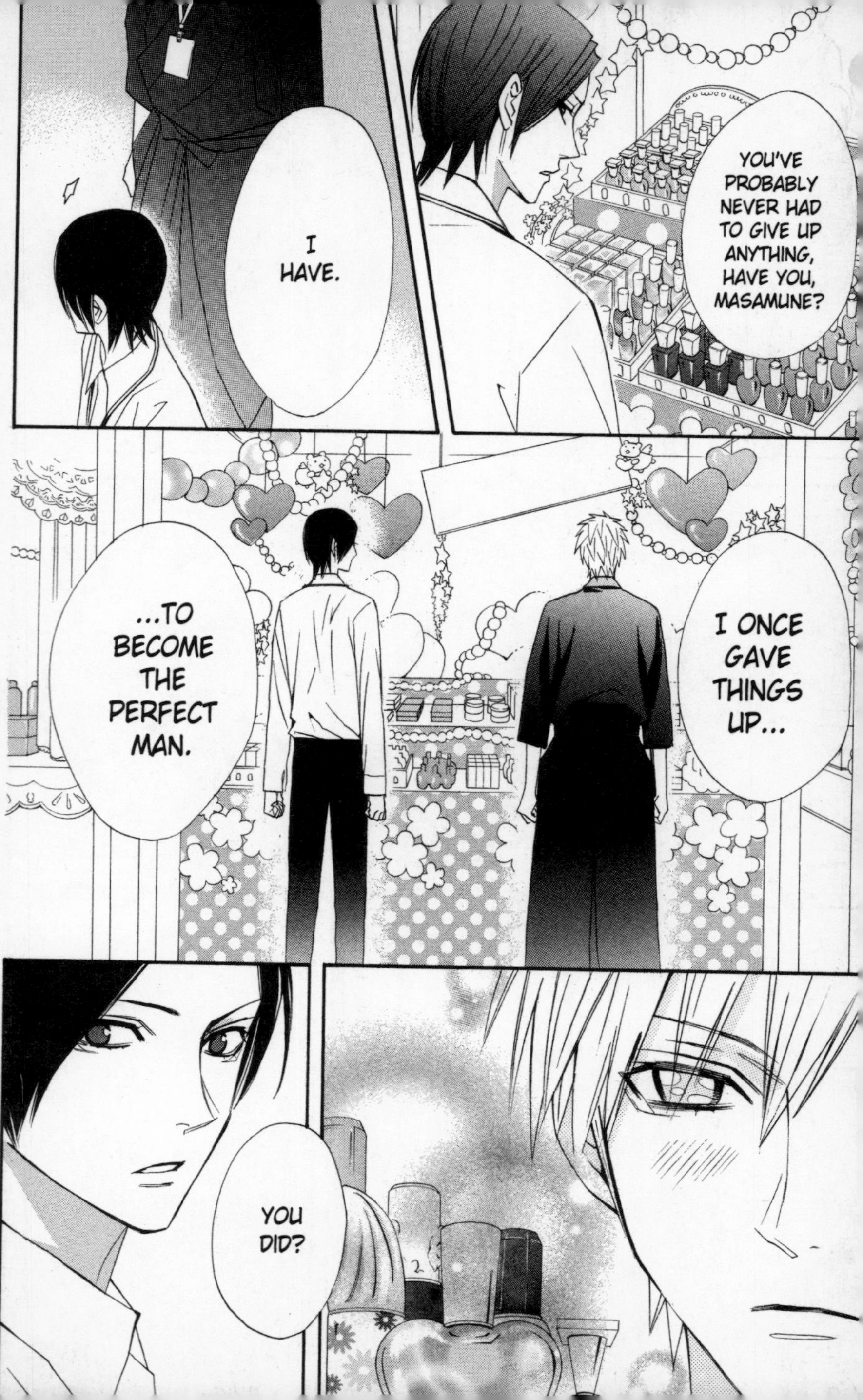
YOU'VE PROBABLY NEVER HAD TO GIVE UP ANYTHING, HAVE YOU, MASAMUNE?
I HAVE.
I ONCE GAVE THINGS UP...
...TO BECOME THE PERFECT MAN.
YOU DID?

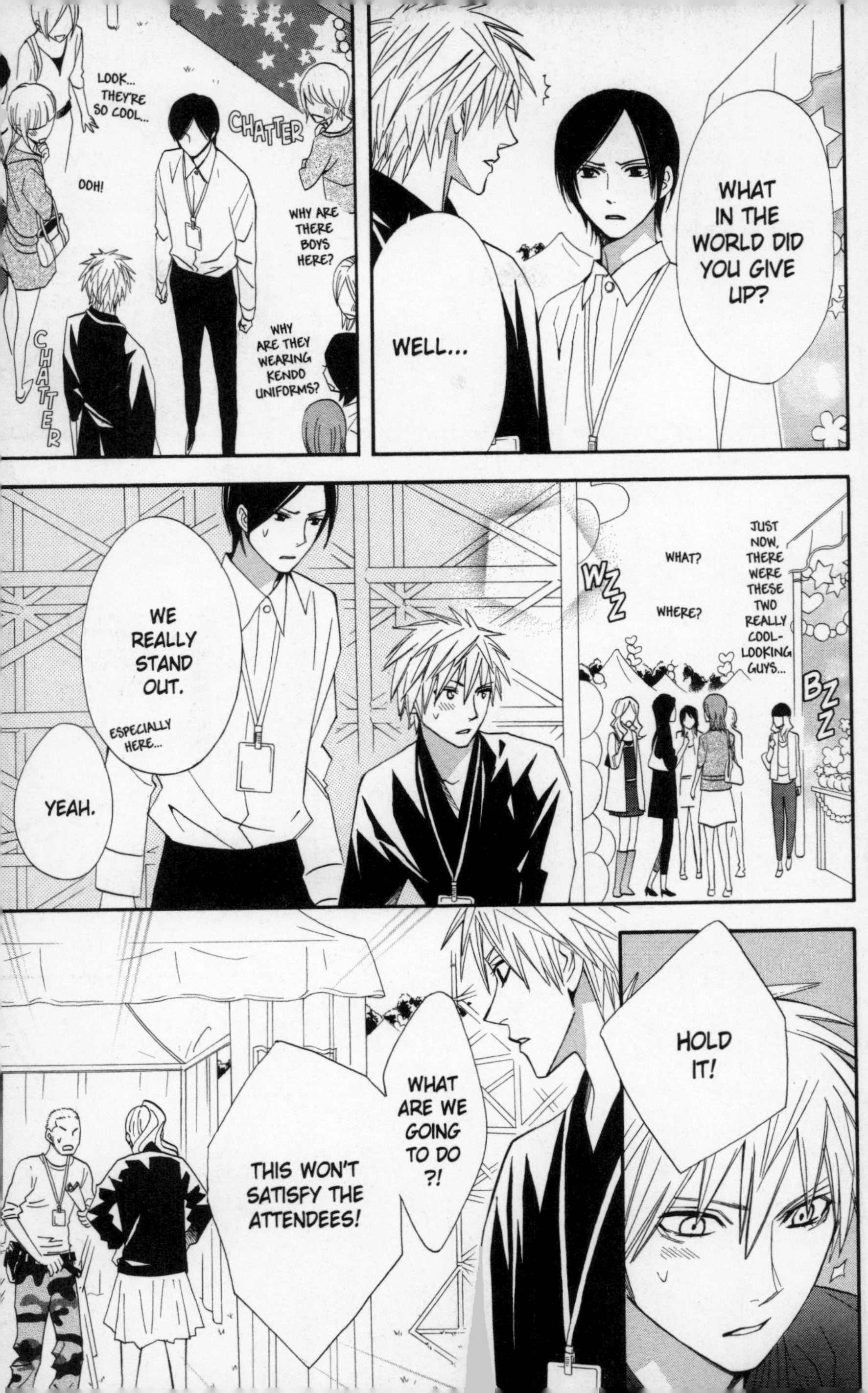
WHAT IN THE WORLD DID YOU GIVE UP?
WELL...
CHATTER
LOOK... THEY'RE SO COOL...
WHY ARE THERE BOYS HERE?
OOH!
WHY ARE THEY WEARING KENDO UNIFORMS?
CHATTER
JUST NOW, THERE WERE THESE TWO REALLY COOL-LOOKING GUYS...
BZZ
WHAT?
WHERE?
WZZ
WE REALLY STAND OUT.
ESPECIALLY HERE...
YEAH.
HOLD IT!
WHAT ARE WE GOING TO DO ?!
THIS WON'T SATISFY THE ATTENDEES!

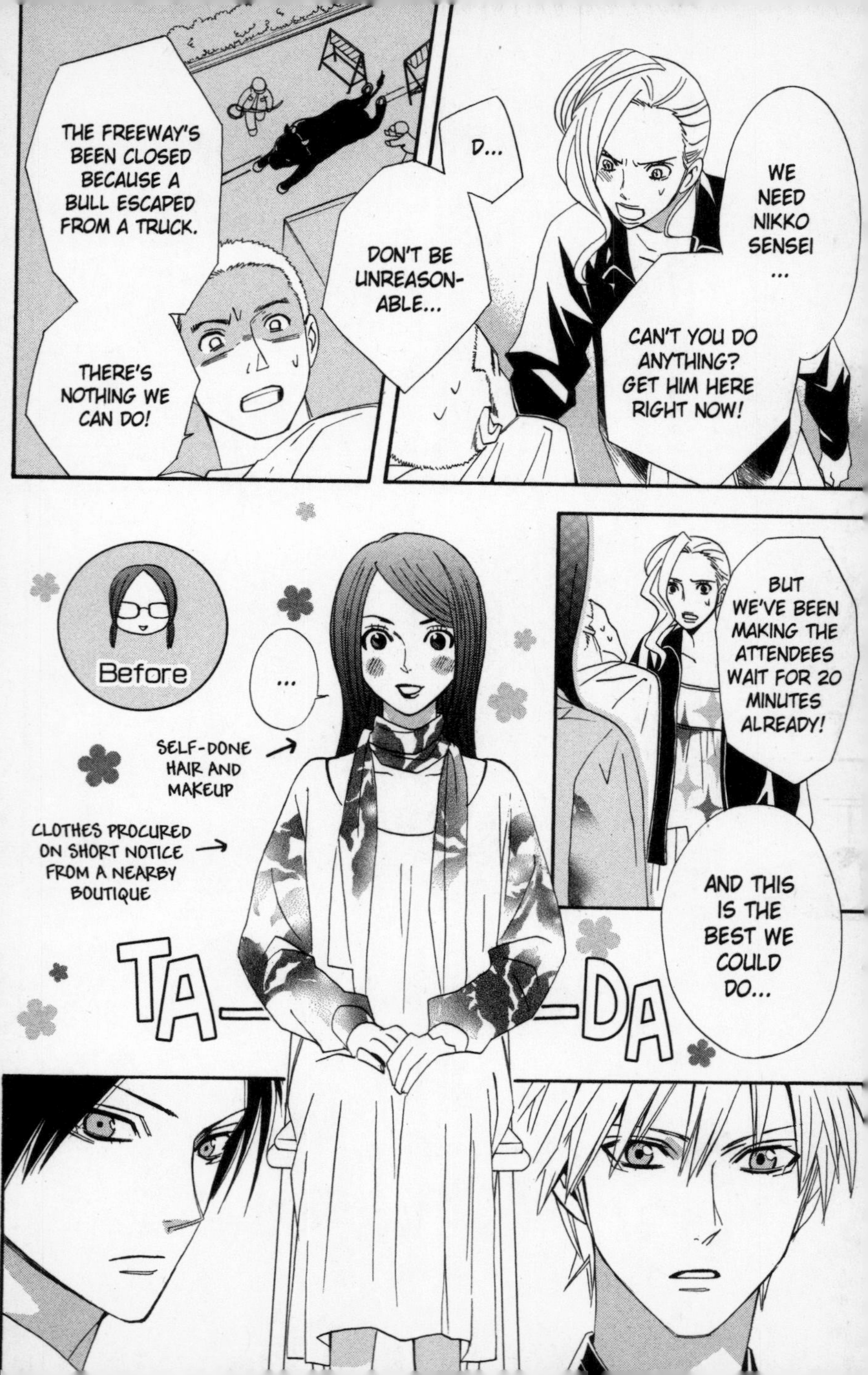
WE NEED NIKKO SENSEI ...
CAN'T YOU DO ANYTHING? GET HIM HERE RIGHT NOW!
D...
DON'T BE UNREASON-ABLE...
THE FREEWAY'S BEEN CLOSED BECAUSE A BULL ESCAPED FROM A TRUCK.
THERE'S NOTHING WE CAN DO!
BUT WE'VE BEEN MAKING THE ATTENDEES WAIT FOR 20 MINUTES ALREADY!
AND THIS IS THE BEST WE COULD DO...
TA—DA
...
Before
SELF-DONE HAIR AND MAKEUP
CLOTHES PROCURED ON SHORT NOTICE FROM A NEARBY BOUTIQUE

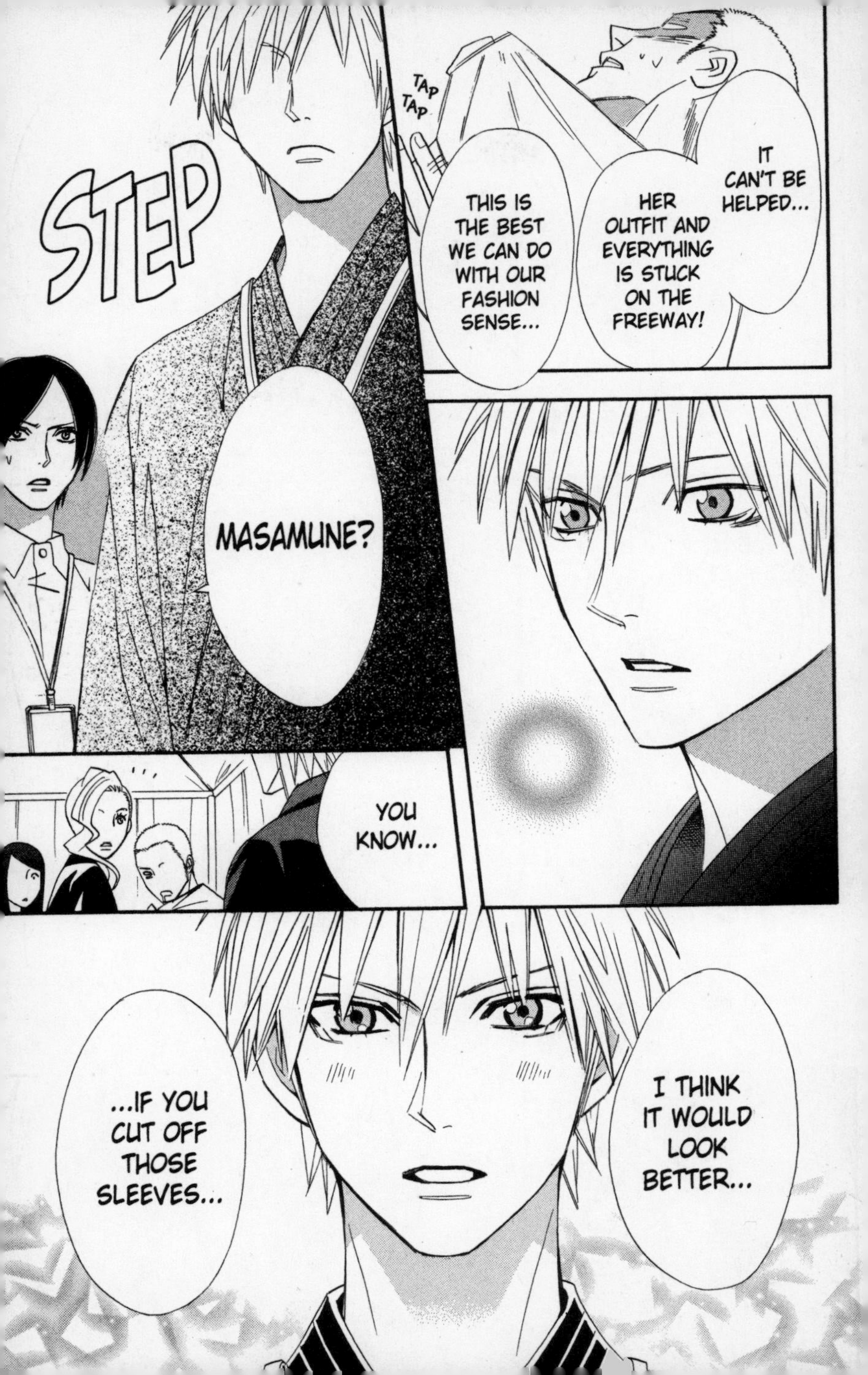
TAP TAP
IT CAN'T BE HELPED...
HER OUTFIT AND EVERYTHING IS STUCK ON THE FREEWAY!
THIS IS THE BEST WE CAN DO WITH OUR FASHION SENSE...
STEP
MASAMUNE?
YOU KNOW...
I THINK IT WOULD LOOK BETTER...
...IF YOU CUT OFF THOSE SLEEVES...

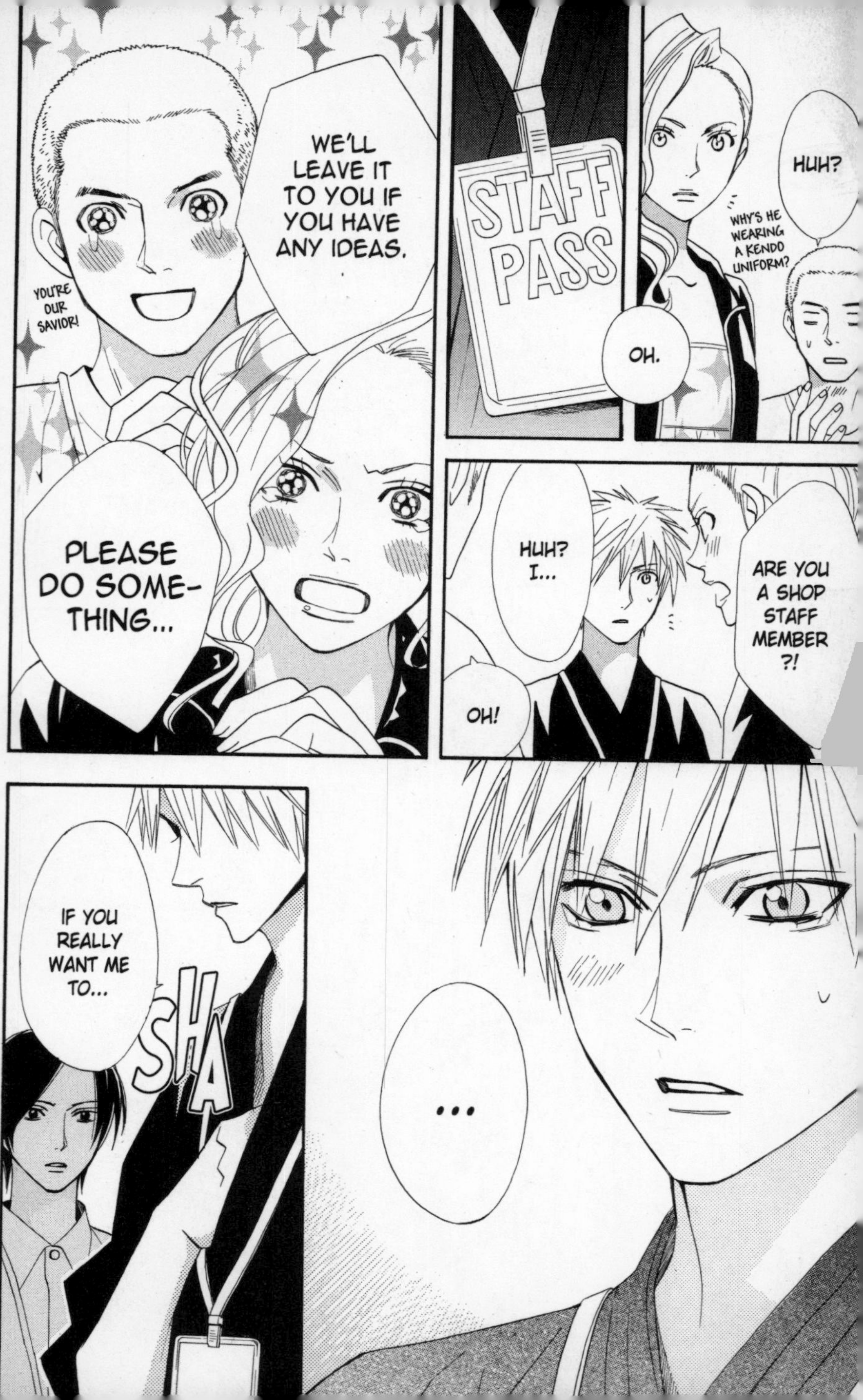
HUH?
WHY'S HE WEARING A KENDO UNIFORM?
OH.
STAFF PASS
ARE YOU A SHOP STAFF MEMBER ?!
HUH? I...
OH!
WE'LL LEAVE IT TO YOU IF YOU HAVE ANY IDEAS.
YOU'RE OUR SAVIOR!
PLEASE DO SOME-THING...
...
IF YOU REALLY WANT ME TO...
SHA

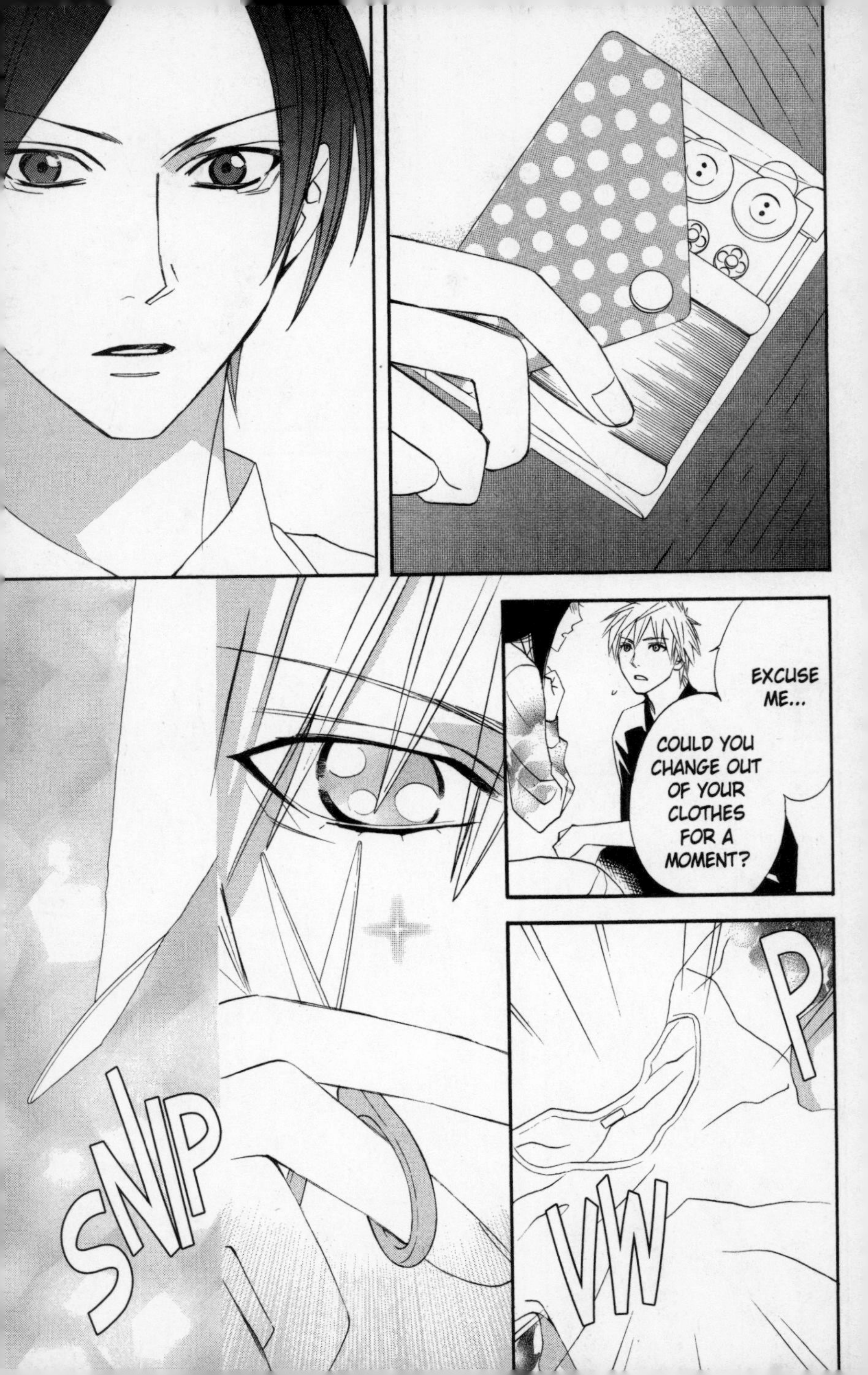
EXCUSE ME...
COULD YOU CHANGE OUT OF YOUR CLOTHES FOR A MOMENT?
SNIP
VWP

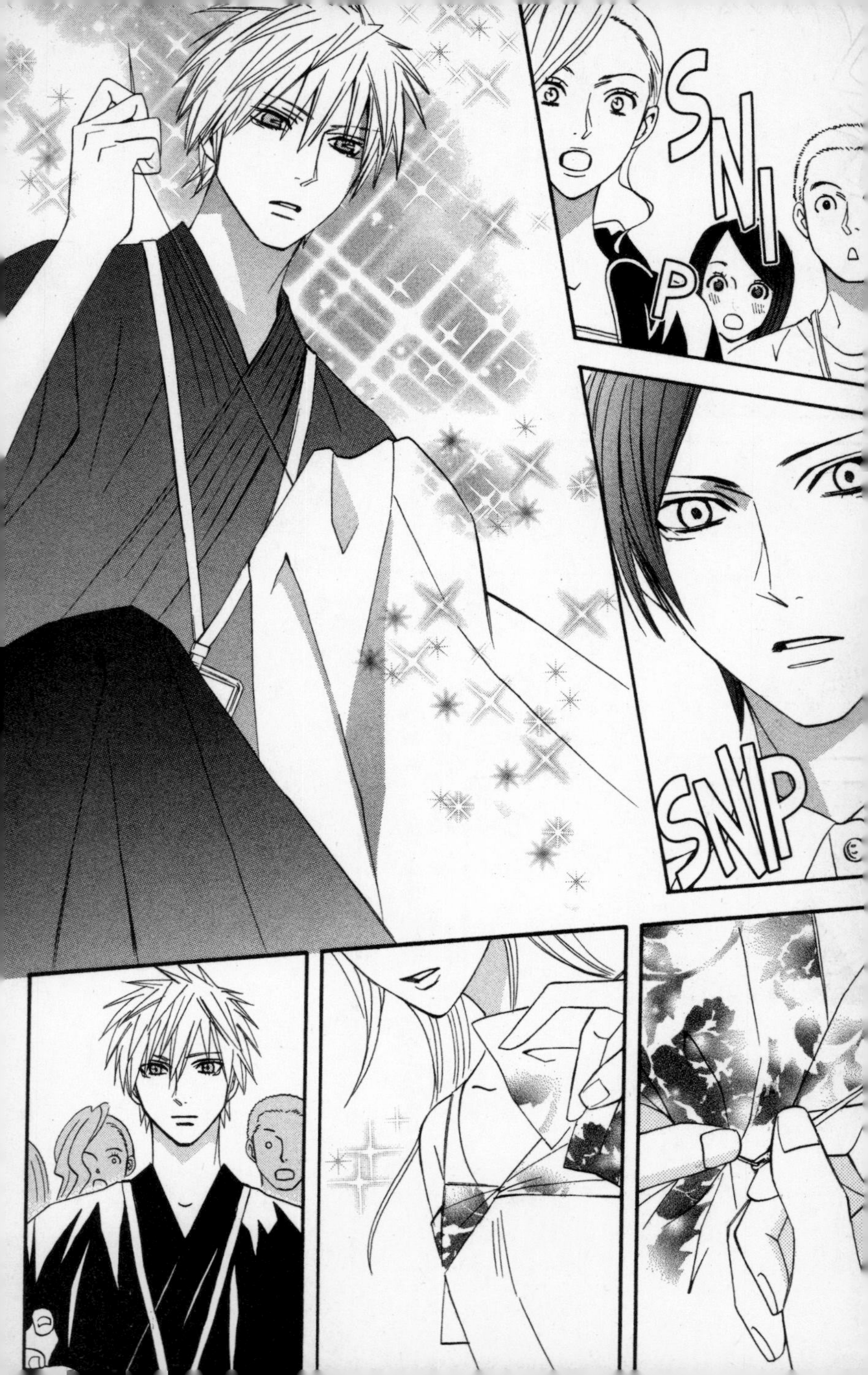
SNIP
SNIP

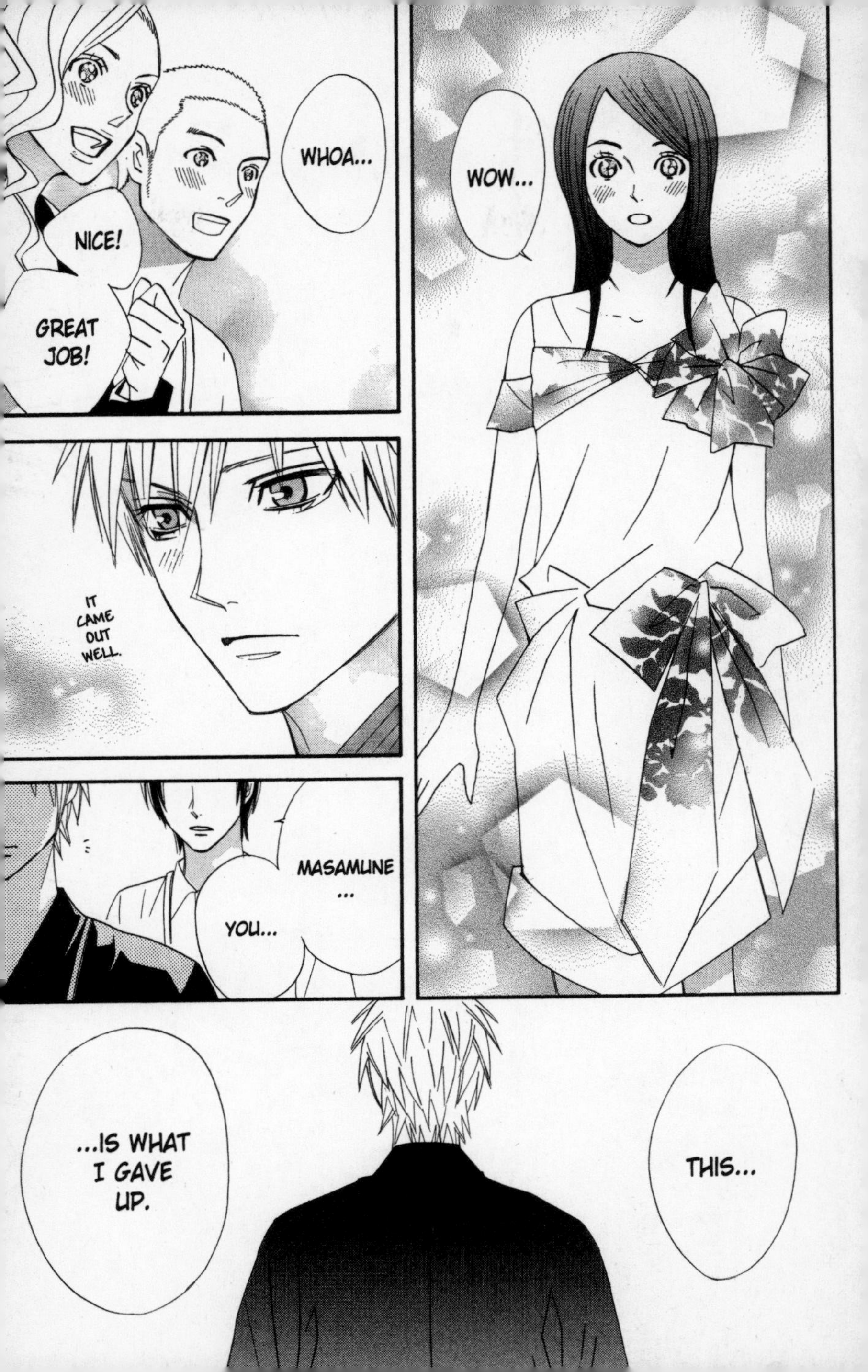
WOW...
WHOA...
NICE!
GREAT JOB!
IT CAME OUT WELL.
MASAMUNE...
YOU...
THIS...
...IS WHAT I GAVE UP.

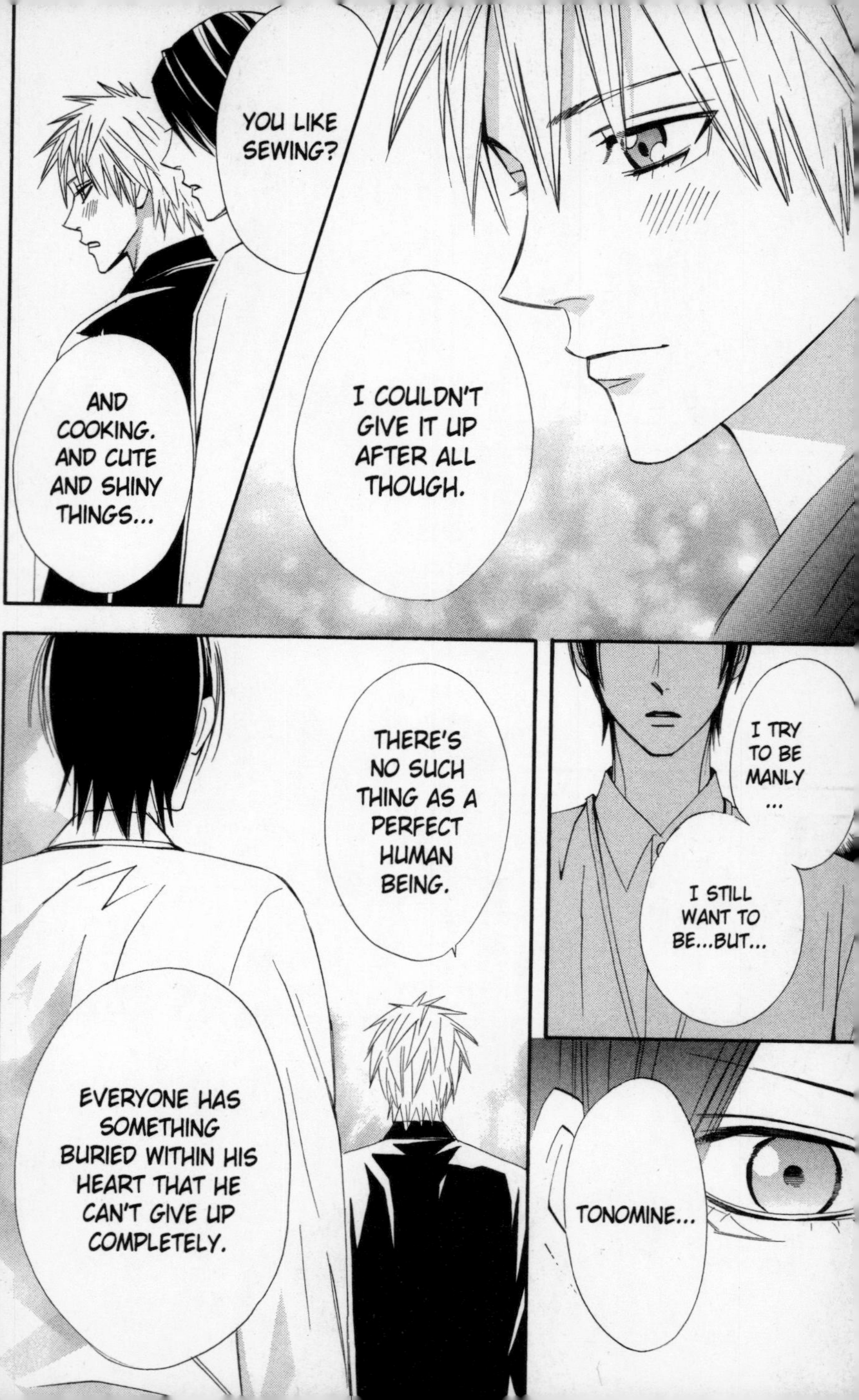

YOU LIKE SEWING?
AND COOKING. AND CUTE AND SHINY THINGS...
I COULDN'T GIVE IT UP AFTER ALL THOUGH.
I TRY TO BE MANLY ...
I STILL WANT TO BE...BUT...
TONOMINE...
THERE'S NO SUCH THING AS A PERFECT HUMAN BEING.
EVERYONE HAS SOMETHING BURIED WITHIN HIS HEART THAT HE CAN'T GIVE UP COMPLETELY.

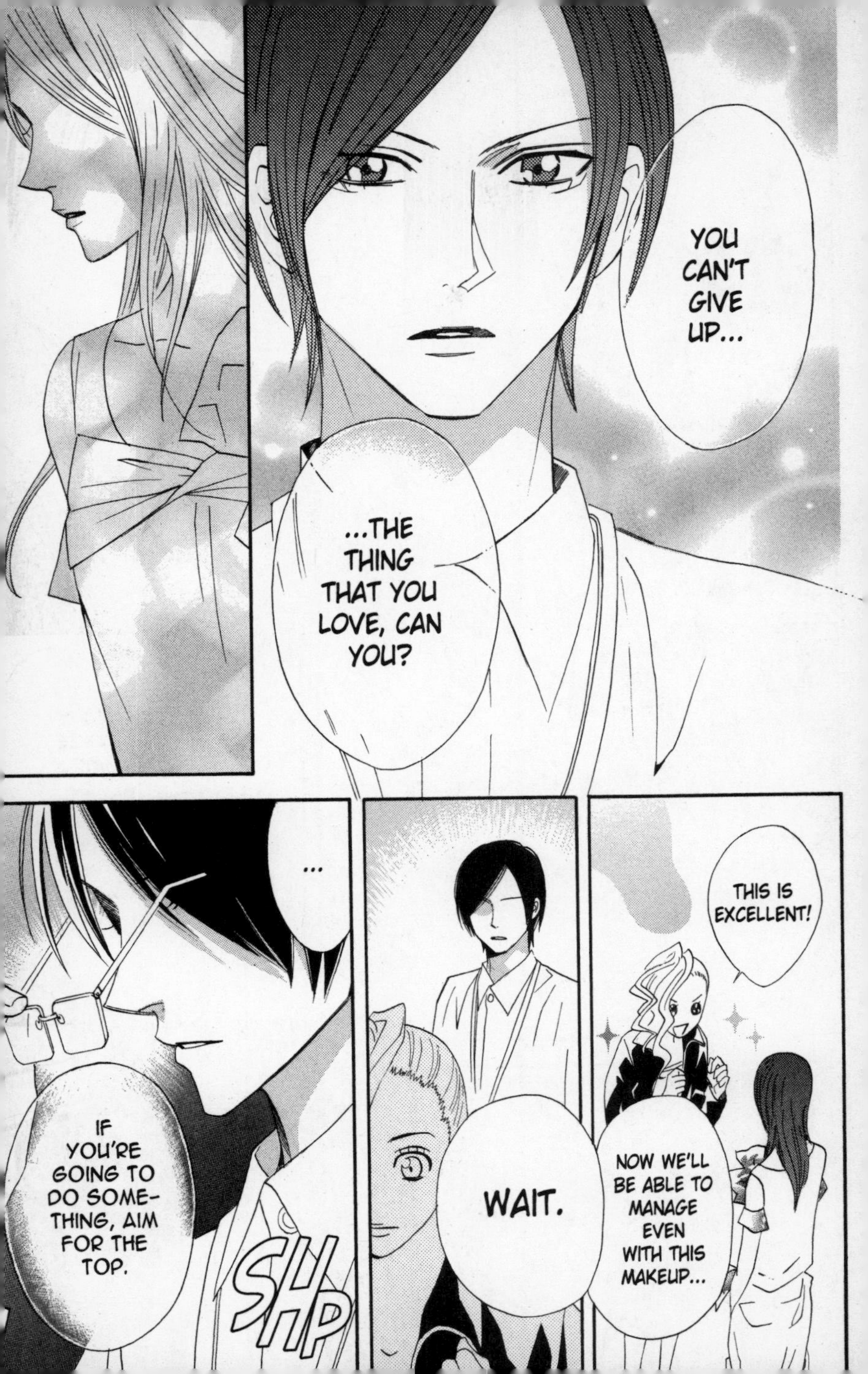
YOU CAN'T GIVE UP...
...THE THING THAT YOU LOVE, CAN YOU?
THIS IS EXCELLENT!
NOW WE'LL BE ABLE TO MANAGE EVEN WITH THIS MAKEUP...
WAIT.
...
IF YOU'RE GOING TO DO SOME-THING, AIM FOR THE TOP.
SHP

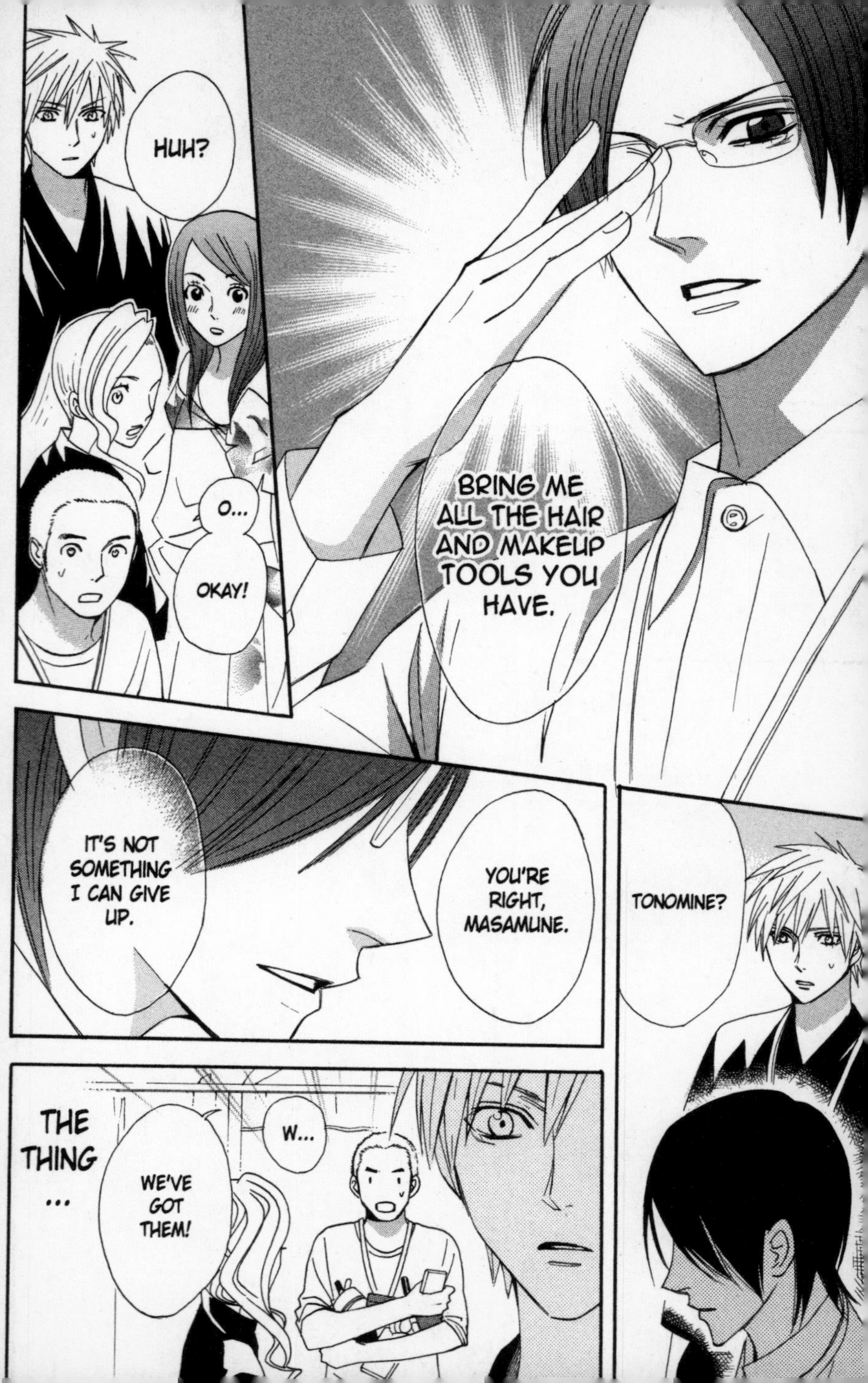
BRING ME ALL THE HAIR AND MAKEUP TOOLS YOU HAVE.
HUH?
O...
OKAY!
TONOMINE?
YOU'RE RIGHT, MASAMUNE.
IT'S NOT SOMETHING I CAN GIVE UP.
W...
WE'VE GOT THEM!
THE THING...

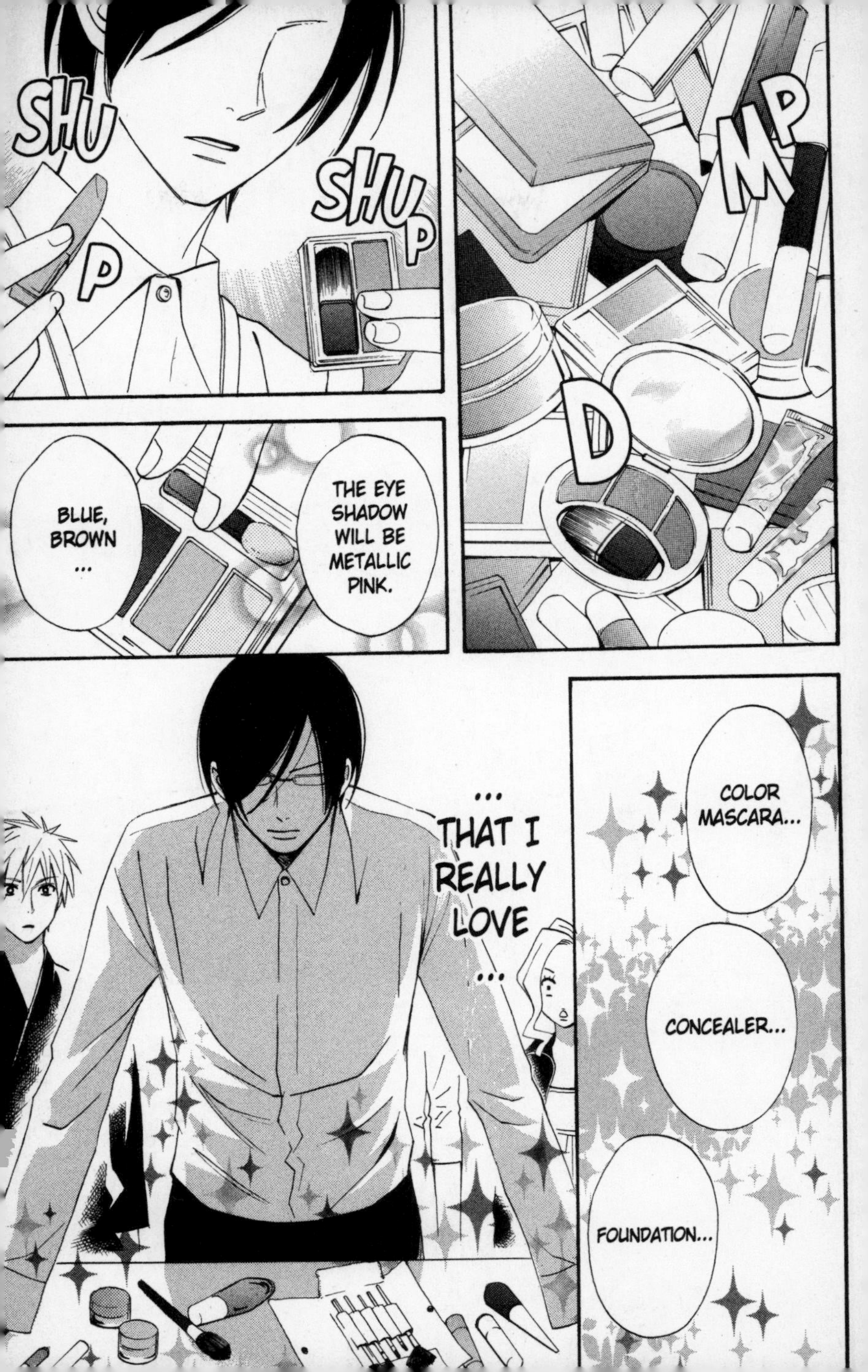
MP
D
SHUP
SHU
P
THE EYE SHADOW WILL BE METALLIC PINK.
BLUE, BROWN ...
COLOR MASCARA...
CONCEALER...
FOUNDATION...
... THAT I REALLY LOVE ...

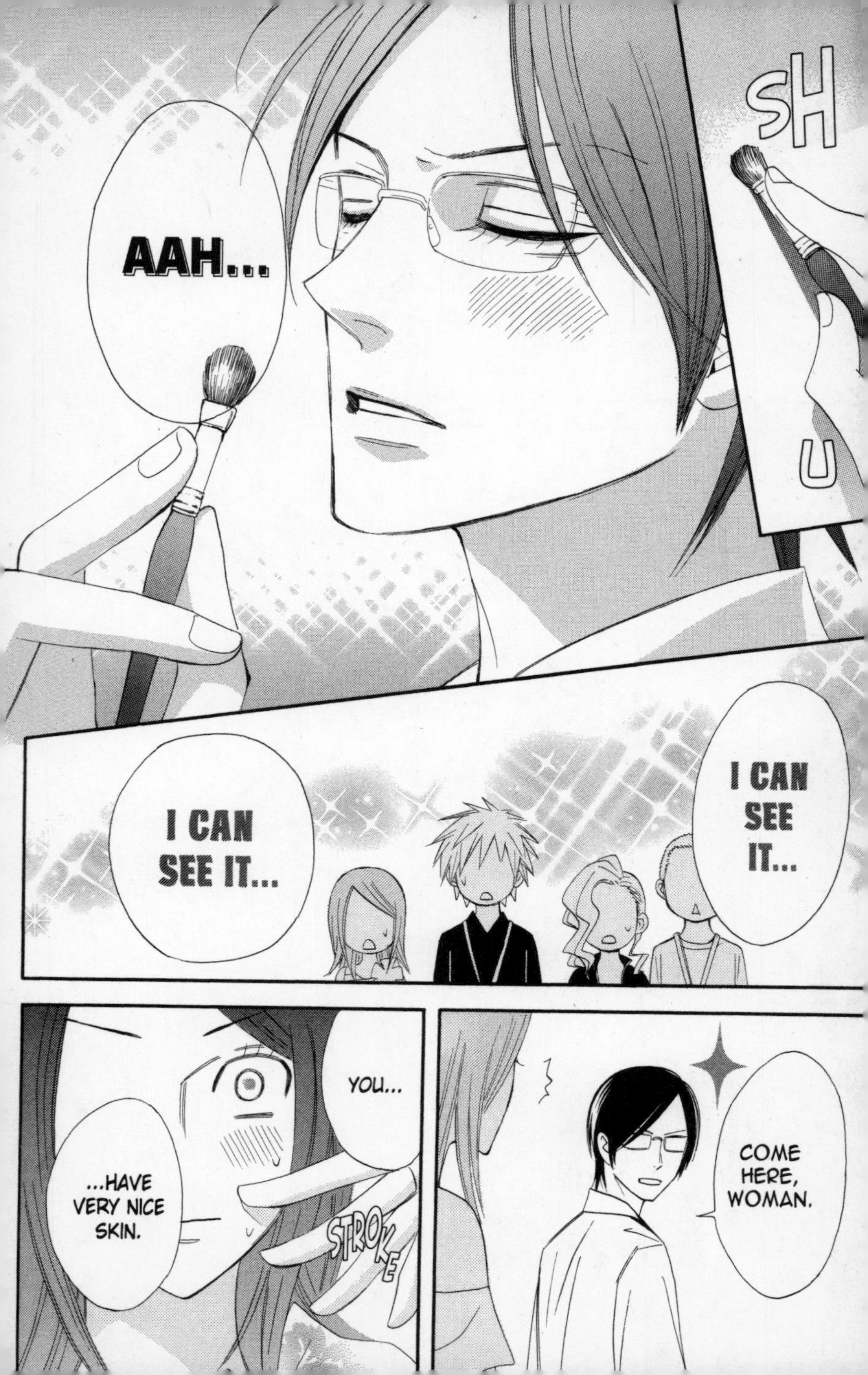
SH
U
AAH...
I CAN SEE IT...
I CAN SEE IT...
COME HERE, WOMAN.
YOU...
...HAVE VERY NICE SKIN.
STROKE

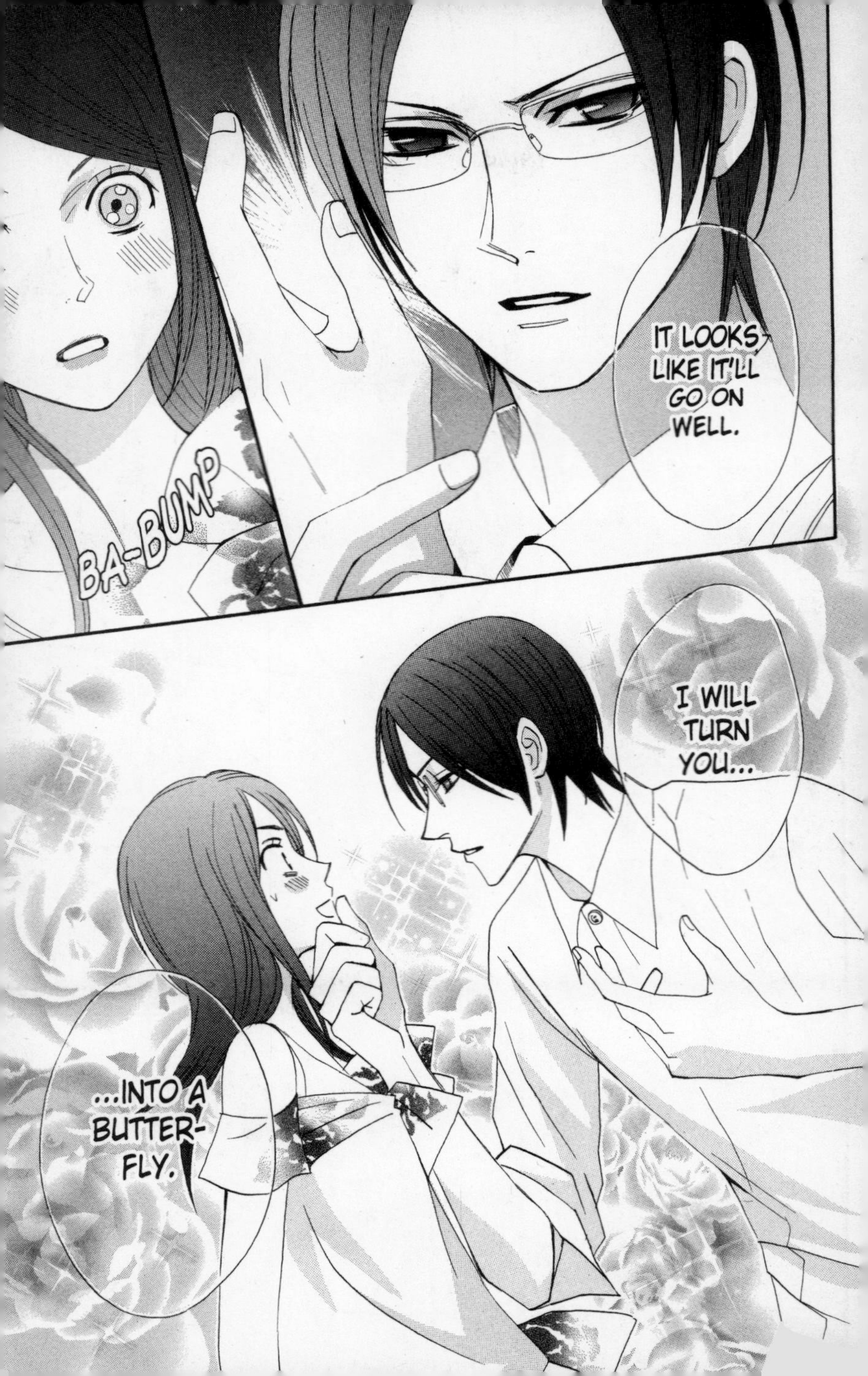
IT LOOKS LIKE IT'LL GO ON WELL.
BA-BUMP
I WILL TURN YOU...
...INTO A BUTTER-FLY.

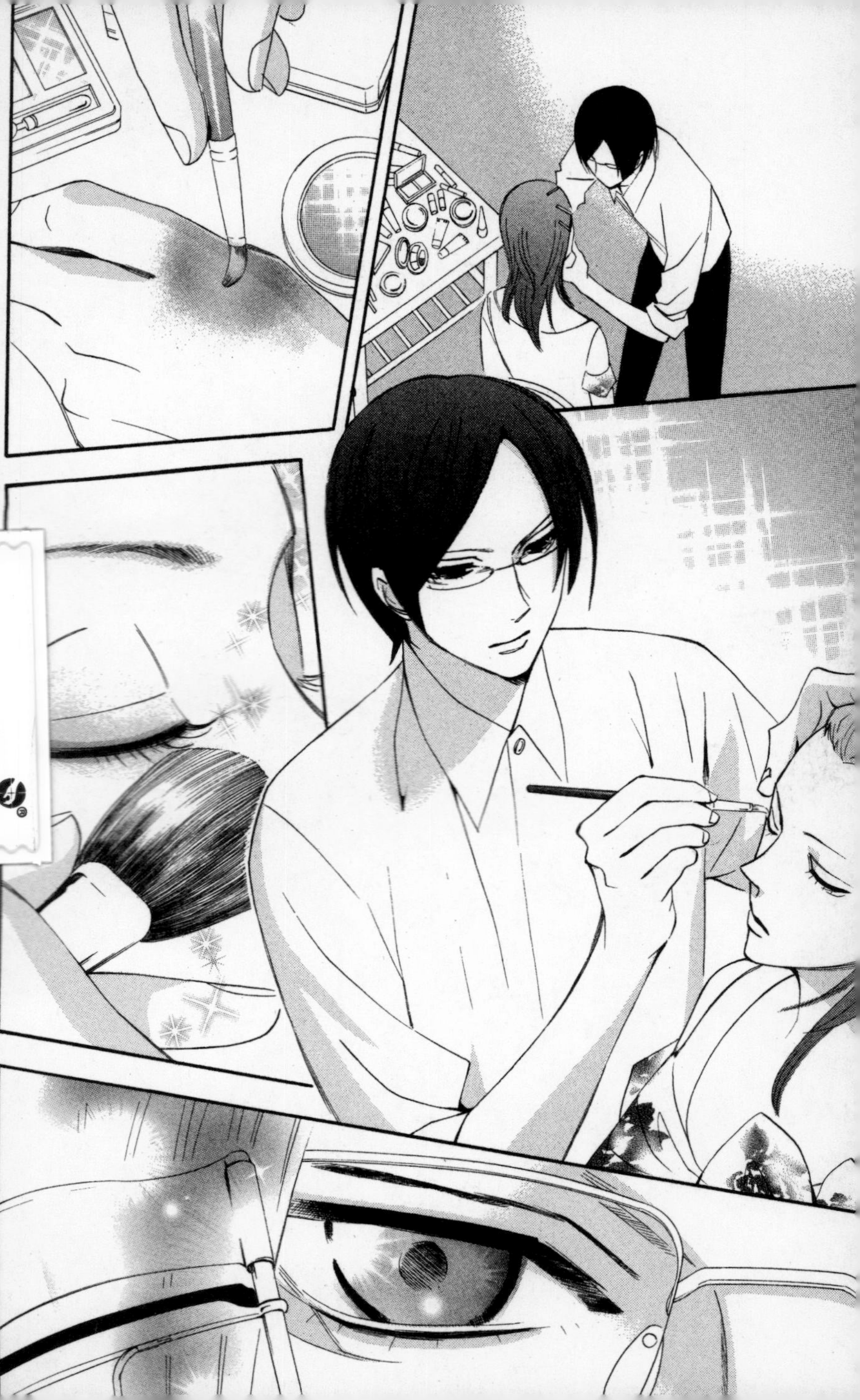

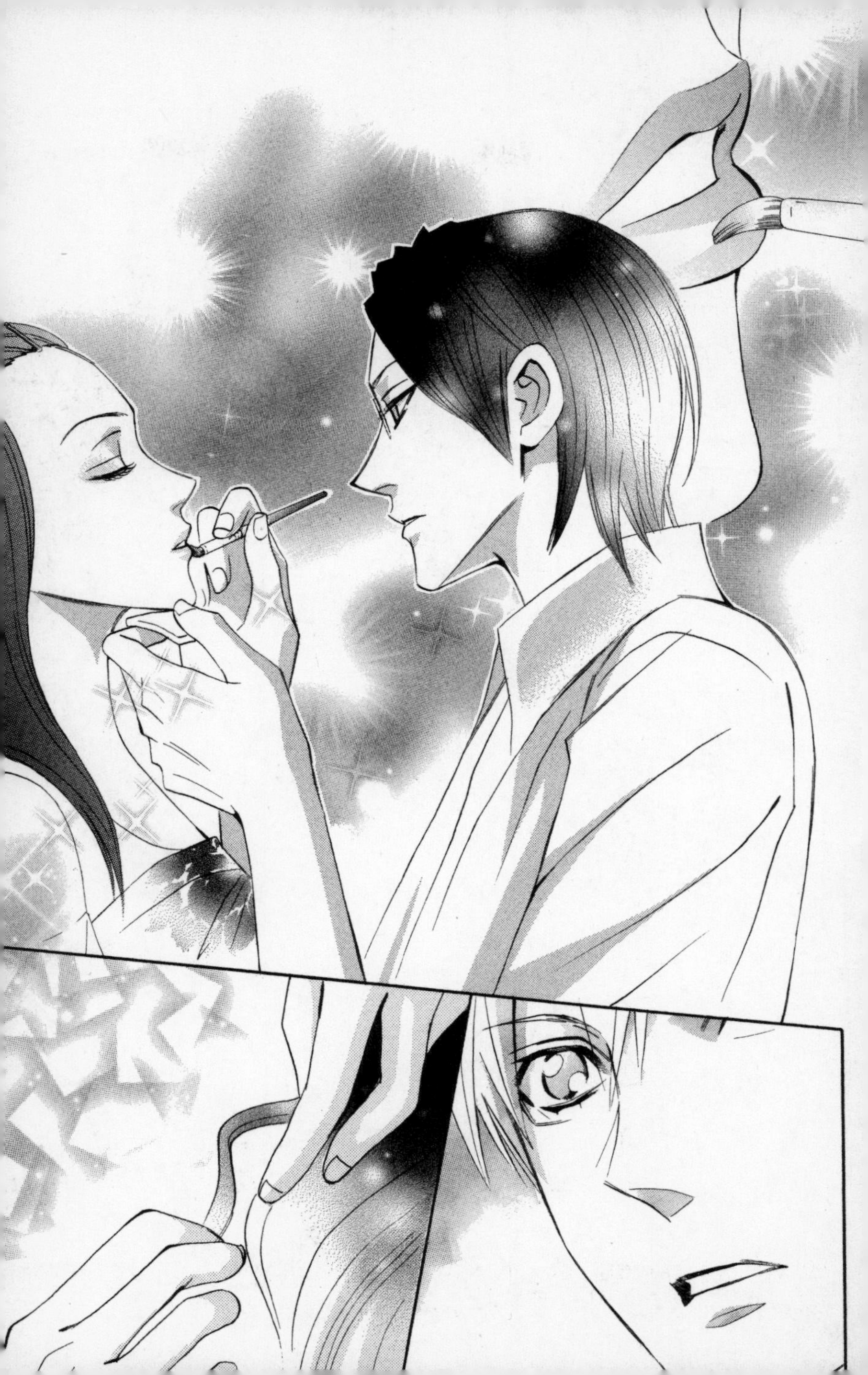

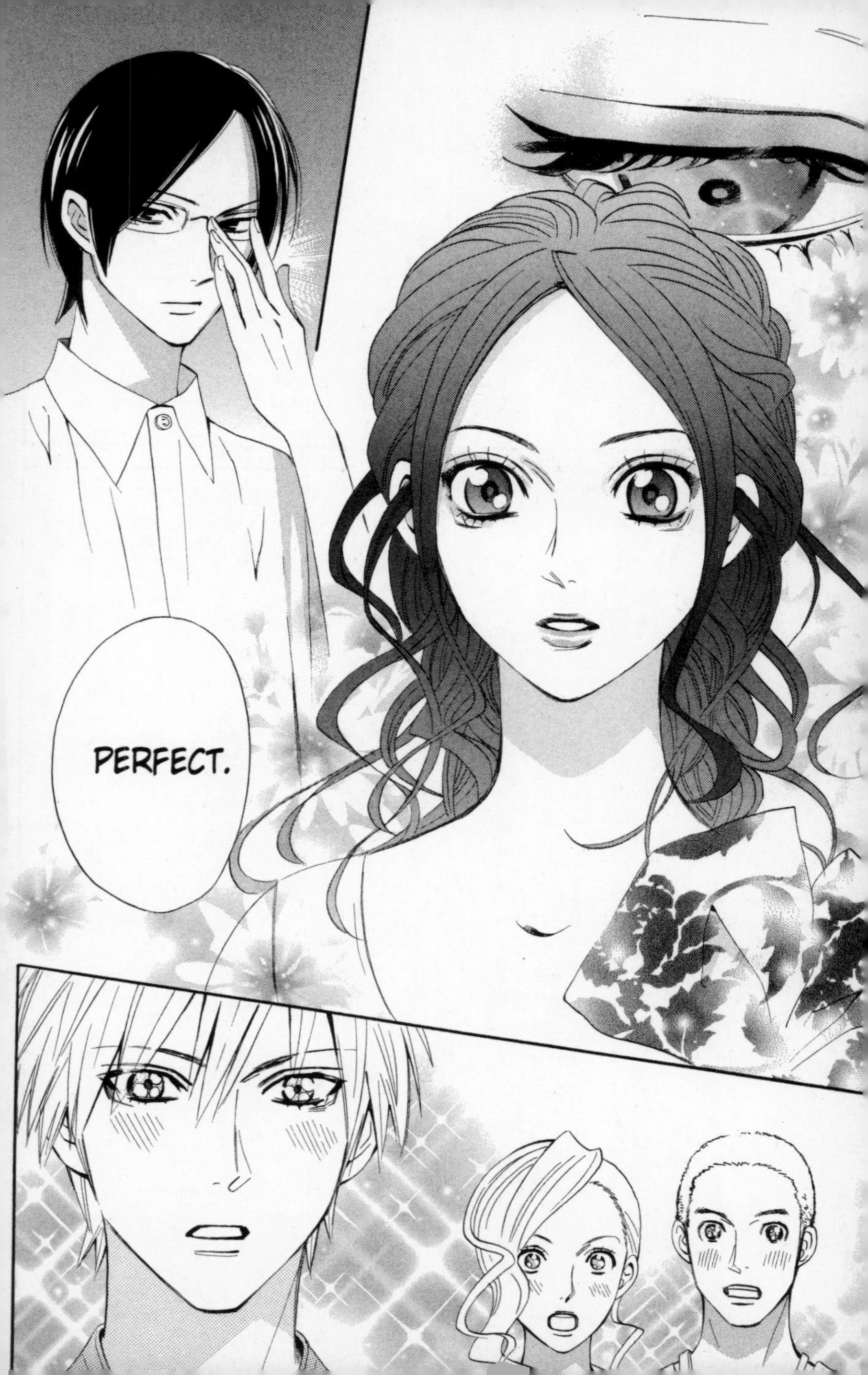
PERFECT.

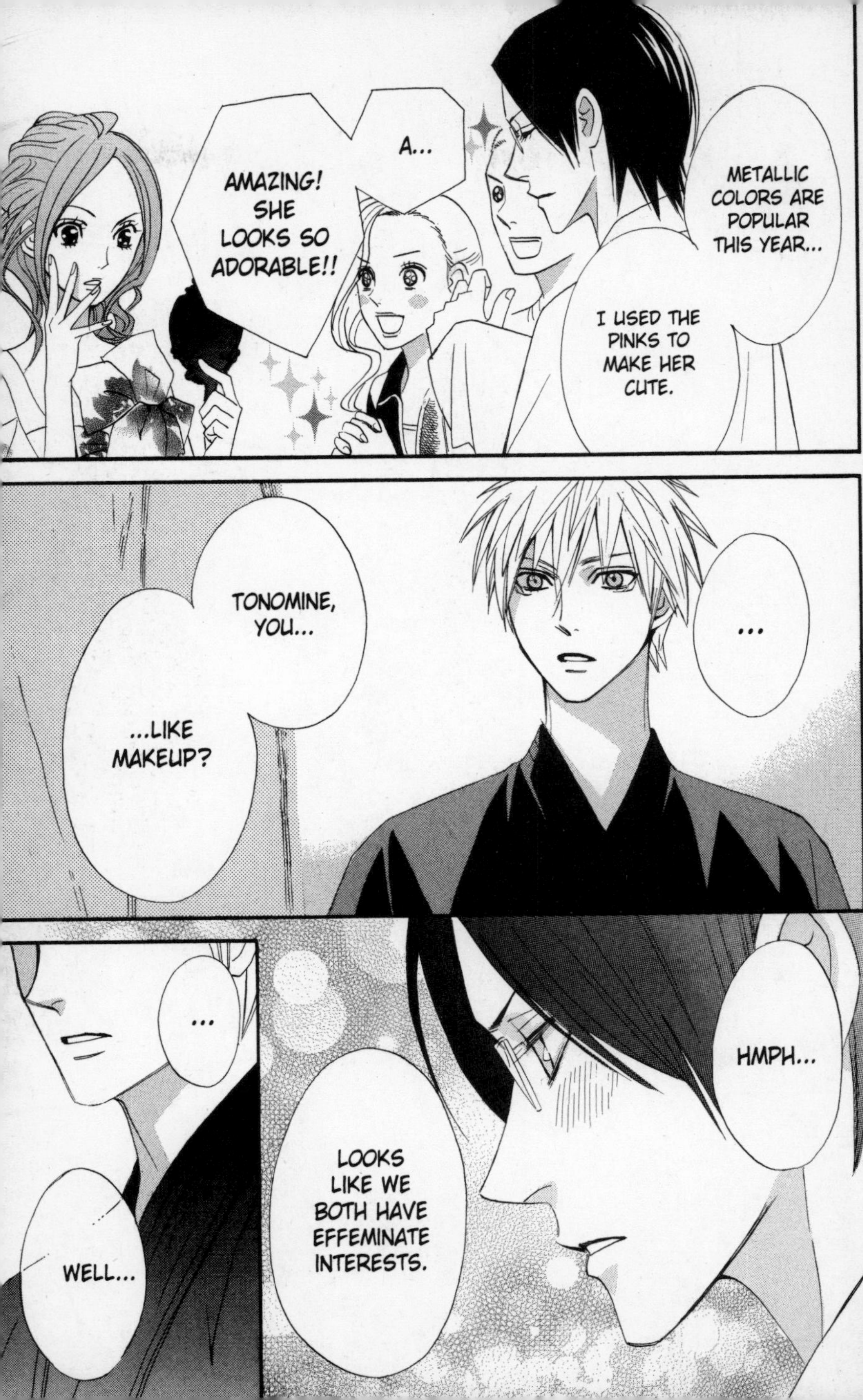
METALLIC COLORS ARE POPULAR THIS YEAR...
I USED THE PINKS TO MAKE HER CUTE.
A...
AMAZING! SHE LOOKS SO ADORABLE!!
...
TONOMINE, YOU...
...LIKE MAKEUP?
HMPH...
LOOKS LIKE WE BOTH HAVE EFFEMINATE INTERESTS.
...
WELL...

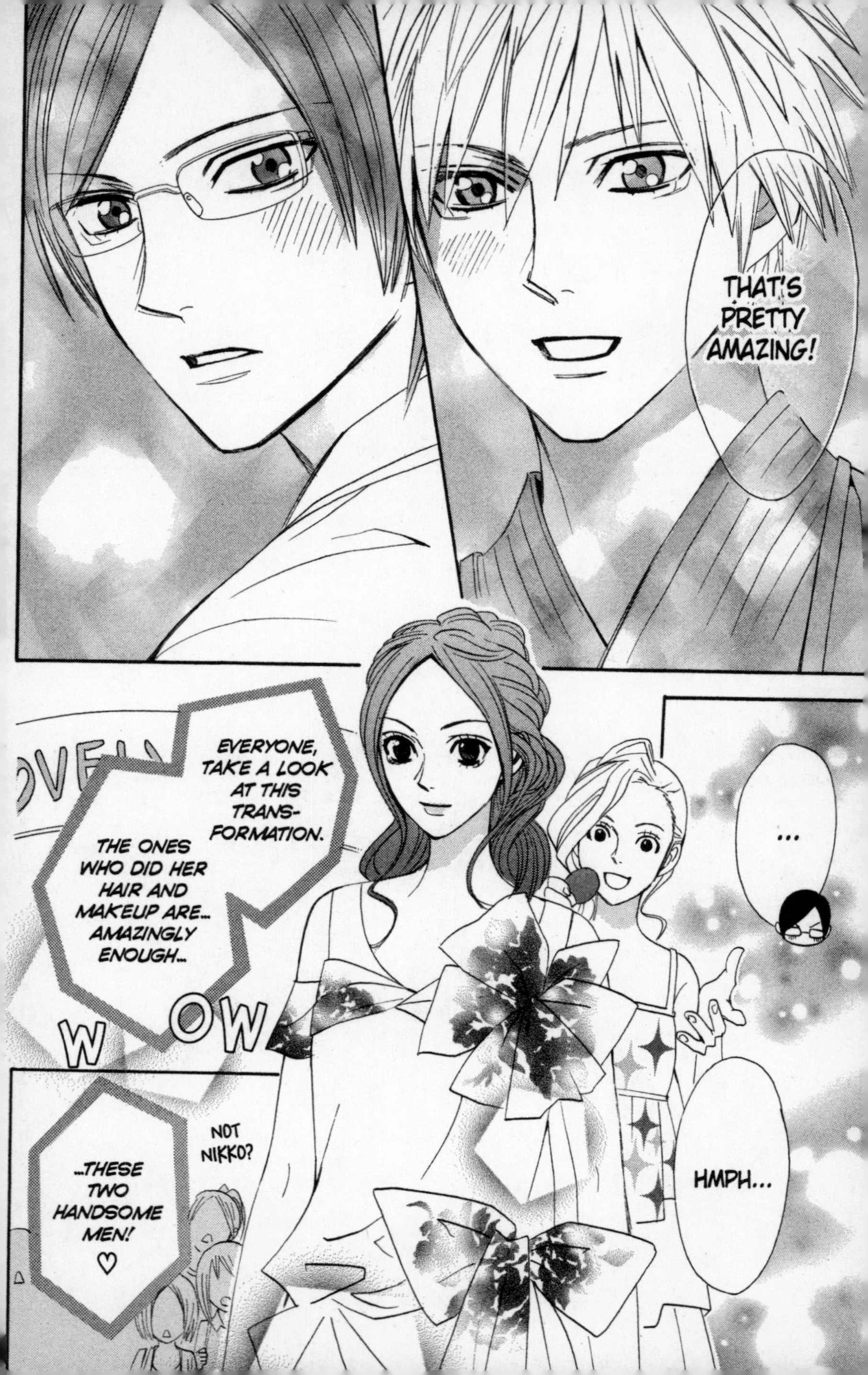
THAT'S PRETTY AMAZING!
...
EVERYONE, TAKE A LOOK AT THIS TRANS-FORMATION.
THE ONES WHO DID HER HAIR AND MAKEUP ARE... AMAZINGLY ENOUGH...
WOW
HMPH...
NOT NIKKO?
...THESE TWO HANDSOME MEN! ♡

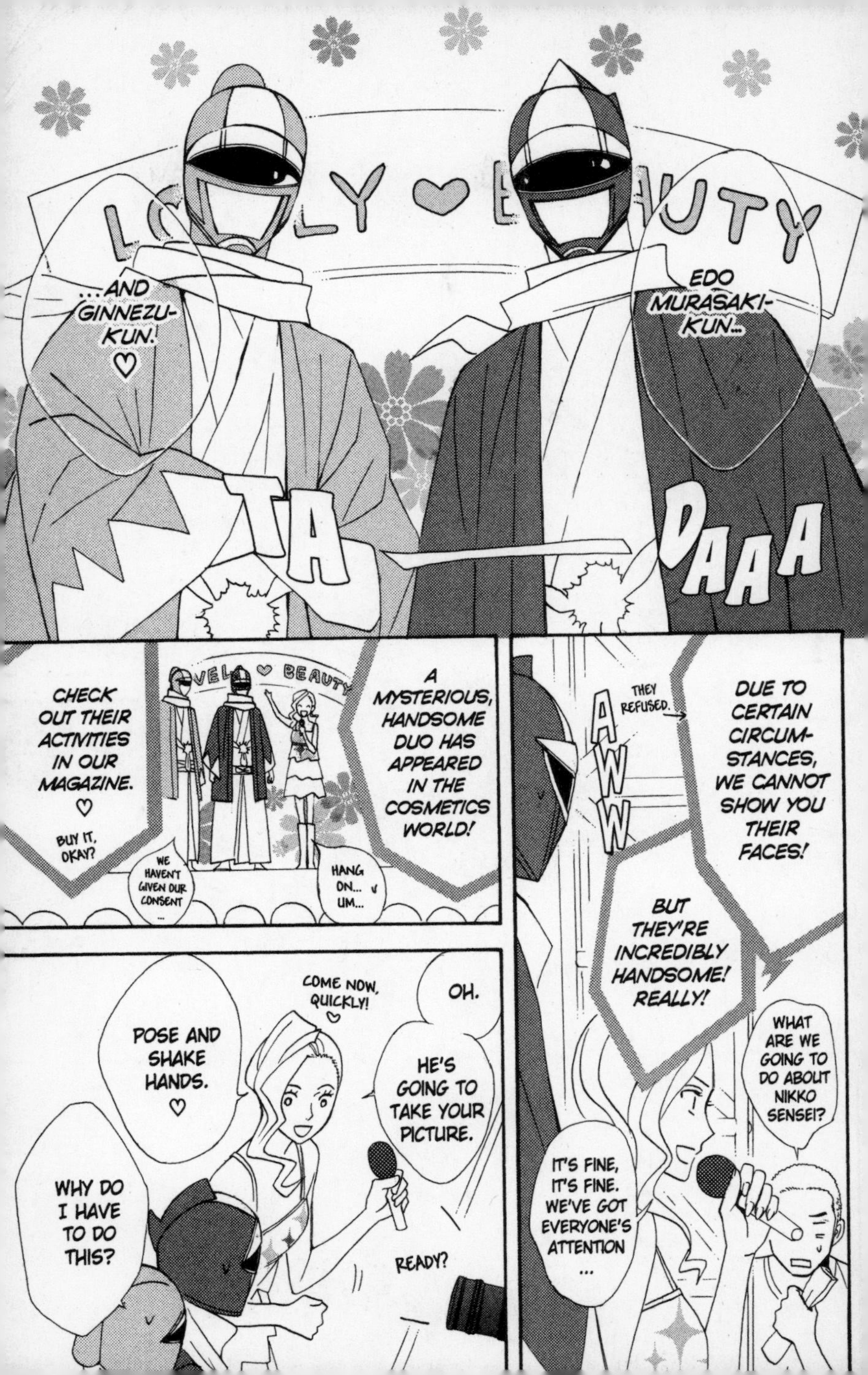
EDO MURASAKI-KUN...
...AND GINNEZU-KUN. ♡
TA DAAA
DUE TO CERTAIN CIRCUM-STANCES, WE CANNOT SHOW YOU THEIR FACES!
THEY REFUSED.
AWW
BUT THEY'RE INCREDIBLY HANDSOME! REALLY!
WHAT ARE WE GOING TO DO ABOUT NIKKO SENSEI?
IT'S FINE, IT'S FINE. WE'VE GOT EVERYONE'S ATTENTION...
A MYSTERIOUS, HANDSOME DUO HAS APPEARED IN THE COSMETICS WORLD!
CHECK OUT THEIR ACTIVITIES IN OUR MAGAZINE. ♡
BUY IT, OKAY?
HANG ON... UM...
WE HAVEN'T GIVEN OUR CONSENT...
OH.
COME NOW, QUICKLY! ♡
HE'S GOING TO TAKE YOUR PICTURE.
POSE AND SHAKE HANDS. ♡
READY?
WHY DO I HAVE TO DO THIS?

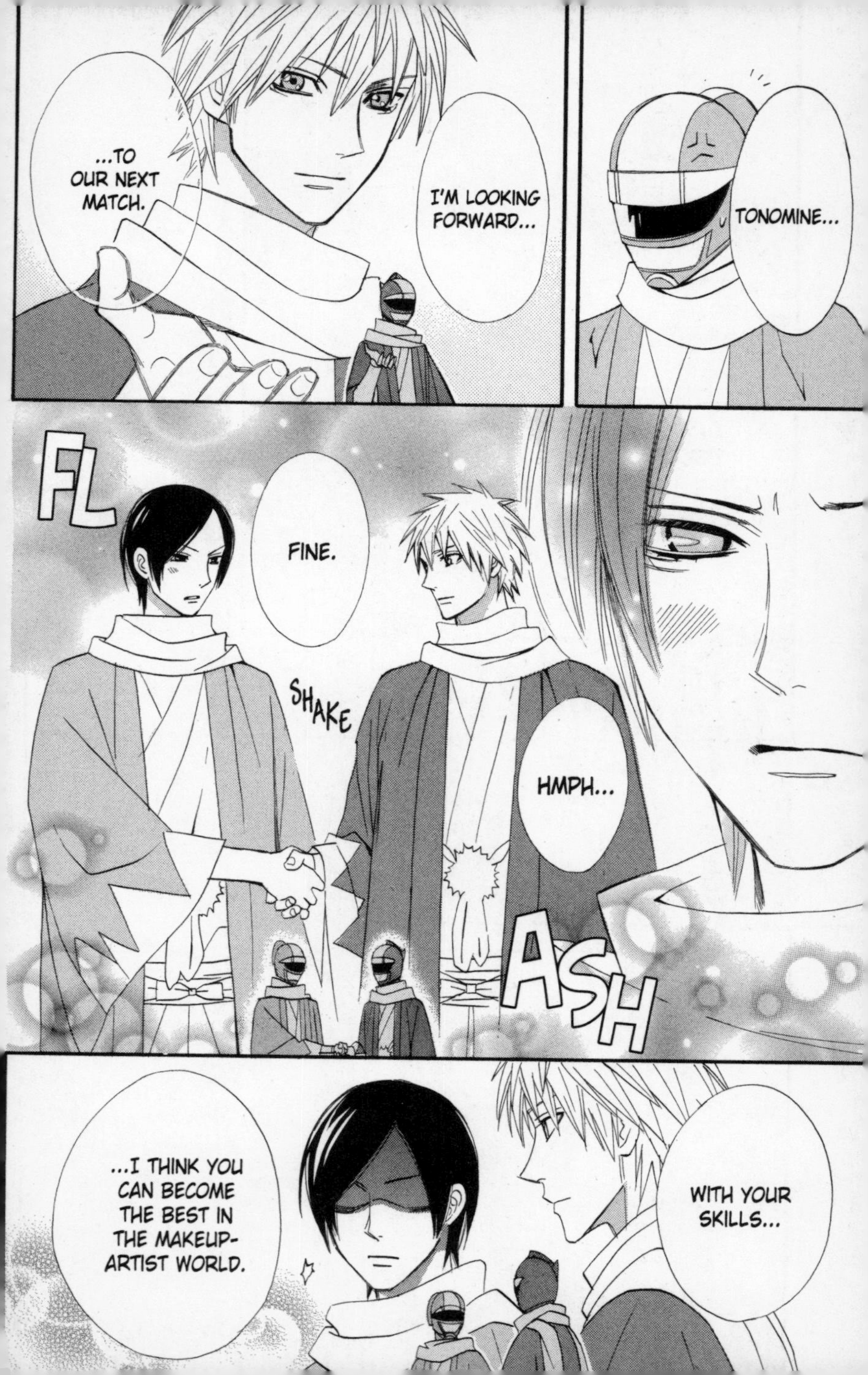
TONOMINE...
I'M LOOKING FORWARD...
...TO OUR NEXT MATCH.
FINE.
HMPH...
FL
SHAKE
ASH
WITH YOUR SKILLS...
...I THINK YOU CAN BECOME THE BEST IN THE MAKEUP-ARTIST WORLD.

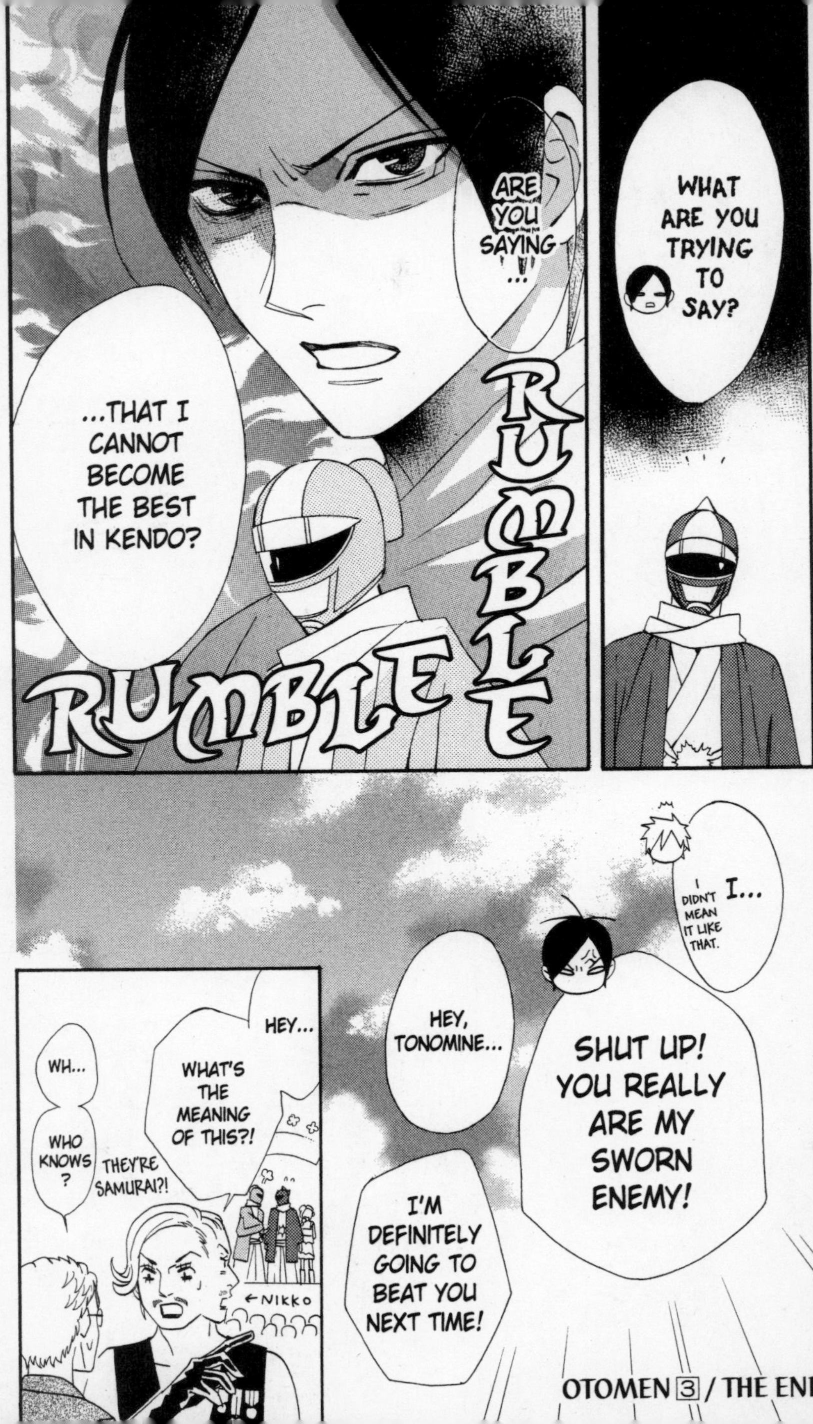
WHAT ARE YOU TRYING TO SAY?
ARE YOU SAYING...
...THAT I CANNOT BECOME THE BEST IN KENDO?
RUMBLE
RUMBLE
I...
I DIDN'T MEAN IT LIKE THAT.
SHUT UP! YOU REALLY ARE MY SWORN ENEMY!
HEY, TONOMINE...
I'M DEFINITELY GOING TO BEAT YOU NEXT TIME!
HEY...
WHAT'S THE MEANING OF THIS?!
THEY'RE SAMURAI?!
WH...
WHO KNOWS?
←NIKKO

OTOMEN 3 / THE END

OTOMEN

Confused by some of the terms, but too MANLY to ask for help?
Here are some **cultural notes** to assist you!

honorifics

Chan – an informal honorific used to address children and females. *Chan* can also be used toward animals, lovers, intimate friends, and people whom one has known since childhood.

Kun – an informal honorific used primarily toward males. It can be used by people of more senior status addressing those junior to them or by anyone addressing boys or young men. Like *chan*, *kun* is often added to nicknames to emphasize friendship or intimacy.

San – the most common honorific title. It is used to address people outside one's immediate family and close circle of friends.

Senpai – used to address one's senior colleagues or mentor figures. It is used when students refer to or address more senior students in their school.

Sensei – honorific title used to address teachers as well as professionals such as doctors, lawyers and artists.

NOTES

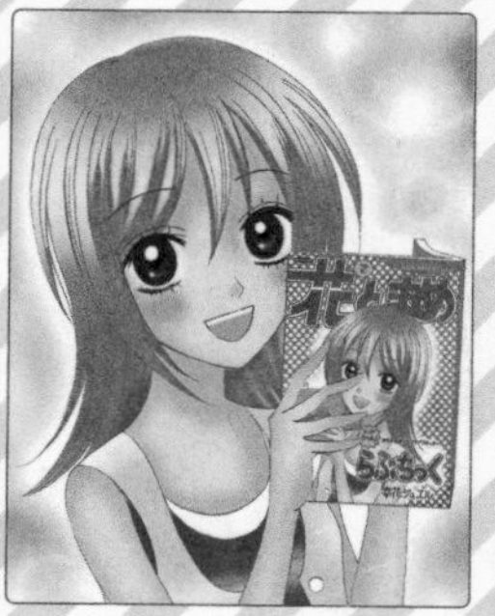
花とまめ
らぶちっく

Page 5 | **Hana to Mame**
The name *Hana to Mame* (Flowers and Beans) is a play on the real shojo manga magazine *Hana to Yume* (Flowers and Dreams) published by Hakusensha.

Page 29, panel 3 | **Girls' Day doll**
Girls' Day, also known as Doll Festival or *Hinamatsuri*, is celebrated in Japan on March 3rd. Ornamental dolls representing the emperor, the empress, attendants and musicians in traditional Heian period court dress are displayed for a period before and after the 3rd.

Page 75, panel 2 | **Bento**
A lunch box that may contain rice, meat, pickles and an assortment of side dishes. Sometimes the food is arranged in such a way as to resemble objects like animals, flowers, leaves, and so forth.

Page 96, panel 3 | **Golden Week**
Golden Week contains four national holidays and is one of Japan's busiest holiday seasons. Depending on what days those four holidays fall on, Golden Week can start around late April or early May.

Page 96, panel 4 | **Obon**
Obon is a festival to honor the dead. It is celebrated toward the end of summer and is another major holiday season in Japan.

Page 159, panel 3 | **Bushido**
Bushido means "the way of the warrior" and is a code of conduct that emphasizes loyalty, bravery, sacrifice, faith, propriety, honor and simplicity.

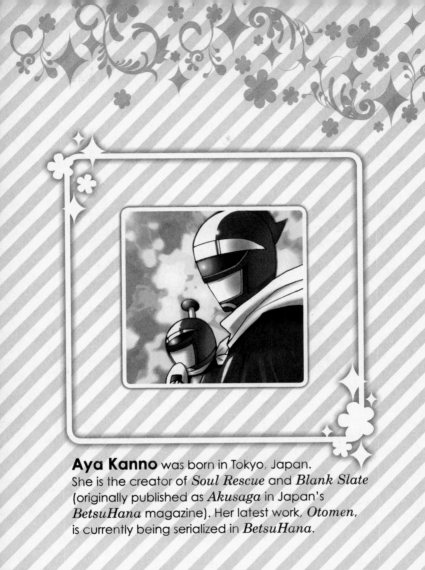

Aya Kanno was born in Tokyo, Japan.
She is the creator of *Soul Rescue* and *Blank Slate*
(originally published as *Akusaga* in Japan's
BetsuHana magazine). Her latest work, *Otomen*,
is currently being serialized in *BetsuHana*.

OTOMEN

Vol. 3
The Shojo Beat Manga Edition

Story and Art by | **AYA KANNO**

Translation & Adaptation | **JN Productions**
Touch-up Art & Lettering | **Mark McMurray**
Design | **Fawn Lau**
Editor | **Amy Yu**

Editor in Chief, Books | **Alvin Lu**
Editor in Chief, Magazines | **Marc Weidenbaum**
VP, Publishing Licensing | **Rika Inouye**
VP, Sales & Product Marketing | **Gonzalo Ferreyra**
VP, Creative | **Linda Espinosa**
Publisher | **Hyoe Narita**

Printed in the U.S.A.

Published by VIZ Media, LLC
P.O. Box 77010
San Francisco, CA 94107

Shojo Beat Manga Edition
10 9 8 7 6 5 4 3 2 1
First printing, August 2009

www.viz.com

PARENTAL ADVISORY
OTOMEN is rated T for Teen and is recommended for ages 13 and up. This volume contains suggestive themes.
ratings.viz.com

store.viz.com

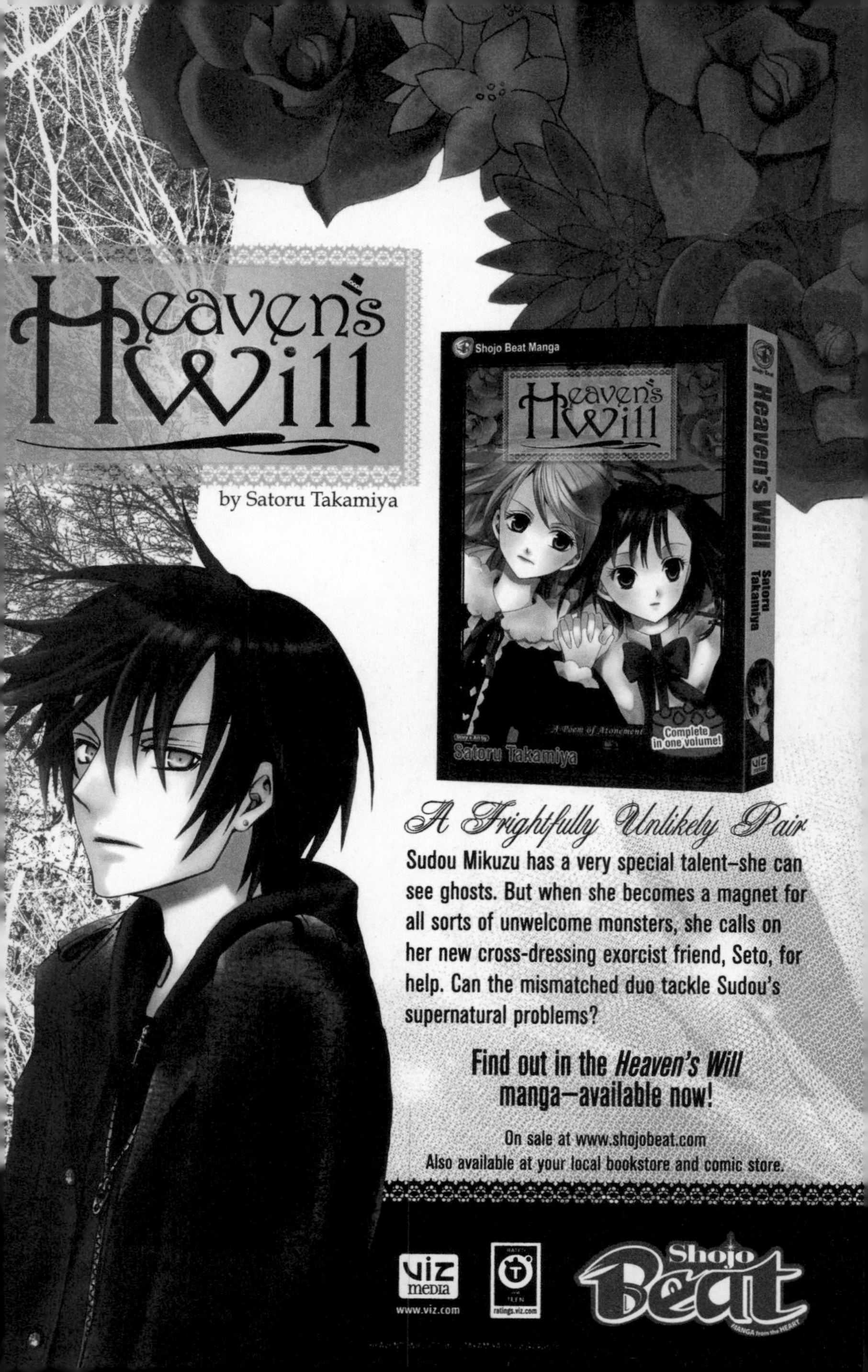
Heaven's Will
by Satoru Takamiya
Shojo Beat Manga
Heaven's Will
Satoru Takamiya
A Poem of Atonement
Complete in one volume!
Satoru Takamiya
A Frightfully Unlikely Pair
Sudou Mikuzu has a very special talent—she can see ghosts. But when she becomes a magnet for all sorts of unwelcome monsters, she calls on her new cross-dressing exorcist friend, Seto, for help. Can the mismatched duo tackle Sudou's supernatural problems?
Find out in the Heaven's Will manga—available now!
On sale at www.shojobeat.com
Also available at your local bookstore and comic store.
viz media
www.viz.com
ratings.viz.com
Shojo Beat
MANGA from the HEART

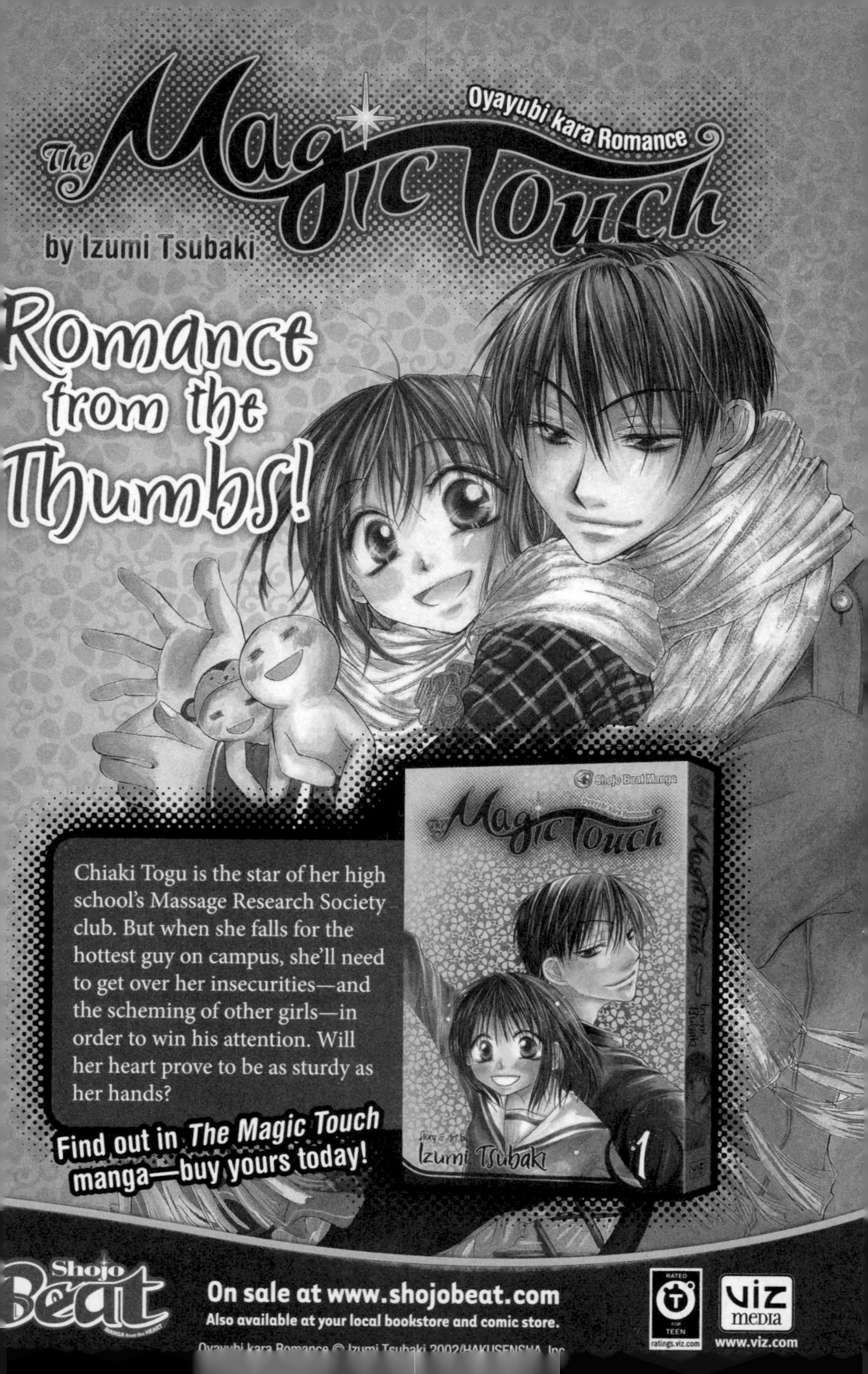
The Magic Touch
Oyayubi kara Romance
by Izumi Tsubaki
Romance from the Thumbs!
Shojo Beat Manga
The Magic Touch
Oyayubi kara Romance
Story & Art by
Izumi Tsubaki
1
Chiaki Togu is the star of her high school's Massage Research Society club. But when she falls for the hottest guy on campus, she'll need to get over her insecurities—and the scheming of other girls—in order to win his attention. Will her heart prove to be as sturdy as her hands?
Find out in The Magic Touch manga—buy yours today!
Shojo Beat
MANGA from the HEART
On sale at www.shojobeat.com
Also available at your local bookstore and comic store.
RATED T FOR TEEN
ratings.viz.com
VIZ media
www.viz.com
Oyayubi kara Romance © Izumi Tsubaki 2002/HAKUSENSHA, Inc.